Ebenezer Josiah Newell

A History of the Welsh Church to the Dissolution of the Monasteries

Ebenezer Josiah Newell

A History of the Welsh Church to the Dissolution of the Monasteries

ISBN/EAN: 9783337162788

Printed in Europe, USA, Canada, Australia, Japan

Cover: Foto ©ninafisch / pixelio.de

More available books at **www.hansebooks.com**

A HISTORY

OF

THE WELSH CHURCH

TO THE

DISSOLUTION OF THE MONASTERIES.

BY THE
REV. E. J. NEWELL, M.A.,
AUTHOR OF
'A POPULAR HISTORY OF THE ANCIENT BRITISH CHURCH,'
'ST. PATRICK: HIS LIFE AND TEACHING.'

'Gwell Duw na dim.'

LONDON:
ELLIOT STOCK, 62, PATERNOSTER ROW, E.C.
1895.

To

RICHARD,

LORD BISHOP OF LLANDAFF,

THIS VOLUME

IS (BY PERMISSION) DEDICATED

BY

HIS OBEDIENT SERVANT AND SON,

THE AUTHOR.

EXPLANATION OF SOME ABBREVIATIONS EMPLOYED IN THE NOTES.

'C. B. S.'   'Lives of the Cambro-British Saints,' with English translations and explanatory notes by the Rev. W. J. Rees, M.A., F.S.A. Published for the Welsh MSS. Society, Llandovery. 1853.

This volume contains lives of Brynach, Beuno, Cadoc. Carannog, David, Gwynllyw, Illtyd, Cybi, Padarn. Winefred, etc., the original Latin and Welsh texts, with translations.

H. and S.   'Councils and Ecclesiastical Documents relating to Great Britain and Ireland,' edited by Arthur West Haddan, B.D., and William Stubbs, M.A. [now Bishop of Oxford]. Oxford, 1869.

J. and F.   'The History and Antiquities of St. David's.' by William Basil Jones, M.A. [now Bishop of St. David's] and Edward Augustus Freeman, M.A. London, 1856.

'M. H. B.'   'Monumenta Historica Britannica,' 1848.

W. S.   'The Tripartite Life of Patrick,' with other documents relating to that saint, edited with translations and indexes by Whitley Stokes, D.C.L., LL.D. Rolls Series, 1887.

PREFACE.

AMONG the prizes offered for competition at the National Eisteddfod, held at Rhyl, in 1892, was one of £25 for the best 'History of the Christian Church in Wales, from the Earliest Times to the death of Elizabeth.' The prize was awarded to the essay bearing the motto, 'Gwell Duw na dim.'[1]

A portion of this essay has been incorporated in this volume; but since the competition I have devoted further time and attention to the subject, with the result that I have added very considerably to the size of the history, and have practically re-written the whole, with the exception of the first three chapters.

One result of my additional labours has been to deepen my impression of the nationality of the Welsh Church, which neither oppression, fraud, nor friendship availed to destroy in the period under consideration. As a matter of historical accuracy, therefore, I have not unfrequently used the expression of Archbishop Peckham, and written of the Church of the four dioceses as the 'Church *of* Wales' (*Ecclesia Walliæ*), a title which in no way invali-

[1] The adjudicators were the Venerable Archdeacon Pryce and Mr. Owen M. Edwards, M.A., Fellow of Lincoln College, Oxford.

dates its claim to be also regarded as an integral part of the great Church of England.

I have to thank Mrs. Gordon, of Nottage Court, Porthcawl, for her kindness in lending me Rymer's 'Fœdera;' 'Monumenta Historica Britannica;' Leland's 'Itinerary' (the third edition); 'Athenæ Oxonienses;' Browne Willis's 'Survey of Landaff;' 'Rotuli Parliamentorum;' Francis's 'Charters of Neath and its Abbey,' and many other valuable works. My thanks are also due to the Very Reverend the Dean of Llandaff, for relaxing in my favour, for the final revision of this History, the rule which confines to the Cathedral Library some of the most important of its volumes.

E. J. NEWELL.

PORTHCAWL, *January* 1, 1895.

CONTENTS.

CHAPTER	PAGE
I. THE CHURCH DURING THE ROMAN PERIOD	1
II. GERMAN AND THE AGE OF THE SAINTS	33
III. EARLY WELSH MONASTERIES	66
IV. THE AGE OF CONFLICT	98
V. THE AGE OF CONFLICT AND THE SUBMISSION OF THE WELSH CHURCH	115
VI. THE AGE OF FUSION TO THE CONSECRATION OF BISHOP BERNARD	151
VII. FROM THE CONSECRATION OF BISHOP BERNARD TO THE VISITATION OF ARCHBISHOP BALDWIN	175
VIII. GERALD DE BARRI AND THE CONTEST FOR ST. DAVID'S	198
IX. THE CONDITION OF THE CHURCH IN THE AGE OF GERALD DE BARRI	238
X. THE NEW MONASTERIES	275
XI. THE AGE OF THE TWO LLYWELYNS	307
XII. FROM THE CONQUEST OF WALES TO THE DEATH OF OWAIN GLYNDWR	338

CHAPTER	PAGE
XIII. FROM THE DEATH OF OWAIN GLYNDWR TO THE DISSOLUTION OF THE MONASTERIES - - -	363
APPENDIX. TRANSLATION OF AN ODE BY LEWIS MORGANWG - - - - - -	399
XIV. THE DISSOLUTION OF THE MONASTERIES - -	403
APPENDIX A.—ANNUAL VALUE OF THE WELSH MONASTERIES AT THE DISSOLUTION - -	419
APPENDIX B.—A LETTER OF BISHOP BARLOW -	423
INDEX - - - - - - -	429

CHAPTER I.

THE CHURCH DURING THE ROMAN PERIOD.

To trace a mighty force, still active in our midst, to its first small beginnings in far-distant centuries, is a task that appeals strongly to the interest of the student. The same attraction which leads men to ascend Plinlimmon to view the sources of the Severn, Wye, and Rheidiol, operates also in the field of history, and causes speculation and research as to the origin of national movements and institutions. But research is toilsome and speculation easy, and men often describe the source without climbing the hill. In the case of Celtic Christianity the conscientious student is embarrassed by the multitude of sources which the fertile imagination of theorists has invented.

The date of the introduction of Christianity into Wales is not recorded, and cannot be determined with precision. Yet there is a certain amount of evidence from which we can draw a probable inference respecting it. Our earliest and best authority on Welsh Christianity is Gildas, who lived in the sixth century, and who supplies us with a picture of the state of society in his time, overdrawn perhaps, but instructive, and corresponding in its main features to the indications found in other sources of information. He states as his belief that the light of the Gospel began to shine upon Britain in the days of Tiberius Cæsar,[1] and although his testimony as to the exact date is

[1] Gildas, 'Historia,' vi.; 'Monumenta Historica Britannica,' p. 8.

weakened by his admission that he gained no information from the records of his own country, which were lost, and by the evident fact that he borrowed his statement from a passage of Eusebius which he misinterpreted, he could not have ventured upon such an assertion if, indeed, Wales had only recently received Christianity. Throughout his writings he speaks of Welsh Christianity as no new thing, but a creed commonly embraced and long established. Paganism as an acknowledged religion was a thing of the past; the diabolical idols of his country, which almost surpassed in number those of Egypt, were still to be seen here and there, within or without the deserted walls, with ugly features and their wonted stiff and savage glare, but they lacked their former worship; the Divine honour that had been paid to mountains, hills and rivers by the nation in the time of its blindness was paid no longer, but these powers of nature, once destructive, were now useful for the service of man.[1] Bitter and incisive as are the increpations of Gildas, he nowhere lays paganism to the charge of those whom he rebukes, and in like manner the successors of Augustine in a subsequent age treated Welsh Christians as an ancient, though schismatical, body, quite free from taint of paganism. If we credit the authority of Gildas, and disregard, as we may safely do, both the scoff of Gibbon[2] and the obstinate incredulity of Mr. Thomas Wright, we are led to infer that Christianity existed and flourished in Britain centuries before the coming of the English people, and that the Christian Church in Wales was at least not much posterior in date to that of the more easterly parts of the island.

It is not improbable that occasional Christian visitors came over to Britain among the soldiers of the Roman armies, or in their wake, at an early period after the

[1] 'Historia,' ii.; 'M. H. B.,' p. 7.
[2] 'Decline and Fall,' chap. xxxviii.

outpouring of the Holy Spirit on the day of Pentecost, but these scattered individuals or families can have had but little influence upon the mass of the people. Various baseless statements have been made as to the visits of Apostles to Britain, and it is even to this day almost an article of faith with some that St. Paul preached the Gospel in this country, to which others add a local and patriotic opinion that Glamorganshire was especially honoured by his presence. A little inquiry soon shows the absence of anything that can be called evidence in favour of these suppositions. Clement of Alexandria has indeed left his testimony that St. Paul taught 'the whole world, even to the boundary of the West,' but, as we know that the Apostle intended to visit Spain, it is more natural to suppose that Clement was referring to that country than to Britain. Chrysostom also, in rhetorical language, has stated that the Apostle went from Illyricum 'to the very ends of the earth.' Theodoret specifies, besides Italy and Spain, 'the islands that lie in the sea' as recipients of the Apostle's aid, but apparently with reference to Crete; and in another passage mentions how 'our fishermen and publicans and the leather-cutter' (viz., St. Paul) 'carried the laws of the Gospel to all mankind, not only to Romans, but to Scythians, Sarmatians, and Britons.' This last passage really approaches nearest of any to being evidence in favour of a visit to Britain; but if it refer to personal visits at all, it may be interpreted of St. Peter or other Apostles quite as properly as of St. Paul. Other quotations adduced from ancient writers are quite beside the mark; the poet Venantius Fortunatus speaks of St. Paul's pen as crossing the ocean 'to the land which the Briton inhabits and furthermost Thule,' but as elsewhere he limits St. Paul's personal travels to Illyricum, he cannot be held to assert that the Apostle and his pen crossed the ocean in company. The only testimony which states in so many words that St. Paul came to Britain is ascribed to Sophronius, Patriarch of Jerusalem in the seventh century, but that is late and not improbably spurious. There is no ancient native tradition in favour of the theory, and the existence of certain Triads called 'Paul's Triads'[1] proves nothing. It may be suspected that Protestant zeal, which has at times set up St. Paul as a rival champion to St. Peter, has availed more than force of argument in gaining acceptance for the supposition that the Apostle of the Gentiles preached in Britain. It must not be forgotten, too, that some Romish writers, as Serenus de Cressy (who is well known as figuring in an interesting passage of 'John Inglesant'), state that St. Peter also came to Britain and there built many churches. The chief authority for this is 'St. Peter's own testimony in a Vision hapning in the dayes of S. Edward the Confessour, wherein himself professed that he had preached the Gospell in Brittany.'[2]

Although there may have been individual Christians in Britain, and even in Wales, before A.D. 176, it may be concluded with a fair degree of certainty that there was no British Church at that date, for Irenæus, enumerating then all the Churches, and more particularly those of the West, makes no mention of Britain. It is, therefore, necessary to dismiss not only the theories of a Pauline and a Petrine origin of the Church, but also the various stories about visits of St. Simon Zelotes, St. Philip, St. James the Great, Aristobulus, and Joseph of Arimathæa. Much ingenuity has been bestowed upon the identification of Claudia mentioned with Pudens by St. Paul, with Claudia, the foreigner from Britain, spoken of by Martial as the wife of Pudens, his friend. But though it has been said that 'no lovelier character than that of the high-born British matron,' in her care of Paul the aged, 'is presented

[1] See 'Poems,' by Edward Williams (Iolo Morganwg), A.D. 1794, vol. ii., pp. 251-253, where these Trioedd Pawl are preserved.
[2] Serenus de Cressy, 'Church History of Brittany,' A.D. 1668, p. 15.

to our admiration in the pages of history,' it must be confessed that the arguments for the identification are not very strong, and that the pretty pictures which have been drawn of the family party assembled in the 'Titulus' at Rome seem more romantic than real. For with an identification which is not quite impossible, have been united hints, traditions, legends, guesses, and inventions which together make up an imposing story of the introduction of Christianity into Wales. Bran, we are told, was taken to Rome with his celebrated son Caratacus, or Caradog.[1] There Caratacus's daughter, Gladys or Claudia, was married to Pudens, and Bran and his son were converted and baptized by St. Paul. The children of Claudia, St. Timotheus, St. Novatus, St. Pudentiana and St. Praxedes, were brought up 'literally' on the knees of the Apostles, and 'in A.D. 59 Aristobulus, brother of St. Barnabas and father-in-law of St. Peter, was ordained by St. Paul first Bishop of the Britons, and left Rome with Bran, Caradoc, and the royal family for Siluria.'[2] A farmhouse in Glamorganshire, called Trevran, has been pointed out as the place where Bran used to live,[3] and St. Donat's Castle, which stands picturesquely on a cliff on the coast of the same county, has been selected as the site of the palace of Caratacus and of the temporary resting-place of the Apostle of the Gentiles.[4]

A genuine local tradition is always respectable, and should not be dismissed without due consideration, for if it be not history, it may contain matter that is historical. But tales which are either the invention of local vanity or have been sophisticated thereby and changed beyond all chance of recognition, fall within a very different category.

[1] Dion Cassius, however, says that the father of Caratacus (or Caractacus) was Cunobelinus. No author of repute knows anything of Bran.
[2] 'The British Kymry,' by Rev. R. W. Morgan, p. 101.
[3] 'Ecclesiastical History of the Cymry,' p. 56.
[4] The spot where St. Paul preached at Llantwit Major is pointed out by sincere believers.

The 'Triads of the Third Series,' which are the chief authority for the story, cannot be accepted as history, and it is doubtful whether they are even genuine traditions. The Triad of the Three Holy Families of Britain, which is the eighteenth of this series, states that the first of the three families was 'the family of Bran the Blessed, son of Llyr Llediaith; this Bran brought the faith in Christ first into this island from Rome, where he had been in prison through the treachery of Aregwedd Foeddawg, daughter of Avarwy, the son of Lludd.' But this triad is merely a corruption of an earlier triad, in which there is no mention of Bran at all.[1] Bran is mentioned as 'Blessed Bran' in the genuine Triads of Arthur and his Warriors, and also in the Mabinogi of Branwen, both of which exist in manuscripts of the fourteenth century. But it is quite uncertain what may be the signification of this title. In the Mabinogi Bran acts a strange part for a Christian missionary, and shows more of the pagan than the Christian in his composition. He is a giant, who wades across the sea from Wales to Ireland, because there is no ship that can carry him. The swineherds of the Irish king Matholwch see him coming, and tell their lord that they see a mountain moving upon the sea, and 'there was a lofty ridge on the top of the mountain, and a lake on each side of the ridge.' Says Branwen, 'It is Bran the

[1] Teir gwelygordd Seynt Kymru. Plant Brychan; a phlant Kunedda Wledig; a phlant Kaw o Brydyn. (The three stocks of Welsh Saints: the children of Brychan, those of Cunedda, and those of Caw of Pict-land.) Triad 18 of the Third Series reckons as the three holy families: (1) the family of Bran Fendigaed, (2) the family of Cunedda Wledig, and (3) the family of Brychan Brycheiniog. Triad 35 of the Third Series amplifies the story a little. It begins thus: 'The three sovereigns of the Isle of Britain who conferred blessings. Bran the Blessed, son of Llyr Llediaith, who first brought the faith in Christ to the nation of the Cymry from Rome, where he had been seven years a hostage for his son Caradog, whom the Romans had taken captive after he was betrayed by treachery and an ambush laid for him by Aregwedd Foeddawg.' For these and other so-called authorities for the Bran story see 'Ecclesiastical History of the Cymry,' pp. 53-56. Compare also for their historical value 'Y Cymmrodor,' xi. 126.

Blessed, my brother, coming to shoal water; there is no ship that can contain him in it.' 'What,' ask the messengers, 'is the lofty ridge with the lake on each side thereof?' 'On looking towards this island,' she replies, 'he is wroth, and his two eyes, one on each side of his nose, are the two lakes beside the ridge.'[1] Bran was on his way to Ireland to avenge the wrongs done by Matholwch to his sister, Branwen, and this object he accomplished. When his army was unable to cross a river, and asked his counsel, he replied, 'He who will be chief, let him be a bridge,' and forthwith he lay down across the river, and hurdles were placed upon him, and the host passed over thereby. At last, being wounded by a poisoned dart, he commanded that his head should be cut off, and borne by the seven who remained of his army to the White Mount in London, and there be buried with the face towards France. On the way the seven tarried for seven years in Harlech feasting, and all that time the head was 'pleasant company,' and at Gwales in Penvro they stayed further for fourscore years, and 'it was not more irksome having the head with them than if Bran the Blessed had been with them himself.' With all its grotesqueness, this wild and wondrous tale is not devoid of elements of beauty, but the deeds and attributes of its hero savour more of heathen god than of Christian missionary.[2]

In A.D. 176, we may conclude, there was no Christian Church in Britain; but a few years afterwards, about A.D. 208, it is pretty clear that some such Church existed, for Tertullian in his work, 'Against the Jews,' makes

---

[1] 'Mabinogion' (Lady Charlotte Guest's translation), second edition, pp. 377, 378.
[2] Elton ('Origins,' pp. 291, 292) thinks Bran to be a war-god, brought to Rome with his fellow deity, Caradoc, through a confusion of Bran with Brennus, and Caradoc with Caratacus. Professor Rhys ('Hibbert Lectures,' pp. 94-97) thinks him to be a god of the nether world, and the counterpart of the Gaulish Cernunnos.

distinct mention of it. 'In whom else,' he says, 'have
all nations believed except in Christ, who now has
come? For to whom have also other nations trusted?'
Then he mentions in order the nations which heard the
Pentecostal message, and adds 'varieties of the Gaetuli,
many territories of the Moors, all the bounds of Spain,
and divers nations of Gaul, and districts of the Britons,
inaccessible to the Romans, but subjugated to Christ
. . . in all which places the name of Christ, who now
has come, reigns . . . since in all these places the people
of Christ's name dwell. . . . What shall I say of the
Romans, who fortify their empire with the garrisons of
their legions, and are unable to extend the might of their
rule beyond those nations? But the rule and name of
Christ are everywhere spread abroad, everywhere believed,
are worshipped by all the above-mentioned nations.'
This testimony is corroborated in A.D. 239 by Origen,
who says in his fourth homily on Ezekiel: 'For when
before the coming of Christ has the land of Britain
assented to the religion of the one God? When the
land of the Moors? When, in a word, the whole world?
But now, on account of the churches, which occupy the
limits of the world, the whole earth shouts out with joy
to the Lord of Israel.' In his sixth homily on St. Luke,
the same Father mentions Britain and Mauritania as two
distant regions to which the Gospel had spread; and
in yet another place, in A.D. 246, he speaks of the British
Church as though it were still comparatively small and
weak, for 'very many' in Britain, he tells us, 'had not
yet heard the word of the Gospel.' There are many
other passages in the works of Christian writers of the
first few centuries attesting the existence of a British
Church.

'Little better than flourishes of rhetoric!' says the
sceptical archæologist. 'When the zealous preacher
wished to impress upon his hearers or readers the

widely-extended success of the Gospel, he would tell them that it extended from India to Britain, without considering much whether he was literally correct in saying that there were Christians in either of these two extremes.'[1] The same author denies the 'authenticity'[2] of the work attributed to Gildas,'[3] and, after rejecting wholesale the testimony of legends, of Christian Fathers, and of council records, concludes, from the absence of Christian remains 'among the innumerable religious and sepulchral monuments of the Roman period found in Britain,' that Christianity was not established in Roman Britain, and entered Cornwall and Wales from Spain or Armorica after the period when the island was relinquished by Rome.[4]

Such criticism savours rather of the 'incurable suspicion,' upon which Gibbon prided himself, than of the judicial mind of a sober critic. The scantiness (not absence) of archæological remains is a significant fact, which is full of meaning, but to its real significance the archæologist himself was blind. Tertullian's testimony may be couched in rhetorical language, but is, nevertheless, pretty precise. A modern preacher in a missionary sermon might speak of the Gospel as spread ' from pole to pole,' but if he gave a list of countries which had become Christian, it would be necessary for him to observe accuracy in his enumeration, and probably it was quite as incumbent upon Tertullian. Nothing but ' the stubborn mind of an infidel ' in the field of history can refuse to accept his witness as conclusive, that in

---

[1] 'The Celt, the Roman, and the Saxon,' by Thomas Wright. Second edition, p. 300.
[2] Probably meaning 'genuineness.'
[3] Dr. Guest sarcastically remarks ('Origines Celticæ,' ii. 157) : 'I am not aware that the genuineness of these works ' (' The Epistle ' and 'History') 'has been questioned by anyone whose scholarship or whose judgment is likely to give weight to his opinion.'
[4] 'The Celt, the Roman and the Saxon,' p. 461.

A.D. 208 there was a Christian Church or a Christian Mission in Britain. His knowledge, indeed, seems to have been of a very precise kind, for he states that there were districts which had submitted to Christ, though they were then inaccessible to the Romans. This may not imply the existence of Christianity outside the ordinary boundaries of Roman rule, for the passage was probably written at a time when Severus was occupied in quelling an insurrection in Britain. But in any case it implies a knowledge, even in detail, of the state of the British Church at the time when Tertullian wrote.

From whence, then, was Christianity introduced into Britain between the years 176 and 208? Various answers have been given to this question: Rome, Gaul, and the East having respectively its advocates as the source of the British Church.

If tradition can be trusted, the mother of British Christianity was the See of Rome. The theories about the visits of Apostles and others fade into insignificance when placed in contrast with the great Lucius story. This is contained in the later form of the 'Roll of Roman Pontiffs,' in Bede's 'Ecclesiastical History,' and his 'Chronicle,' in the 'History of the Britons,' attributed to Nennius, and in the 'Book of Llandaff,' as also in the 'Triads of the Third Series.' In Geoffrey of Monmouth's romance it attains extraordinary proportions as the endowment of a Christian Church with the wealth and privileges of the ancient Druidical priesthood. Later writers give the letter which was written by the Pope in answer to the petition of the British King, and, among comparatively modern historians, Serenus de Cressy devotes one long and elaborate book of his 'Church History' to the acts and death of King Lucius, respecting whom he shows a detailed and minute knowledge, extending even to his motives. On the Protestant side, Usher, whose vast accumulations of learning on the subject were termed by Hallam 'a bushel of chaff,' has pronounced decisively in favour of the legend, and many other later writers have been led by his authority to believe in Lucius and his petition.

The earliest trace of the story is found in the later version of the 'List of Roman Pontiffs,' which is brought down to the year 530, and is, probably, of that date or thereabouts. The earlier version contains no mention of Lucius, but the second, after amplifying a little in other respects the notice of Eleutherius, continues thus: 'He received a letter from Lucius, King of Britain, that he might be made a Christian by his mandate.'[1] Bede, about 731, repeats the story almost exactly in the same words, but with the addition of an erroneous date, and also with a slight change of phraseology, which has been thought to show that Bede did not copy from the 'List' itself, but from some source common to himself, and to the continuator of the 'List.'[2] Nennius, in the ninth century, gives a somewhat various account, stating the Pope to be Evaristus, and mentioning that Lucius was called Lleuer Maur, or the Great Light, on account of the faith which came in his time.[3] The 'Book of

[1] The first version is: 'Eleutherius annis .... fuit temporibus Antonini et Commodi, a consulatu Veri et Erenniani, usque Paterno et Bradua.' The second is: 'Eleuther natione Græcus ex patre Abundantio de oppido Nicopoli, sedit annos quindecim, menses tres, dies duos. Fuit temporibus Antonini et Commodi usque Paterno et Bradua. Hic accepit epistolam a Lucio Britanniæ rege, ut Christianus efficeretur per ejus mandatum.'

[2] Bede's version is: 'Anno ab incarnatione domini centesimo quinquagesimo sexto Marcus Antonius Verus, decimus quartus ab Augusto, regnum cum Aurelio Commodo fratre suscepit: quorum temporibus cum Eleutherus vir sanctus pontificatui Romanæ ecclesiæ præesset, misit ad eum Lucius Britanniarum rex epistolam, obsecrans, ut per ejus mandatum Christianus efficeretur' (Bede, 'H. E.,' i. 4; 'M. H. B.,' pp. 111, 112). Dr. Guest remarks ('Origines Celticæ,' ii. 139): 'Bede, I believe, never uses the plural "Britanniæ" except when he is evidently copying some classical or some foreign ecclesiastical writer, and as the catalogue did not furnish the phrase he must have found it elsewhere.'

[3] 'Anno Dominicæ Incarnationis clxiv., Lucius Britannicus Rex cum universis regulis totius Britanniæ baptismum susceperunt, missa

Llandaff,' which was compiled in the twelfth century, states that in the year 156, Lucius, King of the Britons, sent his ambassadors, Elvanus and Medwinus, to Pope Eleutherius. ' They beg that by his admonition he might be made a Christian, which he obtained from him.' Eleutherius accordingly baptized the envoys, and ordained Elvanus a bishop, and Medwinus a doctor. Through their preaching, Lucius himself and the chief men of all Britain received baptism, and, ' according to the command of the blessed Pope Eleutherius, he established ecclesiastical order, he ordained bishops, and taught the rule of right living.' The date in this version of the story is probably borrowed from Bede, and cannot possibly be correct, as Eleutherius did not become Bishop of Rome until 171 A.D., at the earliest. But the 'Book of Llandaff' contains also another reference to the story. A somewhat later scribe than the original compiler, but also probably writing in the same century, has inserted a life of Eleutherius, evidently derived from the later form of the Roman 'List,' and containing the clause respecting Lucius, with but one slight verbal variation. In tracing the history of the evolution of the legend this significant entry is worthy of no little consideration.[1]

William of Malmesbury adds fresh details to the story, mentioning that Eleutherius sent Phaganus and

---

legatione ab imperatoribus Romanorum et a Papa Romano Evaristo: Lucius agnomine Llever-Maur, id est "Magni-Splendoris," propter fidem quæ in ejus tempore venit ' (' Nennius,' 18 ; ' M. H. B.,' p. 60). Dr. Guest (' Origines Celticæ,' ii. 140) believes that Nennius had the more perfect tradition, and preserved the name of the Roman bishop who sent missionaries to Britain, though he considers the name Lucius an invention, borrowed from one of the names of Commodus, the Emperor under whom Eleutherius flourished.

[1] ' Eleutherius natione grecus ex patre habundio de oppido nicopoli sedit annos xv. menses vi. dies quinque. Fuit autem temporibus antonie et commodi usque ad paternum et braduam. Hic accepit epistolam a Lucio britannio rege ut christianus efficeretur per eius mandatum,' etc. ' The Book of Llan Dâv ' (Evans's edition), p. 26. Compare the notice of Eleutherius above in the ' List of Roman Pontiffs.'

Deruvianus as preachers to Britain; and Geoffrey of Monmouth calls these missionaries Faganus and Duvanus. The untrustworthy 'Triads of the Third Series' make Lucius, or Lleurwg, as they call him, fourth in descent from Caradog or Caratacus, the son of Bran, and so connect him with the Bran legend or imposture. As a Silurian chief, he is naturally brought into connection with Llandaff as the founder of its first church.

It is to be noted that in the 'Book of Llandaff' no connection is asserted between Lucius and Llandaff. The mission to Rome is merely related as the origin of British Christianity, and neither the line of the descent of Lucius nor his capital city is mentioned. The version of the Triads would therefore meet with little consideration were it not for the existence of dedications to Lleurwg, Dyfan, Ffagan, and Medwy in the immediate neighbourhood of Llandaff, and nowhere else. St. Fagan's is a charming little village close to Llandaff, with a 'decent church,' and with the antique mansion of Lord Windsor standing upon a slight eminence amid a lovely country. Merthyr Dyfan, the Church of Dyfan the martyr, is not far off, and on the other side of the great town of Cardiff lie Llanlleurwg, now better known as St. Mellon's, and Michaelston-y-Fedw.[1] These dedications are probably old; Llan Fagan is mentioned at least by the 'Book of Aberpergwm,'[2] under the date 1150, as one of the chief churches of the diocese which had lost their sanctuary since the time of Iestin ap Gwrgan. Neither do they seem to be due to Romanizing influence, seeing that two,

---

[1] In 'Achau a Gwelygorddau Saint Ynys Prydain' (Iolo MSS. 114, 513) we read as follows: 'Saint Lleirwg, King of the Island of Britain, the son of Coel, the son of Cyllin, the son of Caradoc, the son of Bran, the son of Llyr Llediaith; his church is Llanlleirwg; and also another in Llandaff. . . . Saint Ffagan was bishop in Llan-Sanffagan, and there is his church. Saint Dyfan was bishop in Merthyr Dyfan, where he was slain by the pagans, and there is his church. Saint Medwy was bishop in Llanfedwy, where his church is.'

[2] This, however, is by no means trustworthy evidence.

those to Medwy and Lleurwg, gave place in later times to other saints, one of whom, Mellon, was naturally dear to Norman hearts from his association with Rouen.

The phraseology used respecting the petition of Lucius in several versions of this story is evidently borrowed from the Roman List, which was unquestionably well known to Llandaff scribes in the twelfth century, and from which Bede also, notwithstanding one slight verbal difference, probably derived ultimately his notice of Lucius. But this phraseology savours so much of Roman arrogance as to lead to suspicion of the authority of the Roman List in its later form. As has been well remarked, it is 'manifestly written in the time and tone of Prosper.'[1] The later versions do nothing to strengthen the story; but rather weaken it by their inconsistent statements, and the idea of a 'King of Britain' sending an embassy to Rome towards the end of the second century, is in itself rather extraordinary. The story may safely be dismissed to the limbo of interested fictions; but it is possible that the dedications in the neighbourhood of Llandaff indicate that it developed in its Welsh form by association with genuine Welsh saints, and even perhaps with a genuine tradition respecting early missionary operations around Llandaff. It is along the Roman road, which can still be traced between Cardiff and Newport, that the missionary movement would come westward, and Lleurwg, Ffagan, Dyfan, and Medwy, may have been the pioneers of Christianity in the district.

If British Christianity did not come from Rome, there can be little doubt that it was carried from the neighbouring country of Gaul. It is certainly quite unnecessary to suppose that it was brought straight from the East. There is no evidence of this, and the theory in itself is not very probable. Yet it seems to be true that there are traces in the Celtic Church of some Oriental connec-

[1] 'H. and S.,' i. 25.

tion. This has been denied, and some exaggerated statements to the effect have been successfully refuted; but there nevertheless remains a considerable amount of evidence leading to this conclusion. It must of course be admitted that all early Christianity was Greek, that the British Church from its isolated position was conservative of primitive practices and ignorant of later Latin usages, and that, furthermore, the British Easter and other peculiar customs were primitive or old-fashioned, not Eastern. But notwithstanding this, the Celts certainly founded their opposition to Latin customs upon Eastern authority. It is not without significance that at the Council of Whitby, Colman, the spokesman for the Celtic Easter, appealed to the authority of St. John against Wilfrid, who claimed to follow St. Peter. 'Marvellous is it,' said Colman to the Roman champion, ' that you would call our toil foolish, wherein we follow the example of so great an apostle, who was worthy to lean on the bosom of the Lord; since all the world knows that he lived most wisely.'[1] When Wilfrid had replied to this contention, Colman next adduced the authority of another Eastern saint, Anatolius, Bishop of Laodicea. The great missionary Columbanus, when he encountered similar difficulties to those of Colman, in like manner refused to be bound by the authority of Rome, and appealed to the judgment of the Council of Constantinople, and in another eloquent passage plainly owned his greater reverence for Jerusalem than for Rome. So, too, in the legends of the Celtic saints, influenced though they are by the prejudices of late writers of Roman proclivities, there are frequent signs of an ancient tendency to regard Jerusalem as preeminent. David, the patron saint of Wales, Teilo, Padarn, Cybi, Cadoc, and King Arthur, are all taken to Jerusalem by their biographers; and the legends tell how the first three saints arrived at the Holy City together, and were con-

[1] Bede, 'Historia Ecclesiastica,' iii. 25; 'M. H. B.,' p. 201.

secrated by the Patriarch, and enriched with wonderful gifts. Pilgrimages to the East from Celtic countries were undoubtedly numerous, as is proved by the testimony of Palladius and Theodoret.[1] Some of the Celtic clergy appear to have visited Constantinople in the middle of the ninth century to make inquiries, as at the fountain-head of knowledge, concerning the date of Easter and other points of ecclesiastical order.[2] Architectural and palæographical evidence in favour of Eastern influence is not quite clear, and pilgrimages may have introduced Orientalisms at a date long subsequent to the original planting of the British Church; but it must not be forgotten that the existing remains of early Celtic liturgies belong rather to the 'Ephesine,' than to the 'Petrine' family.[3]

All this, however, is quite harmonious with a Gallican origin of the British Church, though it were less explicable, if the Britons had regarded Rome as the source of their Christianity. It is probable that at the time when the British Church was founded, between A.D. 176 and A.D. 208, there was little Christianity in Gaul outside the Churches of St. John in the Rhone valley. These were distinctively Greek Churches, being colonies from Asia Minor. The first bishop of Lyons was Pothinus, who came direct from Asia Minor. Irenæus, who succeeded him, was probably a native of Smyrna, and was instructed by Polycarp, from whom he received the traditions of St. John. In A.D. 177 occurred that terrible persecution of the Churches of the Rhone valley, the details of which are known from the pathetic letter sent by them to the

[1] Palladius, writing in 420, of the years before 410, and Theodoret, writing about 440, but probably concerning A.D. 423. Palladius is treating of the hospitality of Melania the elder to pilgrims at Jerusalem, and Theodoret of the visits of Spaniards, Britons, and Gauls to Telanissus near Antioch, to see Symeon Stylites. See 'H. and S.,' i. 14.
[2] See 'Vita S. Chrysostom.,' quoted by 'H. and S.,' i. 204, *note*.
[3] Warren, 'Liturgy and Ritual of the Celtic Church,' 163, 167, etc.

Greek Churches of Asia Minor. Possibly the mission to Britain had started ere this; or perhaps in this case, as so often happened, the dispersion of Christians from one city caused them to flee to another for refuge, and so the Gallican Christians found safety in distant Britain, and there planted a new Church. 'The chain of these Gallo-Celtic Churches reached up to Langres on the northern side of the watershed, near the springs of the Seine, and through Langres ran one of the great northern roads from Lyons to the British Channel. It was by a route through Arles and Lyons, and then northwards, that Augustine in the sixth century proceeded to Britain, after reaching the Rhone basin from Italy by the easy connection of the Provincia.'[1] Here, then, was the natural road for the approach of Christianity to Britain, and in default of a genuine tradition respecting the origin of the British Church, it appears most probable that Christian missionaries came that way from the churches of the Rhone valley to Britain, and brought with them memories of St. John, which caused the Celts centuries afterwards to appeal to him as the Apostle whose traditions they professed to follow.

There is very little doubt that Christianity entered Wales by the Roman road which led by Glevum or Gloucester through the stations of Venta Silurum (Caerwent), and Isca Silurum (Caerleon) by Cardiff to Nidum (Neath), and Maridunum (Carmarthen). Caerleon itself is probably the City of Legions,[2] mentioned by Gildas as the city of Aaron and Julius, who were martyred in the Diocletian persecution of A.D. 304. Such, at least, was the current belief in the time of Giraldus Cambrensis, who states that two churches at Caerleon had been dedicated respectively to each of these martyrs; and it may be inferred from the Book of Llandaff that there was

---

[1] Dr. Brewer in *Quarterly Review*, vol. cxlvii., p. 516.
[2] Legionum urbs. Gildas, 'Hist.,' 8 ; 'M. H. B.,' p. 8.

a 'territory' of Julius and Aaron at Caerleon during the ninth century.[1] It is also probable, though not wholly unquestioned, that Caerleon was the seat of a British bishopric in the Roman period. Giraldus Cambrensis used and distorted this tradition to suit his own purposes; but it is not for that reason of necessity worthless. Bishop Adelfius, who was present from Britain at the Council of Arles in 314, together with his brother bishops, Eborius of York and Restitutus of London, may very probably have been bishop of this see, but the corruption of the manuscripts precludes absolute certainty. The council was called to consider the case of the Donatists, the followers of Donatus, an African bishop. Constantine the Great had previously summoned a council of twenty bishops at Rome, to settle the questions of discipline and doctrine which this sect had raised; but as their decision was not accepted by the Donatists, the Emperor convened a provincial council at Arles. The names of the British bishops are found towards the latter part of the signatures, and included among those of the bishops of Gaul. The bishops were accompanied by Sacerdos, a priest, and Arminius, a deacon. Adelfius in the entry is called 'Bishop of the City Colonia Londinensium;'[2] but as no 'Colony of Londoners' is known, there is evidently here some mistake. Various have been the suggestions in consequence: Usher supposes the place intended to be Colchester, the Caer Collon of Nennius; Selden and Spelman think it is Camulodunum, whether that be Maldon or Colchester; Whitaker prefers to accept the present reading, and interprets it of Richborough; and Lingard and Routh give their judgment in favour of Lincoln (Col. Lind.). Stillingfleet, with the late Arthur Haddan, and the Bishop of Oxford, substitute 'Legionensium' for 'Londinensium,' and interpret of Caerleon.

---

[1] 'Book of Llan Dâv' (Evans' edition), p. 225.
[2] Episcopus de civitate Colonia Londinensium.

The Bishop of Eboracum, or York, naturally takes the first place in the list from the predominance of York in the time of Constantine; the bishop of the southern capital comes next; and if Caerleon were indeed the western capital, its bishop would naturally come third.

British bishops also attended the Council of Ariminum in A.D. 359. Whether any of these were from Wales, we know not. All the information we possess is that the Aquitanians, Gauls, and Britons who were present were for the most part unwilling to avail themselves of the Emperor's proffered hospitality; but that three only of the British bishops accepted it on account of their poverty.[1] This statement seems to imply that there was a considerable number of British bishops present, so that it is not improbable that one or more came from Wales. The bishops of Britain certainly concurred with the decrees of the Council of Nice[2] (A.D. 325), and with the acquittal of Athanasius by the Council of Sardica[3] (A.D. 347), but there is no proof that any of them were present at those councils. The lists of the bishops present are, however, incomplete; but with regard to the Council of Nice, we learn that its decrees were sent to the West by Hosius, Bishop of Cordova, through two Roman presbyters, Victor and Vincentius, which seems to imply that Gaul and Britain sent no representatives. However this may be, the orthodoxy of the British Church during the period of the Arian heresy is attested by the unimpeachable witness of both Athanasius and Hilary. The Western Churches do not seem to have thoroughly grasped the niceties of Eastern terminology, and for a time hesitated about accepting the new term 'consubstantial'; but they were still less willing to listen to the heretical novelties of the Arians, and although coerced and cheated into agree-

[1] Sulpicius Severus, 'Hist. Sac.,' ii. 41, in ' H. and S.,' i. 9.
[2] 'Athanasius ad Jovian Imp.,' etc., in ' H. and S.,' i. 7, 8.
[3] Athanasius, 'Apol. cont. Arian.,' and 'Hist. Arian. ad Monach.,' in ' H. and S.,' i. 8, 9.

ing to an ambiguous creed at the Council of Ariminum, they speedily disavowed any complicity with heresy, and maintained throughout the purity of their Christian heritage. The presence of British bishops at Ariminum was partly due to the efforts made by the Arian Emperor Constantius to get together the bishops of the West, and partly to the protection afforded at this time to the coast of Britain by the 'Britannic fleet,'[1] which kept the piratical Franks and Saxons in check.

'Happy the nation which has no history.' If this be true of Churches as well as nations, the Church in Wales in the Roman period must have been happy indeed. There is plain, unmistakable evidence that such a Church existed; but of its acts and memorials, apart from those of the British Church in general, there is scarcely a trace remaining. Yet, doubtless, it was doing a good work, for it was pure in doctrine, although unused to theological subtleties and probably unlearned. The dwellers in the gorgeous Roman villas knew little of the work that was going on all around them, and cared less. As had happened earlier still, 'not many wise men after the flesh, not many mighty, not many noble' were called; and the archæologist may search in vain amid the relics of Roman greatness for imposing monuments of British Christianity. Nothing has yet been found at Viriconium, and nothing at Caerleon, except perhaps a sepulchral stone with a 'rough scoring,' which may be a palm-branch, and may perhaps indicate the burial-place of a Christian. The stone at Llanerfil may bear a Christian inscription of this period: 'Hic in tumulo jacit Restice filia Paternini an xiii in pa(-ce).'[2] The words 'in pace,' 'in peace,' are very commonly used on Christian tombs in early times. 'A gold Basilidian talisman, with an inscription, partly

---

[1] 'Classis Britannica.'
[2] 'Here, in this mound, lies Restice, daughter of Paterninus, aged 13, in peace.'

in Greek letters, partly in astral or magical characters,[1] found at Llanbeblic in Carnarvonshire, about twenty yards from the old Roman wall of Segontium, shows that semi-Christian heresies penetrated into Wales at a very early date. There are other traces of Christianity in Britain outside Wales besides these; but these are all that have been detected with any approach to certainty within the borders of Wales. This is certainly significant; it proves, not that the Christian Church was non-existent, but that it lived apart from the patronage of wealthy Roman residents. The same fact is hinted in contemporary history by the statement of Sulpicius Severus, that three British bishops were compelled by poverty, and evidently sorely against their will, to accept the heretical Emperor's bounty at Ariminum. It is a problem of considerable interest, whether the members of the Church were chiefly Roman slaves and freedmen, 'the poorer class of that mixed race of immigrants which clustered round the chief Roman colonies,'[2] or whether they were for the most part native Britons. The names of British Christians in traditions and martyrologies— Alban, Aaron, Julius, Socrates, Stephanus, Augulus, and the rest—have been referred to in support of the former hypothesis, and the connection of bishops with the Roman towns, Eboracum, Londinium, and possibly Caerleon has been thought to tend the same way. Yet Eborius is a British name, appearing in the forms Ebur, Ibarus, and Ywor among the names of British and Irish bishops in later times, and the argument drawn from foreign names is by no means strong. Such names as David, Asaph, Daniel, Samson, and Ismael, which are parallel to Aaron, occur among the later Welsh saints, and suggest either a tendency among the Britons to adopt 'Bible names,' or an adaptation of native names to

[1] 'H. and S.,' i. 40.
[2] Haddan, 'Remains,' p. 218.

Hebrew forms, just as the name of St. Thenew, mother of St. Kentigern, has been corrupted in Scotland into St. Enoch.[1] As regards the Latin forms, we know that Britons occasionally had two names, one Roman and one Celtic. Thus we are told that Patrick in addition to his Roman name had also the native name of Succat.[2] Whatever may have been the character of the British Church in the earliest period of Christianity, it must have been strongly Celtic at the time of the separation of Britain from the empire, otherwise the departure of the Romans would have weakened it, whereas in reality it is from that point that it seems to have acquired fresh vitality and vigour. Patrick, who was born in Britain probably towards the close of the period of Roman occupation, has all the characteristics of a Celt both in his writings and in his work. But he was of a family that had long been Christian; his father Calpornus, or Calpurnius, was a deacon,[3] and also a decurion of a Roman colony. His grandfather Potitus was a priest, the son of Odissus. Perhaps the Roman names may indicate an intermixture of Roman blood; but the Celtic spirit and temperament were in the brave missionary all the same, and his Celtic name proves him to have had Celtic blood as well. As it was with Patrick, so it was with the Church from which Patrick sprung. The Latin and the Celtic strains were blended, but the Celtic in the end predominated. The story of Patrick's work in Ireland explains the problem which has sorely puzzled some of our archæologists, why there are so few remains of churches of the Roman period. St. Martin's, Canterbury, and a few others, none of which are in Wales, contain

---

[1] St. Enoch's Station, Glasgow.
[2] Sochet, so Muirchu, 'Tripartite Life of Patrick, with other Documents,' ii. p. 494 (Whitley Stokes, Rolls Series); Succetus, so Tirechan, *ibid.*, ii. 302; Succat, so Fiacc's 'Hymn,' *ibid.*, ii. 404; Lebar Brecc, Preface to Secundinus, 'Hymn,' *ibid.*, ii. 390.
[3] 'Confession' in 'Tripartite Life' (Rolls Series), ii. 357.

Roman work, and may have been used for Christian purposes even in the Roman period, by the Roman Christians or the Romanized Britons; but probably the majority of the churches throughout Britain, and almost certainly the majority in Wales, were wooden. Occasionally, when wood was scarce, Patrick built a church of earth, as at Foirrgea—he 'made a quadrangular church of earth, because there was no forest near at hand.'[1] At Clebach also, we are told, he made a church of earth.[2] Churches of stone were rare, though probably not without examples even in the time of Patrick. It has been supposed, from the special mention of quadrangular churches at Foirrgea, and in the reign of Conmaicne,[3] that Patrick usually built round churches, and it is inferred from the fact that only one dimension is given for the buildings of the Ferta at Armagh,[4] that they were all circular. It is not improbable that Patrick introduced this custom from Britain, and it has been suggested that the word Côr is a trace. Old churchyards in Wales are often round, and possibly the ashes of rude pagan forefathers lie in many such with the ashes of their Christian sons and successors.

Welsh patriotism would claim St. Patrick as a native of Gower, and asserts that his father's name was Mawon, and that his own name was Padrig Maenwyn. One story even calls him the first principal of the college of Llantwit Major, and states that he was carried away captive thence by the Irish; but this is manifestly inconsistent with Patrick's own narrative. Wherever Bannavem Taberniæ may have been, whether at Old Kilpatrick, near Dumbarton, or elsewhere, it was certainly in Britain,

[1] 'Fecit ibi æclessiam terrenam de humo quadratam, quia non prope erat silva.' Tirechan in 'Book of Armagh'; Whitley Stokes' 'Tripartite Life of St. Patrick,' ii. 327, and other documents.
[2] 'Æclessiam terrenam fecit in eo loco.' Tirechan in 'Book of Armagh'; 'W. S.,' ii. 317.
[3] 'W. S.,' ii. 321.   [4] 'Tripartite Life'; 'W. S.,' i. 237.

not in Gaul, and Patrick's practices and writings are valuable, therefore, as illustrative of the condition of the British Church at the close of the Roman period. It is very clear from his writings that Christianity was the dominant religion throughout the civilized parts of Britain. Of himself, and the companions of his boyhood, he says: 'We had departed from God and had not kept His precepts and were not obedient to our Priests, who admonished us for our salvation;'[1] but his words are clearly the outcome of spiritual contrition for moral faults, not a confession of any relapse into paganism. During his mission some of his Irish converts were carried off into slavery by a British prince, named Coroticus. But this prince himself was no pagan, but a nominal Christian. Joceline in his life of Patrick calls the prince Cereticus, and states that his principality was 'in certain territories of Britain which are now called Vallia,' *i.e.*, Wales. Cereticus would be in Welsh, Ceretic or Ceredig, so that he may perhaps be identified with Ceredig, the son of Cunedda.[2] But the older writer, Muirchu, calls the prince Coirthech, King of Aloo,[3] a place which is probably to be identified with Alclud or Dumbarton. In any case, whether he were of Wales or the north, he was nominally a Christian, though he scoffed at the clerical embassy which Patrick sent to his court, and was for this act denounced by the saint. By the end of the period of Roman occupation, Christianity was the religion of the native population of the Roman provinces, except perhaps in backward districts, although doubtless paganism was largely blended with it in popular beliefs and practices.

'Society was a long time unlearning heathenism; it has not done so yet,' says a recent writer,[4] and in

---

[1] 'Confession,' in Haddan and Stubbs' 'Councils,' ii. 2, 296.
[2] See Rees, 'Welsh Saints,' pp. 108-110; Todd, 'St. Patrick,' p. 352.
[3] Muirchu Maccu-Machtheni in 'Book of Armagh'; 'W. S.,' ii. 271.
[4] Dean Church, 'St. Anselm.'

Patrick's time 'the dead hand' of paganism was still mighty to thwart Christian practice, though not to prevent the Christian profession. The old worships had been many and diverse. The conquest of Britain by the Romans had not destroyed the native heathenism; it only introduced new gods. The Roman raised his altars to Jupiter, best and greatest; to Mars, conqueror and avenger, and to the other gods of his mythology, and the numerous nationalities among the legionaries and settlers—Gauls, Germans, Spaniards, Tungrians, Dacians, Thracians, Dalmatians, and Palmyrenes—joined him in his worship, and adored also their own national gods. Thus all the gods whose worship had been adopted at Rome, and besides these many strange and barbarous deities also, had their temples and altars in this island. The Britons, too, learned to identify their gods with the gods of the conquerors, and the conquerors in turn condescended to adore the British gods. So Maponus, or Mabon, and Grannus, 'the light-bringer,' both received the name of Apollo, and Belatucadrus, 'the god mighty to kill,' and 'the holy god Mars Cocidius' were identified with the Roman god of war. But all these greater gods passed away before the power of 'the dreaded Infant' of Bethlehem, it was the minor superstitions that died hardest; in respect of these it is true that 'the Canaanite dwelt still in the land.' The worship of the three goddesses, the Deæ Matres; of the Genius Loci, of the Nymphs, and of the god of Druidism, was too deeply rooted in the popular mind to be quickly destroyed. The old temples might be pulled down or abandoned, but the convert could still behold the sun, the fire, the wells, the streams, and the stones. He had still a superstitious dread of the powers of Nature, and a fondness for the older rites, and so many a one 'feared the Lord and served his own gods.'

It is sometimes maintained that the early Christianity

of Britain and of Ireland was a compromise between Christianity and Druidism. This is undoubtedly a fairly accurate description of the Christianity of Ireland at some periods, but is not more applicable to Britain than to most of the other countries of Christendom in the early ages of the Church. There was a conflict to be waged with paganism in every country where Christ's Gospel was preached, a conflict which did not cease when the old gods were cast down and when their temples were demolished. It is difficult for us to realize how entirely the everyday life of mankind was interpenetrated by pagan ideas and pagan actions; though we may get a glimpse of the condition of things in the old Roman world from the description of Tertullian. While the Christians were a small, persecuted body, they remained comparatively pure in spite of all the infection around them, though even then, as many examples prove, it was exceedingly difficult, if not impossible, for converts when they embraced Christianity to give up wholly their old ways of thought. But when the world itself became Christian, Christianity necessarily suffered from the adhesion of multitudes who were pagans at heart, and who mixed with their Christianity many of their old beliefs and practices.

These are somewhat trite reflections, which any student of Early Church history can make for himself; but it is necessary to remind those who view British Christianity as a kind of Christianized paganism that the pagan survivals which they notice and upon which they lay undue stress had their counterpart in every nation of Christendom, and that it would be as fair to accuse the Church in other nations of paganism, as it is to accuse the Church in Wales. The dream of a British Church distinguished by ambitious native heterodoxy, wherein 'the Bards, or Druids, continued for many centuries after they became Christians, the ministers of religion, even till, and probably in some places long after, the time of the two Athanasian and incipiently Popish bishops, Germanus and Lupus'[1] (I quote the text of the accusation in all its naked absurdity), is too ridiculous for any serious thinker now to entertain. But the more sober conception which has been sometimes advanced, and which represents the early British Christians as so far influenced by pagan superstitions as scarcely to hold Christianity in any restricted sense of the term,[2] has, I venture to assert, hardly any more support from history than the older dream which I have just quoted from the writings of Iolo Morganwg. Not the slightest shadow of paganism rests upon the writings of St. Patrick, the British missionary of the fifth century, or upon the 'De Excidio Britanniæ' of Gildas in the sixth century. Both writers serve as unimpeachable witnesses to the orthodoxy

[1] 'Poems,' by Edward Williams (Iolo Morganwg), vol. ii., p. 203.
[2] This would almost seem, indeed, to be the view of Professor Rhys. See his 'Arthurian Legend,' p. 369 : 'It is not wholly improbable that some of them (viz., the early recluses who were fond of withdrawing to the islands) expected to derive advantage from the wall of inviolability which the pagans of former ages had built round the person of the islander. At any rate it would be hazardous to treat that consideration as a *quantité négligeable* before the sanguinary advent of the Norsemen ; and it lends some countenance to our conjecture expressed elsewhere to the following effect : " Irish Druidism absorbed a certain amount of Christianity : and it would be a problem of considerable difficulty to fix on the point where it ceased to be Druidism, and from which onwards it could be said to be Christianity, in any restricted sense of that term." This has been characterized as an extreme statement, but after toning it down a little we should be disposed to extend it so as to take in the Celts, not only of Ireland, but of Britain too.' See also Rhys, 'Hibbert Lectures,' p. 224, and my 'St. Patrick' ('The Fathers for English Readers'), p. 221. I acknowledge pagan survivals in Wales ; I acknowledge the existence of a semi-pagan bardic literature, such as the 'Book of Taliessin' ; but I cannot find any evidence that the Church was largely 'tinctured' with paganism, as Iolo Morganwg says, or that the Christianity of Wales was in any proper sense of the term a druidical or semi-pagan Christianity. I find instead in the earlier ages, at least down to the seventh century, traces of a very healthy Christianity, and with all due respect to so eminent an authority as Professor Rhys (to whom all students of Celtic antiquity must owe deep obligation), if he takes an opposite view, I must beg to differ from him.

of the British Church. Even the statement as regards Ireland that 'Patrick engrafted Christianity on the pagan superstitions'[1] in order to accommodate it to the tastes of his Irish converts, cannot be supported by one tittle of evidence from his 'Confession,' his 'Epistle to the Subjects of Coroticus,' or even from the 'Deer's Cry,' but is wholly diverse from the spirit of these writings. If we seek for its basis, we find it in the worthless testimony of late writers of legends, who created a fictitious Patrick, whom they embellished with forgeries of their own evil imaginations.

It is noteworthy that the orthodoxy of the British Church, except for the short period of the Pelagian heresy, which we are immediately about to consider, was never impugned in ancient times by its bitterest assailants, and that the suspicions which have been raised are entirely of modern origin. There were pagan survivals all over Christendom in those old days (as, indeed, there are still), and no branch of the Church could venture to throw stones at another on this account. All over Christendom, too, these practices were more or less condoned by the Church for reasons of expediency. St. Columba was not alone in his policy when he converted a well venerated by pagans into a Christian holy well;[2] the same principle was more or less at work everywhere. Here and there some bold leader would strive to stem the popular tide, but it was too strong for him; for the people forced upon the clergy some compromise with their favourite practices. And so it came to pass that paganism even gained the ascendancy in some points; the conquered one, as so often happens, took the conqueror captive, and mediæval Christianity, in its popular

---

[1] Dr. O'Donovan quoted by Todd; 'St. Patrick,' p. 500. See also my 'St. Patrick' (S.P.C.K.), p. 200.

[2] Adamnan, 'Vita S. Columbæ,' ii. 10; 'Historians of Scotland,' p. 159.

form, was largely adulterated with paganism. But this we usually call mediævalism, or sometimes Romanism, not paganism ; and few, however extreme their Protestantism may be, would refuse to the religion of the Middle Ages the name of Christianity.

We shall not, however, grasp the whole truth of the matter unless we try to understand the true essential nature of Celtic Christianity, which certainly differed very much from the comfortable, unexciting and unexacting compromise which the British Philistine, who makes the best of both worlds, considers his ideal of Christianity; but which critics, even among ourselves, have sometimes stigmatized as a 'civilized heathenism.' We are about to consider the lives of the Welsh saints, and if we hold fast to our modern ideals, cold comforters though they be, we may utterly misconceive these strange, uncouth men of the days of old. When we contemplate their fasts and vigils, or when we read the gloomy pages of Gildas, the Celtic Jeremiah, we may fall into the error of regarding the religion of early Wales as a morbid and repulsive asceticism. But a wider view and a deeper insight will teach us a very different lesson. The Celt then, as now, was eminently sympathetic, and animated by a love for Nature and for the beautiful. It was no sour ascetic that won the heart of the little child Benen, so that he took the feet of the weary missionary in his arms and clasped them to his breast, and placed sweet-scented flowers in his bosom as he lay asleep.[1] No; St. Patrick had the Celtic charm of manner in his dealings with men, as well as decision in action and skill in policy, or he would never have won the tribes of Ireland for his Lord, and succeeded where Palladius had failed. He had, too,

---

[1] The story of Benen, or Benignus, the successor of Patrick in the See of Armagh, is contained in Tirechan's 'Life'; 'Book of Armagh'; 'W. S.,' ii. 303. The mention of the flowers is not in Tirechan's narrative, but in the 'Tripartite Life'; 'W. S.,' i. 37.

the Celtic love of Nature, and resented the claim of the Druids to control it for their purposes, and in his ' Deer's Cry ' ' bound himself to '

> ' The sun with its brightness,
> And the snow with its whiteness,
> And fire with all the strength it hath,
> And lightning with its rapid wrath,
> And the winds with their swiftness along their path,
> And the sea with its deepness,
> And the rocks with their steepness,
> And the earth with its starkness ;'

for he held that the earth was the Lord's, and the fulness thereof, and that the powers of Nature, which so long had been regarded as spirits of dread, to be propitiated with sacrifices, were appointed to serve the servant of the Lord. With a like feeling, in a later age, the Celtic monk could look forth from the little island of Iona upon the sea around him, and with no fear that there was aught sinful or profane in the love of beauty, could sing of ' the level sparkling strand,' ' the thunder of the crowding waves upon the rocks,' ' the song of the wonderful birds,' and ' the sea monsters, the greatest of all wonders,' in a poem[1] which in pathos is almost modern, and in its love of Nature approximates to that intimate feeling of sympathy with her moods which we usually associate with our own century, and with the name of Wordsworth. Celtic Christianity, in spite of its asceticism (or ought we rather to say in consequence thereof?), was no creed of gloom ; it was eminently a joyous Christianity, loving and lovable, which realized, perhaps as nearly as ever has been realized in the history of Christendom, such aspirations after a higher level of pure and gentle Christian practice, as in recent literature breathe in Kenelm Digby's magnificent pages, or, perhaps, in the late Mr. Pater's ideal picture of Marius the Epicurean ;

---

[1] Skene's ' Celtic Scotland,' ii. 92. The poem, which is Irish, is ascribed to Columba.

or, again, in the daringly simple verses of the most Christian of our living poets, Coventry Patmore:

> 'Would Wisdom for herself be wooed,
>   And wake the foolish from his dream?
> She must be glad as well as good,
>   And must not only be, but seem.
> Beauty and joy are hers by right,
>   And knowing this, I wonder less
> That she's so scorned, when falsely dight
>   In misery and ugliness.'

The brightness of joy and hope which the Celtic saints possessed, sometimes illuminated their faces. Said Columbanus to one of his disciples, 'Diecholus, why are you always smiling?' He answered, 'Because no one can take my God from me.' Diecholus was pure, not Puritanical.

This being the standpoint of the leaders of Celtic Christianity, would it not be rash for us to blame them overmuch, or accuse them of paganism, if in our investigation of the acts and teaching of the saints we find at times that they erred from an excess of charity, and evinced too great an anxiety to detect a soul of goodness in things evil? I think, however, that we shall fail to find any certain evidence of such error on the part of the saints of Wales, though we may have to notice it in some of their fellows and compeers of Ireland. But those who are over-keen in detecting pagan tendencies have at times erred themselves by considering as paganism what was only a healthier type of Christianity than they were familiar with. When the Celtic saint refused, from his innate love of Nature and of beauty, to regard this earth and its glories, however profaned, as in themselves common and unclean, he proved his grasp of an essentially Christian and anti-pagan principle, and a discrimination which has not always been attained by those who deem themselves more enlightened. We have differentiated so much that we have restricted religion to a very narrow sphere ; we have feared so much the temptations of art, beauty, and culture, that we have at times altogether divorced them from Christianity. It matters little by what names we may disguise these acts ; we may call them Progress, Puritanism, or Positivism, but really they are Paganism. The essence of paganism is to claim the earth and all that is therein for some other than their rightful Possessor ; and against this claim the Celtic saints contended with all the earnestness of their Celtic nature. If in details we venture to blame them, in their central conception we owe them only respect and imitation, for there is reason to fear that we, not they, are the pagans. The nearer we approach their ideal, the nearer will Christianity approach its realization as the Religion of Humanity.

CHAPTER II.

GERMAN AND THE AGE OF THE SAINTS.

ABOUT the time of the withdrawal of the Roman legions from Britain, Pelagius first began to teach his heresy at Rome. He was, as we learn from his great opponent Augustine and from Orosius, himself a Briton by nation, and his doctrines were afterwards introduced by his disciple, Agricola, into his native land, where they rapidly spread to such an extent, that the orthodox clergy sent to the Church of Gaul for assistance. Constantius of Lyons, who wrote his 'Life of St. German' towards the close of the century, relates that on account of this embassy 'a great synod was gathered; and by the judgment of all two glorious lights of religion were beset by the petitions of the whole body, viz., German and Lupus, Apostolic priests, who possessed earth, indeed, with their bodies, but heaven by their merits. And the more urgent appeared the necessity, the more promptly did the devoted heroes undertake the work, hastening on the business with the goads of faith.'[1] German, one of the selected missionaries, was Bishop of Auxerre. He had been a soldier, and governor of Auxerre, and had been made a clergyman in a curious way, significant of the manners of his time. An enthusiastic huntsman, he was accustomed to hang up his spoils upon an ancient tree. Amator, then Bishop of Auxerre, caused this tree

[1] 'M. H. B.,' p. 122, *note*.

to be cut down, possibly because it was connected with pagan superstition. German was exceedingly angry, and threatened that he would kill Amator. But not long afterwards Amator summoned the people to the cathedral, and having ordered them to lay aside their arms, and the ostiarii to shut the doors of the church, he, with a number of clergy, laid hands upon German and ordained him, tonsuring him and investing him in the clerical habit. This was in A.D. 418, eleven years before the selection of German for the mission to Britain. German's companion, Lupus, was Bishop of Troyes, and a brother of the celebrated Vincent of Lerins. The date of their mission (429) is fixed by the contemporary witness of Prosper the Aquitanian, who relates also that the two bishops were sent by Pope Celestine at the suit of Palladius.[1] This latter statement, at first sight, seems scarcely consistent with the narrative of Constantius, and it has often been questioned on the ground of Prosper's known partiality for the see of Rome. Certainly, if Prosper made a false statement, he did so wilfully, for he must have known the facts; but it is quite possible that both he and Constantius are truthful, and that each relates the circumstances from his own point of view.

The fitness of the two bishops for their work was speedily manifested on their arrival in Britain by their energy and success. At a council held at Verulam the Pelagians were utterly beaten in argument, and the people, in their enthusiasm for German and Lupus, could scarcely refrain from laying hands upon their opponents.

It is not certain that German and Lupus visited Wales, and we do not know how far the Pelagian heresy affected that part of Britain. But one incident in their mission has been popularly connected with Wales ever since the time of Usher, but on somewhat insufficient grounds. This is the Alleluia Victory.

[1] 'M. H. B,' p. 123, *note*.

The Saxons and Picts, so Bede relates, joined their forces at this time and made war against the Britons, who, in their necessity, sought the aid of the holy bishops. 'The sacred days of Lent were at hand, which the presence of the priests made more solemn to such an extent that the people, taught by daily sermons, flocked eagerly to the grace of baptism ; for the greatest part of the army sought the water of the laver of salvation, and a church is constructed of boughs for the day of the Lord's resurrection.' Wet with the baptismal water, the army marches forth ; 'German offers himself as their general ; he picks out some light-armed men, views the circumjacent country, and espies, in the direction by which the arrival of the enemy was expected, a valley enclosed by mountains. Here he himself, as their general, draws up his raw troops. And now the fierce multitude of the enemy was at hand, the approach of which was espied by the men in ambuscade. Then suddenly German, bearing the standard, admonishes and orders the whole body to answer to his voice with one shout, and as the enemy came on carelessly, in their confidence that they were not expected, the priests call out thrice "Alleluia." A single shout of all follows, and the hollows of the mountains multiply the clamour with their reverberations ; the band of the enemy is stricken with panic, so that they fear not only that the surrounding rocks are falling upon them, but even the very vault of heaven itself, and scarcely was the speed of their feet believed sufficient for their haste. They flee in all directions ; they cast away their arms, glad even to have snatched their naked bodies from danger ; many also in the headlong haste of their panic were drowned in re-crossing the river. The guiltless army looks upon its own revenge, and becomes an inactive spectator of the victory granted to it. The scattered spoils are gathered up, and the pious soldiers embrace the joys of the heavenly reward. The bishops triumph in the rout of the foe achieved without bloodshed; they triumph in a victory gained by faith, not by strength.'[1]

The wattled church has been supposed by some to be Llanarmon in Iâl, and the battle-field to be the Vale of Mold. There are several churches in Wales which are dedicated to St. German and which have been supposed to owe their foundation to him. These are[2] Llanarmon in Iâl, and Llanarmon Dyffryn Ceiriog, both in Denbighshire; St. Harmon's, Radnorshire, and Llanfechain, Montgomeryshire. The chapels dedicated to him are: Llanarmon under Llangybi, and Bettws Garmon under Llanfair Isgaer, both in Carnarvonshire; and in Denbighshire Capel Garmon under Llanrwst, and Llanarmon Fach under Llandegfan.[3] Philologists, however, deny that any of these can be traced back to the age of German.[4] German's companion, Lupus, is known in Wales by the Welsh equivalent, Bleiddian. 'The churches ascribed to him are Llanfleiddian Fawr, in Glamorganshire, which bears the same relation to the town of Cowbridge as Llanbeblig and Llannor do to Carnarvon and Pwllheli; and Llanfleiddian Fach, or St. Lythian's in the same county.'[5] Llanfleiddian Fawr is now more commonly known as Llanbleddian.

Some years afterwards, in A.D. 447, German came on a second visit to Britain, where the Pelagian heresy was again making head. This time he was accompanied by Severus, Bishop of Treves, and was equally successful. British traditions preserved by Nennius bring German into Wales and connect him with Guorthigern, or

---

[1] 'Hist. Eccl.,' i. 20; 'M. H. B.,' pp. 126, 127. Bede is here quoting from Constantius.

[2] Rees, 'Essay on the Welsh Saints,' p. 131.

[3] Recently a church has been dedicated to St. German in Cardiff.

[4] 'There are reasons for doubting that the churches called Llanarmon received that name during the period in which St. German lived.' Professor Rhys in *Journal of the British Archaeological Association*, vol. xxxiv., p. 425.

[5] Rees, 'Welsh Saints,' p. 126.

Vortigern. Vortigern, adding this to his other crimes, according to the story, took his daughter to him to wife, and she bare him a son. When this was discovered by St. German, he came to seize the King with all the clergy of the Britons. But the King told his daughter to go to the council and give the boy to German, and say that he was the father. The scheme failed, and Vortigern was cursed and condemned by German and all the council of the Britons. He fled, and German followed him with the clergy into Wales, and for forty days and nights upon a rock prayed God to forgive his sins. Vortigern afterwards fled to a castle on the river Teifi and was followed there by the saint, who, with his clergy, fasted and prayed for three days and three nights. Finally, fire fell from heaven and consumed the castle, and the guilty King and all his company. Guorthemir, or Vortimer, in compensation for the calumny which his father Vortigern had brought against German, gave him the district of Guartherniaun, in which the charge had been made, to be his for ever, whence it got the name Guarrenniaun, 'a calumny justly retorted.'[1]

Guartherniaun, or Gwrtheyrnion, is a district of Radnorshire, being the present hundred of Rhayader, in which at the present day there is a church (St. Harmon's) dedicated to St. German. Historically the stories of Nennius are worthless, and cannot even be accepted as testimony that the saint set foot in Wales, but they indicate clearly enough in what reverence the name of German was held by the Church in that part of the island. The power of his eloquence and the force of his character left indelible traces on the subsequent life of the Church. When Amator 'pressed' the young soldier into the service of his Lord, he doubtless had a clear insight into the wondrous energy and the magnetic attraction of that

---

[1] Nennius, 'Historia Britonum,' §§ 39, 46, 50; 'M. H. B.,' pp. 66, 68, 70.

heroic soul, and deemed that all means were lawful to
save such, and to enlist so brave a champion under the
banner of Christ. Once enlisted, the soldier served faithfully, the instinct of discipline prevailed, and he who
knew how to obey, held thereby the secret of command.
The story of the Alleluia Victory is no fiction, it is well
attested and is in full harmony with German's character,
and German's military training. The marvel would
rather have been if soldiers, led by such a commander, had
failed. Tradition, attracted by his name, has ascribed to
German all the institutions of his own and even of the
next century. Though inaccurate, tradition is not wholly
wrong, for to the spirit which he infused into the British
Church the subsequent glories of its history are due.

'Garmon,' says one authority,[1] 'was a saint and a
bishop, the son of Ridigius from the land of Gallia; and
it was in the time of Constantine of Armorica that he
came here, and continued here to the time of Vortigern,
and then he returned back to France, where he died. He
formed two choirs of saints, and placed bishops and
divines in them, that they might teach the Christian
faith to the nation of the Cymry, where they were become
degenerate in the faith. One choir he formed in Llan
Carvan, where Dyfric, the saint, was the principal, and he
himself was bishop there. The other was near Caer
Worgorn, where he appointed Iltutus to be principal;
and Lupus (called Bleiddan) was the chief bishop there;
after which he placed bishops in Llandaff; he constituted
Dubricius archbishop there; and Cadoc, the saint, the
son of Gwynlliw, took his place in the choir at Llancarvan,
and the Archbishop of Llandaff was bishop there also.'

This narrative is full of anachronisms, but it is quite
possible that German infused the monastic spirit into
the British Church, which produced such monasteries
as Llantwit and Llancarvan. It is scarcely necessary

[1] 'Achau y Saint,' quoted in Rees' 'Welsh Saints,' p. 122.

to discuss the statements that German founded the Universities of Oxford and Cambridge, but, worthless as they are, they testify in a somewhat emphatic manner to the opinion formed of him as an organizer and a leader of men.

The mission of St. German was followed by that interesting, but difficult, period, the Age of the Saints. Tradition gives the names of very few saints before his time: there are those of the Lleurwg story; there is Cadfrawd, who has been supposed to be the same with Bishop Adelfius; there is Ceneu the son of Coel; and the legendary Owain, son of Maximus, and his brothers, Ednyfed and Peblig, have also been accounted saints. The church of Llanbeblig, near Carnarvon, is dedicated to Peblig, and Llannor, or Llanfor, in Carnarvonshire, and also Llanfor in Merionethshire, are assigned to Mor, the son of Ceneu ab Coel, who is considered to be a contemporary of Peblig. There are also a few other names of early saints in the Welsh genealogies, concerning whom tradition states nothing except their parentage; but from the time of German the number and importance of the names increases, so that altogether the roll of Welsh saints is made up to the total of four hundred and seventy-nine.

The Age of the Saints is often passed over with but scanty attention, on account of the difficulty of distinguishing between history and fiction in the records of the period which we possess. These are the writings of Gildas: a few dates in the chronicle known as the 'Annales Cambriæ'; the 'Book of Llandaff'; the Welsh genealogies of the Saints; a number of Welsh traditions, some of which are contained in the Iolo Manuscripts; and the Legends of the Saints. The question of Welsh dedications is also important in connection with this subject. The most ancient churches in Wales are believed to have got their names either from their actual founders or from some other connection with the saints after whom they are called, and not to have received any formal dedication to those saints.[1] The earliest foundations bear the names of native saints; next in point of antiquity are those which are called after St. Michael; and last of all, those which are dedicated to the Virgin Mary and other saints.[2] A dedication to St. Michael is first mentioned in the year 718.[3] The first Church of St. Mary was dedicated in A.D. 973,[4] and this was founded by the English King, Edgar.

Gildas tells us nothing of the Welsh saints; his topic is rather the sins of his countrymen, but he draws a graphic picture of his time. The 'Book of Llandaff' was compiled in the twelfth century by Geoffrey, brother of Urban, Bishop of Llandaff, and contains also numerous entries by other and later hands. The earlier portion comprises the Lucius legend, and the story of the foundation of the see of Llandaff by King Meurig; the lives of Dubricius, Teilo, and Oudoceus, the first Bishops of Llandaff; and a number of charters and synodical records from the sixth century onwards. One of the most important of the subsequent entries is a life of St. Samson. The synodical records contain numerous anachronisms; and the early charters are unquestionably confused and have been much suspected. But even the severest critics admit that 'real materials existed for the compilation of the book,' and it is not improbable that the charters are for the most part genuine.[5]

The Welsh genealogies of the saints appear to have

---

[1] Rees, 'Welsh Saints,' §§ 1, 2, 3.
[2] *Ibid.*, p. 59.
[3] 'Brut y Tywysogion' says, A.D. 717: 'The "Annales Cambriæ" has cclxxiii. Annus (*i.e.*, A.D. 718) Consecratio Michaelis Archangeli ecclesiæ.'
[4] At Bangor. Rees, p. 69, *note;* Pryce, 'Ancient British Church,' p. 128, *note.*
[5] 'H. and S. Councils,' p. 147, *note;* 'Remains of Arthur Haddan,' pp. 239-253; 'The Book of Llan Dâv,' preface, by J. G. Evans. Also 'Archæologia Cambrensis,' 5th Series, x. 332-339.

been drawn up by mediæval antiquaries, and differ to some extent among themselves. One curious feature of these records is the number of names which are thrown together in one group. In the Latin tract 'Concerning Brychan of Brycheiniog and his family,'[1] said to be copied from an ancient manuscript of A.D. 900, or thereabouts, Brychan is credited with ten sons and twenty-six daughters, a most prodigious family. In the 'Bonedd y Saint' twenty-four sons and twenty-five daughters are ascribed to him. The smallest number of children given him by any genealogist is twenty-four.[2] Various explanations have been given of these absurdities, which are far from consistent with one another; but it is a little doubtful whether ingenuity is not wasted in the task.'[3] The genealogies, as has been well said, seem to be 'an attempt on the part of chroniclers to systematize and bring into harmony a mass of pre-existing legends, the subjects of which are thus brought into mutual relation.'[4] At the same time, it is highly probable that they contain

[1] 'Cambro-British Saints,' pp. 272-275.
[2] Rees, 'Welsh Saints,' p. 136. See also Giraldus Cambrensis ('Itin. Kamb.,' i. c. 2), who mentions that the British historians testify that Brychan had twenty-four daughters, all saints.
[3] The children of Brychan may have been merely natives of the county over which he once ruled (Borlase, 'Age of the Saints,' p. 89; *Journal Royal Inst. Cornwall*, 20). Wakeman in a note to the 'Cambro-British Saints' mentions three Brychans (p. 606). Skene also suggests that there were various Brychans, and Borlase mentions that it was a common Celtic patronymic. Rees and others suppose that the names of the grandchildren of Brychan have crept into the list of his children (Rees, p. 137).
[4] Jones and Freeman ('History of St. David's,' p. 252, *note*): 'Hence probably arose the "Triad of Holy Families," and in particular the extremely symmetrical progeny of Brychan Brycheiniog, many of the individuals composing which may have had, very possibly, a real though an independent existence. Compare Mr. Grote (vol. i., pp. 596-601) on the Greek and (pp. 623-625) Teutonic genealogies, and on the process of harmonizing conflicting legends (p. 145). 'The legendary world of Greece,' he says, 'in the manner in which it is presented to us, appears invested with a degree of symmetry and coherence which did not originally belong to it. . . . The primitive elements, originally distinct and unconnected, are removed out of sight, and connected together by subsequent poets and logographers.'

historical matter, and that the relationship they show between the leading saints and the princes of Wales is historically correct.

The legends of the Welsh saints were written with an ethical purpose, and have many of the characteristics of a religious novel. The hero is frequently made the centre of the religious work of the time; around him are grouped his great contemporaries; and, if he be a bishop, his see is magnified to the disparagement of others. His privileges or his person are threatened by some stupid and malignant tyrant, either Maelgwn Gwynedd, 'ever the tempter of the saints,' or a wicked Arthur, strangely diverse in character from the 'white Arthur' of Tennyson, or perhaps some minor chief, who takes a curious pleasure in running upon his own destruction, and whom the saint in the calmest manner causes to be stricken with blindness, swallowed by the earth up to the chin, or in some other way frustrated and punished. The tyrant is an important requisite to act as a foil to the virtues of the saint, and his vices are painted in the darkest colours. It is only minor saints whose legends lack a tyrant. It is curious to note how in some legends the cursing powers of the saint are so insisted upon, that they nearly equal those of the Irish saints. Patrick in the 'Tripartite Life' is represented as cursing friend and foe alike, as cursing the sea[1] and the rivers Buall[2] and Dub,[3] as cursing the stones of Uisnech,[4] as driving his chariot three times over his penitent sister Lupait till he killed her,[5] and as defying the Almighty himself in his wrath upon the peak of Cruachan Aigle.[6] Aedh of Ferns by his curse split a rock in two.[7] Another Irishman 'performed fasting against the Lord' because he thought that a fellow-

[1] Whitley Stokes, 'Tripartite Life,' i. 205.   [2] *Ibid.*, p. 143.
[3] *Ibid.*, p. 147.   [4] *Ibid.*, p. 183.   [5] *Ibid*, p. 235.
[6] *Ibid.*, pp. 113-121.
[7] 'Vita S. Aidui' (Rees, 'C. B. S,' p. 244), 'cum sanctus Aidus illam petram malediceret, statim illa petra in duas partes divisa est.'

clergyman had been better treated by Heaven than himself. So, too, Cadoc of Llancarfan cursed the boorish servant Tidus, because he would not give him fire, and the rustic was burned up with his threshing-floor and corn.[1] Sawyl Benuchel, who offended him by taking meat and drink by force from the monks of Llancarfan, was punished ignominiously by the saint's order: when he and his company were asleep, half their beards and hair was shaven off, and the lips and ears of their horses were cut off. Afterwards the whole troop was swallowed up.[2] Rhun, son of Maelgwn, and his 'eunuchs' were blinded for a time for another offence.[3] At another time Cadoc sailed with two disciples, Barruc and Gwalches, from Echni (the Flat Holme) to Barry. The disciples found that they had left his Manual behind at Echni, whereupon the saint, burning with anger, said, 'Go, not to return!' The two returned to Echni and got the book, but through the saint's curse were drowned on the way back, and Barruc's body was cast upon Barry Island, which to this day bears his name.[4] Since those who offended from forgetfulness were thus punished, it is not strange that wilful offenders suffered heavily. A murderer vanished like smoke before the saint;[5] a swineherd who was going to slay the saint, thinking he was a thief, was blinded and had his arm paralyzed, but was afterwards made whole;[6] and two English wolves which followed their natural instincts so far as to tear Cadoc's sheep on the Isle of Echni, were changed to stone on swimming back, and still remain as two dangerous rocks—The Wolves—in the Bristol Channel.[7] Even after Cadoc's death, his coffin when struck by robbers bellowed like a bull, and an earthquake followed.[8]

[1] 'Vita S. Cadoci,' § 4 ('C. B. S.,' p. 29).
[2] Ibid., § 13 ('C. B. S.,' pp. 42, 43).
[3] Ibid., § 20 ('C. B. S.,' p. 54).   [4] Ibid., § 25 ('C. B. S.,' p. 63).
[5] Ibid., § 12 ('C. B. S.,' p. 42).   [6] Ibid., § 5 ('C. B. S.,' p. 31).
[7] Ibid., § 26 ('C. B. S.,' p. 64).   [8] Ibid., § 37 ('C. B. S.,' p. 77).

The legend of Cadoc is especially notable for miracles of the revengeful type, which are not particularly noticeable in most of the other legends, for a few judgments upon the ordinary legendary tyrant served to point a moral to the princes and nobles for whose behoof the legends were in part compiled. This characteristic of Cadoc's legend is probably to be explained by Irish influence, which manifests itself in various other ways in the story.

It may be inferred from the foregoing remarks that the historical element is rather overlaid in the legends by the ethical, and that they are full of extravagant miracles. It has been seen that these miracles sometimes savour more of the spirit of a cruel and relentless paganism than of Christianity; at other times they are merely ridiculous. When Brynach invited Maelgwn to supper, he had nothing to give him, whereupon he went to a neighbouring oak and pulled off as many wheaten loaves as he required, and then drew wine from the river Caman, and made fishes of its stones.[1] At Teilo's death three churches quarrelled for his body, but in the morning, lo! there were three Teilos, so that each was contented.

One strange peculiarity of the Welsh saints is their partiality for pigs. Several churches of the first importance have their sites pointed out by a white boar or a white sow. In this wise Kentigern was directed to the site of St. Asaph;[2] Dyfrig to the site of his church at Mochros, 'the moor of the pigs'; Brynach to a spot by the banks of the Caman;[3] and Cadoc to Llancarvan,[4] and to Cadoxton-juxta-Neath.[5] Probably the story is adapted from Roman legend, though it has been suggested

---

[1] 'Vita S. Bernaci' ('C. B. S.,' p. 12).
[2] 'Vita Kentegerni auct. Jocelino,' § 24 ('Hist. of Scot.,' v. 202).
[3] 'Vita S. Bernaci' ('C. B. S.,' p. 9).
[4] 'Vita S. Cadoci,' § 5 ('C. B. S.,' p. 34).
[5] *Ibid.*, § 31 ('C. B. S.,' p. 67).

in the case of St. Asaph that local names, such as Sarn Sws, Berwyn and *aper* (*i.e.*, *aber*), may have helped.¹

The legend of an Irish saint, as has been well said, 'too often bids defiance to truth, reason, and decency; and, instead of history, presents a specimen of the meanest fiction.'² The legends of the Welsh saints are not of quite so low a grade as the Irish legends, but they are exceedingly poor as literature, and cause somewhat painful feelings when we reflect that they supplied much of the religious wants of the people in the Middle Ages. Yet here and there occur brighter and better parts which make us feel that, amid all their extravagance, they show that a better era of gentleness had dawned upon the world, and that the old days of force and fraud were doomed. Oudoceus's pity for the stag which sank upon his cloak as if taking refuge there from Prince Einion and his troop; Illtyd's protection of another stag, which was chased by King Meirchion, are pretty stories, which a cold, hard age would not have appreciated. The stories of vengeance taken by the saints upon aggressors may be pardoned at a time when the poor needed the defence of the spiritual arm against many a local tyrant, as wicked as Maelgwn, Meirchion, or the wicked Arthur. But if, from an ethical point of view, we can discern good as well as evil in the legends, can we also find history as well as fiction? Are we to believe in Cadoc's power of cursing, and in his possession of two wooden horses, exceeding swift, or, if we reject these wonders, what are we to receive?

There are two ways of solving these problems, which have been often tried, but neither of which is perfectly satisfactory. One is to reject the legends altogether as monkish impostures—' blasphemous fables and damnable deceits'; the other is to rationalize the myths, to strip

---

[1] 'St. Asaph' ('Diocesan History,' S.P.C.K.), by Ven. Archdeacon Thomas, p. 1. *note*.
[2] Reeves, 'Columba' ('Hist. of Scot.,' vi. 223).

them of their miraculous element, and serve up all the rest as genuine history.

The latter plan is, to the critical student, utterly false and wrong; the first is rash. Though the stories are not history, they contain history. They have traces of old ecclesiastical customs, which frequently the writers of the legends themselves did not understand, and could not have invented; they bear testimony to a state of society which the pages of Gildas prove to have existed in reality; they evince a conflict between ancient national habits of thought and Roman habits, some of the legends, as that of Beuno, being strongly national, and others, as that of Cadoc, strongly Roman; and they have here and there touches of paganism, and even of a tenderness for Druidism which help us to understand what a composite thing early British Christianity was. In all these respects they are of the utmost value. Furthermore, if one attentively studies these legends, and carefully compares them one with another and with the legends of other nations, he will gain a discernment between the genuine original tradition and the false later accretions. Some stories, as the wickedness of the monastic cook and steward, the pointing out of sites by a white boar or a white sow, and the judgments upon princes, are the stock-in-trade of the professional legend writer, and may be treated accordingly. Some legends will have to be rejected altogether as wholly fictitious. But in others a basis of early tradition may be traced, just as the 'Tripartite Life of St. Patrick,' with all its marvellous absurdities, is built up upon the substructure of the early, rational, and sober life by Tirechan. The life of St. Samson in the 'Book of Llandaff' corresponds closely in its main features to an early life of the saint still extant, which was written probably about A.D. 600, and whose author states that he crossed the sea to Britain, and obtained information from Samson's own cousin. The lives of St. David are, in the main, the same, and Giraldus, who despised his predecessors in the work, was content to steal from them. Rhygyfarch, the biographer of St. David, and Joceline, the biographer of St. Kentigern, both profess to use earlier materials, existing in their time, and there is no reason to doubt their statements, but rather the contrary.

The legend writers were poor inventors after all; that is proved by their constant repetition of the same stories with the names altered ; when they had materials to go upon they were very glad to avail themselves of them, and did so. It is not often that the lives of one saint differ so much from each other as do the lives of Gildas ; but, of course, if Arthurian fictions are introduced as they are in Caradoc's 'Life of Gildas,' the historical value of the legend is at once ruined. But, with care and discrimination, a certain historical residuum may be gathered from some of the legends, even with regard to the lives of the saints themselves.

The Age of the Saints was an age of conflict and sin, of 'fightings without and fears within.' The pagan English were driving the Britons back westward, step by step, and the defence of the Christians was enfeebled by reason of their sins. If the obscure verses of Aneurin are interpreted aright,[1] the drunkenness of the Britons lost them the battle of Cattraeth. There was wickedness in high places. 'Britain,' says Gildas, 'has kings—nay, tyrants; it has judges—they are unrighteous; ever plundering and terrifying the innocent; avenging and protecting—aye, guilty brigands; having a multitude of wives—nay, harlots and adulteresses; frequently swearing, but falsely; vowing, and almost immediately breaking their vow; warring, but in unjust and civil warfare; chasing zealously thieves through the country, and yet not only loving, but even rewarding the brigands who sit

---

[1] 'Gododin,' 11, etc., 'Mead they drank, yellow, sweet, ensnaring ;' also 17, etc., Ab Ithel's edition, pp. 96, 106.

with them at table; giving alms lavishly, yet heaping up, on the other hand, an immense mountain of crimes; sitting in the seat to judge, but rarely seeking the rule of right judgment; despising the guiltless and humble, raising to the stars, to the best of their power, the bloody, the proud, murderers, comrades, and adulterers, enemies of God, who ought earnestly to be destroyed together with their very name; having many bound in prisons, whom they trample under foot rather by their own treachery than for any fault, loading them with chains; tarrying among the altars to take oaths, and shortly after despising these altars as though they were muddy stones.'[1]

These are not mere rhetorical antitheses; Gildas gives particulars in the case of five princes. Constantine of Damnonia, the same whose later repentance was one of the most notable events of the sixth century, had perpetrated a sacrilegious murder in the very year that Gildas was writing. After having bound himself with a dreadful oath that he would do no wrong to the citizens, this prince, in the dress of an abbot, had killed two princely boys 'among the sacred altars.' His previous life had not been stainless, for he had put away his lawful wife. In like manner Gildas accuses Aurelius Conan[2] of murder, fornication, and adultery, and Vortipor, the prince of the Demetæ, 'the wicked son of a good prince, like Manasseh, the son of Hezekiah,' of murder, adultery, and of divorcing his wife. Cuneglas,[3] a fourth prince, had not only divorced his wife, but had married her sister, who was under a vow of celibacy. Against all these Gildas turns the bitterness of his indignation,

---

[1] 'Epistola Gildæ.' See 'H. and S.,' i., pp. 48, 49; 'M. H. B.,' p. 16.

[2] 'Catule leoline Aureli Conane.'

[3] 'Tu, ab adolescentiæ annis, urse multorum sessor, aurigaque currus receptaculi ursi, Dei contemptor, sortisque ejus depressor, Cuneglase, Romana lingua Lanio-fulve.'—'Ep. Gild.,' 'M. H. B.,' p. 17.

and summons them to repentance. But the chief outburst of both reproach and entreaty is directed to Maglocunus, or Maelgwn Gwynedd, in whom, at one time, there had been some signs of goodness. He, 'the dragon of the island, who had deprived many princes of their territories and their lives,' was the 'first in evil, greater than many in power and in wickedness, more lavish in giving, more profuse in sins, powerful in arms, but bolder in the destruction of the soul.' He had not lacked a good training, for he had had as his instructor 'the elegant master of nearly the whole of Britain.' Yet, in the first years of his youth, he had 'crushed most vigorously with sword, spear, and fire, the king, his uncle, with almost the bravest soldiers, whose countenances seemed in battle not greatly unlike to those of a lion's whelps.' After this he had repented and taken the vow of a monk; but he sinned again, and this time more grievously than before. Led astray by a wicked woman, the wife of his nephew, he had murdered his wife and his nephew, and having thus got rid of the two obstacles to the gratification of his guilty passion, he then married his temptress.

It is not without significance that Gildas includes in his rebukes the priests of Britain, as well as its princes. 'Britain[1] has priests, but they are foolish; a multitude of ministers, but they are shameless; clergy, nay, crafty ravishers; shepherds, as they are called, but they are wolves ready to slay souls, for they provide not for the good of their people, but seek to fill their own bellies; having the houses of the Church, but approaching these for the sake of base gain; teaching the people, but showing them the worst examples, vices, and wicked manners; rarely offering the Sacrifice, and never standing among the altars with pure hearts; not reproving the people for their sins, for they do the same themselves; despising

[1] 'Ep. Gild.' 'M. H. B.,' p. 29.

the commands of Christ, and taking care by all means to satisfy their own lusts; usurping with foul feet the seat of the Apostle Peter, but falling by their covetousness into the pestilent chair of the traitor Judas; hating truth as an enemy, and favouring falsehoods as dear brothers; looking with fierce countenances upon the righteous that are poor, as if they were frightful serpents, and venerating the wicked, who are rich, without any regard for shame, as if they were angels from heaven; preaching with their lips that alms should be given to the needy, and themselves not giving even an obolus; keeping silent with respect to the wicked crimes of the people, and magnifying their own wrongs as if done to Christ; driving from home, perchance, a religious mother or sister, and indecently welcoming strange women as familiar friends, as it were, for some more secret office, or rather, to speak truth, though folly (but the folly is not mine, but theirs who act thus), humiliating them; seeking after ecclesiastical preferment more eagerly than the kingdom of heaven, and defending it when received like tyrants, and not adorning it by lawful manners.' They are 'hoarse like bulls with fatness,' 'they roll in the mire like pigs,' they imitate Simon Magus, and yet sin more desperately than he, 'for they buy their priesthood, counterfeit and never likely to profit, not from the Apostles or the successors of the Apostles, but from tyrants and from their father, the devil.'[1] They are 'enemies of God and not priests, veterans in evil and not bishops, traitors and not successors of the holy Apostles, and not ministers of Christ.' They are 'shameless, double-tongued, drunken, covetous of evil gain, holding the faith and, to speak more truly, the lack of faith in an impure heart, ministering, not approved in good, but known beforehand in an evil work, and having innumerable crimes.'

[1] 'M. H. B.,' p. 30.

This is indeed a dark picture of the Age of the Saints. Gildas admits that his description of the priesthood of his times was not universally applicable. He says: 'But perhaps someone may say, "Not all the bishops or priests are wicked as above described," because they are not stained with the infamy of schism, or pride, or impurity, which we also do not vehemently deny. But though we know that they are chaste and good, yet we will briefly reply: What profited it Eli the priest, that he alone did not violate the commands of the Lord . . . seeing that he was punished by the same fatal wrath as were his sons?'[1] In his denunciation of the worldliness and immorality of the clergy, we may discern the monk's dislike of a secular and married clergy; but there are some charges precise and definite enough, for which there must have been some ground.

The Penitentials also which remain testify to the existence of the foulest crimes even among the clergy. There is one set of rules which is ascribed to Gildas himself, another to a Synod of Northern Britain, a third to the Synod of the Grove of Victory (Luci Victoriæ), and a fourth to St. David. Some of the crimes mentioned in these can scarcely have been of common occurrence, but it is appalling to find them included at all, and the mild punishment in one for drunkenness may suggest that it was not an unfrequent offence. 'If anyone from drunkenness cannot sing through being unable to speak,' says the rule of Gildas, 'he is to lose his supper.'[2] In the rules of St. David[3] it is ordered that priests about to minister in church, who drink wine or strong drink through negligence, and yet not ignorance, are to do penance for three days; but if they do it wilfully, they are to do penance for forty days. Those who are drunk through ignorance have penance for fifteen

[1] 'M. H. B.,' p. 31.   [2] No. X., 'H. and S.,' i. 114.
[3] 'H. and S.,' i. 118-120.

days; those through negligence, forty; those wilfully, thrice forty days. He who causes anyone to get drunk from courtesy is to do the same penance as the drunken man. He who makes others drunk to laugh at them is to do penance as a murderer of souls.

These Penitentials would hardly have been drawn up in a period of general virtue and holiness. But indeed it is quite a modern conception of the Age of the Saints to represent it as such a period; and those who object to the genuineness of the Epistle of Gildas on the ground of its severe criticisms of the princes and priests of Britain might equally well object to other authorities also. The legends of the saints do not represent all the clergy and monks as alike holy. The 'Life of St. David' contains a story of an attempt to poison the saint, which was made by the steward, the cook, and a deacon of the monastery of Menevia.[1] We are led to suppose, indeed, that the steward and the cook were frequently wicked, or, at least, were unpopular with the writers of the legends, for these officials in the monastery of Llancarfan, together with the sexton, annoyed the Irish visitor St. Finnian, and were cursed by St. Cadoc.[2] St. Padarn, while he was in Brittany, suffered much from false brethren, and one wicked monk was seized by a demon for a trick he played on the saint.[3] The legends of St. Samson draw a dark picture of monastic life in Wales. A nephew of St. Illtyd, who was anxious to succeed his uncle as abbot, but feared that the superior merits of St. Samson might cause him to be chosen in preference, sought, in conjunction with his brother, to poison his rival and so remove him out of his way. Samson drank the poisoned cup, but, as might have been expected, felt no hurt, and

---

[1] Rhygyfarch, 'Vita S. David;' 'Cambro-British Saints,' pp. 131, 132. For stories of wicked stewards, see also Todd, 'St. Patrick,' pp. 167-169.
[2] 'Vita S. Cadoci,' § 9, 'C. B. S.,' p. 38.
[3] 'Vita S. Paterni,' 'C. B. S.,' p. 190.

the guilty clergyman was soon afterwards seized by the devil. Soon afterwards Samson visited another monastery on an island near Llantwit, and here also he found matters in an evil state. ' One gloomy night,' says the old ' Life,'[1] 'the venerable Abbot Piro took a solitary stroll into the grounds of the monastery; but what is more serious, he was in a very tipsy condition, and tumbled headlong into a deep pit. The brethren were alarmed by his loud cries for help, and hurrying to the spot, they dragged him out of the hole in a helpless state, and before morning he was dead.' When Samson visited Ireland he found there an abbot possessed with a devil, whom he delivered. St. Kentigern, according to his biographer Jocelin of Furness, was especially careful to denounce hypocrisy, and on one occasion supernaturally detected a British clergyman, ' of great eloquence and much learning,' who was nevertheless guilty of a most abominable crime, and who finally perished by a sudden destruction.

The testimony of Gildas to the vices of the princes and of the world at large is abundantly corroborated by all our other authorities. The legends, as has already been said, ordinarily introduce some wicked tyrant who molests the saint, but is continually worsted. Maglocunus, or Maelgwn, whom Gildas rebukes, is a familiar figure to a reader of these lives. The ' Book of Llandaff' records excommunications pronounced, and penalties imposed, upon princes for crimes of violence and unchastity. Two princes of Glamorgan, Meurig,[2] and Morgan,[3] as well as Tewdwr, prince of Dyfed,[4] and Clydri, or Clotri, prince of Ergyng,[5] were excommunicated for murder committed after they had sworn to friendship upon relics. Gwaednerth,[6] prince of Gwent, was excommunicated for fratricide

---

[1] This story is told in the old life of Samson, written at the request of Bishop Tigerinomalus. The later life in the 'Book of Llandaff' discreetly omits it.
[2] 'Book of Llan Dâv,' Oxford edition, p. 147.   [3] *Ibid.*, p. 152.
[4] *Ibid.*, p. 167.   [5] *Ibid.*, p. 176.   [6] *Ibid.*, p. 180.

and sent on a pilgrimage for a year to Brittany. Gwrgan,[1] prince of Ergyng, was excommunicated for incest with his step-mother. Margetud,[2] King of Dyfed, was punished for the murder of Gufrir, 'a man of St. Teilo,' whom in a frenzy of rage and cruelty he had murdered in front of the altar. Tutuc,[3] a rich man, gave certain lands to the see of Llandaff, as an atonement for the murder of a young nephew of St. Teilo, named Tyfei, whom he killed while he was attempting to slay a neglectful swineherd, who had allowed his pigs to damage Tutuc's corn. Another curious story of the same age illustrates the prevalent savageness of manners when left unrestrained. A prince of Dyfed, Aircol Lawhir,[4] was holding his court at Lircastell; but every night some quarrel happened, and murders were frequent. The cause was drunkenness; but the murders became so customary, that even in that wild age the prince and his court became alarmed, and feared that the devil was let loose among them. So, after fasting and prayer, the prince sent to Penaly to St. Teilo, that 'he might bless him and his court, so that the accustomed murder should not take place any more therein.' Teilo came and blessed him and his court, and sent two of his disciples to distribute meat and drink to all in future by measure; 'and by the grace of the Holy Spirit no murder was committed that night, nor afterwards in his court, as had been usual.'

Although some of the above stories may not be history, they are correct in their picture of the Age of the Saints. As in the age of Antony and the first hermits, men's hearts were 'failing them for fear, and for looking after those things which were coming on the earth.' The world was full of savage violence and unbridled lust; the appointed pastors were not always faithful to their flocks, they spoke softly to the rich and roughly to the poor, and

---

[1] 'Book of Llan Dâv,' Oxford edition, p. 189.
[2] *Ibid.*, p. 125.   [3] *Ibid.*, p. 127.   [4] *Ibid.*, p. 125.

so earnest men fled to the wilderness to save their souls, in solitude, apart from the world, for it seemed impossible to save them in the world and amid its wickedness. Some lived as hermits on the islands or rocky promontories of Wales, or retired across the British Channel to Devon and Cornwall, for Cornwall has been called 'the Thebaid of the Welsh saints.' Some of these may have lived a solitary life continually in the places which they had chosen; but most became monks or abbots in one of those great camps wherein the soldiers of the Cross kept ever watch and ward against their spiritual adversaries.

Thus, though the age was an evil one, and merited the terrible rebukes of Gildas, it was also an age of religious revival and of Church progress. The sixth century witnessed the foundation of the Welsh bishoprics and of the great Welsh monasteries, which latter were the especial glory of the Church in Wales. Gildas says nothing of these, and the omission has been thought strange. But those who thus criticise his writings fail to perceive their purpose. His Epistle is a stern denunciation of the world outside the monasteries; he deals with the sins of the princes, and of the secular priests who live in that outside world; those within the monastic pale are men of quite a different sphere; to them he utters no word of praise or of blame in this treatise. His mission, to use modern phraseology, is only to the unconverted; and he seeks to rouse such to a sense of sin, with all the force of Celtic impetuosity and Hebrew rhetoric, until the Latin language nearly breaks down under the strain that is put upon it. There is no need, therefore, to infer from the gloomy picture of Gildas that the saints were not saintly, and that the religious revival in the Church was unreal, or that there was merely progress in Church institutions, not in Christian morals. The testimony of the hostile English controversialist, Aldhelm, in a somewhat later age, proves that Wales was noted for the purity of its clergy and the sanctity of its hermits. His words, which we shall consider later, lead rather to the conclusion that the temperament of Gildas led him to put matters in the very worst light. However great were the sins and failings of the Welsh, they were at least superior in morality to the English converts of Aldhelm's age, and Aldhelm can only blame them for a Pharisaic contempt of sinners, and not for being sinners themselves.

It is probable that even among the monastic saints Gildas was exceptionally severe in his abhorrence of the secular world. There are legends which seem to show that antiquity esteemed the mildness attributed to the gentle Cadoc rather than the terrible severity of the stern Gildas. Celtic Christianity has frequently presented two different aspects in the same age: there has been the awful earnestness of Gildas which doubts the goodness even of the good, and applies the test of its rigid rules to prince and priest alike; and there has been the gentleness of Cadoc[1] and of Columba,[2] which seeks to discover the 'soul of goodness in things evil,' which bridges over the space between paganism and Christianity, which believes that 'nothing is common or unclean,' and which gently invites even such as Maelgwn 'to brighter worlds and leads the way.' Perhaps in each case 'wisdom is justified of her children.'

The Welsh bishoprics were the creation of the new monastic spirit, and the Welsh princes whom Gildas criticises so severely, co-operated with the monastic saints in their foundation. Maelgwn gave lands for the see of Bangor, of which Deiniol Wyn, who died in A.D. 584, was the first bishop. Meurig is said to have endowed Llandaff, which was founded by Dyfrig or Dubricius, who

---

[1] Cadoc in Breton legends, and others, is represented as a gentle saint.
[2] I incline to accept Adamnan's picture rather than the Irish stories.

died in A.D. 612.¹ Dubricius seems to have resigned the see before his death, and to have retired to Bardsey. St. Teilo, who was his successor, is also reckoned a founder of the see. Padarn, an Armorican saint, appears to have established a bishopric at Llanbadarn Fawr, near Aberystwith. He was another sixth-century saint, being a contemporary of David and Teilo. Kenauc or Cynog, who died in A.D. 606, was transferred from Llanbadarn to succeed St. David in his see. The bishopric of Llanbadarn was finally united to St. David's, perhaps on account of the murder of Idnerth, one of its bishops. St. David founded the bishopric of Menevia or St. David's. He is said to have died in A.D. 601.² Llanelwy or St. Asaph was founded by Cyndeyrn or Kentigern, who is said to have left his disciple, St. Asaph, in charge on his return to his bishopric of Glasgow. Kentigern died in A.D. 612.³ These five bishoprics seem to have corresponded fairly well to the Welsh principalities then existing; Bangor being the bishopric for Gwynedd, St. Asaph for Powys, St. David's for Dyfed, Llanbadarn for Ceredigion, and Llandaff for Gwent and Morganwg. None had any jurisdiction over the others, although the term archbishop is applied loosely, as a mere term of honour to various bishoprics, as it was also used in Ireland, and claims of archiepiscopal jurisdiction were advanced by more than one of the five. Giraldus Cambrensis made a bold but fruitless stand on behalf of St. David's, but his arguments merely show how fictitious the claims were; and the 'Book of Llandaff' claims the same privilege for the see of Llandaff.

The Welsh diocesan bishops of the sixth century were abbots as well as bishops—a fact which attests the predominance of the monastic spirit in the Church. It also

---

¹ 'Annales Cambriæ,' p. 6.
² *Ibid.*, p. 6. 'clvii. Annus . . . David episcopus Moni judeorum.'
³ *Ibid.*, p. 6. 'clviii. Annus. Conthigirni obitus.'

seems probable that there were abbot-bishops in Wales who had no dioceses. Such is the tradition respecting Paulinus or Pawl Hên, who was abbot of Tŷ Gwyn, and was the instructor of St. David.[1] Cybi, founder and abbot of the monastery of Caergybi, is also called a bishop in his legend, which, however, contains an anachronism in relating his consecration by Hilary of Poitiers, who lived some two centuries before his time.[2] Tradition hands down also the names of Tudwal Befr,[3] Cynin,[1] and Guislianus or Gweslan, as non-diocesan bishops. Of these three, the two former were not abbots, and the evidence regarding them is not very strong. Gweslan was cousin, or uncle, of St. David, and lived at Old Menevia (Hen-meneu) as a bishop, and possibly also as an abbot over a small monastery.[5] But the legend of the consecration of David, Padarn, and Teilo at Jerusalem by the Patriarch, without reference either to dioceses or abbacies, and the similar story of the consecration of Samson to be bishop without a see, shows that the idea of a non-diocesan episcopate was perfectly familiar to Welsh churchmen. Rhygyfarch[6] also states that at the synod of Llanddewi Brefi 'there were gathered together 118 bishops, and an innumerable multitude of presbyters, abbots, and other orders.'[7] A Bishop Afan is found among the saints of Wales, and a mediæval inscription at Llanafan Fawr, in Breconshire, marks his burial-place and preserves the tradition

---

[1] Rhygyfarch, 'Vita S. David,' 'C. B. S.,' p. 122.
[2] 'Vita S. Kebii,' 'C. B. S., p. 183.
[3] Rees' 'Welsh Saints,' p. 133. [4] *Ibid.*, p. 144.
[5] Rhygyfarch, 'Vita S. David,' 'C. B. S.,' p. 124; cf. 'Buchedd Dewi Sant,' 'C. B. S.,' p. 108.
[6] Frequently called Rhyddmarch, the form of the name in the so-called *Gwentian Brut*, against which form Mr. Egerton Phillimore has protested. He calls himself in Latin, Ricemarchus. The 'Annales Cambriæ' (p. 32) calls him Regewarc, the *Brut y Tywysogion* Rychmarch (p. 62).
[7] 'C. B. S.,' p. 136.

that he was a bishop.[1] It has been conjectured that Llanafan Fawr was for a short time the see of a bishop, but this is not very probable. In a mediæval list of the seven bishops who met St. Augustine, a bishop of Wig and a bishop of Morganwg are mentioned. The Bishop of Morganwg has been conjectured to have had his see at Margam, and a list of bishops of the see has been preserved. But all other than the five Welsh sees of St. David, St. Asaph, Bangor, Llandaff, and Llanbadarn, are exceedingly doubtful, and the traditions respecting them, so far as they have any truth, may not improbably rest upon the existence of non-diocesan bishops.

The Dimetian form of the laws of Hywel Dda contains a curious entry, which may bear upon the same matter. It runs as follows: 'There are seven bishop-houses in Dyfed: 1. One is Menevia, a principal seat in Wales; 2. The second is the Church of Ismael; 3. The third is Llan Ddegeman; 4. The fourth is Llan Usyllt; 5. The fifth is Llan Deilo; 6. The sixth is Llan Deulydog; 7. The seventh is Llan Geneu; 8. The abbots of Teilo, Teulydog, Ismael and Degeman, should be graduated in literary degrees; 9. Their ebediws, due to the lord of Dyfed, are ten pounds, and those who succeed them are to pay them; 10. Menevia is to be free from every kind of due; 11. Llan Geneu and Llan Usyllt are free from ebediws, because there is no church-land belonging to them; 12. Whoever draws blood from an abbot of any one of these principal seats before mentioned, let him pay seven pounds; and a female of his kindred to be a washer-woman, as a disgrace to the kindred, and to serve as a memorial of the payment of the saraad.'[2]

---

[1] This stone is traditionally said to mark the site of the bishop's martyrdom. The inscription is 'HIC IACET SANCTUS AVANUS EPISCOPUS.' There is a brook near called Nant-yr-escob (The Bishop's Brook), and a dingle, Cwmesgob (Bishop's Dingle), and not far off the little parsonage, still known as Perth-y-saint.

[2] 'Cyvreithiau Hywel Dda,' ii. 24, in 'H. and S.,' i. 281.

Whatever may be the exact signification of this section, which is not quite clear, this much is certain, that the heads of the bishop-houses were abbots, and it is not improbable that originally, at least, they were abbot-bishops.

The existence of a non-diocesan episcopate in Wales, although doubted by some high authorities, is certainly rendered probable by the hints afforded by tradition, especially when interpreted by the usages of the daughter Church of Ireland. St. Patrick, who was a British priest, introduced into Ireland a non-diocesan episcopate on rather an extensive scale. The 'Catalogue of the Saints of Ireland,' an authority which is referred by Dr. Todd to the middle of the eighth century, states that the first order of Catholic saints in the time of Patrick 'were all bishops, famous and holy, and full of the Holy Ghost, 350 in number,'[1] or 450, according to another manuscript. Tirechan, in his 'Life of Patrick,' states that he came to Ireland with a multitude of holy bishops and other clergy, and that he consecrated afterwards 450 bishops.[2] The 'Tripartite Life' mentions 370 bishops as consecrated by Patrick;[3] Nennius mentions '365 or more;' the Chronological Tract in the 'Lebar Brecc'[4] mentions 'seven fifties;' and the Litany of Angus the Culdee invokes 'seven times fifty holy bishops.' The numbers in these estimates need not be taken as exact, being in some cases influenced by a prejudice in favour of the sacred number seven; but the fact that there was a prodigious number of bishops in Ireland is beyond question.[5] St. Bernard complained that in his time 'one bishopric was not content with one bishop, but almost every

---

[1] Usher, 'De Brit. Eccl. Primord.,' p. 913; 'H. and S.,' ii. 292.
[2] Tirechan's 'Collections' in 'Book of Armagh,' 'W. S.,' ii. 303, 304.
[3] 'Tripartite Life,' 'W. S.,' p. 261.
[4] Quoted in 'W. S.,' p. 553.
[5] See Skene, 'Celtic Scotland,' ii. 14-26.

church had its separate bishop.' It is, therefore, highly probable from the connection of Patrick with the British Church that there was also a goodly number of British bishops without dioceses. We know that Wales was very closely connected with Ireland in the sixth century, and that Gildas, David, and Cadoc in particular were intimately associated with the Saints of the Second Order. This order of Irish saints had, however, fewer bishops, being composed mostly of presbyters.

Groups of seven bishops are frequently found in the Irish Church. The Litany of Angus the Culdee invokes one hundred and fifty-three groups of seven bishops, and six are mentioned in the Martyrology of Donegal. An arrangement in sevens was common both in Ireland and Wales. The seven bishop-houses in Dyfed suggests the working of the same principle. There were seven British bishops at the meeting with Augustine of Canterbury. Oratories were clustered together in groups of seven at Glendalough, at Cashel, at the river Fochaine, at Cianacht, and among the Hui Tuirtri. So, too, we are told that at Llantwit Major 'Illtyd founded seven churches, and appointed seven companies for each church, and seven halls, or colleges, in each company, and seven saints in each hall or college.'[1] Bede tells us of Bangor Iscoed that it was divided into seven companies with provosts set over them, and no company had less than three hundred monks.[2]

There is no trace in the traditions of the Church in Wales of anything parallel to the authority of the abbots over the bishops, which prevailed in the Irish and Scottish Churches. Columba, though only a priest, had bishops subject to him, as Bede relates with wonder,[3]

---

[1] 'Iolo MSS.,' p. 555.
[2] Bede. 'H. E.,' ii. 2; 'M. H. B.,' p. 151. See further, 'St. Patrick' (S.P.C.K.), pp. 121-123.
[3] Bede, 'H. E.,' iii. 3.

and this example was followed by the subsequent abbots of Hy. Even a woman, like St. Bridget, kept a bishop in connection with her monastery to perform the necessary functions, for, although the abbot or abbess was superior in jurisdiction to the bishop, none but a bishop could convey holy orders.

The ascertained customs of the Irish Church throw much light upon hints and traditions concerning the Welsh Church, which might otherwise be very obscure. But the two Churches had their differences as well as their similarities. The civilization of Britain was superior to that of Ireland, and the age of its paganism was more remote. In the sixth century the Irish Church suffered severely from paganism, and the Saints of the Second Order virtually effected a compromise between paganism and Christianity. Ireland at this time received effectual aid from Wales, and especially from the monasteries of Menevia and Llancarfan. Of the Second Order of Irish Saints the Catalogue states that 'they received a mass from Bishop David and Gillas and Docus, the Britons.' Gillas is Gildas, and Docus is Cadoc, of Llancarfan. The legend of Cadoc represents him as studying in Ireland at Lismore under Muchutu, who may be the same as Mochuda.[1] Finnian of Clonard and others are said to have accompanied Cadoc on his return to Llancarfan.[2] Rhygyfarch relates that 'almost the third or the fourth part of Ireland serves David.'[3] Aedh of Ferns, Bar of Cork, Finnian of Clonard, Scuthin and Senanus are brought by various legends to Menevia to study there under St. David. St. Canice also 'went across the sea into Britain to Doc (Cadoc), a wise and most religious man, and read with him diligently and learned good morals.'[4] Gildas is said to have been invited to Ireland

[1] 'Vita S. Cadoci,' § 7, 'C. B. S.,' p. 36.   [2] *Ibid.*, § 8.
[3] 'Vita S. David,' 'C. B. S.,' p. 133.
[4] 'Vita S. Cannechi,' p. 3, quoted by Todd; 'St. Patrick,' p. 100, note.

by King Ainmire, 'because almost all the inhabitants of that island had abandoned the Catholic faith.' He consented, and 'went around all the country of the Irish, restored churches, and instructed the whole clergy in the Catholic faith and the worship of the Holy Trinity. He healed the people who had been grievously wounded by the bites of heretics, and drove away from them heretical deceits with their authors.' The date of this mission, according to the 'Annales Cambriæ,' was A.D. 565. The Irish annals mention the death of Gildas variously under the dates 569 and 570.

All these scattered hints tend one way: they prove that in the sixth century Ireland was much more affected by paganism than was Wales, and that the Church in Wales did a good work in restoring the Christianity of at least the centre and south of that country, for the north seems to have been chiefly under the influence of Ninian's foundation of Whitherne. It is plain, then, that in some respects Ireland and its Church differed widely from Wales and its Church, although in other respects they were similar, and we must not conclude that, because we find one state of affairs in Ireland, a similar condition existed in Wales. There is no proof of any subjection of bishops to abbots in Wales, and no traditions to that effect; hence it is rash to assume it, merely because it was a custom in the Irish churches, both of Ireland and Scotland. Bede's astonishment at the existence of such a custom in the case of Hy and his silence with respect to Wales proves that he knew nothing of it in the latter country. Neither can we infer because Irish Christianity was largely tinged with paganism, that British Christianity was affected by it to the same extent. There is no trace of paganism in the writings of Patrick, his 'Deer's Cry' containing instead a very healthy Christianity, and the compromise with paganism finally effected by the Irish Christian leaders appears to have resulted from the policy of the Second Order of Saints rather than from the Briton, St. Patrick. In North Britain we trace the influence of paganism on Christianity down to the time of Kentigern, for the story of his mother's delusion shows how the two were liable to be blended in the case of a Christian daughter of a half-pagan father.[1] But Gildas brings no charge of paganism against the people of Wales, though unquestionably the crimes he mentions were in part the result of a struggle between pagan ethics and Christianity. The curious statement of the Triad that the family of Brychan Brycheiniog taught the faith in Christ to the nation of the Cymry 'where they were without faith' does not seem consistent with the pictures presented either by Gildas or by our other authorities. David is said to have contended with Baia or Boia, an Irishman and a 'magus,'[2] and 'magus' usually in the Irish legends means a Druid. Boia was eventually slain by his enemies, and his castle, which is traditionally identified with Clegyr Foia at St. David's, was destroyed by fire from heaven, which is scarcely suggestive of compromise on the part of the Welsh saint. The 'Magi' prophesied of the birth of St. David, just as the Irish Druids foretold the coming of St. Patrick. But the most that these stories preserved by Rhygyfarch can indicate is that there may have been in the remote district of Menevia near the western coast, some Gaelic or Irish settlers, perhaps planted by an Irish invasion, who were pagans. A similar influence may have inspired the reference to the Druids in the legend of St. Beuno, the Abbot of Clynnog Fawr. At his death he sees heaven open and exclaims, 'I see the Trinity, the Father, the Son, and the Holy Ghost, and Peter, and Paul, and the Druids, and Deiniol,

---

[1] See the old life of St. Kentigern, of which only a fragment is preserved, 'Vita Kentegerni Imperfecta,' §§ 1-3 (Forbes' edition, pp. 245-247, 'Hist. of Scot.,' v.).
[2] 'Vita S. David' (Rhygyfarch), 'C. B. S.,' p. 124.

and the saints, and the prophets, and the apostles and the martyrs appearing to me.'[1]

There is no doubt, however, that pagan ideas entered largely into the beliefs of the common people, and that they tainted their practice even with the consent of the clergy. The wells that had previously received Divine honours were consecrated to the saint, who used them for baptism, and too often the rites that had been performed of old were continued with a change of names. The superstitious practices connected with the wells of St. Elian, St. Dwynwen, St. Cynhafal, St. Cynfran, St. Winifred, and St. Peris, among others in Wales, even down to modern times sufficiently prove this. The pagan reverence for stones, which was long preserved in Ireland and Cornwall, left also its traces in the legends of Wales. Nimanauc, we are told, crossed from Brittany to Britain on a stone, Carannog's altar floated on the Severn; and Cadoc saw three stones at Jerusalem which he liked and which he willed to fly thence like birds to Llancarfan. St. Canna's stone, near Llangan, Carmarthenshire, was long credited with magical powers, and another in St. David's Church, at Llanfaes, was pointed out as having caught a thieving boy and held him fast for three days and nights.

It may be also that the association of the saints with the islands off the Welsh coast, as also the superstitious reverence of the Welsh for bells and for books, of which there is abundant testimony in the legends and in the writings of Giraldus Cambrensis, are survivals or transferences of pagan ideas. It would have been strange indeed if such ideas had not survived in Wales, as they did in every other country of Christendom, but there is no reason for us to conclude therefrom that Welsh Christianity was in early times of a lower type than existed in Western Europe generally.

[1] 'Buchedd Beuno Sant,' 'C. B. S.,' p. 20.

CHAPTER III.

EARLY WELSH MONASTERIES.

MONASTICISM appears to have reached Britain by way of Gaul. Ninian, the apostle of Whitherne, dedicated his church to St. Martin of Tours, of whose death he heard while he was building it (A.D. 397); and Patrick's connection with the Gallican Church, of whose saints he speaks with reverence and affection, is mythically illustrated by the tradition that he was a nephew of St. Martin. The British Church, near Canterbury, where Bertha had her Christian service, was dedicated to the same saint. All these indications point to the influence which St. Martin's name and fame exerted on the British Church. It is natural, then, that his monastic system, as exhibited at Liguge and Marmoutier, should have been copied more or less by the Britons. But the mission of St. German and St. Lupus appears to have given the necessary impetus to the monastic movement. We find that in Patrick's Church, which was planted by Gaul and Britain, acting in conjunction, the full monastic rigour was unknown. 'They rejected not the service and society of women, because, founded on the Rock of Christ, they feared not the blast of temptation.'[1] Yet there were pretty certainly monasteries or 'insulæ,' as they are called in the legends, in the Church of Patrick. The

[1] 'Catalogus Sanctorum Hib.,' Usher, p. 913.

Second Order of Irish saints, who were in close connection with the monastic leaders of South Wales, were much more rigid in their customs than the earlier saints had been; for 'they refused the services of women, separating them from the monasteries.'[1] The leaven of the teaching of German and Lupus had had time to work, the outburst of monastic zeal in Wales had taken place, and Ireland in its turn was affected thereby. To German, traditions ascribe the foundation of several monasteries,[2] and these traditions, though literally inaccurate, correctly represent the effects of his mission.

Among the native leaders of this great movement in South Wales were the trio who have already been mentioned for their work for Ireland, David, Gildas, and Cadoc, to whom may be added Dyfrig, Teilo, and Padarn. Probably a little earlier than these were Paulinus and Illtyd, the former of whom founded the monastery of Tŷ-gwyn ar Dâf or Whitland in Carmarthenshire, and is said to have instructed both David and Teilo. A stone, formerly at Pant y Polion in the parish of Caio near Llanddewi Brefi, and now at Dolau Cothi, preserves the memory of a Paulinus, who is perhaps to be identified with this saint. The inscription runs thus:

'SERVATUR FIDÆI
PATRIEQUE SEMPER
AMATOR HIC PAULIN
US IACIT CULTOR PIENTI
SIMUS ÆQUI.'

'A maintainer of the faith and ever a lover of his country, here Paulinus lies, a most pious observer of justice.'[3] Although Paulinus was a notable saint, there is no legend of his life extant.

Illtyd 'Farchog,' Illtyd 'the knight,' as he is called by Welsh authorities, is said to have been an Armorican

---

[1] 'Catalogus S. H.,' Usher, p. 914.
[2] Paulinus is called his disciple by Rhygyfarch, 'C. B. S.,' p. 122.
[3] There are in all three Paulinus stones in Wales.

by descent. His legend[1] represents him as a contemporary of Dyfrig, the first Bishop of Llandaff, and of a Glamorganshire prince named Meirchion, who alternately patronized and persecuted the saint. The one thing certain about him is his foundation of Llanilltyd Fawr or Llantwit Major, in which monastery, according to a tradition already quoted, there were seven churches, each with seven companies, and seven colleges in each company, and seven saints in each college. 'Illtyd,' says another tradition, 'made on the banks of the Hodnant eight score and eight colleges, where two thousand saints resided, leading a life according to the faith of Jesus, practising every godliness, fasting, abstinence, prayer, penance, almsgiving, and charity, and all of them supported and cultivated learning.'[2] The Triads give the number of the Llantwit monks as two thousand four hundred; other traditional estimates are three thousand, and two thousand one hundred. The monastery was so notable that its origin was traditionally carried back many years before Illtyd, and was ascribed to the Emperor Theodosius, in conjunction with Cystennyn Llydaw. It was regulated, so runs the story, by Balerus, a man from Rome, and its first principal was St. Patrick.[3]

The wooden huts of the first monks have long since decayed or been destroyed, but around and within the curious old church of Llantwit Major stand some curious monuments of early Welsh Christianity. On the south side of the church against the wall of the porch may be seen the old stone which Iolo Morganwg rescued, after it had lain for many years in the tomb of a local celebrity. It is a tall narrow pillar, on which are inscribed in twenty or twenty-one short lines the following words, so far as

[1] 'Vita S. Iltuti,' 'C. B. S.,' pp. 158-182.
[2] 'Iolo MSS.,' p. 549.
[3] *Ibid.*, p. 537. One story is that Eurgen, daughter of Caractacus, first founded there a college of twelve saints ('Iolo MSS.,' p. 554). Of course these stories are not historical.

they can be deciphered: 'In Nomine Di Summi Incipit Crux Salvatoris Quæ Preparavit Samsoni Apati Pro Anima Sua Et Pro Anima Iuthahelo Rex Et Artmali Tecani'[1]—'In the name of God Most High begins the cross of the Saviour, which Abbot Samson prepared for his soul and for the soul of King Iuthael and Arthmael the Dean.' There was a Iuthael, King of Gwent, and he was killed in battle in A.D. 848, according to the 'Brut y Tywysogion' and the 'Annales Cambriæ.' Within the church, on the west, is a most beautiful carved wheel cross, unfortunately broken. Its inscription, which for the most part is extremely clear, is as follows: 'In Nomine Di Patris Et Speretus Santdi Anc Crucem Houelt Properabit Pro Anima Res Patres Eus'—'In the name of God the Father and the Holy Spirit Howel prepared this cross for the soul of his father Rhys.' There was a Howel, King of Glamorgan, whose death is fixed by the 'Annales Cambriæ' and the 'Brut y Tywysogion' in the year 885. On the north side of the church in the middle of the churchyard stands a richly-carved stone with three inscriptions, one, 'Iltet Samson Regis'; the second, 'Samuel and Ebisar'; the third, on the reverse side, 'Samson Posuit Hanc Crucem Pro Anima Eius'— 'Samson placed this cross for his soul.' Against the north wall of the church, not far from this cross, there leans a curious cylindrical stone, which has been supposed to be a corner-piece of a pedestal of another cross. It is not strange that with these relics of ancient Christianity ever witnessing to the world, there have arisen numerous stories respecting the antiquity and importance of the old monastery of Llantwit Major.[2]

One of the most notable pupils of Illtyd at Llantwit

[1] This word is doubtful.
[2] For a full description of these crosses see 'Archæologia Cambrensis,' Fifth Series, vol. vi., pp. 118-126. See also Mr. Edward Williams's ('Iolo Morganwg') account of these crosses in 'Arch. Camb.,' Fifth Series, x. 326-331.

Major was St. Samson, son of Amwn Ddu and of Anna, said to be daughter of Meurig, King of Morganwg. Samson, according to his legend, which is a very early one, removed from Llantwit to some adjacent island, perhaps Barry or Sully, where, notwithstanding the lax morals of Piro, its abbot, 'he led a glorious and angelic life,' and eventually on Piro's unhappy death, which we have already related, he was elected as his successor. After a short visit to Ireland he returned to Britain, and for a time lived the life of a hermit in a cave near the river Severn. He was consecrated bishop by Dubricius at Llantwit, without appointment to any particular see, and some time afterwards left Llantwit for Brittany, which was then ruled by Count Commorus, a tyrannical foreigner who had slain the native count Jonas, and given up his son Judual to King Hildebert. Samson is said to have obtained the release of Judual in spite of the opposition of the queen which he miraculously overcame. Commorus was defeated, and Judual was restored to his authority. Samson founded the monastery of Dol, and in later times, when it became definitely recognised as a bishop's see, he was accounted as its first bishop. He was present at the Council of Paris held about 557.[1] Besides the legendary miracles which have gathered around Samson's name, other fictions were added with the purpose of exalting respectively the sees of Dol and of St. David's, and so both Giraldus Cambrensis, and the clergy of Dol gave him the title of archbishop in the later sense of the term, and Giraldus asserted that he was Archbishop of St. David's, and carried the pall away with him to Dol, whereby St. David's had lost its token of being a metropolitan see. The romancer Geoffrey of Monmouth puts Samson a century earlier than his real date, and makes him Archbishop of York and afterwards of Dol. There is nothing of all this in the legends,

[1] See Usher, 'De Brit. Eccl. Prim.,' p. 532.

which in this case furnish us with more history than the professed historians. But unquestionably few of the legends of the Welsh saints are so certain in their main outlines as the legends of St. Samson.[1]

Within a short distance of Illtyd's foundation of Llantwit Major stood Cadoc's foundation of Llancarfan, or rather of Llanfeithin, for the original monastery was probably at a short distance from Llancarfan. Cadoc, otherwise called Cathmael, Doc, and Cattwg, and known generally in Welsh tradition as Cattwg Ddoeth, or Cattwg the Wise, owed much of his position as a leader in the Welsh Church to his birth, for he was son of a Monmouthshire prince, named Gwynlliw. His legend represents his power at Llancarfan as princely: 'He daily fed a hundred clergy and a hundred soldiers, and a hundred workmen, and a hundred poor men, with the same number of widows. This was the number of his household, besides servants in attendance, and esquires, and guests, whose number also was uncertain, and a multitude of whom used to visit him frequently. Nor is it strange that he was a rich man and supported many, for he was abbot and prince' (*abbas enim erat et princeps*); 'besides his father, Gunluc, from Ffynnon Hên, that is, the Old Well, as far as the mouth of the river Rymni, and he possessed the whole territory from the river Gulich as far as the river Nadauan, from Penntirche right on to the valley of Nantcarvan, from the valley forsooth to the river Gurimi, that is the Little Remni towards the sea.'[2]

---

[1] Mr. Egerton Phillimore accepts the early life of Samson as written at its professed date, viz., about 600 ('Y Cymmrodor,' xi. 127). So does also Adams ('Chronicles of Cornish Saints,' iv. 4, 5), though he believes that it is largely interpolated. See also for the later legend 'Book of Llan Dâv,' Evans' edition, pp. 6-24.

[2] 'Vita S. Cadoci,' by Lifris. § 15, 'C. B. S.,' p. 45. The Gulich, according to the notes in Rees' 'C. B. S.,' is a tributary of the Daw, the Nadauan is the Dawon or Daw, which enters the sea at Aberthaw, and the Gurimi is conjectured to be a stream running near Cadoxton-juxta-Barry.

This picture is probably exaggerated, but making all due deductions, we can infer from it what in some cases was the power of a prince-abbot, and how it was that his monastery was so much resorted to. When thousands left the world and became monks, they very often did so as clansmen, dutifully following the example of their chief. The populousness of Celtic monasteries admits of no question; Bede testifies to it in the case of Bangor Iscoed, and it was equally common in Ireland as in Wales. Their tribal character is another feature which the Irish and Welsh monasteries had in common. 'In Ireland,' says Dr. Todd, 'the land granted in fee to St. Patrick, or any other ecclesiastic, by its original owner, conveyed to the clerical society, of which it became the endowment, all the rights of a chieftain or head of a clan; and these rights, like the rights of the secular chieftains, descended in hereditary succession. The com-arb, or co-arb, that is to say, the heir or successor of the original saint who was the founder of the religious society, whether bishop or abbot, became the inheritor of his spiritual and official influence in religious matters. The descendants in blood or "founder's kin" were inheritors of the temporal rights of property and chieftainship, although bound to exercise those rights in subjection or subordination to the ecclesiastical co-arb.'[1] This principle is illustrated by the particulars given in the curious story of the foundation of the church of Trim, contained in the 'Book of Armagh,'[2] and also by the succession of the abbots in the monastery of Hy.[3] In

---

[1] Todd, 'St. Patrick,' p. 149.
[2] 'Additamenta ad Collectanea Tirechani,' in W. Stokes' 'Trip. Life,' etc., ii. 334, 335.
[3] Reeves' 'Vita S. Columbæ auctore Adamnano,' Introd., cvi. ('Hist. of Scot.,' vol. vi.). 'In the election, preference was given to founder's kin, and hence it happened that of the eleven immediate successors of the founder there is but one (Suibhne, sixth abbot) whose pedigree is uncertain, and but one (Connamail, tenth abbot) whose descent was confessedly from another house.'

Wales the same principle prevailed; bishoprics, canonries, and parochial benefices passed from one to another member of the same family, and frequently from father to son. Celtic monasticism undoubtedly developed on Celtic lines, and though there are some unusual features, such as that of abbot-bishops, in which Gallican customs may have been followed, there are others which are purely Celtic.

Little can be affirmed with certainty concerning Cadoc, the abbot-prince, save his foundation of Llancarfan, and his efforts in the cause of the Irish Church. But there are a large number of churches which preserve his name, and of many of which he probably was in some way the founder.[1] He appears to have visited Brittany, and Breton legends attest his piety and gentleness. A large body of Welsh proverbial philosophy is ascribed to him, and he is connected by some traditions with the mythic Arthur and his court. Altogether there is a mass of curious lore connected with his name, but the facts we can gather therefrom are few.

Gildas, another great leader of the Welsh monastic movement, and the author of the 'History' and 'Epistle,' was born in the year of the battle of Mount Badon, viz., about A.D. 516. So much is certain, for he tells us this himself. He is said to have been the son of Caw, a prince of Northern Britain, who was driven from his principality by hostile incursions, and to have been born at Alclud,[2] before the removal of the family. Illtyd was his reputed instructor. His mission to Ireland has been already related. He appears to have been associated in various ways with Cadoc, and to have visited Brittany. He died in A.D. 569 or 570.

St. David, or Dewi Sant, was another saint of noble

---

[1] Rees' 'Welsh Saints,' p. 177, enumerates fourteen of which he considers him to be the founder. Two other subordinate churches are dedicated to him.
[2] Dumbarton.

descent, though the story of his birth points to a deplorable state of society.¹ Such stories are not altogether uncommon in the 'Legends of the Saints,' and may perhaps arise from a popular belief in the ability of the children of such unions. The name Non in this case may have originated the idea that David's mother was a nun, and so caused the legend. His father is said to have been Sant, or Sandde, who is called a son of Ceredig, and grandson of the great Cunedda. David was brought up, it is said, at Old Menevia, and afterwards settled in Glyn Rosyn, where he founded his monastery of Menevia. He was present at the Synod of Llanddewi Brefi, and also at the 'Synodus Victoriæ,' held at Caerleon. He did a good work for Ireland, and made his monastery a place of instruction for the Irish clergy. He died on March 1, A.D. 601, according to the 'Annales Cambriæ.'[2]

With regard to David's synods, the customary story regarding the revival of Pelagianism cannot be regarded as historical, and is exceedingly improbable in itself. The date of the 'Synodus Victoriæ' is given by the 'Annales Cambriæ' as A.D. 569.[3] The canons which remain and purport to be those of a 'Sinodus Luci Victoriæ' are of a penitential character, and fix the penalties for various crimes, some of which are of the most detestable character. The 'Annales Cambriæ' records a Synod of Caerleon in A.D. 601, the year of David's death.

Dyfrig, or Dubricius, is said to have founded colleges at Henllan and Mochros, both on the river Wye, and also one at Caerleon.[4] He was the first Bishop of

---

[1] His father was Sanctus, Sant, or Sandde, a prince of Ceredigion, who, while walking in Dyfed, met Non or Nonnita, whom he ravished, 'Vita S. David,' 'C. B. S.,' p. 119. 'Buchedd Dewi Sant.,' 'C. B. S.,' p. 103.
[2] P. 6.
[3] MS. 'B.,' p. 5.
[4] Life in 'Book of Llan Dâv,' Evans' edition, pp. 78-86.

Llandaff, and retired before his death to Bardsey Island, where he died on November 14, 612. His bones were removed in 1120 to the cathedral of Llandaff, and there buried.

Teilo, Dyfrig's successor in the See of Llandaff, is always reckoned as a founder of the see, and figures more prominently in tradition than Dyfrig himself. The 'Book of Llandaff' is the 'Book of Teilo,' and the Bishop of Llandaff is 'Escob Teilaw,' the Bishop of Teilo. Teilo is one of the representatives of the Welsh Church in the mythical pilgrimage to Jerusalem, which the writers of the legends delight in describing. Rhygyfarch represents St. David as the saint specially honoured by the patriarch, but the author of the 'Life of St. Teilo,' with local patriotism, dwells rather upon the honour paid to the saint of Llandaff. He records that trial was made of the three pilgrims by offering them three seats in the church.

'There were in the church from ancient times three seats placed by the elders, two of divers metals, and wrought with wondrous art, the third of cedar, having no outward adornment save what nature had given, which lowly seat the lowly Eliud chose for himself, yielding the more costly ones to his brethren through reverence. On seeing this, all they who were present fell down on their faces before holy Eliud, saying: " Hail, Teilo, saint of God, and grant that thy prayers may avail for us with the Lord, because to-day thou art exalted above the rest of thy brethren, sitting in the seat of our Lord Jesus Christ, in which He preached the kingdom of God to our fathers." But the holy man hearing this was sore amazed, and arose and prostrated himself on the ground, saying : " Blessed is the man who hath not walked in the counsel of the ungodly, nor stood in the way of sinners, and hath not sat in the seat of the scornful. And blessed be the Saviour who chose

that a seat should be made for Him of wood, who by
wood willed to succour the perishing world." Thus, the
humble man humbly adored the seat; nay, rather Him
who had sat thereon, because he, a creature, had sat in[1]
the seat of the Creator.' Teilo was then requested to
preach, and when he had ended he bade the people
listen to his brethren, David and Paternus, who also
preached to them—a circumstance which suggests that
something like the modern Welsh *cymanfa* was known
and was popular in early times. After these things 'they
were raised to the pontifical dignity: Teilo in the stead
of Peter, David in the stead of James, and, as it were
for a testimony of the grace which they had received
there from the bounty of the Lord, three precious gifts
were given to them according as it suited each. To
Paternus a staff and a choral cope,[2] woven of very
valuable silk, because they saw he was an excellent
singer. To St. David, moreover, a wondrous altar,
whereof no one knew of what material it was wrought;
nor was such a gift bestowed on him unfitly, for he used
to celebrate in a more pleasing manner than the rest.
Last of all, yet not the least of the gifts, was given to
the blessed Bishop Teilo a bell more famous than large,
more precious than beautiful, for in sweetness of sound
it seems to excel every organ. It condemns the perjured,
it heals the sick, and, what seems more wonderful still,
it used to sound every hour without being moved, until,
through the sin of men preventing it, who were handling
it rashly with defiled hands, it ceased from so sweet a
service. Nor was he presented with such a gift un-
suitably, for, like as a bell invites men to church from
the torpor of sleep and of sloth, so the glorious Bishop
Teilo, being made a herald of Christ, incessantly by

---

[1] 'Considerat in,' so Oxford edition. The Llandovery edition
(p. 99) has 'consideratur.'

[2] Not 'cap,' as in Rees' translation (Llandovery edition, p. 342).

preaching invited to heaven.'[1] It would appear from this eloquent eulogium that good preaching was as much admired in Wales in the days of Teilo, or, at least, of his biographer, as it is at the present day. The sweet singer of the service and the popular celebrant have in the legend to yield to the eloquent preacher.

Teilo thus for some reason was regarded with more reverence by the Llandaff clergy than was Dyfrig. The college at Llandaff was called Bangor Deilo (Teilo's monastery), and he is accounted its founder. His descent is traced from Ceredig, the son of Cunedda, so that he is placed as a member of the same family as St. David. During his bishopric, the terrible Yellow Plague overran Wales, an event that must be regarded as historical. Its date is given by the 'Annales Cambriæ' as 547, in which year Maelgwn Gwynedd is said to have died of it. But if the Epistle and History of Gildas are indeed one work, as seems probable, Maelgwn must have been alive in 560. The date of Dyfrig's death, A.D. 612, seems also inconsistent with Teilo's succession to the See of Llandaff as early as 547. The plague broke out at various times, and Teilo's abandonment of his see, and Maelgwn's death, may have happened on a subsequent occasion to the visitation of 547; for Teilo left his diocese for a time during the plague, and retired to Brittany. He was succeeded in his bishopric on his death by Oudoceus, who is said to have been his nephew.

Padarn, or Paternus,[2] the third saint of the trio who went on pilgrimage to Jerusalem, is said to have been an Armorican. He founded the monastery and bishopric of Llanbadarn, and is said to have received lands from Maelgwn Gwynedd. He is called in the Triads one of the three blessed visitors of the Isle of Britain. He is said to have returned to Brittany, and then to have gone

---

[1] 'Book of Llan Dâv,' Evans' edition, pp. 104-107.
[2] 'Vita S. Paterni,' 'C. B. S.,' pp. 188-197.

to France and become Bishop of Vannes; but this seems to be due to confusion with an earlier namesake, for of the two Bishops of Vannes, named Paternus, one died in A.D. 448, and the other was consecrated in A.D. 465; whereas Paternus, or Padarn, of Wales, was a saint of the sixth century.[1]

Perhaps the most prominent saints of North Wales were Dunawd Fyr and his son Deiniol. They, in conjunction with Dunawd's other sons, Cynwyl and Gwarthan, are reckoned founders of the monastery of Bangor Iscoed by the Dee in Flintshire, not far from the present town of Wrexham. Bede states that 'Dinoot' was the abbot in the time of Augustine of Canterbury, and that 'so great was the number of the monks, that although the monastery was divided into seven companies with provosts in charge over them, no company had less than three hundred men, who all were accustomed to live by the work of their hands. From Bangor Iscoed came a large number of the learned men who accompanied the Welsh bishops in their conference with Augustine; and the destruction of the monks of Bangor by the pagan Æthelfrith at the battle of Chester, in A.D. 613, was regarded by Bede as a fulfilment of Augustine's denunciation of the Welsh for not uniting with him. A large number had come to the battle-field to pray for the success of the British arms. The English King noticed them where they were standing under the protection of Brocmail, and inquired who they were. Being informed, he said, 'Then, if they call to their God against us, they assuredly fight against us, even though they do not carry arms, and they attack us with hostile prayers.' Accordingly, he ordered them to be attacked first, and about twelve hundred were slain, only fifty escaping by flight.[2]

Dunawd is said to have been originally a chief of

---

[1] 'H. and S.,' i. 145, *note*.
[2] Bede, 'H. E.,' ii. 2; 'M. H. B.,' p. 151.

Northern Britain and a great warrior. His brother, Sawyl Benuchel, is also accounted a saint, and is said to have died as a monk of Bangor Iscoed. He is the patron saint of Llansawel in Carmarthenshire.[1] In his early life he is said (by a Triad of the Third Series) to have been a tyrannical ruler, and the 'Legend of St. Cadoc' represents him as oppressing the people of Llancarfan, and swallowed up in consequence through the anger of the saint.[2] His son Asaph was the successor of Kentigern as Bishop of Llanelwy.

Deiniol Wyn, the celebrated son of Dunawd, was the founder of the monastery known as Bangor Deiniol or Bangor Fawr, now Bangor in Carnarvonshire, which Maelgwn Gwynedd made the see of a bishopric, Deiniol being the first bishop. The 'Annales Cambriæ' gives the date of his death as A.D. 584,[3] and he is said to have been buried at Bardsey.

The foundation of the monastery and bishopric of Llanelwy, or St. Asaph, is commonly ascribed to St. Cyndeyrn or Kentigern. This saint was of noble descent, but the story of his birth is somewhat similar to the story about St. David. His chief work was done around Glasgow, of which place he became bishop. He was driven thence by a tyrant named Morken, and retired to Wales, on his way converting the pagans of Cumbria, and erecting a cross at Crosthwaite by Derwentwater. He visited David at Menevia, and afterwards in North Wales founded the bishopric of Llanelwy. But he was recalled to his northern see by Rhydderch, called Hael or 'the Liberal,' the prince of the Strathclyde Britons, who had overthrown the pagan party of the north at the battle of Ardderyd, probably Arthuret, near Carlisle,

---

[1] Rees' 'Welsh Saints,' p. 207.
[2] Rees' 'Camb. British Saints,' p. 43 : 'Vita S. Cadoci,' § 13.
[3] P. 5.

A.D. 573. He died, according to the 'Annales Cambriæ,' in the year 612.[1]

Joceline of Furness, the biographer of St. Kentigern, gives a somewhat detailed account of his sojourn in Wales, which was doubtless derived from those old lives which Joceline despised, on account of their primitive simplicity, and their variations from the orthodoxy of the twelfth century,[2] but from which nevertheless he copied. He relates how David and Kentigern were associated together at Menevia, 'like the two cherubim in the Holy of holies in the temple of the Lord, having their faces bent down towards the mercy-seat. They lifted their wings on high in the frequent meditation upon heavenly things; they folded them down in the ordination and arrangement of earthly things.' It would seem that Kentigern also visited Cadoc's monastery of Llancarfan (which Joceline calls Nautcharvan[3]), though Joceline's narrative is here confused. In building his monastery at St. Asaph, Kentigern was aided by Maelgwn Gwynedd, though at first, according to Joceline (to whom, as a biographer, all princes appear naturally tyrants), that prince violently opposed him.[4] Then follows a good description of the ideal of a Celtic monastery:

'There flocked to the monastery of the man, old and young, rich and poor, to take upon themselves the easy yoke and the light burden of the Lord. Nobles and men of the middle class brought to the saint their children to be trained unto the Lord. The tale of those who renounced the world increased day by day both in number and importance, so that the total number of those who enlisted in God's army amounted to 965, professing in act and habit the life of monastic rule according to the

---

[1] P. 6.
[2] 'Vita Kentegerni, Prologus' (Forbes' edition, p. 160, 'Hist. of Scot.,' vol. v.).
[3] A mistake for Nantcarvan.
[4] He calls the prince Melconde Galganu, apparently a corruption of Maelgwn and Maglocunus.

institution of the holy man. He divided this troop that had been collected together, and devoted to the Divine service, into a threefold division of religious observance. For he appointed 300, who were unlettered, to the duty of agriculture, the care of cattle, and the other necessary duties outside the monastery. He assigned another 300 to duties within the cloister of the monastery, such as doing the ordinary work, and preparing food, and building workshops. The remaining 365, who were lettered, he appointed to the celebration of Divine service in church by day and by night; and he seldom allowed any of these to go forth out of the sanctuary, but ever to abide within, as if in the holy place of the Lord. But those who were more advanced in wisdom and holiness, and who were fitted to teach others, he was accustomed to take along with him, when at the urgent demand either of necessity or reason, he thought fit to go forth to perform his episcopal office. But dividing into troops and choirs those whom he had appointed for the service of God, he ordained that as soon as one choir had terminated its service in the church, immediately another entering should commence it, and that again being concluded, a third should enter to celebrate. Thus the sacred choirs being conveniently and discreetly arranged so as to succeed in turn, while the work of God was celebrated perpetually, prayer was regularly made to God without ceasing of the church there; and by praising God at every time, His praise ever resounded in their mouths. Very excellent things were said in that and of that city of God, for as it became the habitation of all who were joyful therein, so one might well apply the prophecy of Balaam: 'How goodly are thy tents, O Jacob! and thy tabernacles, O Israel! As the valleys are they spread forth, as gardens by the river's side.'[1]

[1] 'Vita S. Kentegerni,' § 25. The translation from Bishop Forbes' edition, 'Historians of Scotland,' v., pp. 78, 79.

Cadfan, an Armorican saint, was another of the monastic leaders in North Wales. The legend of Saint Padarn relates the departure from Brittany of his company. 'At that time,' it says, ' an ecclesiastical company of monks, leaving Letavia, were purposing to seek the shores of Britain,[1] for as the winter hive, when spring smiles, becomes bold and, prudently intent on increasing its people, sends forth another first and especial swarm to gather honey elsewhere ; so Letavia, the quietude of religion increasing, sends across bands of saints to the original home whence they came forth, under the leadership of Hetinlau, Catman and Titechon.' Padarn was filled with like zeal, ' and so all the companies assemble, with one consent, desiring to sail across to Britain ; soon Padarn is made the fourth leader of a band.' Catman and Titechon appear to be Cadfan and Tydecho. Eight hundred and forty-seven monks are said to have followed Padarn, so that if the other three leaders had any similar following, a fair army would have landed on the coast of Wales.

The continual journeying of the Celtic monks is a fact beyond dispute, whatever may be thought of the accuracy of the above passage. The Anglo-Saxon Chronicle tells us of three Irishmen who landed in Cornwall in the reign of Alfred, and who had set out from Ireland in a vessel without sails and oars, desiring to be in a state of pilgrimage. Irish missionaries traversed the whole of Western Europe, and even founded six monasteries in Italy. Between Britain and the neighbouring Celtic population of Ireland and Brittany there was constant communication. The saints of Breton extraction constitute an important section of the Welsh saints.[2]

[1] 'Vita S. Paterni,' ' C. B. S.,' p. 189. The translator in this edition has invented a new saint ' Corus,' translating ' In illo tempore Corus ecclesiasticus monachorum, etc.,' as ' At that time Corus, a monk, left Armorica,' etc.

[2] Rees (' Welsh Saints,' pp. 213-224) enumerates Cadfan, Cynon, Padarn, Tydecho, Trinio, Gwyndaf, Dochdwy, Mael, Sulien, Tanwg,

Cadfan is the reputed founder of two churches in Wales, one of which, the fine church of the pleasant watering-place, Towyn, contains a rude stone pillar, called St. Cadfan's pillar, with a Welsh inscription which has been variously interpreted; some authorities considering it to signify that the pillar marked the burying-place of Cadfan and of Cyngen, King of Powys, and others opposing this view. Cadfan's chief work in Wales was the foundation of the monastery in the island of Enlli, now commonly known as Bardsey. This was done with the co-operation of Einion Frenhin. Bardsey became a place for pilgrims to flock to, and was the sacred island of Wales. Dubricius and Deiniol were buried there, and so many saints retired thither, that it was believed that the island was hallowed by the bones of twenty thousand saints. The poet Meilyr, about 1137, in his 'Death-bed of the Bard,' uttered his wish that he might die at Enlli, 'the holy isle of saints.'[1]

Other saints of North Wales were Cybi, the founder of the monastery of Caergybi (Holyhead), and Beuno, the founder of Clynnog Fawr. Cybi's name is perhaps most generally known in connection with the story of his meetings with Seiriol, abbot of the monastery of Penmon, which is the subject of one of Matthew Arnold's sonnets.[2]

Eithras, Sadwrn, Lleuddad, Tecwyn, Maelrys, Amwn Ddu, Hywyn, Umbrafel, Cristiolus, Rhystud, Derfel, Dwywau, Alan, Llonio, Llynab, Canna, Crallo, Gredifael, Fflewyn, Trillo, Tegai, Twrog, Baglan, Llechid, Tyfodwg, Ilar, Ust, Dyfnig, Llywan and Durdan; also Budic (p. 251), Illtyd (p. 178), and Samson, born, however, in Glamorganshire (p. 253). Welsh saints also visited Brittany (see p. 256).

[1] Stephens, 'Literature of the Kymry,' p. 23.
[2] The poet, however, has altered or mistaken the legend: 'From the circumstance of Seiriol travelling westward in the morning, and eastward in the evening, and Cybi, on the contrary, always facing the sun, they were denominated Seiriol Wyn a Chybi Felyn, Seiriol the Fair, and Cybi the Tawny' (Rees, 'Welsh Saints,' p. 267). Matthew Arnold makes Seiriol the Bright saint because the sun was on his face, and Kybi the Dark one because he was 'in shade.'

> 'In the bare midst of Anglesey they show
> Two springs which close by one another play;
> And "Thirteen hundred years agone," they say,
> "Two saints met often where these waters flow.
> One came from Penmon westward, and a glow
> Whitened his face from the sun's fronting ray;
> Eastward the other, from the dying day,
> And he with unsunn'd face did always go."
> *Seiriol the Bright, Kybi the Dark!* men said,
> The seër from the East was then in light,
> The seër from the West was then in shade.
> Ah! now 'tis changed. In conquering sunshine bright,
> The man of the bold West now comes array'd;
> He of the mystic East is touched with light.'

The Welsh life of Beuno[1] is strongly national and anti-Saxon, and in many respects exceedingly curious and interesting. After his father's death, we are told, Beuno 'resided in the township of his father and there he built a church, which he consecrated in the name of the Lord Christ; and he set an acorn on the side of his father's grave, which there grew to an oak of great size, height, and of a fine form, and on that tree grew a branch which reached the ground, and from the ground again upwards as high as the boughs of the tree; and there was a part of this branch in the ground, as it is at present; and if an Englishman should go between that branch and the body of the tree, he would immediately die; but should a Welshman go, he would be nothing worse.' Beuno stayed some time at Aberrhiw, or Berriew, in Montgomeryshire, but left the place for a curious reason. 'On a certain day, as Beuno was travelling near the river Severn, where was a ford, lo! he heard a voice on the other side of the river inciting dogs to hunt a hare, being that of an Englishman, who spoke as loud as he could, "Cergia," which in that language incited the dogs. And when Beuno heard the voice of the Englishman he immediately returned, and coming to his disciples said to them, "My sons, put on your clothes and your shoes, and let us leave this place, for the nation of this man has

[1] 'C. B. S.,' pp. 13-21.

a strange language and is abominable; and I heard his voice on the other side of the river inciting the dogs after a hare; they have invaded this place, and it will be theirs, and they will keep it in their possession."[1]

Besides the monasteries already mentioned, there were others in Wales, such as 'those of Dogfan in Mochnant, of Gwyddvarch in Meifod (Mechain), of Dyfnog in Cinmeirch, of Jeuan Gwas Batuc in Dinmael,'[2] and the monastery of Caerwent. The abbot of Docwinnus is mentioned in the 'Book of Llandaff' as one of the three chief abbots of the see, the others being the abbots of Llancarfan and Llantwit Major. His monastery may perhaps have been situated at Llandough.

The monastic life in Wales was at first exceedingly ascetic. Bishop Morgeneu, of St. David's, in the ninth century, broke through the strictness of the rule, and ate meat. He was killed by the Danes, and, after his death, his ghost appeared to an Irish bishop and said, 'I ate meat, and I have become meat.' The greater saints were renowned for their austerities. Kentigern, at St. Asaph, would recite the Psalms standing naked in cold water, even in time of frost.[3] Illtyd, at Llantwit, bathed at midnight before matins, staying in the cold water as long as it took him to say the Lord's Prayer thrice.[4] David, at Menevia, sought, by standing long in cold water, to subdue the heat of the flesh, and imitated in his self-discipline, so Rhygyfarch reports, the methods of the Egyptian monks.[5] Sometimes these heroes of the faith

---

[1] 'Buchedd Beuno Sant' ("C. B. S.," pp. 14, 15, 301, 302).
[2] Thomas, 'St. Asaph' (S. P. C. K.), p. 8. See also 'Iolo MSS.,' p. 557.
[3] 'Vita S. Kentegerni,' § 25.
[4] So I interpret the passage in 'Vita S. Iltuti,' § 7; 'C. B. S.,' p. 164. 'Nocte media ante matutinas abluebat se aqua frigida, sic sustinens, quamdiu posset terdiei oratio dominica.' Surely 'diei' ought to be 'dici.' The editor translates the latter clause (p. 472): 'thus sustaining as long as he could the Lord's command thrice a day,' which seems to me nonsense.
[5] 'Vita S. David,' 'C. B. S.,' p. 129.

would leave the monasteries altogether for awhile, and seek in utter solitude to die to the world and lead the angelic life. Samson, as we have seen, retired to a cave near the Severn; Illtyd himself left Llantwit for awhile (partly, however, to avoid the persecution of King Meirchion), and stayed in a cave beside the pleasant Glamorganshire stream Ewenny for a year and three days, sleeping every night on a cold stone.[1] Other Celtic saints, both of Britain and of Ireland, did the like; the caves of St. Ninian and of St. Medana are still pointed out on the coast of Galloway.[2] The Irish saint Fiacc used to retire to a cave during Lent, so one grotesque story tells, and would take five cakes with him, and when he came out on Easter Saturday, 'there always remained with him a bit of the five cakes.'[3] Cadoc was wont to leave Llancarfan[4] at the approach of Lent, and to keep that season in comparative seclusion in the neighbouring islands of Barry and Echni.[5] The heremitical life was full of attraction to men of this type, and the hardships it entailed were the object of their highest ambition. The austerities of the Irish monks were extreme, and, as related by the writers of legends, are frequently incredible. One would sleep with corpses, and hang himself up on sickles placed under his arm-pits; another would keep a stone in his mouth during the whole of Lent; a third mixed his bread with sand; and a female saint, named Ite, let a stag-beetle eat away her side.[6] St. Patrick himself is related by Tirechan to have fasted for forty days and forty nights on Cruachan Aigle. Seven of St. Comgall's monks died of cold and hunger, being unable to live so hard a life as their abbot.[7] There is at

[1] 'Vita S. Iltuti,' § 17.
[2] Bishop Forbes' 'Lives of St. Ninian and St. Kentigern,' p. 284.
[3] 'Tripartite Life of Patrick,' p. 243.
[4] 'Vita S. Cadoci,' § 15.
[5] Echni is the Flat Holme in the Bristol Channel.
[6] See Whitley Stokes, Introduction to 'Tripartite Life,' cxcv.
[7] 'Vita,' § 12, quoted by Bishop Reeves in 'Notes on Adamnan,' p. 233, in 'Historians of Scotland' Series.

times a touch of insanity in the legends, which suggests that occasionally some Celtic saint went mad under the infliction of prolonged fasting and mortification of the flesh, and that his wild ravings and bursts of frenzied passion were regarded as signs of inspiration by the awe-struck and wondering people. The frequent cursings which we find in legends of the Irish saints, and their irascible and revengeful temper, which caused astonishment in Giraldus Cambrensis, probably had some historical foundation, and some members of the company may have been more like fakirs or dervishes than Christian saints. Probably in Wales there were fewer saints of this type than in Ireland, and in general the ideal of the saintly life was higher, though the varied estimates of Sawyl Benuchel may indicate that a late retirement to a monastery has been in some cases the chief qualification for enrolment in the list of saints.

The great ambition of a monastery, according to some traditions, seems to have been to keep up the 'laus perennis,' the perpetual worship of God day and night. But perhaps the most characteristic feature of a Welsh monastery was the manual labour of its occupants. The ideal of the monastic life is well depicted by Rhygyfarch.

'The holy father' (David), he says, ' decreed such strictness in the zeal of monastic life, that every monk working hard daily with his hands should pass his life in community, as, saith the Apostle, " He who doth not work, neither let him eat." For knowing that rest without care was an incentive and mother of vices, he bent the shoulders of the monks beneath Divine labours, for those who devote their time and attention to easeful rest, without rest beget the unstable spirit of melancholy,[1] and

---

[1] 'Accidia.' In 'C. B. S.,' p. 429, it is translated 'accident' (!). See Du Cange. 'Glossarium,' i. 42, 43.

incitements to lust. Therefore, with zealous efforts they labour with feet and hands; they put the yoke to their shoulders; they fix stakes with unwearied arms in the earth, and in their holy hands carry hoes and saws for cutting. . . . They make no use of oxen for ploughing . . . every one is an ox to himself. When the work was done, no murmur was heard, no conversation was held beyond what was necessary, but each one, either by praying or by rightly meditating, performed his appointed work.

'Moreover, when their rural work was completed, returning to the enclosure of the monastery, they spent the whole day till evening in reading, or writing, or praying; but at evening, when the ringing of a bell was heard, everyone left his study . . . and so in silence, without any idle conversation, they go to the church. Having ended the chanting of the psalms with harmonious effort of heart and voice, they continue the service kneeling, until the stars being seen in the sky marked the close of day; but the father alone, when all had gone out, poured forth his prayer to God in private for the state of the church. At length they meet at table, and they relieve their weary limbs with the refreshment of supper, yet not to satiety. For excess, though it be of nothing but bread, breeds licentiousness; but then, according to the difference of health or age, each takes his supper. Nor do they set on dishes of various flavours, nor more palatable kinds of food; but, having fed on bread and vegetables seasoned with salt, they quench their burning thirst with a temperate kind of drink. The infirm and the old, and those who are wearied by a long journey, are provided with some little delicacies, for the same measure must not be meted out to all alike. But after grace they go to church at the canonical ringing, and there for three hours they continue in watching, prayer and kneeling. But as long as they were praying in the church, no one dared to yawn, to sneeze, or to expectorate. When these things are finished, they compose their limbs to sleep; but, awakening at cock-crow, and devoting themselves to kneeling in prayer, they spend the whole of the rest of the day without sleep from morning to night, and so they do the other nights.

'From the night of the Sabbath, until the light has shone after daybreak in the first hour of the Lord's Day, they devote themselves to watching, to prayer and to kneeling, save only one hour after Matins on the Sabbath; they make known their thoughts to the father, they ask the father's leave even for the necessities of nature. All things are in common; there is no mine and thine. For whoever should speak of "my book," or the like, would forthwith be set a hard penance. They wore mean garments, chiefly of skin. Unfailing obedience to the father's command was required of all. . . . For he who desired the fellowship of the holy life, and craved to enter the company of the brethren, had first to remain ten days before the doors of the monastery as an outcast, and be loaded with abuse. But if he should patiently abide until the tenth day, he was received, and being put under the elder who happened to preside, served him, and after working hard there for a long time, and being subdued by many afflictions, at last he merited to enter the company of the brethren. No superfluity was retained; voluntary poverty was beloved; for whosoever desired their fellowship, the holy father would receive none of his substance, which he gave up when he renounced the world; not even would he take, so to say, a single penny for the use of the monastery. But he was taken in naked as a man escaping from shipwreck, lest in any way he should lift up and exalt himself among the brethren, or, relying on his substance, should not do an equal share of work with the brethren, or, wearing the garb of religion, should wrest by force from the monastery what he gave up to it, and stir firm patience to wrath.'[1]

The monastic buildings in Wales probably resembled those of an Irish monastery, such as that of St. Cainnech at Aghaboe, or of Columba at Hy. Adamnan has left us a number of particulars respecting the latter in his life of the saint. The Irish monasteries were surrounded by a rampart and ditch, generally of circular form; the rampart being either of stone, or of earth, or of earth mixed with stones. Within this stood the village of huts, made originally of wattles or of wood, where the monks lodged. A little apart from the rest stood the abbot's house and the guests' house, the former being usually on an eminence. There was also a refectory, or perhaps more than one in large monasteries, and connected with these were the kitchens; but chief among the buildings was the church. Sometimes there were groups of seven churches, as perhaps was the case at Llantwit Major. The church was usually built of wood, and there was a sacristy adjoining, where, probably, was kept the bell by which the congregation was summoned. Other buildings within the enclosure were the smithy and the carpenter's workshop. It is uncertain whether the cemetery stood within or without the enclosure, but probably it was within. Outside were such buildings as the barn, the kiln, and the mill.[2]

Such is the picture we have drawn for us of one of those Irish camps, in which the soldiers of the Cross kept ever watch and ward in the midst of a hostile world. The indications we find in the legends respecting Welsh monasteries show that they corresponded pretty closely to these.

Cadoc, when he came to Llancarfan, or rather Llan-

[1] 'Vita S. David,' 'C. B. S.,' pp. 127-129. The text, however, is very faulty. I have *not* adopted the editor's translation.
[2] See Skene's 'Celtic Scotland,' ii. 59. Reeves' 'Introduction to Adamnan,' cxix.-cxxi. ('Historians of Scotland,' vi.).

feithin, built in three several places in the valley a church of wood, a refectory, and a dormitory. Afterwards he raised a vast mound of earth, and there made a very fair cemetery dedicated to the honour of God, where the bodies of the faithful might be buried round about the church. He also raised another round mound like a city, whereon the abbot's house was built, which, in the British tongue, was called Castell Cadoc (Cadoc's Castle). We are told, too, that he made four great paths.[1] Nothing is said in the legend respecting any enclosure, but we read in St. Illtyd's life how that saint constructed an immense rampart and ditch of earth and stones to prevent the inundations of the sea and river which approached his cemetery.[2] Illtyd's barn was the scene of an amusing miracle, worked by the benevolent Samson, who imprisoned therein the wicked birds which robbed the monks' cornfields.[3]

From these and like scattered hints we may gather some idea of the picture which a Welsh monastery, such as that of Llantwit Major, presented to a visitor in the sixth century. Llantwit is even now, despite some recent improvements, one of the most delightful places in our still delightful isle. Its quaint old cottages with small windows, and low, broad doorways; its ruined castle, and plain town-hall, with St. Illtyd's bell in the belfry; its grassy heights that look out over the silver-bright waters of the Severn Sea to the glad English hills beyond, and its narrow valley stretching seaward between sides of strangely regular slope: its British camp and its monastic ruins, and, more than all, its church, which is not one, but three churches—a monastic church at the east end, a parish church in the middle, and a Galilee at the west end—and the old monuments that stand therein, and among the flowers of the churchyard, with their

[1] 'Vita S. Cadoci,' §§ 5, 6. [2] 'Vita S. Iltuti,' § 13.
[3] *Ibid.*, § 14.

precious memories of the ancient saints; these all unite to produce an impression that is quite unique. Usually, elsewhere, the old is blended with the new; but here, until quite recently, the nineteenth century had scarce dared to intrude, and it seemed that here, at least, one might find a haven from its commonplace mediocrity, as Illtyd found in his time a haven for his spirit to rest in. Even the simplicity of the people, which is proverbial in Glamorganshire, was not lacking to complete the spell.

The monk who tells us the story of St. Illtyd's life felt the strange, subtle charm of the spot in his day. When Illtyd came there, he says, it pleased him well, for it was a delightful place; there was a fertile plain with no ruggedness of mountain or of hill, a thick wood with trees of various kinds, the dwelling-place of many wild creatures, and a river flowing between pleasant banks. It was in truth the most beautiful of all spots.[1]

To this place of retirement many a visitor doubtless came in the sixth century and received a cordial welcome, for hospitality was a prominent monastic virtue. After passing over the pebbly beach and entering the narrow valley, the visitor would come to the embankment which Illtyd had constructed to keep the sea from encroaching on his cemetery. Crossing this he enters the monastic town, and after climbing the hill, he comes in sight of the guest house and the principal buildings.[2] Standing here

---

[1] 'Pulcherrimus iste locorum.'

[2] I am inclined to think from my own investigation of the valley and the town of Llantwit Major that, at least, much of the original monastery of Illtyd must have been in the valley. At present the town and church are on a hill, and the valley is only reached by road after a walk of about a mile from the church. The legend represents Illtyd as building in the valley where the sea invaded his cemetery. Possibly the monastery was removed later to the hill away from the sea to escape the depredations of the Danes, or perhaps, as I have supposed in the above description, the monastic settlement, which certainly must have covered a large extent of ground, was much more extensive than the present town, and was not only in the valley, but also occupied the site of the present town.

he sees on all sides the multitudinous round huts in which the monks dwell, with their walls built of wooden props with wattles and daub between, and covered with roofs of thatch. Should he enter one of these, he has to step down, for the floor is sunk considerably under the level of the ground outside, so as to give the props security against spreading outwards under the weight of the roofs. The guest house on the hill in which he lodges, and the refectory in which he dines, are quadrangular in shape, but built of similar materials.

As he goes on his way to the abbot's house, to which he is being conducted by the monk who has chanced first to meet him, he sees but few of the brethren; for most are now in the fields, busy with farm work. The few whom he meets are clothed in rough garments of leather or of wool, with sandals on their feet, and all have the ugly Celtic tonsure, which leaves the front part of the head bare with a ridge of hair coming round in the shape of a crown, while the back hair hangs down unshorn in shaggy locks over their shoulders. As the visitor passes a church he hears within the sound of choral melody, for in each of the seven the community are keeping up the perpetual service of prayer and praise which they regard as their especial duty.

Arrived before the abbot, he is welcomed with a kiss of brotherhood, and he is afterwards lodged in the guest house. It is a fast day, but in his honour the fast is relaxed and better food than usual is served out to the whole of the community.[1]

At daybreak on the Lord's day he attends a celebration of the Holy Communion at one of the seven churches. The churches are small, of some twenty-nine feet[2] in

---

[1] Adamnan, 'Vita S. Columbæ,' p. 15. Reeves, 'Hist. of Scot.,' vi. 127.

[2] This is the length of the old church of Perranzabuloe, which some suppose to be the original British building. Haslam's 'Perranzabuloe,' p. 67.

length, built of planks of oak and covered with reeds. At the east end[1] is the sanctuary, parted off by a screen,[2] and within stands a stone altar,[3] covered by an altar-cloth.[4] A chalice and dish of bronze are placed thereon.[5] The monks come to the church in their surplices, and two priests in conjunction[6] ' offer the sacrifice,' standing before the altar facing eastward, wearing over albs full white chasubles with embroidered orphreys. The maniple is worn over the wrist, hanging from the forefinger of the left hand.[7] The service is in Latin, wholly choral and broken by many collects.[8] There is a sermon after the Gospel. At the oblation of the elements water is mixed with the wine,[9] and circular wafer bread (unleavened) is offered.[10] After the oblations, a deacon brings forward a diptych with the names of the faithful departed written upon it, which are recited by the celebrant, and the prayers of the church are then offered on their behalf.[11] During the communion of the priests a hymn is sung:

> 'Draw near and take the Body of the Lord,
> And drink the sacred Blood for thee outpoured.'[12]

---

[1] See so-called prophecy of Patrick, 'W. S.,' i. 35 : 'His dish in the east of his house.'
[2] There was a screen in St. Bridget's Church. 'Cogitosus, V. S. Brigidæ,' quoted by Warren, ' Liturgy and Ritual,' pp. 89, 90.
[3] Gildas, ' M. H. B.,' p. 16.   [4] *Ibid.*
[5] St. Gall refused to use silver vessels for the altar, saying that St. Columbanus used bronze, because his Saviour was nailed to the Cross with bronze nails. Walafrid Strabo, ' Vit. S. Galli,' i. 19, quoted by Warren, p. 143.
[6] Adamnan, 'Vita S. Columbæ'; Reeves, ' Hist. of Scot.,' vi. 142.
[7] Warren, pp. 112, 114.
[8] A multiplicity of collects was urged against the Celtic liturgy at the Council of Maçon, A.D. 624 or 627 ; ' H. and S.,' i. 154.
[9] See Adamnan, ' Vita S. Columbæ,' ii. 1 ; ' Hist. of Scot.,' vi. 152.
[10] Warren, pp. 131, 132.
[11] Warren, p. 106 ; Adamnan, 'Vita S. Columbæ,' iii. 13 ; Reeves, ' Hist. of Scot.,' vi. 202.
[12] 'Ymnum quando Commonicarent Sacerdotes':
>   'Sancti venite, Christi corpus sumite ;
>   Sanctum bibentes quo redempti sanguine,' etc.
>   Warren, pp. 187-189.

Immediately before the communion of the people the kiss of peace is given, each of the officiating clergy and of the members of the congregation kissing the one who stands next to him. Then the laity receive in both kinds, and the cup is presented to each communicant by the deacon.[1] When the liturgy is ended, a loaf of bread is brought forward and cut into small pieces with a consecrated knife, and the people come forward and each receives a piece from the priest's hands.[2]

During his stay at Llantwit, the visitor would become familiar with the monastic routine. He would walk out over the cliffs towards the Nash Point, and see the monks busy making clearings in the woods, or tilling the soil that had already been cleared. He would watch them, and, may be, help them, building huts for fresh refugees from the perishing world outside, who had been admitted to join the community of brethren. He would sit among the students, and join with them in reading the Holy Scriptures, and in learning by heart portions of the Book of Psalms, and would listen while one of the more learned monks gave instruction in Latin or in Greek, or while one read the 'Lives of the Saints' to an attentive audience. He would watch the skilful scribes illuminating with all manner of complex and lovely ornament the books of the Gospels that they were writing, or in another place some artificer fashioning one of those little bells that the saints loved, or metal cases for the monastic books, or perhaps patens and chalices for the service of the altar.

It might chance, too, that before he left, Dubricius might come over from Llandaff, attended by some of his clergy. Then the abbot and the brethren would go forth to meet the guest and conduct him and his party to church, where thanks would be offered for their safe arrival. On Sunday

---

[1] 'Excerpta de Libro Davidis,' 'H. and S.,' i. 119.
[2] The 'Eulogiæ,' Warren, pp. 139, 140.

the bishop would 'offer' alone, crowned,[1] and wearing on his breast the rationale, a breastplate of gold or silver, studded with precious stones, after the fashion of the breastplate of Aaron.[2] He would wear also, as other badges of his authority, the episcopal ring and a pectoral cross, and would carry in his hand on occasion his short pastoral staff.[3]

In such peaceful wise the life of the monks sped on. There were at least four of such retreats within easy distance of each other, in the pleasant vale of Glamorgan: Llantwit, Llancarfan, Llandaff, and Llandough; a well-girt traveller might visit them all in the space of a single day. All too, we may reasonably believe, were doing an excellent work; men who would have perished in that rough and dangerous world, in these retreats lost the world and were lost thereto, but gained their souls in exchange.

Rhygyfarch's picture of monastic discipline may be ideal; but it may have been realized in well ordered communities, such as Menevia and Llancarfan. Not every monk was holy, but the average of piety was a high one, and though the monkish conception of sanctity was in part mistaken, the aim was sincere. There were hypocrites among the brethren as there are among Christians of the nineteenth century; and probably there were not more then than there are now. Even serious slips such as that of Abbot Piro may be judged leniently, if we remember the long fasts of the monks, and reflect how a very slight indulgence might affect a man who had been thus weakened. The monks were undoubtedly superstitious, paganism had made their forefathers so; and though paganism was probably dead as a creed in Wales, its survivals must have been powerful. Consequently

---

[1] Warren, pp. 119, 120.   [2] *Ibid.*, p. 113.
[3] One of these short staves, that, possibly, of Mochuda, may even now be seen in the castle of Lismore. See my 'St. Patrick,' pp. 127, 128, where I have described it.

they dreaded the evil, malignant powers with which they peopled the world of nature, and to which their forefathers had offered sacrifices to propitiate their wrath. They looked for miracles and they found them; some are ridiculous enough, especially when contained in late legends; but some of those related of Columba by Adamnan are reasonable and are well attested, and if miracles are to be expected anywhere, they are to be expected in connection with missions to the heathen. The monks dreaded devils and saw visions of angels. Perhaps while they weakened their bodies by fasting, they increased their spiritual perception; or are we to conclude that bad health produced in them delusions? Certainly Adamnan's picture of the monastery of Hy represents a community in which miracles and angelic appearances were recognised as matters of common occurrence, as sanctified 'human nature's daily food,' accepted by all, and questioned by none. And these men were heroes by virtue of their faith. Even if our own eyes are holden, and do not descry the chariots of fire and horses of fire that compass us around, we need not rashly deny that others placed in the outposts of Christendom on the borders of heathendom, in times when Christians were militant and aggressive, may have had such visions vouchsafed to them for their comfort and encouragement. The fact that some stories of the supernatural are absurd does not discredit them all; far from it. Adamnan's 'Life of Columba' is a well-attested and an astounding work, which should not be ignored, but in some way or other should be accounted for.

CHAPTER IV.

THE AGE OF CONFLICT.

UNTIL the end of the sixth century the Church in Wales had come into no direct contact with the See of Rome. While Britain was part of the Roman empire, and was becoming so far affected by Roman civilization that, as Gildas rhetorically says, it was rather to be deemed Romania than Britannia, the British Church, in common with the rest of Western Christendom, had recognised the primacy of the Imperial city and its bishop. What that primacy involved, and how distinct it was from the later conception of the papacy, may be clearly seen from the canons of the Council of Arles (A.D. 314), at which British bishops, including possibly one from Wales, were present. These canons were sent to Pope Sylvester as primate, and the first of them ordained that notice of the proper time of observing Easter should be given by the Bishop of Rome; but at the same time the council treated him as a 'brother,' and as *primus inter pares*, and not as a superior in authority. 'To the most holy lord, Brother Sylvester' (so their letter begins), 'Marinus[1] and the assembly of bishops, who have met together in the town of Arles, have signified to thy Charity what we have decreed in common council, that all may know what they

---

[1] The Bishop of Arles.

ought to observe for the future.'[1] They expressed regret that the Pope had been unable to be present, and sent him the canons which they had decreed, that he might publish them to the Churches of the West.

After the separation of Britain from the Empire, Pope Celestine, if Prosper is to be credited, sent St. German in 429 to check the Pelagian heresy in this country, and two years later sent Palladius as a bishop to the sister island of Ireland. Even as late as the middle of the same century, in 455, according to the 'Annales Cambriæ,' the orders of Pope Leo were followed in Britain respect-

---

[1] See Spelman, 'Concilia,' pp. 39-43, where the canons, etc., of this Council are given. The Latin for the above is as follows : 'Domino sanctissimo fratri Silvestro, Marinus vel cætus Episcoporum, qui adunati fuerunt in oppido Arelatensi, quid decreverimus communi concilio charitati tuæ significavimus, ut omnes sciant quid in futurum observare debeant.' The first canon is : 'Ut uno die et tempore Pascha celebretur. Primo loco de observatione Paschæ Dominici, ut uno die et uno tempore per omnem orbem a nobis observetur, et juxta consuetudinem litteras ad omnes tu dirigas.' See further for comments on the tone of this Council towards the Pope, and its incompatibility with any theory of Papal Supremacy at this date, Collier's 'Ecclesiastical History,' i. 27. 28 : 'The form of saluting that See is very different from that of later ages. Here's no signs of submission, no acknowledgment of supreme pastorship or universal supremacy. By their language we may plainly understand that they looked upon the authority of the Council to be perfect in its legislative capacity without the concurrence or after-consent of the Bishop of Rome. Their words run thus : *Quæ decrevimus communi concilio.* . . . Now one would hardly have imagined that Baronius should have found out the necessity of the Pope's confirmation from hence. For don't they plainly tell him, the points were already settled by common consent, and that they sent them to him to make 'em more publick ? . . . Would such freedom as this have been allowed in a Council since the claim of the Papal Supremacy ? Would it not have been looked upon as a great failure of respect in a provincial Council, even within any of the Eastern Patriarchates ? But at this time of day the fathers assembled at Arles thought *Charitati tuæ*, your Friendliness, ceremony enough, even for the See of Rome. They likewise call him Dear Brother, as St. Cyprian had often done before 'em. . . . Was it possible for this Council, who declared the compleatness of their authority, and treated the Pope with such familiarity, was it possible, I say, for 'em to look upon that Bishop as their Supream Head, or that he had any paramount jurisdiction to confirm, or null the Acts of the Council ? By what has been said we may understand what opinion the British bishops of this century, and the rest of their order, had of the Pope's Supremacy.'

ing the date of Easter. But the entry in the 'Annales' is certainly confused and may be altogether incorrect.[1] Two years later, when a new rule for the calculation of Easter was adopted by the churches in union with Rome, the Britons certainly took no notice of the change. They were then too fully occupied with their struggle with the pagan English, who in that year overthrew their army in the Battle of Crayford.[2] Henceforward they were cut off from Roman influence, and the subsequent development of the Celtic churches of Britain and of Ireland took place in isolation.

We have seen how marvellous that development was in Wales, in spite of the civil commotions due to the progress of the invaders, and to the rivalries of the various petty princes who claimed the name and style of *kings*, but acknowledged the leadership of a Dux or Gwledig. Chieftains whose dominions had been taken from them by the Picts and Scots or by the English, retired to Wales, and exchanged a life of conflict for the quiet of the monasteries, and probably their followers did the same, which will account in great measure for the multitude of monks in Wales. Caw, the father of Gildas, and his family; Pabo Post Prydain, and his son Dunawd, the founder of Bangor Iscoed, and grandson Deiniol, first bishop of Bangor; Elaeth Frenhin, a monk of Seiriol's college in Anglesey; and Clydno Eiddyn and

---

[1] The 'Annales Cambriæ' ('M. H. B.,' p. 830) has: 'A.D. 453. ix Annus. Pasca commutatur *super diem Dominicum* cum papa Leone episcopo Romæ.' There was a dispute at this time between the Eastern and the Western Churches as to the date of Easter in A.D. 455, whether it should be on April 17th or 24th. Pope Leo finally agreed to the computation of Alexandria. But in the entry in the 'Annales Cambriæ' the words 'super diem Dominicum' are a blunder, as there was no question then whether Easter should be kept on a Sunday or a week-day, and there is no reason to suppose that the Britons ever kept it on a week-day.

[2] 'A.D. 457. This year Hengest and Æsc, his son, fought against the Britons at the place which is called Crecganford, and there slew four thousand men; and the Britons then forsook Kent, and in great terror fled to London.'—'Anglo-Saxon Chronicle,' 'M. H. B.,' p. 299.

his brothers are accounted by tradition among such fugitives. Cunedda himself, the founder of a great family to which many of the most illustrious saints, including David and Teilo, belonged, was originally a chieftain of northern Britain, who retired to Wales in consequence of an irruption of the Picts. The concourse of fugitives in Wales was so great and their number so constantly increasing, that they found their bounds too strait for them, and many of them sought a home across the sea, some in Ireland, and others in Armorica, called also by the Welsh, Letavia, or Llydaw, which we know now as Brittany, where already a British colony had been settled since the time of Maximus. We have already seen that many of the Welsh saints were Armorican by birth or descent; but the Britons who settled in Armorica far exceeded these in number. Armorica was the Briton's health resort in time of pestilence, and his place of refuge, when pressed by the invasions of the hated Saxon, or driven to despair of the world in which he lived, by reason of its wickedness and irreligion. Thither in the fifth century came Fracan, cousin of Cathow, a British king, fleeing from a pestilence which had been sent to punish his nation for their 'acts of sacrilege and improper marriages, and lawless feasts, and debauchery forbidden by God.'[1] His wife, Gwen Teirbron and his three sons, Guethennoc, Jacut, and Winwaloe, are still held in veneration by the Bretons. Jacut was the founder of a monastery called by his name, about five miles distant from St. Malo. But, Winwaloe or Gwennolé is the most renowned of the three brothers. The austerities related of him are equal to those of the Irish Saints. From his twentieth year to his death he was never seen to sit in church. 'Every

---

[1] 'Cartulary of Landevennec,' quoted in 'Arch. Camb.,' 3rd Series, 1864, p. 41. This represents Fracan to have come from Britain with his wife and Guethennoc and Jacob (Jacut), and Winwaloe to have been born in Brittany. Another story makes Winwaloe born in Britain about A.D. 418.

day he repeated the hundred and fifty psalms, sometimes standing with his arms stretched forth in the figure of a cross, sometimes fallen on his knees. From the day that he began to build his habitation, he never used any garment of wool or linen, but made use only of goat skins. Neither on his bed had he either feathers or clothes; but instead of feathers he strewed under him nutshells, and instead of blankets, sand mingled with pebbles, and two great stones he put under his head. He used the same garments day and night. He never eat wheaten bread, and but a small proportion of bread made of barley, with which was mingled an equal measure of ashes. He took his refection once only in two, and sometimes three days. His other diet was a mixture of meal and cabbage, without any salt at all. Upon Saturdays and Sundays he would add a little cheese sodden in water, and at Easter a few small fishes.'[1]

Winwaloe founded the celebrated monastery of Landevennec, the rule of which was exceedingly severe. Its brethren sustained themselves by the work of their hands, we are told, 'like the Egyptian monks; for they were running by the path, not only of monks, but even of hermits.' Their days of relaxation were 'the Sabbath and the Lord's day,' on which they were permitted, like their founder, to eat sparingly of cheese boiled in water, and on Sunday also of a little fish.[2] Louis le Débonnaire abolished the rule in 817, with all their Celtic customs, and substituted the rule of St. Benedict, for the old rule was too strict for the weaker brethren, especially in the matter of dress.

The second abbot of Landevennec, St. Guenhael or Guenant, was also a Briton, and other Armorican saints of the fifth century who came from the old country were St. Corentin, first bishop of Quimper; St. Brioc, founder

[1] Capgrave, quoted in Cressy's 'Church History of Brittany,' p. 183.
[2] 'Vita S. Guingaloëi,' quoted in ' H. and S.,' ii. 79.

The Age of Conflict

of a monastery, and St. Ninnocha, one of the numerous daughters of King ' Brechan,' who founded the nunnery of Lan Ninnok, but who may perhaps be a little later in date.

At the beginning of the sixth century, in 513, there was a large immigration of Britons, and the stream continued constant during the whole century. Fresh monasteries were founded by the settlers, one by St. Mevanius, or Méen, in the depth of the terrible forest of Brecéliande, the barrier which Gallican missionaries could not cross, a region of enchantment and romance, where, as trouvères afterwards told, the fairies dance by the fountain of Baranton, and where Merlin lies for ever beneath the whitethorn bush, snared by the device of the fair and faithless Vivien. Another Breton monastery, that of Ruys, was founded by the great saint of South Wales, Gildas.

Constant communication was kept up between Wales and Brittany during this century by journeys to and fro. Both Cadoc of Llancarfan and Illtyd of Llantwit are said to have visited Brittany, and Illtyd is said by his legend to have died at Dol.[1] Cadoc is said to have built a stone church on an island of the archipelago of Morbihan, called Ynys Cathodw, *i.e.*, the island of Cathodw, or Cadoc.[2] Breton legends describe the saint's fondness for Virgil, and say that he made his scholars learn his verses by heart. 'One day, while walking with his friend and companion, the famous historian Gildas, with his Virgil under his arm, the abbot began to weep at the thought that the poet whom he loved so much might be even then perhaps in hell. At the moment when Gildas reprimanded him severely for that *perhaps*, protesting that without any doubt Virgil must be damned, a sudden gust of wind tossed Cadoc's book into the sea. He was

---

[1] 'Vita S. Iltuti,' § 24; 'C. B. S.,' p. 179.
[2] 'Vita S. Cadoci,' § 32; 'C. B. S.,' p. 68.

much moved by this accident, and returning to his cell, said to himself, " I will not eat a mouthful of bread, nor drink a drop of water, before I know truly what fate God has allotted to those who sang upon earth, as the angels sing in heaven." After this he fell asleep, and soon after dreaming, heard a soft voice addressing him. " Pray for me, pray for me," said the voice ; " never be weary of praying; I shall yet sing eternally the mercy of the Lord."' The next day the book which Cadoc had lost was restored in a wonderful manner.

'Eight centuries after his death,' says Montalembert,[1] who dwells lovingly on the character of Cadoc, ' the great Celtic monk and patriot was still invoked as their special patron by the Breton knights in the famous battle of the Thirty, where Beaumanoir drank his own blood. On their way to the field they went into a chapel dedicated to St. Cadoc, and appealed to him for aid, and returned victorious, singing a Breton ballad, which ends thus:

' " He is not the friend of the Bretons who does not cry for joy to see our warriors return with the yellow broom in their casques ;

' " He is no friend of the Bretons, nor of the Breton saints, who does not bless St. Cadoc, the patron of our warriors ;

' " He who does not shout, and bless, and worship, and sing, ' In heaven, as on earth, Cadoc has no peer.' " '

The Breton See of Léon had two British bishops, the first being Paul Aurelian, who came from Cornwall, and was a cousin of St. Samson, and who was made Bishop of Léon by King Childebert in 512, and died in 573; the other being St. Golven. The family of Samson figures largely in Breton church history ; and the fiction of his own archbishopric of Dol was put prominently forward after the creation of the See of Dol by Nomenoë in the ninth century. St. Mevanius, the founder of the abbey

---

[1] Montalembert, 'Monks of the West,' bk. viii. c. 2 (authorized translation).

of St. Méen in the Forest of Bréceliande, was a cousin of St. Samson, and came from Gwent. Another kinsman was Maclovius, founder of the See of Aleth. He came from Cadoc's monastery of Llancarfan, and according to his legend, being evilly entreated by the Bretons, he cursed them and passed into France, but on their repentance absolved them. He is known also as Machutes, or Machutus. Maglorius, another cousin of Samson, and a disciple of St. Illtyd, of Llantwit, succeeded Samson at Dol, probably as episcopal abbot. According to Welsh stories the father of St. Samson was himself a Breton chieftain, who had settled in South Wales and married the daughter of Meurig, King of Glamorgan; and this may possibly explain the prominence of Samson himself and of his relations among the saints of Brittany.

Llantwit Major and Llancarfan seem to have taken the lead among Welsh monasteries in work for Brittany. The former is said to have sent over a fifth saint, Leonorius, or Lunaire, in addition to Illtyd, Samson, Gildas, and Maglorius. So intimate was the connection between Brittany and the diocese of Llandaff, that when, according to his legend, St. Teilo with his people fled from the Yellow Plague, which passed over the country 'in the column of a watery cloud, sweeping one head along the ground, and dragging the other through the air,' he crossed the seas to Samson in Brittany.[1] So, too, Teilo's successor, Oudoceus, when the excommunicated Guidnerth of Gwent asked pardon of him, sent him on a pilgrimage to the 'Archbishop of Dol into Cornugallia (viz., Cornouaille in Brittany), on account of the ancient friendship and acquaintance which the holy fathers, their predecessors, had had between them, to wit, St. Teilo and St. Samson, first archbishop of the city of Dol. And also for another reason because Guidnerth himself and the Britons and the archbishop of that land were of one

[1] 'Book of Llan Dâv,' p. 107.

tongue and of one nation, although they were divided by a space of land.'[1] The identity of nationality thus claimed by the 'Book of Llandaff' on the part of the Cymry of Wales was asserted also by the Cymry of Brittany as late as the ninth century. 'We sojourn in France in exile and captivity'[2] was the lamentation of the Bretons in the days of the English King Athelstan, when the Normans, under Rollo, depopulated Brittany, and many of its inhabitants sought refuge in England.

These statements, legendary and historical, point to the intimacy of the union which existed at the end of the sixth century between the British Church and the Church in Armorica. The latter had become practically merged in the former, for it had by this time shaken off the supremacy of the Archbishop of Tours, which its earlier bishops had recognised. Tours had now become a Frankish see, so that racial jealousy promoted the estrangement, and Armorican Christians looked rather towards Llandaff for support and sympathy, and the saints of Llandaff were their saints. Nor must it be forgotten that Irish monks, who had now begun to overrun the Continent of Europe in their restless zeal and missionary enterprise, settled in Brittany also, and contributed their quota to swell the army of its saints. Brittany was a miniature Britain, wherein the same conflict was already going on, which was soon to begin in the parent country. It had Saxons on its border, who attacked the Bretons on the Vilaine in 578; it had its own Easter question, and its own disputes about the form of the tonsure; it had its quarrel with a see which was in union with Rome, and was situated in the land of alien Teutons; it had, too, its allies and friends in the other Celtic Churches. The See of Tours resented its

---

[1] 'Book of Llan Dâv,' p. 181.
[2] 'In exulatu atque in captivitate in Francia commoramur.' 'Epist. Radbodi Dol. Epis.,' quoted by Lingard, 'Hist.,' i. 125 (Dolman, 1855).

independence, as the See of Canterbury a few years later resented the independence of the Britons; and at the second Council of Tours, held in 567, a canon was passed asserting the Metropolitanship of Tours over Brittany. 'We add also,' so it runs, 'that no one presume to ordain a Briton or a Roman as bishop in Armorica without the consent or letter of the metropolitan or the co-provincials. But if anyone shall attempt to resist, let him observe the sentence published in former canons, and recognise that he is removed and excommunicated from our charity until a greater synod; because those are deservedly separated from our charity or our churches who despise the decrees of the Fathers.'[1] But this canon was as little regarded by the clergy of Brittany as were Augustine's threats by the Church of Wales.

Brittany was not the only outpost of the British Church at this period. There were Britons and a See of Bretoña in Galicia, in the north-west corner of Spain. 'To the See of Bretoña,' so runs the record of the Council of Lugo (A.D. 569), 'belong the churches which are among the Britons, together with the monastery of Maximus, and the churches which are in Asturia.'[2] A bishop of Bretoña, with the Celtic name of Mailoc, was present at the second Council of Braga in 572, and subscribed its canons.[3] Spain, according to the testimony of Gregory of Tours, seems generally to have adhered to the older date of Easter at that time, so that there was no divergence of the Britons from the other churches in this matter, as there was in Gaul. Gregory notices with complacency that in the years 577 and 590, and probably also, he would believe, in other years as well, the springs in Spain, which were filled by Divine command, were

[1] 'Conc. Turon.,' ii., can. 9, in 'H. and S.,' ii. 77.
[2] See 'Conc. Hisp.,' iii. 188, quoted in 'H. and S.,' ii. 99.
[3] Mailoc, Britonensis Ecclesiae Episcopus, his gestis subscripsi. 'H. and S.,' ii. 99.

filled on the Easter-day which he and his party considered the orthodox one. A difference from the Spanish usage in respect of the tonsure which prevailed among the lectors of Galicia—probably the Britons of that district and those under their influence—is noted in the next century by the Council of Toledo (A.D. 633). The forty-first canon complains that these lectors, 'letting their hair grow long like laymen, shave a small circle on the top of the head only. For this custom in Spain has been hitherto that of heretics. Whence it behoves that to remove a scandal to the Church this sign of disgrace be done away ; and there be one tonsure or dress, as is the use of the whole of Spain. But he who shall not observe this, will be an offender against the Catholic faith.' The Easter question was also settled by this council. The See of Bretoña seems to have continued, but with other than Celtic bishops, until about A.D. 830, at which time it was merged in the Sees of Oviedo and Mondeñedo because of the destruction of the town of Bretoña by the Moors.

Brittenburg, at the mouth of the Rhine, has also been mentioned as a British colony, settled by Christian Britons in the time of Maximus; but it would be rash to consider this an outpost of the British Church. On the other hand, the Church of Ireland, founded by St. Patrick, who had among his bishops both Britons and Romans from Britain, and revived in its time of declension by the efforts of the Welsh monks, Gildas, David, and Cadoc, and of the North British monks of Whitherne, was at the end of the sixth century and in succeeding centuries so active and vigorous in its intellectual and spiritual life, and so full of new-born zeal in missionary effort, that its glory quite eclipsed that of the parent Church. Yet, none the less, it was in intimate union and communion with the Christians of Wales and of Britain in general ; its customs were similar, if not in all respects identical; and its sympathies were likely to be enlisted in favour of the Britons in any conflict with a non-Celtic communion in which they should become involved.

In 563 the great Irish missionary, St. Columba, who had been trained by St. David's pupil, Finnian of Clonard, and by the Whitherne student, Finnian of Moyville, and thus inherited the British traditions of Wales and of Strathclyde, settled in Hy, otherwise called Iona, with his missionary colony, which was destined eventually to evangelize the northern English. About ten years later another Irish missionary with a similar name, St. Columbanus, landed in Gaul. At the foot of the Vosges he founded the celebrated monastery of Luxeuil, and afterwards, in Italy itself, the monastery of Bobbio. 'Armies of Scots,' *i.e.*, Irish, sallied forth from their native land and covered Western Europe with their monasteries, overrunning England, Scotland, Brittany, France, Alsatia and Lorraine, and penetrating into Bavaria, Rhetia, Helvetia, Allemania, Thuringia and Italy, and in the North invading both Norway and Iceland. It would be out of place to enumerate their monasteries here, and to record in detail their labours, but it may be permitted to quote the brief and pregnant summary of one of their eloquent panegyrists. 'First,' says Mr. Haddan, 'by armies of monastic missionaries, and next by learned teachers—first, by attracting pupils to Irish schools from all Christian Europe north of the Alps and the Pyrenees, and, next, by sending forth men to become the founders of schools, or monasteries, or churches abroad—the churches of St. Patrick and St. Columba stand out, from the sixth century forward, as the most energetic centres of religious life and knowledge in Europe; the main restorers of Christianity in paganized England and Roman Germany; the reformers and main founders of monastic life in northern France; the opponents of Arianism, even in Italy itself; the originators in the West of the well-meant, however mistaken, system of the Penitentials; the leading preservers in the eighth and ninth centuries (though under strange guise) of theological and classical culture, Greek as well as Latin; the scribes, both at home and abroad, of many a precious Bible-text; the teachers of psalmody; the schoolmasters of the great monastic schools; the parents, in great part, as well as the forerunners, of Anglo-Saxon learning and missionary zeal; the senders forth of not the least bright stars among the galaxy of talent gathered by Charlemagne from all quarters to instruct his degenerate Franks; the founders of the schoolmen; the originators, it must be confessed (to add a dark touch to the picture), of metaphysical free-thinking and pantheistic tendencies in modern Europe, yet (we must maintain) not open as a Church to the charge of Pelagianizing so commonly laid against them; the hive, lastly, whence, long after Charlemagne, Germany and Switzerland drew a never-failing supply of zealous and learned monks, driven from home probably by Danish ravages and intestine brawls, down to the very time of the Normanizing of the Celtic Churches in the entire British Isles in the eleventh and twelfth centuries.'[1]

We must not forget, too, that all this energy and enthusiasm of the Irish Churches was originally kindled by British missionary zeal, which Mr. Haddan unduly disparages, and was due, first to Patrick, the saint of Alclyd, or Dumbarton, and afterwards to the Welsh saints, Gildas, David, and Cadoc.

When, therefore, Augustine landed in Thanet in A.D. 597, on his mission to the pagan English, and our island was thereby again brought into connection with the See of Rome, the British Church was in a far different position from that which it had held when the Roman legions had left our shores. Although it had lost to paganism the

[1] 'Scots on the Continent,' in Haddan's 'Remains,' pp. 260, 261.

greater part of Britain, and was there confined within much narrower limits, yet it had gained largely in self-reliance and in spiritual power; it no longer looked towards Gaul for leaders and instructors, but itself sent its saints abroad on missions of succour; and, further, it had planted colonies in other lands, which in magnitude and importance exceeded what had been lost at home. Celtic Christianity, too, had developed its own customs and modes of thought, distinct from those of the rest of Western Christendom, from which it had so long been severed. The British Church was no longer a weak and dependent branch of the Gallican Churches, as it had been at the Council of Arles, where its bishops were reckoned as among those 'from the Gauls'; it was independent and self-sufficient, itself the Mother Church of a great and powerful Celtic confederacy, which might challenge the dominion of the West with the See of Rome. But fortunately for Rome, the confederacy was a loose one, liable to fall in pieces from the common Celtic fault of defective organization.

It was not long before the Roman mission came into conflict with the Christians of Wales. The holiness of Pope Gregory did not save him from that disregard of national rights which has been the besetting sin of the Roman See, and in reply to Augustine's question how he should conduct himself towards the bishops of Gaul and Britain, the Pope informed him that the bishops of Gaul were outside his jurisdiction; but 'as to the bishops of the Britains, we commit them all,' he wrote, 'to thy Fraternity, that the unlearned may be taught, the weak strengthened by persuasion, the perverse corrected by authority.' Augustine was not the man to waive any of the privileges to which he thought himself justly entitled, and in the year 603 or thereabout, he sought a conference with the British bishops. The story of what followed is told with some fulness of detail by the Venerable Bede.

The two parties met at Augustine's Oak, on the borders of the Huicii and West Saxons, possibly Austcliffe, on the Severn. Here Augustine urged the Britons to unite with him in the work of converting the heathen English, and pointed out certain differences of use between the British and Roman Churches, especially in the date of Easter. After a long discussion, when the Britons maintained their own traditions and would not yield to the foreign missionary, he is said to have proposed to settle the matter by a miracle: 'Let some sick man be brought, and let the faith and practice of him by whose prayers he shall be healed, be believed acceptable to God, and to be followed by all.' A blind Englishman was brought, whom the Britons could not cure, but whom Augustine restored to sight by his prayers. The Britons then confessed that Augustine taught the right way; but pleaded that they could not abandon their ancient customs without the consent of their people. Wherefore they asked for a second conference.

At the second conference seven British bishops were present, and many very learned men, chiefly from the monastery of Bangor Iscoed. Before going to the conference, they had asked advice of a certain holy anchorite, who answered them, 'If he be a man of God, follow him.' 'And how can we prove that?' they replied. He said: 'The Lord saith, "Take My yoke upon you and learn of Me, for I am meek and lowly of heart." If, then, this Augustine be meek and lowly of heart, it is to be believed that both he carries the yoke of Christ himself, and offers it to you to carry; but if he be hard and proud, it is plain that he is not of God, nor are we to regard his words.' They asked again, 'And how can we discern even this?' 'Contrive,' said he, 'that he may first arrive with his friends at the place of the conference, and if at your approach he shall rise up to you, hear him submissively; but if he shall despise you and will not rise up to you, although you are more in number, let him also be despised by you.'

The advice was taken. They found Augustine sitting in a chair, and he did not rise up; consequently they rejected his overtures. Augustine on his part offered to tolerate other differences of ritual, if they would conform in three points: 'to celebrate Easter at the right time; to complete the administration of baptism, whereby we are born again to God, according to the custom of the holy Roman and Apostolic Church; and to preach the word of the Lord jointly' with him and his mission. The Britons refused to comply or 'to receive him as archbishop,' and the conference broke up angrily, Augustine foretelling that if they would not preach the way of life to the English, they should at their hands undergo the vengeance of death.

This is Bede's version of the conferences, and in its main particulars it is pretty certainly accurate. The attempt of Augustine to assert the supremacy of Canterbury had failed, and his curse recoiled upon his own party. Within a few years the Canterbury mission, disturbed by the general hostility of the Celtic Churches, adopted a much more moderate tone, and Augustine's successor, Laurence, in the letter to the Irish bishops and abbots, sent by him jointly with Mellitus and Justus, used language of gentle complaint and entreaty. He saluted his opponents as his 'most dear brethren the lords bishops and abbots,' and stated that when they came into Britain, before they knew the facts, they held both the Britons and the Irish in great reverence for holiness; but when they became acquainted with the Britons, they thought the Irish were better. But, continues the letter, 'We have learned from Bishop Dagan, coming into this island, which we have before mentioned, and the Abbot Columbanus in Gaul, that the Irish in no wise differ from the Britons in their manner of life. For Bishop Dagan, coming to us, not only would not take food with us, but not even in the same house in which we ate.' Laurence also and the other bishops sent like letters, we are told, to the priests of the Britons, whereby he strove to confirm them in Catholic unity. But, adds Bede with a touch of bitter sarcasm, 'how far he profited by doing these things, the present times still declare.'[1]

[1] Bede, 'H. E.,' ii. 4; 'M. H. B.,' p. 153.

CHAPTER V.

THE AGE OF CONFLICT AND THE SUBMISSION OF THE WELSH CHURCH.

IT is no matter for astonishment that the Roman missionaries were dismayed at the tempest which their pretensions had aroused. The difference between them and the Celtic Christians was no mere local quarrel of Bangor Iscoed with Canterbury, as it is sometimes represented; nor a mere outburst of hostility on the part of the Church of the Briton against the Church of the invader. National hatred, and the sense of old and of recent injuries, ever rankling in the breasts of the Britons, unquestionably had their part in embittering hostile feelings in Britain itself; but Dagan, the Irish bishop of Inverdaoile, in Wexford, and Columbanus, the Irish missionary in Gaul, had no such antipathy and wrongs to stir their blood, and yet they too joined in the struggle as loyally as Dunawd and his associates. The churches of the Celtic communion were united in defence of their ancient customs and in opposition to the claims of the See of Rome, which to the majority of Celtic Christians was little else than an abstraction and a name. It was a struggle for independence. The Irish Church might claim, as Columbanus claimed on its behalf, that Ireland had never been part of the Roman Empire, and was therefore from the first outside of the Roman Patriarchate, belonging to the churches of the Barbarians, which, according to the judgment of the Council of Constantinople, were to live according to the laws taught them by their fathers. The Britons for their part were no longer willing to concede to the Bishop of Rome even that harmless primacy which before the Saxon invasion they had acknowledged; it had lapsed long ago when their Church was in its infancy, and its revival, to secure acquiescence, needed more caution and moderation than Augustine, or even Gregory, had shown. The Celtic Churches were of one heart and of one mind. The exiles of Landevennec and St. Méen, while keeping their rigorous fasts and vigils, would learn from British visitors that a contest had begun for their brethren in the mother country similar to that which they were sustaining with Tours—a contest for the customs of Winwaloe, of Illtyd, and of Samson, and would be encouraged by their steadfastness to abide themselves more firmly by the old paths. Through all the monasteries of Ireland it would be told how a bishop from the distant city of Rome had presumed to censure the Easter and the baptismal rite that had been held sacred by Gildas, David, and Cadoc, who had given them their liturgy, and by the saints before them, and had even cursed the Welsh brethren because they would not lightly abandon these usages. The monks of Iona, to whom Columba had been as an angel of God—nay more, for had he not been a discerner of spirits, and held constant communication with angels, who delighted to wait upon him?—would learn with astonishment and disgust that an arrogant foreigner, who had been sent to teach the pagan English, had pronounced the way of truth that Columba held so dear a by-path of error, and had threatened its adherents with destruction. It is not easy to imagine the indignation which must have passed through the whole Celtic community at the news. If Rome had its saints, so had they, attested by as notable miracles, and more successful in missionary work. If Rome had its antiquity in its favour, the Church of Ireland had, at least, youth and vigour on its side; if the one could plead tradition, the other might lay claim to a clearer spiritual instinct. Augustine had treated the Britons with the haughtiness of a superior who expected as a Roman that his commands would be obeyed. The Britons and the Irish with equal spirit treated him and his followers as schismatics, and would not eat in their houses. Columbanus, encountered on the Continent with similar censures to those which the Britons sustained at home, lectured various Popes with a freedom of language, which even in those days, when papal supremacy was not yet developed, must have been to its recipients an exceedingly unpleasant, if wholesome, tonic, and if used in the present day, would appear to a Romanist rank blasphemy. He acknowledged the authority of the See of Rome over the Churches of the Roman Empire; but, as we have seen, claimed exemption for his own Church and for himself. He gave all honour to 'the chair of St. Peter,' and admitted that Rome was the chief see in the world—*except Jerusalem*. He reasoned with Pope Gregory, because, with all his wisdom, he supported the dark Paschal system, out of regard, he supposed, to the authority of Pope Leo; but he urged him to think for himself on the ground that a living dog was better than a dead lion (leo), 'for a living saint might correct errors that had not been corrected by another greater one,' a left-handed compliment that would scarcely be appreciated by a nineteenth-century Pope, were such now called upon to correct the errors of an infallible predecessor. He urged Pope Boniface to watch, for Vigilius had not kept vigil well, and to cleanse the chair of Peter from all error, for it were a sad and lamentable thing if the Catholic faith were not kept in the Apostolic See. In a later age, St. Columbanus would have run a considerable risk of being burned alive as a heretic, and his epistles would have been placed upon the Index.

A great blow was inflicted upon the Britons and the British Church in A.D. 613 by the battle of Chester, at which Æthelfrith defeated the Britons, and massacred the monks of Bangor Iscoed, who were praying for his defeat. Bede and English churchmen of his day regarded the massacre of the monks as the fulfilment of Augustine's curse. But a far worse result of this battle for the British was the severance it effected between Wales and Strathclyde. Before 577 the Britons had held the entire west of the island south of the Clyde. In that year the brothers Ceawlin and Cutha had won the battle of Deorham, and forced a wedge of English between the Cymry of what is now Wales, and the Cymry of the south-western peninsula. During the next few years they had gradually advanced up the valley of the Severn, until in 584 they destroyed Viriconium, 'the White Town in the bosom of the wood,' and made desolate the hall of Cynddylan.[1] But they were defeated soon after at Fethan leag (Faddiley), and Cutha was slain, and so they failed to reach Chester. Now Æthelfrith finished what Ceawlin had only half carried out—the isolation of Wales. Henceforth begins the history of Wales and the Welsh as a separate country and people.

The inevitable result of this isolation, so far as the Church was concerned, was to turn the attention of Welsh Christians more especially to home affairs, and to separate them in some measure from the common current of Celtic feeling. At the same time, the interest of the Celts outside of Wales in the Church of Wales tended gradually to diminish. Communication between Wales and the bishoprics of Candida Casa and Glasgow could only be kept up by sea; and although to a travelling people like

---

[1] See Dr. Guest's paper, and his translation of Llywarch Hên's elegy in 'Origines Celticæ,' ii. 282-312.

the Britons, who were wont to send their saints to Ireland and Brittany, this difference from the earlier state of things might seem to be a slight one, it proved in the end very real. In the sixth century, Kentigern was a saint and bishop both of Wales and of Glasgow; no one afterwards filled a like place, and the immigration of northern Britons into Wales seems to have ceased. Wales had hitherto been in communication through Strathclyde with the stream of life and energy flowing from Iona, and Kentigern, the friend of David, was, according to his legend, a friend of Columba; the battle of Chester weakened this connection also.

Though the travelling bent of the Celts softened the blow a good deal at first, until the Danish pirate fleets rendered all communication by sea exceedingly perilous, yet the Celtic confederacy of churches was necessarily thereby weakened in its struggle against Rome. The Welsh sees were the leading sees in the war of independence; the monastery of Bangor Iscoed the leading college; and when the monks were massacred, and the Welsh sees isolated, the Celtic cause suffered, and the anti-national party gained a corresponding advantage. The battles of Deorham and Chester not only cut the British civil community into three parts, they also divided the British Church. Its three parts acted separately, and while one part was comparatively friendly to the missionaries who kept the Roman Easter, another part would be bitterly hostile. Wini, the Gallican Bishop of Wessex, even procured the co-operation of two British bishops, probably of West Wales, *i.e.*, Devon and Cornwall, in the consecration of Chad (A.D. 665). But it would appear that the Church of Wales at this time had in no degree relaxed its stern, unbending attitude.

The first part of the Celtic body to desert the Celtic cause was the south of Ireland, where it was decided in 634, after a synod and the despatch of deputies to Rome, to accept the Roman Easter. But the decisive point in the struggle was the synod of Whitby,[1] held by Oswiu of Northumbria, the murderer of the gentle Oswini. The rivalry between the Churches caused a very practical difficulty at Oswiu's court. He was himself a disciple of the Irish mission, whereas his wife Eanfled followed the usages of Canterbury. As the two kept Easter at different dates, it happened, that while the queen was still observing the fast of Lent, Oswiu was celebrating the joyous festival of Easter. The good Aidan during his life had contrived to keep peace between the Christians of the rival communions, and prevent any breach of amity. But in the time of Colman, the dispute ran so high, that the intervention of the royal authority became necessary, and it was agreed that both parties should meet and discuss their differences at Whitby. Wilfrid argued on the Roman side, and Colman for the Celtic Easter. The rude king, after hearing the speeches of both parties, succeeding in grasping one point, that Wilfrid claimed to have in his favour the authority of St. Peter, who held the keys of the kingdom of heaven, and as Colman could not claim any such authority for his Columba, Oswiu thought it wisest to conciliate the door-keeper of heaven, lest he might afterwards refuse to open for him. He therefore decided in Wilfrid's favour, and Colman retired from Northumbria (A.D. 664). From this time all the English Christians were united in observing the Roman usage.

Wilfred gained at Whitby something even of more importance than the decision of the canny Northumbrian king, and that was the adhesion of the able and saintly Cuthbert. There is no sadder proof of the bitterness with which the struggle was often carried on, than the last charge of this holy man, who had himself been trained among the Scottish clergy, and who, so men told, had seen the spirit of Bishop Aidan carried to Paradise.[2] Yet,

[1] Streanaeshalch. [2] Beda, 'Vita S. Cudb.,' iv.

after with his dying breath charging his friend, Abbot Herefrid of Lindisfarne, and the brethren around to keep peace with the household of faith, and despise them not, he thus continued: 'But with those that err from the unity of Catholic peace, either by not celebrating Easter at the proper time, or by living perversely, have no communion. And know and hold in memory, that if necessity should compel you to choose one of two evils, I would much rather that you should dig up my bones from the tomb, and carrying them away with you, desert these parts, and dwell wheresoever God may provide—much rather, I say, than that by giving any consent to the iniquities of schismatics, you should submit your neck to their yoke.'[1] The same appellation of schismatics is applied to the Britons and Irish by Eddius, the biographer of the Roman partisan, Wilfrid.[2] Wilfrid himself would not be consecrated in England by Irish bishops, or by those who had been consecrated by the Irish; but went over to Gaul and received consecration from Bishop Agilberct.[3] Archbishop Theodore, in like manner, would not acknowledge the validity of Celtic orders. He upbraided Chad, who, as we have seen, was consecrated by Wini with the assistance of British bishops, and told him that he had not been duly consecrated, but as Chad answered submissively, he did not depose him, but 'himself consummated his ordination anew after the Catholic manner.'[4] The Penitential which bears

---

[1] Beda, 'Vita S. Cudb.,' xxxix. I quote the English translation by Stevenson in 'The Historical Works of the Venerable Beda,' 'The Church Historians of England,' i., pt. ii. 595.
[2] 'Schismatici Britanniæ et Hiberniæ,' 'Vita S. Wilf.,' v.
[3] Bede, 'H. E,' iii. 28; Eddius, 'Vita S. Wilf.,' xii.
[4] *Ibid.*, iv. 2: 'Ipse ordinationem ejus denuo catholica ratione consummavit.' 'M. H. B.,' p. 211, where also is this note: 'Duo in Ceaddæ ordinatione Theodorus erroris arguebat. Primum, quod ordinatus est ad sedem quæ Uilfridi electione jam plena fuit. Secundum, quod in ordinatione ejus, episcopi in Uini societatem pro ministerio adsumpti, ex iis erant qui Brittanicum Paschæ morem sequebantur.'

Theodore's name, treats the Britons as schismatics, whose orders, and very baptism, were of doubtful validity. Its rules are of the most stringent character. 'Those,' it says, 'who have been ordained by bishops of the Irish or of the Britons, who are not Catholics in Easter and the tonsure, are not united to the Church; but are to be confirmed again by a Catholic bishop with the laying on of his hand. In like manner also the churches which are consecrated by the bishops are to be sprinkled with holy water and confirmed with a collect. Also we have no permission to give the chrism or the Eucharist to those asking, unless they shall first confess that they desire to be with us in the unity of the Church. And in like manner, if anyone from their race, or another, whosoever he be, shall have scruples as to his baptism, let him be baptized.'

It seems impossible to find any justification for canons such as these. Even if the Britons and Irish were the schismatics that the Roman party considered them, they were not guilty of heresy. The charge of Pelagianism which Pope John IV. brought against the Irish Church is not proven,[1] and was never even alleged against the Britons at this period. Moreover, as even heretical baptism is held valid by the Church, heresy itself, were such proved against the Celts, would not militate against their baptism, so that in the absence of any proof of carelessness on their part in the administration of the rite, the order for the re-baptism of converts to the Roman party must be considered an act of wanton provocation, and utterly contrary to Catholic usage. The controversial policy of Rome seems to have been then what it is now, to alarm the weak-minded by raising doubts as to the orders and sacraments of their opponents, even though the Roman controversialists knew then well enough, as they know now, the utterly baseless character of those suspicions. The policy of the Popes varied: Gregory did

[1] Bede, 'H. E.,' ii. 19.

not deny the validity of British orders, and wrote of the British bishops to Augustine as if they were genuine bishops; yet, at the same time, he did not advise him even before the schism to seek the co-operation of British bishops in his consecrations, but referred him rather for help to the Gallican bishops, wherever such might be in England.[1] Pope John IV., when Pope Elect, in writing to the Irish bishops and priests respecting Easter, addresses them as most beloved and holy, and gives them their proper style as bishops and priests.[2] But Pope Vitalian, writing to Oswiu, about 665, tells him that he was seeking a bishop for him, who might root out all the enemy's tares throughout the island,[3] which appears from the context to be an uncomplimentary reference to the British and Irish Christians. In the next century, Boniface, the English missionary in Germany, did his utmost in the spirit of this letter to root out his British and Irish rivals. He had a quarrel with Virgilius, or Ferghal, and Sidonius, two Irish missionaries, the former of whom became the saintly bishop of Salzburg. In the first place they appealed to Rome against an order which he had issued for the re-baptism of one, at whose baptism the Latin words had been mispronounced by an ignorant priest. The Pope decided against Boniface; but soon afterwards the Englishman accused Virgilius of heresy in believing that there were antipodes, and nearly procured his deposition from the priesthood. Two other Irishmen were more unlucky than Virgilius. Boniface obtained the deposition and excommunication of a bishop named Clement, for various alleged heresies, and also of a priest named Samson. He recommended that the former should be imprisoned for life; but it is uncertain whether this was carried out.[4] The manner in which

---

[1] Bede, 'H. E.,' i. 27. Answer 6. [2] *Ibid.*, ii. 19. [3] *Ibid.*, iii. 29.
[4] Neander, 'History of the Christian Religion' (Bohn's edition), vol. v., pp. 73-87.

Boniface regarded the British missionaries is probably reflected in the letter wherein Pope Gregory III. recommends him to the Bavarian and Allemanic bishops as his legate. He bids them at the same time to 'reject and forbid the rites and doctrines of paganism, or of Britons coming among them, or of false priests and heretics, whencesoever they may be.'[1] This was in the year 739, before the Britons had submitted.[2]

Facts like these prove the completeness of the separation of Wales from Rome for more than a century and a half, during which it set the Pope and his agents at defiance. It was Wales that incurred the curse of Augustine, and it was Wales that held out longest against the excommunicatory canons of Theodore. Good men such as Abbot Ceolfrid and the Venerable Bede could yield so far to Christian charity as to respect and love the holiness of St. Aidan and other of the saints of Hy, and to excuse their Celtic customs on the ground of ignorance. But for the Welsh, the leaders in the rebellion, Bede cannot find a good word. To him they are 'a perfidious race,'[3] and their army 'an impious army.' He speaks of the massacre of the monks of Bangor Iscoed by the pagan Æthelfrith as though it were almost a Christian work; yet he bitterly complains of the alliance between the Christian Welshman Cadwallon and the heathen Penda, and the devastation the Welsh wrought

---

[1] 'Inter Epistt. St. Bonifacii,' Ep. 45, quoted in 'H. and S.,' i. 203: Gentilitatis ritum et doctrinam, vel venientium Brittonum, vel falsorum, sacerdotum et hæreticorum,' etc.

[2] Even as late as 816, when both the British and Irish Churches had made their peace with the See of Rome, and abandoned their ancient customs, it was ordered by the Council of Celchyth, held under the presidency of Archbishop Wulfred of Canterbury, that no Irishmen should be allowed to minister in any way in the Church of England, because of a doubt whether they were ordained or not. But this may indicate a suspicion as to the good faith of many of the wandering Irishmen, rather than a disposition to question the validity of Irish orders. See Canon V. in 'H. and S.,' iii. 581.

[3] Bede, 'H. E.,' ii. 2; 'M. H. B.,' p. 151: 'gentis perfidæ ... nefandæ militiæ.'

in Northumbria, though surely, if ever man might be excused on the ground of provocation received, Cadwallon might. As for the state of things in his own day, he tells us that it was 'the custom of the Britons to hold the faith and religion of the English of no account, and to have no dealings with them in anything more than with pagans.' 'Through domestic hatred,' he says again, 'they are adverse to the race of the English, and wrongfully and by wicked customs oppose the appointed Easter of the whole Catholic Church.'

It is certainly strange in view of facts such as the above, the curse pronounced upon the Britons by St. Augustine, their treatment as schismatics by St. Cuthbert, the denial of their orders and of the validity of their baptism, and the refusal to them of chrism and the Eucharist by Archbishop Theodore, their denunciation as tares by Pope Vitalian, and their classification with heathens and heretics by Pope Gregory III., that some controversialists attempt to minimize the dispute between Wales and Rome, and even have the audacity to claim the Welsh saints as orthodox Roman Catholics. Those who so argue go perilously near to incurring the charge of heresy themselves, for they cannot be sincere believers in Papal Infallibility, seeing that they give the lie to their own popes, Vitalian and Gregory III. Cardinal Baronius in a former age did not venture upon so unhistorical a paradox, but classed the Britons and the Irish alike as guilty of schism for their breach of unity with Rome. It must be remembered, too, that if the chronology of the 'Annales Cambriæ' be accepted, some of the most notable of the Welsh saints are included in the charge of wilful schism. St. David just escapes, for he died in 601, though it has been supposed that the Synod of Caerleon, which he held in the year of his death, was connected with the overtures of Augustine. But St. Dubricius and St. Kentigern were certainly wilful 'schismatics' in the Roman sense, for they did not die until 612. St. Teilo and St. Oudoceus, the successors of Dubricius in the See of Llandaff, probably both come under the same category, and as for St. Dunawd, he was the arch-schismatic of all. Five only out of the four hundred and seventy-nine Welsh saints whom Professor Rice Rees enumerates in his learned 'Essay' are posterior in date to the submission to Rome, and of the remaining four hundred and seventy-four, the vast majority belong to the three hundred years of entire isolation and independence. All such, if the Roman postulates be admitted, must be pronounced guilty of error from the unity of the Church and of disobedience to the See of Rome, whether committed in ignorance or through wilful perversity. It is difficult, therefore, to see how Romanists can claim the Welsh saints as their own, except on the assumption that all good men are Roman Catholics, whatever else they may choose to call themselves, and however much they may oppose the See of Rome during their lifetime. But if this be so, we have no reason to desert our own Church for an allegiance which the Welsh saints of old rejected and repudiated.

It will be interesting in this connection to consider the letter of St. Aldhelm, Bishop of Sherborne, written in 705 to Geruntius, the British King of Damnonia (*i.e.*, Devon and Cornwall), and the British priests of his principality. This both shows that the Roman party of his time considered the Britons to be guilty of schism, which would cut them off from heaven at the last, and also gives us a contemporary picture of Wales, proving that the Welsh regarded the Roman party exactly as the Roman party regarded them. There cannot be a clearer proof of Welsh independence of Rome at the beginning of the eighth century than this interesting letter affords.[1]

[1] The passages which I quote verbatim I take from the vigorous translation of Serenus de Cressy, contained in his 'Church History of

At the outset, Aldhelm states that the duty of writing had been unanimously imposed on him by a synod of bishops at which he had been present, that he might acquaint the Britons 'with their fatherly suggestion and request that they would be careful not to break the unity of the Catholic Church, nor admit opinions not suiting with the Christian faith, since so doing they would deprive themselves of future rewards in heaven. For what profit,' he continues, ' can anyone receive from good works done out of the Catholic Church, although a man should be never so strict in regular observance, or retire himself into a desert to practise an anchoretical life of contemplation ?'

He informs them further that it was reported that their priests did 'very much swerve from the rule of Catholic faith enjoined in the Scriptures, and that by their quarrels and verbal contentions there had arisen in the Church of Christ a grievous schism and scandal, whereas the Psalmist said, "Great peace is to those who love Thy name, and among them there is no scandal."' He points out that the British tonsure, which they retained as being 'the tonsure of their predecessors, whom with pompous phrases they exalted, as men eminently illustrated with Divine grace,' was in reality the tonsure of Simon Magus, whereas the Roman tonsure was that of St. Peter. Besides this, 'there was among them another practice, far more pernicious to souls,' which was their observance of an incorrect date of Easter. He then proceeds to complain of the behaviour of the Christians of Wales.

' But besides these enormities, there is another thing wherein they do notoriously swerve from the Catholic faith and Evangelical tradition, which is that the priests of the Demetae inhabiting beyond the bay of Severn,

Brittany' (*i.e.* Britain), A.D. 1668 (no place given), bk. xix., chap. xvii., pp. 481-483.

puffed up with a conceit of their own purity, do exceedingly abhor communion with us, insomuch as they will neither join in prayers with us in the church, nor enter into society with us at the table; yea, moreover, the fragments which we leave after refection they will not touch, but cast them to be devoured by dogs and unclean swine. The cups also in which we have drunk, they will not make use of, till they have rubbed and cleansed them with sand or ashes. They refuse all civil salutations or to give us the kiss of pious fraternity, contrary to the Apostle's precept, "Salute one another with a holy kiss." They will not afford us water and a towel for our hands, nor a vessel to wash our feet. Whereas our Saviour, having girt Himself with a towel, washed His disciples' feet, and left us a pattern to imitate, saying, "As I have done to you, so do you to others." Moreover, if any of us, who are Catholics, do go amongst them to make an abode, they will not vouchsafe to admit us to their fellowship till we be compelled to spend forty days in penance. And herein they unhappily imitate those heretics who will needs be called Cathari. Such enormous errors and malignities as these are to be mournfully bewailed with sighs and tears, since such their behaviour is contrary to the precepts of the Gospel, and suiting with the traditions of Jewish Pharisees, concerning whom our Saviour saith, "Woe unto you, Scribes and Pharisees, who cleanse the outsides of cups and dishes." On the contrary, our Lord disdained not to be present at feasts with publicans and sinners, thereby showing himself a good physician, who was careful to provide wholesome cataplasms and medicines to heal the corrupt wounds of those that conversed with him. Therefore he did not, like the Pharisees, despise the conversation of sinners, but on the contrary, according to his accustomed clemency, he mercifully comforted the poor sinful woman who bewailed the former pollutions of her life, and casting herself down at our Lord's feet, washed them with showers of tears, and wiped them with the curled locks of her hair, concerning whom He said, " Her many sins are forgiven her, because she hath loved much."'

Aldhelm then goes on to implore Geruntius and the clergy of Damnonia to be reconciled to the See of St. Peter.

'Since, therefore, the truth of these things cannot be denied, we do with earnest humble prayers and bended knees beseech and adjure you, as you hope to attain to the fellowship of angels in God's heavenly kingdom, that you will not longer with pride and stubbornness abhor the doctrines and decrees of the blessed Apostle St. Peter, nor pertinaciously and arrogantly despise the tradition of the Roman Church, preferring before it the decrees and ancient rites of your predecessors. For it was St. Peter who, having devoutly confessed the Son of God, was honoured by Him with these words, " Thou art Peter, and upon this rock will I build my Church. . . ." If, therefore, the keys of the kingdom of heaven were given to St. Peter, who is he, who, having despised the principal statutes and ordinances of His Church, can presumingly expect to enter with joy through the gate of the heavenly paradise ?'

'Some nice disputer,' Aldhelm admits, may urge that the Britons hold and teach the doctrines of the Catholic faith, and it is noteworthy that Aldhelm does not deny the truth of such a statement, showing that so far as doctrine was concerned, the British Church was quite orthodox. His answer to such a contention is, ' That man does in vain boast of the Catholic faith, who does not follow the dogma and rule of St. Peter.'

Geruntius and the Britons of Damnonia were persuaded by the letter of Aldhelm, as Naiton and the Picts were persuaded five years later, in 710, by a letter from Abbot Ceolfrid. Probably in both cases the recalcitrant clergy were already tired of their separation from their brother Christians, and were glad to avail themselves of some pretext for abandoning their attitude of opposition. The Britons of Strathclyde had conformed to the Roman usages as early as 668; the Northern Scots of Ireland, with the exception of the Columban monasteries, followed their example in 697, and in 704 there began to be a Roman party in Hy itself. After the submission of the Picts, Wales was left almost alone in its opposition to Rome, though the national customs did not altogether lose their hold of Hy till 772, and Landevennec in Brittany certainly retained its Celtic tonsure until 817.

The importance of Aldhelm's letter, however, does not lie in the conversions it effected, so much as in the contemporaneous picture it presents of the struggle, and especially of the condition of the Church in Wales, which now from its isolated position may be called also the Church *of* Wales. It is evident from the language of Aldhelm that the Welsh Christians were pure in doctrine, and at least so far pure in morals, that none of the English Christians could venture to cast the first stone against them. They even seem to have laid claim to a morality superior to that of the English, which Aldhelm for his part could not deny, and only disparages as Pharisaic self-righteousness. The Britons generally held their former saints in great reverence, and still had saints and anchorites whose strictness of life Aldhelm is forced to acknowledge, though he deems such holiness worthless on account of their state of schism. It does not appear that he refrained from offensive charges out of courtesy to those whom he addressed; he rather magnified their faults, or, at least, used much plainness of speech, so that his testimony to the virtues of the Britons, and especially of the Welsh, is the more valuable, as extorted from an enemy. It is the fashion with some authors to represent the Welsh Christians as corrupt in morals and utterly lacking in religious zeal, except such as manifested itself in a gloomy and selfish asceticism. It would be well, therefore, for those who may have been misled by such misrepresentations, to study not only the pages of Gildas, but also the 'Epistle' of Aldhelm. Undoubtedly the age was dark and troublous, and the increpations of Gildas, though one-sided, had their foundation in fact. But what readers of his gloomy 'Epistle' too often forget, is that the same crimes were to be found also elsewhere than in Wales; the English converts were not immaculate either, and had Aldhelm denounced the Welsh for sin, they might have advised him to look at home. Wales at the beginning of the eighth century was at least not worse than England, and probably was rather better. Nay, I would be inclined to go even beyond this, and maintain that Wales in Aldhelm's time was no worse than Wales is to-day. We must not make too much of growth in civilization as though it were the same as growth in grace; outward manifestations vary in different ages, but the sum total of human corruption probably varies less than we may think. A modern Gildas might fill as goodly and as forcible a volume as that of the saint of Llancarfan, with the crimes and follies of Christian Englishmen and Welshmen of the nineteenth century.

It is stupid to blame harshly the Britons for not sending missionaries among the pagan English; it is false to accuse them of lack of missionary zeal. The facts of the conversion of Ireland and of the revival of its Church are a sufficient answer to the latter charge. There were also British missionaries on the Continent, otherwise Pope Gregory III. would not have warned the Bavarian and Allemanian bishops against them. There was a Briton with St. Gall in Switzerland. Their fame on the Continent has been obscured by that of the Irish with whom they were associated, but we have sufficient indications to prove that Britons were there. That they did nothing for the conversion of the English is true enough; for the story told by Nennius that Rum map Urbgen baptized Edwin of Northumbria and 'all the race of the Ambrones,' and that through his preaching many believed in Christ,[1] seems somehow to have arisen, from a confusion with Paulinus, the origin of which is not apparent. But those who censure the Britons for not preaching to the English should first make it clear that it was even possible for them to do so; it does not follow that because the Celts of Ireland could do missionary work, therefore the national enemies of the English, the conquered race, would also have been welcomed. Short, probably, would have been the shrift of the intrusive Briton who had ventured among the Saxons to overthrow their belief in their national gods. Neither can we determine with any certainty whether Bede, who half applauds the massacre of the monks of Bangor, would have chronicled him as a martyr or as a miscreant.

Eventually Wales also accepted the Roman Easter. The circumstances are unknown, but the leader was Elbod or Elfod, Bishop of Bangor, and the date given for the change by the 'Annales Cambriæ' and the 'Brut y Tywysogion' is 768. The 'Book of Aberpergwm,' sometimes called the 'Gwentian Brut,' asserts that Easter was changed in 755 in Gwynedd by the advice of Elfod, but that the other bishops did not concur therein, on which account the Saxons invaded the Cymry in South Wales, where the battle of Coed Marchan took place, and the Saxons were defeated. The same book gives A.D. 777 as the date of the alteration in South Wales. In 809 Elbod died, a date upon which all the chronicles are in agreement. The 'Book of Aberpergwm' adds that in the same year 'a great tumult occurred among the ecclesiastics on account of Easter; for the Bishops

[1] 'M. H. B.,' p. 76.

of Llandaff and Menevia would not succumb to the Archbishop of Gwynedd, being themselves archbishops of older privilege.' But all these statements of the 'Book of Aberpergwm' are extremely questionable, for the book cannot be regarded as possessing any historical value.

Thus terminated the struggle for independence, after it had continued for more than a century and a half. Wales at the beginning was the head of a great and powerful Celtic confederacy; at the end it was left almost alone. A party in Hy, and perhaps also the Breton clergy, remained faithful to the last to the cause of Celtic independence, but Wales had no other allies. The Church of Ireland had so entirely turned against it that by its canons it had put restrictions upon the ministrations of such clergy as came from Britain, and had condemned their churches for separating from the Roman customs and from the unity of Christendom. The prolongation of the struggle only completed the isolation of Wales, and though by its submission to Rome it again entered nominally into fellowship with the rest of Western Christendom, it was long separated in feeling from the English Church and the Churches of the Continent, and it never quite regained the old connection with its Celtic brethren. It had lost alike its headship and its colonies. Communication with Ireland was still kept up, but Wales was never again to Ireland what it had been in the days of Gildas, David, and Cadoc; the relative positions of the two Churches rather tended to be reversed.

The differences of the British customs from the Roman have not always been understood. It is clear that the Britons agreed in doctrine with the rest of Christendom; there was no taint of heresy or of paganism about them, and their differences in practice do not at this distance of time appear important enough to be worth a struggle. The chief differences which were made matter for discussion were whether Easter Sunday should come a week or so earlier in the year or not, and how the priests should be tonsured. The discussion upon these two points tends to become wearisome to a modern reader; but such an one should bear in mind that the real matter at issue was the important question whether the Celtic churches were to retain their independence or to submit to the authority of Rome. This fact invests this old-world controversy with abiding interest, and stands out clearly from dull verbiage about minor points, in the letters of Ceolfrid and Aldhelm and the speeches of the Synod of Whitby, as it came to the front, too, at the very first, when the Britons rejected Augustine's overtures, not from stupid conservatism, but because of his arrogant claim to their obedience as their superior sent to them from Rome.

The British Easter was undoubtedly merely the result of an older calculation of the date, which the Roman Church and Western Christendom generally had abandoned during the period of British isolation. The difference was very similar to that which existed in the last century, when Britain retained the unreformed calendar, whereas the countries under the Roman obedience had adopted the Gregorian calendar. The Church of Rome in 457, for purely astronomical reasons, made an important change in their mode of reckoning Easter; and in 525 made another. Isolated and distracted, the British Church either remained in ignorance of these changes or gave no heed to them; and hence it was, that in the time of Augustine, when the British Church was rediscovered by Continental Christendom, it was found to be using the antiquated cycle, frequently, but erroneously, attributed to Sulpicius Severus. Ignorant or prejudiced persons accused the Britons of being Quarto-decimans and Judaistic; but this charge was false and calumnious, and is contradicted by Bede, whom no one can accuse of being prejudiced in favour of the Britons. The Celtic Easter was the Sunday which fell next after the equinox, between the 14th and the 20th days inclusive of the moon, whereas the Roman Easter was the Sunday between the 15th and 21st days. The Celts determined the moon by the old eighty-four years' cycle, whereas the Roman party settled it by the nineteen years' cycle of Dionysius Exiguus.

The Celtic tonsure was the subject of much criticism from the Roman party, and was doubtless abandoned by the Britons simultaneously with their adoption of the modern Easter. The British priests shaved all the hair in front of a line drawn over the top of the head from ear to ear, shaping the ridge of hair in front like a crown, and suffered the back hair to grow long, so that they must have presented a strange and uncouth appearance.[1] The Roman party, as we have already seen from Aldhelm's letter, stigmatized this tonsure as the tonsure of Simon Magus, whereas they claimed that their own tonsure was that of St. Peter, who, according to the well-known legend, had overthrown Simon at Rome. It has been supposed that the Celtic tonsure was Druidical. The Druids are called magi in the old Irish and Welsh legends, and Simon himself is called in Irish Simon Drui, or Simon the Druid; and according to one Irish story, he was accounted the ancestor of the Fir Bolg, a mythic people of ancient Erin.[2] It is possible that the Celtic tonsure may have had some likeness to that of the Druids; at any rate, the custom of wearing the hair long seems to have prevailed among the heathen, for there is an early Welsh canon forbidding it as a practice 'of the barbarians.'[3] But it is not probable that the tonsure of the Celtic

---

[1] See 'Du Cange,' sub voce *tonsura*.
[2] Rhys, 'Celtic Heathendom,' p. 213.
[3] 'Si quis Catholicus capillos promiserit more barbarorum, ab Ecclesia Dei alienus habeatur et ab omni Christianorum mensa, donec delictum emendat.'—'H. and S.,' i. 137.

priests was identical with that of the Druids. In the beautiful story of Ethne the fair and Fedelm the ruddy, related by Tirechan in his 'Life of St. Patrick,' we are told that when the druid Mael was converted, 'the hair of his head was taken off, that is, the magical rule which before was seen on his head, *airbacc giunnæ*, as it is called.'[1] This seems decisive against the identity of the two tonsures, especially if *airbacc giunnæ* be rendered, as it is by Dr. Todd, 'a band of hell.' The slightest similarity would be sufficient for the Roman party as a basis for their calumny, or some skilful controversialist might originate it purely from his own imagination, because of the beautiful antithesis of Simon Magus and Simon Peter. That controversialists were no more scrupulous then than they often are now is proved by another ridiculous story which attributes the invention of the Celtic tonsure to the swineherd of the Irish King Laoghaire, who ruled over Meath in the time of St. Patrick.

One of Augustine's requirements was that the Britons should 'complete the administration of baptism according to the custom of the holy Roman and Apostolic Church.' What this refers to cannot be certainly discovered ; but probably it is to the custom of single immersion, which prevailed in a Breton diocese as late as the year 1620. It cannot be that the Britons omitted chrism, as the Irish are said to have done in the time of Lanfranc, for Patrick accuses Coroticus of carrying off his converts while the faith was shining on their foreheads, and the neophytes having been baptized, and having received the chrism, were wearing their white garments or chrisoms. Neither is it credible that the defect referred to was a lack of confirmation, a charge brought by St. Bernard against the Irish of his time, for so serious a fault would have been commented upon by others than Augustine, and

[1] Tirechan in 'W. S.,' ii. 317.

more precisely. The later Irish appear to have been rather careless with regard to baptism, as it is said that it was customary for the infant's father, or someone else present, to immerse it thrice in water by way of baptizing it immediately on its birth; and this apparently without always using the correct formula in the name of the Three Persons of the Blessed Trinity. If the babe were the son of a rich man, he was immersed in milk. There is no warrant, however, for attributing these customs to the Britons. Augustine could not have referred to the Celtic custom of the Pedilavium, or ceremonial washing of the feet after baptism, preserved in the Stowe Missal, for this was rather an addition than a defect.[1]

These were the most important differences of usage between the Celtic churches and Rome. There were, however, a large number of minor differences. The Britons differed, we are told in a passage falsely attributed to Gildas, 'in the Mass,' and there is some reason for supposing that they used either the Gallican liturgy,

[1] The Stowe Missal is the earliest surviving missal of the Irish Church. The earlier portion was assigned by Dr. Todd to the sixth century, but Mr. Warren attributes this portion doubtfully to the ninth century, and the latter portion to the tenth century. Trine immersion, with the alternative of aspersion, is enjoined, as well as three separate acts of unction, and the 'pedilavium.' The following is the passage referring to the last curious rite, which is found also in early Gallican 'Ordines Baptismi':

'*Tunc lavantur pedes eius, accepto linteo accepto.*
'Alleluia! Lucerna pedibus mieis verbum tuum, domine.
'Alleluia! Adiuva me, domine, et saluus ero.
'Alleluia! Uisita nos, domine, in salutare tuo.
'Alleluia! Tu mandasti mandata tua custodire nimis.
'Mandasti misericordiam tuam, opus manuum tuarum ne despicias.
'Si ego laui pedes uestras dominus et magister uester, et uos debetis alterutrius pedes lauare; exemplum enim dedi uobis ut quemadmodum feci uobis et uos faciteis aliis.
'Dominus et saluator noster ihesus christus, pridie quam pateretur, accepto linteo splendido, sancto, et immaculato, precinctis lumbis suis, misit aquam in piluem, lauit pedes discipulorum suorum. Hoc et tu facias exemplum domini nostri ihesu christi hospitibus et peregrinis tuis.'—'The Stowe Missal,' in Warren's 'Liturgy and Ritual of the Celtic Church,' pp. 217, 218.

or one of the same family. There is no indication of the existence of a Welsh Prayer-Book, or of a Welsh Bible; but Gildas, though he sometimes uses the Vulgate, appears to have been also familiar with a different Latin translation, probably a special Celtic revision of the Old Latin version. It is a little doubtful whether the Vulgate was known at all to St. Patrick.

The Celtic practice of consecrating churches and monasteries was peculiar, and caused astonishment in Bede, who records how Bishop Cedd, who had been trained in Celtic customs, consecrated the monastery of Lastingham by prayer and fasting during the forty days of Lent. This he told Ethelwald, King of Deira, was the custom which he had learned among the Scotic clergy of Lindisfarne. We are told that Cybi stayed forty days and forty nights in Mida before he built a church there,[1] and that Beuno stayed forty days and forty nights in Meifod, where he built a church,[2] statements which appear to be made by the writers of their lives in ignorance of any particular significance attaching to them, but which are probably to be connected with the peculiar Celtic usage of consecration. It has been already mentioned that instances of dedication to departed saints are rare in early times, and that the British churches were generally wooden. Bede mentions that the cathedral of Lindisfarne was built 'after the manner of the Scots, not of stone, but of hewn oak,' and was covered with reeds. It was dedicated to St. Peter, not, however, by Finan, its founder, but afterwards by Archbishop Theodore, when it had passed under Anglican authority.

The hands of deacons and priests were anointed at ordination in the British Church, as Gildas testifies, and this custom passed also into the Pontifical of the English

[1] 'Vita S. Kebii,' 'C. B. S.,' p. 185.
[2] 'Buchedd Beuno Sant.,' 'C. B. S.,' p. 15.

Archbishop of York, Egbert. Certain other Anglican peculiarities have been supposed to be derived from British sources, such as the prayer at the giving of the stole to deacons at their ordination, the rite of delivering the book of the Gospels to them, and the rite of investing priests with a stole. The sections of Scripture used in ordination are quoted by Gildas,[1] and differ from those in the Gallican and the Roman Ordinals.

The Celtic customs differed from the Roman also in the consecration of bishops. Joceline of Furness is led to dwell on this matter in his 'Life of St. Kentigern.' He states that the British use was merely to anoint the head by pouring on it the sacred chrism with invocation of the Holy Spirit, and benediction, and laying on of hands. The consecration, moreover, was performed by a single bishop, a custom which he confesses did not invalidate the act, though it was irregular. Kentigern himself was thus consecrated, and single consecration is assumed as customary in several of the legends of the Welsh Saints. The celebrated story of the journey of David, Teilo, and Padarn to Jerusalem, and of their consecration thereat, mentions the patriarch only as consecrator. So, too, Patrick was consecrated in Gaul by Amatorex, and, it would seem, without the presence of other bishops; and Patrick in like manner consecrated bishops in Ireland. Augustine was not likely to cavil at single consecration, as Pope Gregory had permitted him to practise it himself, owing to the peculiar circumstances of his mission. It can scarcely have been always prevalent in the British Church, seeing that the British bishops at the Council of Arles had consented to a canon forbidding the practice.

It would be outside the scope of this history to discuss the various ecclesiastical usages, which can only be

[1] They are 1 St. Peter i. 3, 13, 14, 22; ii. 1, 9; Acts i. 15, 16; 'Secunda Lectio Pauli'; 1 Tim iii. 1 etc.; St. Matt. xvi. 16-18.

proved of the Church of Ireland. As David, Gildas, and Cadoc gave a mass to the Second Order of Irish saints, it is exceedingly probable that many of these usages were common to Wales and Ireland, and some, therefore, have already been mentioned in the picture which I have drawn of sixth-century life at Llantwit Major. But to treat of them further would be wearisome and unprofitable. On the other hand, it would be rash to assume the accuracy of the 'Book of Llandaff,' and the legends of the Welsh saints, when they mention customs of the mediæval Church as existing in the earlier centuries before the submission to Rome. To mediæval readers the use of anachronisms by an author appeared to be a virtue, not a fault, and every compiler of ancient documents did his best to impart to his work the colour of his own time.

There are numerous relics of the period of the early Celtic Church in Wales, but most of them are monumental stones. There are no churches, and we can only conjecture that when such buildings were not of wooden construction, they resembled the stone oratories on Skellig Mhichel, or the oratory of Gallerus,[1] in county Kerry, Ireland. The earliest monumental stones belonging to the period of Celtic Christianity are rough unhewn pillars, varying from four to nine feet in height. The inscriptions which they bear are either in the Latin language, and written in debased Latin capitals; or in Celtic, and written in Oghams. Altogether there are 90 such inscribed stones in Wales, 66 being inscribed with Latin capitals only, 6 with Oghams only, and 18 biliteral, with both Oghams and Latin capitals. Those with Oghams only are thus distributed: 4 in Pembrokeshire, 1 in Glamorganshire, and 1 in Carmarthenshire. Of biliteral stones there are 8 in Pembrokeshire, 4 in Carmarthenshire, 3 in Brecknockshire, and 1 in Cardigan-

[1] Figured in Miss Stokes' 'Early Christian Art in Ireland,' p. 155.

shire, Glamorganshire, and Denbighshire respectively. Of those with Latin capitals only, Carmarthenshire has 14, Carnarvonshire 13, Glamorganshire and Pembrokeshire 7 each, Anglesey and Brecknockshire 6 each, Cardiganshire 5, Merionethshire 4, Denbighshire 2, and Flintshire and Montgomeryshire 1 each.[1] It is to be noted, by way of caution against a tendency to suppose that early Irish and Welsh customs were always identical, that in Ireland there are no rough pillar-stones with inscriptions in Latin capitals only, and only two with biliteral inscriptions, whereas there are no less than 186 with Oghams only, of which 160 are in the three counties of Kerry, Cork, and Waterford. Of the 24 Welsh stones with Oghams, either alone or in conjunction with Latin capitals, exactly half are in Pembrokeshire, the nearest county to the south of Ireland. Cornwall, however, has no Ogham stones, and Devonshire only 2, both biliteral; but the Isle of Man has four.

It has been disputed how far the Ogham stones are Christian, and opposite conclusions have been come to on this subject. In Wales six of such stones bear incised crosses. In all the early pillar-stones that have a cross, that cross is incised and not sculptured in relief. The formula *hic jacit* (for *hic jacet*) is frequently employed in the Latin inscriptions; and in two cases *in pace* is found. On one very early monument at Penmachno church, Carnarvonshire, the Chi-Rho monogram is used above the inscription, CARAUSIUS HIC IACIT IN HOC CONGERIES LAPIDUM (Carausius lies here in this cairn). At Bedd Porius, near Trawsfynydd, in Merionethshire, the monogram forms the beginning of the word *Christianus*. The inscription runs thus: PORIUS HIC IN TUMULO IACIT HOMO XPIANUS FUIT. At Trawsmawr in Carmarthen-

---

[1] I derive these statistics from Mr. Romilly Allen's excellent 'Monumental History of the British Church,' p. 68.

shire a pillar-stone is found, marked with an incised cross, without an inscription.[1]

One of the most interesting of these early stones is the Maen Llythyrog or Letter-Stone on Margam Mountain in Glamorganshire, about which there used to be a popular superstition that whoever read the inscription would die soon after. The pillar is 5 feet high, 1 foot 6 inches wide, and 1 foot thick. On the top is an incised cross of the Maltese form, which is continued by a narrow line over the angle towards the inscription, which runs down the face of the stone perpendicularly in four lines, and is as follows: BODVOCI HIC IACIT FILIUS CATO-TIGIRNI PRONEPVS ETERNALI VEDOMAVI. The name Bodvoc is also found on two ancient coins, which are possibly British.[2]

These early pillar-stones, with inscriptions in Oghams or in debased Latin capitals, probably date between A.D. 400 and 600. After this period minuscules, or small letters, were introduced for inscriptions. There is an intermediate class between the early stones and the later elaborate sculptured stones, in which minuscule inscriptions are found on rough unhewn pillar-stones. Some of the stones in this class belong to the period of Welsh Church history which we are now considering, namely, that prior to the submission of Elfod. One of these is the celebrated stone of St. Cadfan, the Armorican saint, who is said to have come over to Britain with St. Padarn, and to whom is ascribed the foundation of the first church of Towyn. The stone now lies at the west end of the fine church of Towyn, and is to the student one of the

---

[1] This and the Pennachno stone are both figured in Romilly Allen's 'Christian Symbolism in Great Britain and Ireland,' pp. 87, 99, where, as also in Westwood's 'Lapidarium Walliæ,' the various volumes of the 'Archæologia Cambrensis,' etc., a large amount of information on these early inscribed stones may be found.

[2] See 'The Maen Llythyrog,' by J. O. Westwood, in 'Archæologia Cambrensis' for 1859, pp. 287-292, where the stone is figured and described.

chief attractions of that pleasant and growing watering-place. It is a rude pillar, 'about 7 feet long, and about 10 inches wide on the two widest sides, the other two sides being considerably narrower.' The inscription is in old Welsh, and seems to import that the stone marks the burial-place of Cadfan and Cyngen. The latter was a King of Powys.[1] Another notable stone of the same type as that of Cadfan may be seen in the church of Llanddewi Brefi, which stands in a fine position near a wild and romantic gorge, which is one of the most attractive points in the scenery in the neighbourhood of Lampeter. Tradition says that St. David leaned against this stone when he addressed the synod of Brefi.

Others of these early stones, besides the stone of Cadfan, commemorate persons about whom we have some small amount of information from tradition or history. The stone of Paulinus, formerly at Pant y Polion, has been mentioned in a former chapter. Pascent, a legendary son of Brychan, has (or had)[2] his stone at Towyn; Saturninus, or Sadwrn, a brother of St. Illtyd, is commemorated, together with his wife, at Llansadwrn, in Anglesey; and King Catamanus, or Cadfan, at Llangadwaladr, in the same island. Near the church and holy well of St. Canna, a cousin of St. Illtyd, at Llangan, in Carmarthenshire, is her stone chair with her name inscribed upon it.

The subject of the early inscribed stones of Wales is one of exceeding interest, especially as many are certainly, and all are probably, connected with its early Chris-

---

[1] See further 'Archæologia Cambrensis,' Old Series, iii. 364; New Series, i. 90-100 (two articles by J. O. Westwood and Rev. J. Williams ab Ithel); i. 205-212 (a discussion of St. Cadfan's history and connection with Armorica by T. Wakeman); ii. 58-65 (a criticism of previous interpretations by T. Stephens). See also Rees, 'Welsh Saints,' p. 215.

[2] I speak doubtfully, because I cannot remember seeing it there; and that stones sometimes disappear I know full well, having to my astonishment discovered a curious case of disappearance at Penaly.

tianity. They are so numerous that familiarity too often breeds a measure of contempt, and they are not always regarded with that interest and treated with that veneration which such precious and sacred monuments of antiquity deserve. Too often they are left exposed to suffer from the ravages of the elements, or from the profaning hands of the British Philistine, and so the inscriptions fade and the stones themselves disappear. Yet, while men hold their peace, these stones cry out and remind all who have ears to hear, of the lives and labours of early saints, and of the illumination of that loving and lovable Celtic Christianity which they shed around them.

Some curious bronze spoon-like objects, which have been found at Llanfair, in Denbighshire, and at Penbryn, in Cardiganshire, as also at various places in England and Ireland, have been supposed by some to be connected with the early British Church, whether for administering the consecrated wine at the Holy Communion, or for conveying a little water into the chalice of wine before consecration, or for the administration of the consecrated wafer after being dipped in the chalice, or for aspersion in baptism, or for the use of oil in that sacred rite. The spoons seem to have been made in pairs, and some stress has been laid upon the fact that one of each pair has transverse lines upon it, something like a cross. But there is absolutely no proof that these objects were used for any sacred purpose at all, nor even any real evidence pointing to that conclusion.[1]

Much more important are the hand-bells, which we know from the legends of the saints were much reverenced in ancient times. There are nine of these still existing in Wales or in the borders. There are also fifty-five similar bells in Ireland, fifteen in Scotland, two in France, and

---

[1] See an exhaustive paper on the subject (with illustrations) by Mr. Albert Way in 'Archæologia Cambrensis,' Series iv., 1870, pp. 199-234. See also 'Arch. Camb.,' Series iv. 5, pp. 1-20, for an article by Dr. Rock on the same subject.

one in Switzerland. The most remarkable of all these early relics is the iron bell of St. Patrick, which ' is at once the most authentic and the oldest Irish relic of Christian metal-work that has descended to us. It possesses the singular merit of having an unbroken history through fourteen hundred years.'[1]

One of the Welsh bells, which I have had the privilege of handling and examining, is known as the bell of St. Ceneu, and was dug up 'on a farm, eastward of the present church, called Penydaren, in the parish of Llangeney, Breconshire.'[2] It is now preserved in the library of the University College at Cardiff. It is quadrangular, made of two iron plates hammered and riveted together, and has a loop of metal at the top to serve as a handle. This is continued through to the inside to form a smaller loop to hold the clapper, which, however, has disappeared. The whole was covered with bell-metal, but the bell has suffered so much that the bell-metal has peeled off altogether in many places, and it is impossible to say whether it was chased or not. It is ten inches in length without the handle; the size at the top is five and a half by three inches, and at the mouth seven and three-quarter inches by six, so that it is considerably larger than St. Patrick's bell. The weight is a little more than six pounds fifteen ounces.[3]

Another very important class of relics of early Celtic Christianity are those left in language. The number of Llans in Wales seems to an English visitor almost end-

[1] Miss Stokes, 'Early Christian Art in Ireland,' p. 58.
[2] Jones, 'History of Breconshire,' ed. 1809, iii. 469.
[3] See 'Cymru Fu,' i. 365. I have consulted also Mr. Thomas Kerslake's 'Catalogue,' in which this bell was offered for sale in 1859, and have examined the bell myself. Mr. Kerslake thought that the bell-metal was 'applied by dipping or washing the finished iron utensil in fluid metal, as all the joints, and the rivets themselves, are covered, and the seams and interstices filled with it. Being corroded through in some places, the amalgamated contact of the metals is apparent. The result is similar to that of electrotype.' Mr. Kerslake finally presented the bell to University College, Cardiff.

less. I have just counted 510 in Professor Rees' list of churches in Wales,[1] but many of these have other and more generally used English names, and some are now extinct. All these mark the site of an old church, and in many of the place-names the second part of the word indicates the saint or saints who are the reputed founders, or in some cases to whom the church is dedicated, though, as has before been pointed out, instances of dedication are exceedingly few in the period which we are now considering. The dedications to St. Michael, which are denoted by the numerous Llanfihangels in the Principality, and those to St. Mary, indicated by the Llanfairs, are all later. The name Llanddewi, which is fairly common, signifies the church of David, Llandeilo is the church of Teilo, Llangollen the church of Collen, Llandudno the church of Tudno, Llanbadarn the church of Padarn, Llanelly the church of Ellyw, Llanrwst the church of Grwst, and Lantwit, or Llanilltyd, the church of Illtyd. I select these examples out of the list of Llans because most of them will be familiar to English visitors to the Principality. The term *llan* is the earliest in use for church or sacred enclosure; late subordinate chapels are known by the terms *capel* or *bettws*, as Capel Curig and Bettws-y-coed, two neighbouring places well known to lovers of the Snowdon district, which mean respectively, 'The Chapel of Curig,' and 'The Chapel in the Wood.' *Eglwys*, a church, from the Latin *ecclesia*, is sometimes used in place-names, but rarely.

The kinship which in early times existed between Wales and Brittany, as also between Wales and Cornwall, is well illustrated by place-names and (so-called) church dedications. Brittany and Cornwall have place-names beginning with *lan*; Cornwall has *eglos* for *eglwys* (the Breton equivalent for which is *ilis*), as in Eglos Hayle, and also one unique *Altar* in Altarnun, the church

[1] He includes Monmouthshire and also Herefordshire south-west of the Wye.

of St. David's mother, Nonna. Altogether there are twenty-six Cornish parish churches with the prefix *lan* (of which four are aliases); there are five compounded with *eglos* (of which two are aliases), and there are two in which *lan* and *eglos* are found together. Mr. Borlase makes the following statement with respect to Cornish dedications:[1] " Out of a list of 210 Cornish churches (22 of which bear uncertain or modern names) I find 9 dedications to St. Mary, 5 to St. Michael, 29 to well-known Calendar saints, 28 to obscure saints (some in the Roman Calendar, but most of them of foreign origin, contained in early Celtic lists), while no less than 117 retain their native British name. Out of a list, however, of 200 chapelries, holy wells, cells, and oratories, collected from the MSS. of Dr. Borlase, but of which 35 have lost their identity, I find that 20 are dedicated to St. Mary, 8 to St. Michael, 84 to well-known Calendar saints, 8 to obscure saints, while 45 bear a native Celtic name.' The saints of Wales have numerous churches and place-names in Cornwall. Teilo, who was also called Eliud, has the churches of St. Issey and Philleigh,[2] of Endellion,[3] and possibly others; David has Dewstow; his mother, Nonna, has Altarnun; Samson has St. Samson's Island, at Scilly, and also churches at Golant and Southill; Padarn has North and South Petherwyn; Petroc, who is claimed by Lifris as an uncle of Cadoc,[4] has Petrockstow, or Padstow, and Little Petherick; Cadoc has a chapel at Padstow, and may have left his name to St. Cadix, Quethiock or Quedock, and Landock or Ladock; Mabon, the brother of Teilo, may have a church at St. Mabyn; Illtyd has a chapel, that of St. Ilduictus, in St. Dominick; and Cyby has a church and well at Duloe, and also the parish of Cuby.

---

[1] 'The Age of the Saints,' in *Journal of the Royal Institution of Cornwall*, 1878, p. 74.
[2] Both ascribed to St. Filius, viz., Felians or Theliaus.
[3] Viz., Landelian.   [4] 'Vita S. Cadoci,' Prefatio.

Various other dedications which are more obscure have also been referred to Welsh saints.[1]

The Welsh language retains from the times of the early Celtic Church the terms of ritual and the names of Church seasons. This appears certain from a comparison with Cornish and Breton, in which the same words are found, with too much resemblance in some cases to make it probable that each formed the word from Latin independently. In old canons ascribed to St. David we find the phrase 'to offer the sacrifice' (*offerre sacrificium*) used of the Eucharist, and the deacon 'holds the chalice' (*tenere calicem*).[2] The reader (*lector*) and sub-deacon are mentioned in addition to the three orders of bishops, priests and deacons. In Welsh, as also in Breton and Cornish, the Eucharist is *offeren*, 'the offering,' and in Welsh the priest is *offeiriad*, 'the one who offers,' the Cornish equivalent being *oferiat*; but here the Breton differs, being *bælec*. *Esgob* is Welsh for 'bishop,' and the Breton and Cornish have *escop*. Vespers is *Gosper* in Welsh and *gousper* in Breton; Sunday is *Dydd Sul* in Welsh and *Dissul* in Breton; Trinity Sunday is *Dydd Sul y Drindod* in Welsh and *Dissul an Dreindet* in Breton. Christmas is *Nadolig* (*natalis*) in Welsh, *Nadelic* in Cornish, and *Nedelec* in Breton. Lent is *Carawys* (*Quadragesima*) in Welsh and *Corais* in Breton. Easter is *Pasg* (Pascha) in Welsh, *Pasch* in Cornish, and *Pasc* in Breton. There are other similarities between the three languages, and when taken all together they point to the common use of Church ordinances and festivals in bygone ages, when the Churches of Wales, Cornwall and Brittany were practically one. One of the most curious identifications, however, is connected with the word *Plygain*, or *Pylgain* (*pulli cantus?*), which is used for Matins in the Welsh Prayer-Book in the Calendar of Proper Lessons, but in ordinary speech

---

[1] 'Age of the Saints,' pp. 70-102.
[2] 'Excerpta Quædam de Libro Davidis,' 'H. and S.,' i. 118.

means the early service which is held in many Welsh churches on Christmas Day. 'Some years ago,' says the present Bishop of St. David's, 'being in Brittany, I asked one of the people whether a *messe de minuit* was celebrated on Christmas Eve, and, if so, by what name it was popularly known. The answer was, "Pelguent." This word, which I do not find in any Breton book of devotion, or in Lhuyd's "Armoric-English Vocabulary" (I have no better Breton dictionary at hand), seems to be confined to that particular service. *Matins* are called *Matinesou*. Now the word *Pelguent* is not merely similar to, but . . . absolutely identical with, *Pylgain*, a popular pronunciation of *Plygain*. And, so far as one can judge, it is of purely Celtic origin. The coincidence appears to me to favour the supposition that this particular usage was common to the British and Gallican[1] Churches at a very early period.'[2]

These relics which survive in language are perhaps the most permanent of all the relics of early Welsh Christianity. The monumental inscriptions may become obliterated through lapse of time and the carelessness of their custodians; they may even be used as garden-rollers,[3] or as targets for frolicsome tourists.[4] The sacred bells, hallowed by the use of ancient saints, may pass into secular hands, and, instead of gracing their churches, may be gazed at in museums, sometimes doubtless by reverent eyes, but often in mere heedless curiosity, and at times, even by the scientific antiquary, in the spirit of him who would 'peep and botanize upon his mother's grave.' But the place-names of Wales will remain and be known

[1] I should myself prefer to say Armorican, as the Church of Brittany was for some time, as I have shown, distinct from the Gallican.
[2] 'Arch. Camb.' for 1854, pp. 90, 91. I have to own my obligations to this article generally for the comparison of Welsh terms with Breton and Cornish.
[3] The Victorinus Stone was once used thus. See 'Arch. Camb.' for 1851, p. 226.
[4] As was the case not long ago with the cross at Penmon, Anglesey.

of all when the monuments have decayed and the bells are hidden away, and the names which the Welsh of old gave to the ordinances and seasons of the Church will live too, to testify to the antiquity and nationality of the Catholic faith in Wales as long as the Cymric language lives, in which, as every pious Welshman believes, the Welsh nation 'shall, in the day of severe examination before the Supreme Judge, answer for this corner of the earth.'

CHAPTER VI.

THE AGE OF FUSION TO THE CONSECRATION OF BISHOP BERNARD.

THE Celtic lack of cohesion in the struggle with Rome was unquestionably due in part to the weakness of the Celtic position on the subject of Easter. Irishmen went to Rome and inquired into the matter for themselves, and as a result, felt that it was presumptuous on their part to say, 'Rome errs, Jerusalem errs, Alexandria errs, Antioch errs, the whole world errs, the Irish and the Britons alone know what is right.'[1] But it was nevertheless a lamentable proof of Celtic disunion, that not only did Irish Christians renounce their peculiar customs of Easter and the tonsure separately from the Britons, and earlier than they, but also the South of Ireland acted independently of the North. In spite of the untrustworthiness of the 'Book of Aberpergwm,' there is unfortunately some plausibility in its statement as to a like disagreement on the Easter question between North and South Wales. Celtic Christianity, it must be admitted, did not weld tribes and people together as Latin Christianity did. In England the Church unified the

---

[1] Cummian thus sums up the matter in his letter to Segienus, Abbot of Hy: 'Quid autem pravius sentiri potest de Ecclesia matre, quam si dicamus, Roma errat, Hierosolyma errat, Alexandria errat, Antiochia errat, totus mundus errat, soli tantum Scoti et Britones rectum sapiunt.'

various states, and brought about one kingdom; in Wales, no such effect was ever experienced. The opposition between North and South Wales, of which traces remain even to the present day, appears very plainly in the history of the Welsh Church. In the Period of Fusion which we have now reached it was a mere aggregation of four independent units, and not one organized whole. 'Ni bydd dy-un dau Gymro,' 'Two Welshmen will never be unanimous,' is a proverb that may be amply illustrated from this period of the history of the Welsh Church and people.

There are indications also which point to the conclusion that the Period of Fusion was a time of spiritual declension, and this also may have been a result of faults inherent in the Celtic type of Christianity. The Christianity of the Celt was more spontaneous, more enthusiastic, and less mechanical than Latin Christianity; but it was less sustained; it was inferior in discipline, and utterly lacking in organization; and so it came to pass, that after it had won souls for Christ, not only in Britain and in Ireland, but all over Western Europe, the Latin Church 'entered into its labours.' And we must confess that it was well that it was so, for otherwise when the enthusiasm of the first love was spent, the disciples of the Celtic teachers might have relapsed into semi-paganism, as from time to time happened in Ireland. It is to this period of declension, and not to earlier centuries of spiritual advance, and certainly not to the Age of the Saints, which was an era of spiritual fervour—that I should be inclined to refer any recrudescence of paganism that may be traced in Welsh history or genuine literature, though I cannot find any justification for connecting such traces with the Church of the Welsh people.

From the time of Elbod, the Churches of Wales and England ceased from active hostility towards one another, and in various ways the two became little by little connected together. But the history of the Fusion is by no means clear, inasmuch as certain of the chroniclers have been largely influenced by local prejudice. The compiler of the 'Book of Llandaff,' writing in the twelfth century, was anxious to establish a connection between his see and that of Canterbury at an early period, and records the consecration of Oudoceus, third Bishop of Llandaff, at Canterbury at the beginning of the seventh century. This is a manifest absurdity, and only serves to discredit more or less other more plausible statements of the same chronicle regarding later consecrations. English records such as the Canterbury Rolls are open to a similar suspicion. Considerable confusion also is introduced by the discordant statements of our various authorities, and if the evidence of the 'Book of Aberpergwm' were to be accepted as trustworthy, this confusion would only become more confounded. It is possible, as I hope has been made evident, to gain a fairly accurate idea of the religious movements of the Age of the Saints, and of the general political and social condition of the time; but after this period of mingled gloom and glory we have for some time only short and scanty notices respecting ecclesiastical affairs. The historians of the diocese of St. David's lament that as far as concerns the history of that part of the Church of Wales, 'from the era of St. David to the middle of the ninth century, a period of two hundred and fifty years, is an almost total blank.'[1] With regard to the diocese of Llanelwy, or St. Asaph, 'a deep silence' prevails for a much longer period. We know, indeed, of the slaughter of the monks of Bangor Iscoed in 613; but we have no distinct mention of any bishop of the diocese from the time of Tysillio (*circa* 600)[2] to the consecration

---

[1] Jones and Freeman, p. 257.
[2] Rees, 'Welsh Saints,' p. 277. He was son of Brochwel, Prince of Powys, and is said to have been a bard, and to have written an ecclesiastical history of Britain.

of Melanus[1] about 1070, with the single[2] exception of Cebur,[3] named as one of the bishops who went to Rome in the time of Hywel Dda, to compare his laws with the law of God, and 'to obtain the authority of the Pope of Rome for the laws of Hywel.' The only diocese of which any continuous history can be made out, is that of Llandaff.

The Age of Fusion is accordingly exceedingly obscure. It must not be forgotten that the Welsh dioceses acted independently, so that while one was submissive to the See of Canterbury, the others might be in full possession of their ancient rights and privileges. Unquestionably the political ascendancy of the English King went hand in hand with the ecclesiastical supremacy of the English primate. In the ninth century, according to the testimony alike of the English and Welsh chronicles, Wales was for a time more or less in subjection to the rule of Egbert. 'The Saxons,' says one manuscript of the 'Annales Cambriæ'[4] under A.D. 816, 'invaded the mountains of Ereri and the kingdom of Roweynauc,' and again under A.D. 818 the same manuscript says, 'Ceniul[5] devastated the regions of the Demetæ.' Another manuscript[6] records, under A.D. 822, 'The fort of Diganwy[7] is destroyed by the Saxons, and they brought the kingdom of Powys under their power.' The Brut y Tywysogion relates the same events.[8] But it does not appear to have been so much these hostile operations of the English,

---

[1] Consecrated by Bedwd, Bishop of St. David's, according to a statement of the chapter of St. David's to Pope Eugenius. 'De Invectionibus,' ii. 6 : Gir. Camb., Op. iii. 57.

[2] Renchidus Episcopus is mentioned in conjunction with Elbod of Bangor in one MS. of Nennius. 'H. and S.' (i. 144) say he 'may have been Bishop of St. Asaph.' Archdeacon Thomas ('Diocesan History of St. Asaph,' p. 113) includes him in the list of bishops, but see his 'History,' p. 23.

[3] His name is mentioned by the Dimetian copy of the laws ; the Venedotian mentions 'the Bishop of Asaph' without giving the name.

[4] MS. B in Rolls edition.   [5] I.e. Cenulf.

[6] A.   [7] 'Arcem Decantorum.'

[8] Under A.D. 817, A.D. 819, A.D. 823 respectively.

as later friendliness on their part, that caused the first approximation to union. The first indications of such friendliness are connected with the names of Alfred and Asser. No pleasanter picture is found in our history than the friendship of these two good men. Asser was nephew of Novis, Bishop[1] of St. David's, and both himself and his uncle were expelled by the local tyrant, Hemeid, or Hyfeidd, King of Dyfed, 'who often used to plunder the monastery and See of St. David's.'

'At that time and long before' (so Asser relates) 'all the districts of the southern part of Britain belonged to King Alfred, and still belong. Hemeid, with all the inhabitants of Dyfed, forced by the violence of the six sons of Rotri, had submitted to the King's authority. Howel also, son of Rhys, King of Glewyssig, and Brochmael and Fernail, sons of Mouric (Meurig), Kings of Gwent, forced by the violence and tyranny of Earl Eadred and the Mercians, of their own accord sought the same King, that they might have government and defence from him against their enemies. Helised also, son of Tewdwr, King of Brecknock, forced by the violence of the same sons of Rotri, of his own accord, sought the government of the aforesaid King. Anaraut[2] also, son of Rotri, with his brothers at last deserting the friendship of the Northumbrians, from which he had had no good but loss, eagerly seeking the King's friendship, came to his presence; and when he had been honourably received by the King, and had been received as son by confirmation at the bishop's hand, and had been enriched by very great gifts, he submitted to the King's government with all his people on the same terms that he should be obedient in all things to the King's will in the same way as Æthered with the Mercians.'[3]

[1] Asser calls him 'Novis *archiepiscopum* propinquum meum.' 'De Rebus Gestis Ælfredi,' 'M. H. B.,' p. 488.
[2] King of Gwynedd.
[3] 'De Rebus Gestis Ælfredi,' 'M. H. B.,' p. 488.

Wales, accordingly, was at this time subject to the King of England, and its people were more or less inclined at times to look to him for protection against their own petty kings. Alfred, too, was an enlightened ruler, who saw in the Church a bond of brotherhood that should knit all nations and peoples together, and it mattered not to him whether the Church he befriended was the Church of England or the Church of Wales. He was wont to give money 'some years in turns to the churches and servants of God in Britain[1] and Cornwall, Gaul, Armorica, Northumbria, and sometimes even in Ireland.'[2] It was natural, therefore, that the clergy of St. David's should look to him for succour against the oppression of Hemeid, and that when Alfred sent for Asser, of whose wisdom and learning he had heard, and pressed him to take up his abode in England, they should advise Asser to consent to stay with Alfred six months in the year, for they hoped that by means of this friendship they might secure some abatement of the wrongs they were enduring.

Asser, accordingly, went to live with Alfred at his court, and became his instructor, and in return he was presented to the monasteries of Cungresbury[3] and Banwell, in Somersetshire, and afterwards to the bishopric of Sherborne, an evident proof that Welsh orders were recognised as valid by the Church of England in the ninth century. Asser had a genuine love and admiration for his royal pupil, as can plainly be seen in his 'Life of Alfred,' which is worthy alike of its subject and its author; and these feelings seem to have been fully reciprocated by Alfred. It is the first instance we find recorded of friendship between Welshman and English-

[1] Viz., Wales.
[2] 'De Rebus Gestis Ælfredi,' 'M. H. B.,' p. 496.
[3] So MS. B. But another reading is Amgresbyri, *i.e.*, Amesbury, in Wiltshire. See 'M. H. B.,' p. 488, the editor of which prefers the reading Cungresbury.

man, and, therefore, is the more interesting. Hitherto the Irish alone of the Celtic nations had done anything for the English, but now Asser was to Alfred what Aidan had been to Oswini. In Alfred's youth learning was at a very low ebb in England, and although he was most desirous then of gaining knowledge of the liberal arts, he could find no good teachers, because 'at that time there were no good readers in the whole kingdom of the West Saxons.'[1] It would appear from Alfred's recourse to Asser that the Church of Wales was at that time superior in learning to the Church of England.

Asser gives a most interesting narrative, how under his instruction Alfred began ' on one and the same day to read and interpret.' 'On a certain day,' he says, ' we were both sitting in the King's chamber, talking on all kinds of matters, as was our wont, and it happened that I read to him a quotation from a certain book. He listened to it attentively with both his ears, and anxiously examined it with his inmost mind, and suddenly showing me a little book, which he carried carefully in his bosom, wherein were written the daily course and certain psalms and prayers which he had read in his youth, he bade me to write that quotation in the same book. Hearing this, and perceiving his willing aptness and devout desire of the study of Divine wisdom, I silently gave great thanks to Almighty God, who had implanted so great a devotion to the study of wisdom in the King's heart. But I could not find any vacant space in that little book in which to write the quotation, for it was quite full of various matters; and so I made a little delay, especially because I was anxious to provoke the King's apt wit to a greater knowledge of the Divine testimonies. So, when he pressed me to make haste and write it, I replied, " Is it your pleasure that I should write this quotation on some leaves separately? For we know not whether we

[1] 'De Rebus Gestis Ælfredi,' ' M. H. B.,' p. 474.

shall find sometimes one or more other like quotations which may please you; and if that shall happen unexpectedly, we shall be glad we kept them apart." "Your plan is approved," he said; and I gladly, with haste, prepared a volume, at the beginning of which I wrote as he bade; and on that same day I wrote at his bidding in the same volume as I had said before, no less than three other quotations which pleased him. And afterwards, by our daily conversation and investigation of these things, other quotations were found which pleased him equally; and so the volume became full, and deservedly so, as it is written: " The just man builds upon a moderate foundation, and little by little flows to greater things." Like a most productive bee, flying far and wide and asking questions,[1] he gathered eagerly and incessantly divers flowers of holy Scripture, with which he filled full the cells of his heart.

'For when that first quotation was written, he was eager forthwith to read and to interpret in the Saxon tongue, and then to teach more; and as we are warned of that happy robber, who recognised the Lord Jesus Christ, his Lord, aye, and the Lord of all, hanging by his side on the venerable gibbet of the holy cross, and turning on Him, as he prayed, his eyes only, because otherwise he could not move, for he was wholly pierced with nails, cried with lowly voice, " Lord, remember me when Thou comest into Thy kingdom"; who first began to learn the rudiments of the Christian faith on the gallows. So, too, the King, although his lot was different, by Divine inspiration began to study the rudiments of holy Scripture on the venerable solemnity of St. Martin (November 11); and these flowers, collected from various quarters by certain masters, he learned, and gathered

---

[1] Latin: 'Longe lateque gronnios interrogando discurrens.' What is *gronnios?* Du Cange ('Glossarium Latin. Med. et Infim.'), s. v., says, 'Forte *gronniens*, aut *grunniens.*'

into one book, although diverse, as he could, and this he enlarged so much that it became at last almost as large as a psalter. This he called his Enchiridion or Manual, because he most diligently kept it at hand day and night, and found therein, as he then used to say, no small solace.'[1]

The good Asser died in A.D. 906 or 908, and the compiler of the 'Brut y Tywysogion,' proud of his illustrious countryman, calls him, in his record of his death, 'Asser, Archbishop of the isle of Britain'—a notice which may have led to his inclusion in some lists of the Bishops of St. David's.[2]

One cause of the growing kindness between England and at least a part of Wales about this time was their exposure to a common foe, 'the black pagans' or 'black Normans,' as the Welsh chronicles call them; that is, the Northmen or Danes. In 853[3] Anglesey was laid waste by them; in 890[4] they came a second time to Castle Baldwin, and in 894[5] they devasted England, Brecheiniog, Morganwg, Gwent, Buallt, and Gwenllwg.

In 915, or thereabout,[6] there was a notable invasion of South Wales by the Danes, which gave opportunity for another act of kindness on the part of England. 'The pagan pirates' who, about nineteen years before, had left

---

[1] 'De Rebus Gestis,' 'M. H. B.,' pp. 491, 492.

[2] 'Annales Cambriæ,' p. 16 : '908, cccclxiv. Annus. Asser defunctus est.' MS. B has 'Asser episcopus defunctus est.' C has 'Asser episcopus Britanniæ fit.' 'Brut y Tywysogion,' p. 18 : 'dccccvi. Ac y bu uarw Asser archescob ynys Prydein.'

[3] 'Annales Cambriæ.' [4] 'Brut y Tywysogion.'

[5] So *ibid.* 'Annales Cambriæ' gives 895.

[6] 915 is the date of Florence of Worcester, 'M. H. B.,' p. 570. The 'Brut y Tywysogion' (Rolls edition, p. 19), says : '910 was the year of Christ when Other came to the island of Britain,' but the marginal chronology from MS. D gives 911. The 'Annales Cambriæ' (Rolls edition, p. 17) says : '913. cccclxix. Annus. Otter venit [in Brittanniam].' The 'Anglo-Saxon Chronicle' ('M. H. B.,' p. 377) narrates the invasion under A.D. 918, but MSS. C and D agree with Florence of Worcester. Henry of Huntingdon ('Historiæ Anglorum,' lib. v. ; 'M. H. B.,' p. 743) relates the invasion as happening in the eleventh year of King Edward.

Britain and gone to Gaul, returned from Brittany with a great fleet, under the command of Other and Hroald; and (as the 'Anglo-Saxon Chronicle' relates) 'they went west about till they arrived within the mouth of the Severn, and they spoiled the North Welsh everywhere[1] by the sea-coast where they then pleased. And in Ircingfeld they took Bishop Cameleac, and led him with them to their ships; and then King Edward ransomed him afterwards with forty pounds. Then after that the whole army landed, and would have gone once more to plunder about Ircingfeld. Then met them the men of Hereford and of Gloucester, and of the nearest burhs, and fought against them, and put them to flight, and slew the eorl Hroald, and a brother[2] of Ohter, the other eorl, and many of the army, and drove them into an inclosure, and there beset them about, until they delivered hostages to them, that they would depart from King Edward's dominion. And the King had so ordered it that his forces sat down against them on the south side of Severnmouth, from the Welsh coast westward, to the mouth of the Avon eastward; so that on that side they durst not anywhere attempt the land. Then, nevertheless, they stole away by night on some two occasions, once to the east of Watchet, and another time to Porlock; but they were beaten on either occasion, so that few of them got away, except those alone who there swam out to the ships. And then they sat down, out on the island of Bradanrelice,[3] until such time as they were quite destitute of food; and many men died of hunger, because they could not obtain any food. Then they went thence to Deomod (Dyfed), and then out to Ireland; and this was during harvest.'[3]

[1] *I.e.* the Welsh of Wales as opposed to the Welsh of Devon and Cornwall.
[2] Henry of Huntingdon calls him Geolcil, 'M. H. B.,' p. 743.
[3] Henry of Huntingdon calls it Stepen, Florence of Worcester ('M. H. B.,' p. 570) calls it Reoric. It is now the Flat Holme.

Age of Fusion to Consecration of Bernard

Cameleac, whom Florence of Worcester calls 'Cymelgeac, a bishop of the Britons,' and whom Henry of Huntingdon calls Camelegeac, is the Cimeilliauc, or Civeilliauc (in modern Welsh, Cyfeiliawg), of the 'Book of Llandaff,' and comes in the register between Bishops Nudd and Libiau. Two disputes are recorded to have taken place between him and Brochmael, son of Meurig, the King of Gwent, mentioned by Asser, and on one occasion it was adjudged that Brochmael should pay the bishop 'the price of his face in length and breadth in pure gold,' instead of which, however, he gave Tref Peren with six modii of land, and 'with all its liberty, and all commonage in field and in woods, in water and in pastures.'[1]

It is not surprising that, at a period of comparative friendliness such as is indicated by these acts of kindness on the part of English kings towards Asser and Cyfeiliawg and the Welsh Church in general, we find records of consecrations of Welsh bishops by archbishops of Canterbury. These records are confused, but it is highly probable that they contain a measure of truth, and a good deal may be done in the way of harmonizing them, if we altogether decline to admit the evidence of the untrustworthy 'Book of Aberpergwm.' Ralph de Diceto records that Æthelred, Archbishop of Canterbury, whose tenure of his see lasted from 870 to 889, consecrated at Canterbury Chevelliauc, Bishop of Llandaff, and after him Libau, Bishop of Llandaff, and after him Lunverd, Bishop of St. David's. By Chevelliauc he must mean Cyfeiliawg, the bishop who was afterwards ransomed from the Danes, and who died, according to the 'Book of Llandaff,' in 927.[2] This date is corroborated by the authority of Florence of Worcester, who records Cyfeiliawg's captivity under date A.D. 915. It is impossible, therefore, that Æthelred can have consecrated Libiau, who was

[1] 'Book of Llan Dâv,' pp. 233, 234. [2] *Ibid.*, p. 237.

Cyfeiliawg's successor, but he may have consecrated Lunverd, or rather Llunwerth, of St. David's, who became bishop in 874,[1] in succession to Bishop Nobis, or Novis. Asser's invitation to the court of King Alfred is generally supposed to have been given about A.D. 884, so that both the consecrations of Cyfeiliawg and of Llunwerth, if they are historical, must have been prior to his visit; but Asser's invitation need not have been the first act of kindness on the part of the English court.

In the next century, according to the 'Book of Llandaff,' the limits of the diocese of Llandaff and of the kingdom of Morganwg were determined by the English King, Edgar, acting as suzerain over Morgan Hên, King of Morganwg, and Hywel Dda, King of Deheubarth.

Hywel Dda had attempted, it is said, to deprive Morgan Hên wrongfully of Ystradyw and Ewyas, but Edgar awarded those districts to Morgan Hên and to the diocese of Landaff. The document which professes to record the decision of Edgar claims for the diocese of Llandaff seven cantrefs: (1) Cantref Bychan, or the district round Llandovery; (2) the Cantref of Gower, Kidwelly and Carnwillion; (3) Cantref Gorwenydd, in Glamorgan; (4) Cantref Penychen, also in Glamorgan; (5) the Cantref of Gwenllwg and Edelygion, in Monmouthshire; (6) Cantref Gwentiscoed, also in Monmouthshire, and (7) the Cantref of Gwentuwchcoed, with Ystradyw and Ewyas, of which part is in Monmouthshire, but Ewyas is in Herefordshire, and Yystradyw is in Brecknockshire.

The claim thus advanced is practically to an inclusion

---

[1] 'Annales Cambriae,' MS. B. The 'Brut' calls him Lwmbert, the 'Liber Landavensis' Lumberth. The 'Book of Aberpergwm' states under 871 that Einion died and 'Hubert the Saxon was made Bishop in his room.' See also Jones and Freeman, p. 262: 'Giraldus finds room for seven, and Godwin's Catalogue for eight, prelates between' Novis and Llunwerth. Among these are Asser and Sampson, the latter of whom, according to the discredited story of Giraldus, carried the pall away from St. David's to Dol.

in the diocese of Llandaff of the district between the Tawe and Towy with a portion of Brecknockshire and Archenfield, in Herefordshire, districts which eventually became parts of the dioceses of St. David's and Hereford. The document may not be genuine, for it contains one decided anachronism, as Hywel Dda died several years before Edgar became King of England;[1] and further, it was not inserted by the compiler of the 'Book of Llandaff,' but by a somewhat later hand.[2] It is curious also that it is stated that it was entered in the 'Book of Llandaff' because the original document was in danger of falling to pieces from extreme age,[3] whereas there are many charters in the earlier part of the book which purport to be much older.

As we shall see later on, there was a dispute in the twelfth century between the See of Llandaff on the one hand, and the Sees of St. David's and Hereford on the other, respecting the districts mentioned in this document, for St. David's claimed the country between Towy and Tawe with the Brecon district, and Hereford claimed Archenfield. Those who take a sceptical view of the older charters in the 'Book of Llandaff' say that there can be little doubt that we owe these to a desire on the part of the Llandaff clergy to support their claim by written evidence as well to these districts as to other possessions in dispute. But on the other hand, some of these early documents are couched in an archaic Welsh which it is averred could not have been written in the twelfth century, and this is an argument of considerable force, for if the Welsh documents be not forgeries, probably the majority of the other documents are also

---

[1] The 'Book of Aberpergwm' attempts to get rid of this difficulty by recording the dispute as one between Morgan Hên and Owain of Deheubarth, which is possible. See 'Gwentian Brut,' p. 27, in 'Archæologia Camb.,' supplement for 1863, Third Series, vol. x.
[2] See 'Book of Llan Dâv' (Evans' edition), xxix. Evans ascribes the writing of hand 'Fc' to 'early thirteenth century.'
[3] *Ibid.*, p. 247.

genuine. The narrative of the Danish invasion of Wales in 915, which is gathered from English and unprejudiced sources, has shown that a Bishop of Llandaff was captured in Archenfield, and it would appear probable from this that Archenfield, which was one of the districts in dispute, was at that time reckoned in the diocese of Llandaff. The document which purports to record the decision of Edgar in favour of Morgan Hên, whether it be genuine or not, shows clearly that the diocesan boundaries were considered the same as the civil boundaries, and the limits of the different dioceses probably varied very much from time to time, and thus the dispute arose. It is certainly probable that matters had been maturing for a long period before the final great cause of the twelfth century.

There are other doubtful records of this period of Welsh history, which are contained in the 'Book of Aberpergwm.'

Under 961 it relates that 'Padarn, Bishop of Llandaff, died, and Rhodri, son of Morgan the Great, was placed in his room, against the will of the Pope, on which account he was poisoned, and the priests were enjoined not to marry without the leave of the Pope, on which account a great disturbance took place in the diocese of Teilo, so that it was considered best to allow matrimony to the priests.'[1] As the date given would put this in the time of Dunstan, the great adversary of the secular clergy, it may be that the compiler in this case is relating, more or less accurately, actual facts due to the influence of the English archbishop and his party, but the authority is too weak to enable this to be confidently accepted. The same book relates a visit of Edgar to Caerleon in A.D. 962, and under 972 relates the death of the same King, stating also that 'he erected the monastery at

[1] 'Gwentian Brut,' in 'Arch. Camb.,' Third Series, x., supplement, p. 28.

Bangor Fawr, and many other monasteries in Wales and England, and recompensed the churches of Wales for the injuries he did them in his youth.' Edgar really died in 975, so that the date at least is wrong. The genuine 'Brut' records that Edgar 'collected a very great fleet at Caerleon upon Usk' in 971, but says nothing of any previous visit.

The next records of any acts of supremacy on the part of England are those contained in the 'Book of Llandaff' of the consecration by Archbishops of Canterbury of three Bishops of Llandaff, Gucaunus or Gwgan in A.D. 982, Bledri in A.D. 983, and Joseph in A.D. 1022. The 'Canterbury Rolls' confirm the testimony of the Llandaff authority, and Ralph de Diceto also relates the consecration by Archbishops of Canterbury of Bledri and Joseph, Bishops of Llandaff, and of Tramerin, Elfod, and Bleduc, Bishops of St. David's. Unfortunately the dates are in such hopeless confusion that it is difficult to ascertain the truth. Elfod is a Bishop of St. David's otherwise unknown to fame, but the historians of the diocese incline to accept Diceto's testimony for the other consecrations.[1] In any case, friendliness with the English Church must have been increasing, for during the last thirteen years of the life of Bishop Æthelstan of Hereford, while he was incapacitated by blindness, Tremerin, or Trahaiarn, of St. David's acted as his vicar.

With the Norman Conquest the claims of the Anglican bishops grew more imperious than before. The saintly and gentle Anselm, who likened himself to a tame old sheep in comparison with the fierce young bull, William the Red, behaved in nowise tamely towards the Church of Wales. He placed Herwald, Bishop of Llandaff, under an interdict, and in a letter to Ralph, Abbot of Séez, forbade that the orders of a certain man whom

[1] Jones and Freeman, p. 267. See also Canon Bevan, 'St. David's,' p. 50.

Herwald had consecrated should be recognised as valid.
He also suspended temporarily Wilfrid, or Gryffydd,
Bishop of St. David's. What were the causes or pretexts
for these high-handed acts on the part of Anselm cannot
be determined. It has been conjectured that Wilfrid
was suspended for an alienation of Church property
which he made. Herwald, the offending Bishop of
Llandaff, may possibly have received consecration from
an Anglican source, though the accounts vary extremely,
Lanfranc of Canterbury, Joseph of St. David's, and Kinsi
of York, being respectively named as his consecrators.
Lanfranc of Canterbury is manifestly impossible, as
Herwald was consecrated in or about A.D. 1056. About
the same time as Herwald of Llandaff was placed under
an interdict by Anselm, Hervé, a Breton, was consecrated
to the See of Bangor[1] by Thomas, Archbishop of York
(A.D. 1092). This is the first instance of any encroach-
ment by the English Church upon the independence of
the northern dioceses of Wales, and is therefore the more
significant. Hervé was promoted to his see by reason
of the favour of William Rufus. However, he did not
retain his position long; for, as we are informed by a
sympathetic chronicler, 'he treated the fierce people with
too great austerity, seeing in their manners so great a
perversity as no one could easily endure.' When he
began to take strong measures to coerce his irreverent
flock, they rose in rebellion against him, and slew his
brother, and 'were ready to punish him in like manner
if they could lay hands upon him.' Many of his friends
were wounded and slain, and Hervé himself fled for protection to Henry I. He was anxious to be transferred
to another see, and after failing to obtain the bishopric
of Lisieux, was finally translated to Ely (1109) through

[1] Previous Bishops of Bangor are mentioned by the chapter of
St. David's in their letter to Pope Eugenius ('De Invectionibus,'
ii. 6, Gir. Camb., op. iii. 57); Morgleis and Duvan, consecrated by
Joseph of St. David's, and Revedun by Julienus of St. David's.

the intervention of Pope Paschal II., who pitied him for the cruelties which he and his kindred had suffered at the hands of the 'barbarians.'

South Wales by this time had been conquered by the Normans. In 1079, as the 'Brut' states, 'William the Bastard, King of the Saxons and the French and the Britons, came for prayer on a pilgrimage to Menevia,' a pilgrimage which very probably had more of a political than a religious purpose. In 1091, Rhys, son of Tewdwr, King of South Wales, was overthrown and slain by the Normans, 'and then,' says the 'Brut,' 'fell the kingdom of the Britons. . . . And about the calends of July,' continues the same authority, 'the French came into Dyved and Ceredigion, which they have still retained, and fortified the castles, and seized upon all the land of the Britons.' There were many alternations of fortune in subsequent years, but the Norman dominion was never altogether overthrown, and the conquerors dealt with the Church of the subject principality as they dealt with the English Church. Upon the death of Wilfrid of St. David's, whom the chronicle calls Jeffrey, the clergy of the diocese elected Daniel to succeed him. Daniel had especial claims as son of a noted former bishop, Sulien; but King Henry put him aside 'against the will and in contempt of all the scholars of the Britons.' Bernard, 'a man from Normandy,' was preferred instead to the vacant see; he was not even in priest's orders at the time, so that he was ordained priest on a Saturday, and consecrated bishop on the next day. There was some little dispute about the place of his consecration, one baron asserting that it ought to take place in the royal chapel, which called forth an indignant protest from the Archbishop of Canterbury. The King smoothed the angry waters by a few polite words to the archbishop, and in compliment to the Queen, who wished to be present at the ceremony, the primate agreed to alter the place of consecration from Lambeth to Westminster Abbey. Bernard made formal profession of canonical obedience to the See of Canterbury, and was consecrated by Archbishop Ralph with the co-operation of various suffragans, among whom is mentioned Urban of Llandaff, Sept. 19, 1115.[1] The death of the unfortunate Daniel ab Sulien, who had been set aside in Bernard's favour, is mentioned by the 'Brut' under 1124. 'In the end of that year,' it says, 'died Daniel, son of Sulien, Bishop of Menevia, the man who had been arbitrator between Gwynedd and Powys, in the trouble between them; and there was none of them who could find blame or dispraise in him, for he was peaceful and beloved by all; he was likewise the Archdeacon of Powys.'[2]

The Church in South Wales had now finally lost its independence, for Urban of Llandaff, although not imposed so violently upon his diocese as was Bernard, was apparently equally a nominee of the Normans, and was consecrated by Archbishop Anselm in 1107, when he professed canonical obedience to the See of Canterbury.[3] Urban, however, was probably a Welshman, for he is called Worgan, *i.e.*, Morgan, in the 'Brut.'[4] It remains, therefore, now that the process of fusion or absorption has been traced to its close, so far as South Wales is concerned, to gather from such scanty materials as we have at our disposal some idea of the general condition of the Church during the period.

It would appear that the strictness of the monastic ideal had been very considerably relaxed. Gildas would probably have found very much more to censure in this age than in the sixth century. The Age of the Saints was indeed not closed for many years after Augustine landed; but very few saints are chronicled after A.D. 664.

---

[1] Eadmer, 'Hist. Nov.,' 5, in 'H. and S.,' i. 306. The 'Brut' gives the date of Wilfrid's death as A.D. 1112 ('Brut y Tywysogion,' p. 118).
[2] 'Brut,' p. 152.
[3] See 'H. and S.,' i. 302, 303. [4] P. 80.

Elbod of Bangor, who ended the Easter controversy; Sadyrnin, Bishop of St. David's, who died in A.D. 832; Cyfeiliawg, Bishop of Llandaff, who died in A.D. 927; Caradog, a hermit, and Gwryd, a twelfth-century friar, bring up the rear of the noble army.[1] The passion for asceticism had died out, and though the monasteries were still resorted to, the austerities of the monks were not quite so severe. Morgeneu, the thirty-third bishop from St. David, was murdered by Danish pirates in A.D. 999, and the popular voice proclaimed that his death was a judgment for his violation of the rule not to eat flesh. 'Because I ate flesh, I became flesh,' was the ghastly message which his ghost told an Irish bishop, so Giraldus informs us. But the spectral warning probably went unheeded. Clerical celibacy was not universal in the time of Gildas; but it may be supposed that all the bishops contemporary with that ascetic saint, whether diocesan bishops or others, were celibates. At a later age, however, clerical celibacy seems to have been the exception rather than the rule, and parochial cures passed from father to son. This was the case, too, with the canonries of St. David's cathedral, and even in some measure at one time with the bishopric of St. David's itself. Sulien, one of the most notable of the pre-Norman bishops of that see, was the father of four sons.

> 'Quattuor ac proprio nutrivit sanguine natos,
> Quos simul edocuit dulci libaminis amne,
> Ingenio claros; iam sunt hæc nomina quorum,—
> Rycymarch sapiens, Arthgen, Danielque, Johannes.'[2]

Of these 'Rycymarch,' or Rhygyfarch, the biographer of St. David, succeeded his father in A.D. 1089. Daniel, the third son of Bishop Sulien, was the nominee of the Welsh clergy, who was set aside in favour of Bernard. Rhygyfarch was himself a married man, and had a son, named Sulien after his grandfather. A certain Cuhelm,

---

[1] Rees, 'Welsh Saints,' p. 305.
[2] 'Carmen de Vita Sulgeni,' in 'H. and S.,' i. 666.

'the son of a bishop,' is mentioned in a memorandum on the margin of the 'Book of St. Chad.'

This prevalence of marriage among all ranks of the clergy was scandalous in the eyes of the Norman ecclesiastics, accustomed to the greater severity of the rule of Latin Christendom. But herein the Welsh Church was only preserving the ancient usage, which had not been abrogated even during the outburst of religious enthusiasm in the sixth century. Some hint of a feeling against the custom may be discovered in the 'Laws of Hywel Dda,' which draw a distinction between a son born before his father had taken priest's orders and one born after: 'Where a clerk takes a wife by gift of kindred, and has a son by her, and afterwards the clerk takes priest's orders, and subsequently, when a priest, has a son by the same woman; the son previously begotten is not to share land with such son, as he was begotten contrary to decree.'[1] But more than two hundred years after this enactment, even in the Norman period, the custom still flourished.

The curious succession system, whereby benefices descended from father to son, led in some cases to a strange abuse, the custom of dividing benefices between various incumbents. The church of Keri, in Montgomeryshire, had two rectors; one in Radnorshire had six or seven; and the rectory of Hay, in Brecknockshire, was divided between two brothers, one a clergyman and one a layman. This was due no doubt to the Celtic rule of gavelkind.[2] It was mentioned in the foregoing chapter that the succession system was probably analogous to the rule which prevailed in the Church of Ireland and the monastery of Hy.

Though Wales showed a sturdy spirit of independence in retaining some of her ancient customs, such as the right of the clergy to marry, there had been a growing

[1] 'Cyvreithiau Hywel Dda,' in 'H. and S.,' i. 279.
[2] See Jones and Freeman, p. 274.

awe and reverence for the See of Rome ever since the submission of Elfod. We hear no more of visits to Jerusalem and the East, whether legendary or otherwise, but, on the contrary, Rome became a favourite place of resort for such of the Britons as were still, like the older saints, 'born under a travelling planet.' It has been questioned whether the visit of Hywel Dda to Rome on the occasion of drawing up his code is historical or not, but there can be little doubt that some of the visits of Welsh and other British Kings to Rome recorded by the 'Brut' really took place. Cadwalader's visit to Rome and death thereat in 681, when the schism was at its height, is exceedingly improbable in itself, and is also opposed to the authority of the 'Annales Cambriæ';[1] but there is less reason for doubting the death at Rome of Cyngen, King of Powys, in 854,[2] of Hywel of Glamorgan, whose cross is at Llantwit, in 885,[3] or of Joseph, Bishop of Llandaff in 1043,[4] all which are recorded by the 'Brut.' From the same source we learn of a visit to Rome in 974 of the Briton, Dunwallon, King of Strath Clyde.

But though Wales had altogether changed its attitude towards Rome, it had in no way relaxed its friendship with other Celtic communities, except in so far as circumstances hindered the interchange of friendly acts. The compilers of the Welsh chronicles, the 'Annales Cambriæ' and the 'Brut y Tywysogion,' record the chief events in Irish history and the deaths of eminent Irishmen so commonly that they must have had access to Irish sources of information. It is evident that they regarded all Celts as their kinsmen, and preserved the old British traditions in this respect inherited from Patrick and from the three great Welsh saints, David, Gildas and Cadoc.

[1] 'Annales Cambriæ,' '682 : ccxxxviii. Annus. Mortalitas magna fuit in Britannia, in qua Catgualart filius Catguolaum obiit.'
[2] 'Brut y Tywysogion,' p. 12 ; 'Annales Cambriæ,' p. 13.
[3] Ibid., p. 16 ; ibid., p. 15.
[4] Ibid., p. 41. In the 'Annales' the date appears to be 1045.

If we can trust the 'Book of Aberpergwm,' Cydifor, an abbot of Llancarfan, carried on the same work for Ireland as his predecessor Cadoc, and 'sent six learned men of his abbey to Ireland to instruct the Irish.'[1] The 'Manuscript Juvencus,' which is now preserved in the library of Cambridge University, and is certainly Welsh of the ninth century, contains entries about Nuadu and Fethgna, Bishops of Armagh, who died respectively in A.D. 811 and 874, and must clearly have been taken to Ireland in the lifetime of Fethgna. If the 'Book of Aberpergwm' contains in this case a genuine piece of history, it is possible that the manuscript was taken from Llancarfan, and in any case its presence in Ireland proves intercourse between the Churches of Ireland and Wales in the ninth century. Jeuan, the son of Bishop Sulien of St. David's, relates that his father, who was reputed 'the wisest of the Britons'[2] in his day, 'being moved by desire of study, went to the Irish renowned for marvellous wisdom,' a renown, by the way, that was well deserved. Sulien's son, Rhygyfarch, proves by his 'Life of St. David' that he was a master of that florid and viciously rhetorical style which was one of the most cherished products of Irish training. But without any doubt there was also much real scholarship as well as artistic skill in the Irish monastic schools.[3]

Further evidence in favour of the existence of intercourse between Ireland and Wales in this period is found in the inscribed stones. These differ from the earlier ones in the elaborateness of their ornamentation, in which they resemble the Irish stones. There are about sixty-four stones of this class in Wales, of which forty-two are found in Glamorganshire and Pembrokeshire, so that it would appear that the south of the principality was most affected by Irish influence. The best known and most

---

[1] 'Book of Aberpergwm' under A.D. 883 in recording the death of Cydifor.
[2] 'Brut y Tywysogion,' p. 54.
[3] See Stokes' 'Ireland and the Celtic Church,' Lectures x., xi.

remarkable of those of North Wales is that called Eliseg's Pillar in the lovely valley near Llangollen, which holds also the ruins of the beautiful abbey of Valle Crucis. Eliseg, to whose memory it is inscribed, seems to have lived in the eighth century, and the stone was erected about a hundred years after his death. In Glamorganshire there are inscribed stones with Celtic ornament at Kenfig, Bryn Keffneithan, Baglan, Llandough, two at Merthyr Mawr, two at Coychurch, three at Llantwit Major, and five at Margam. Pembrokeshire has similar inscribed stones at Nevern, Penaly, Carew, Pen Arthur, and St. David's. The stones of Llantwit Major have already been described, and, together with the beautiful crosses of Margam, which may easily be visited by a pedestrian in the same day, for they are only about twenty miles distant, will give the investigator a high opinion of the artistic ability of the early Welsh sculptors.

There was, therefore, much intercourse between the Irish and Welsh Churches during the Age of Fusion, but probably less than in the Age of the Welsh Saints, for the seas were so much infested at times by Danish and Norse pirates that intercourse must have had its perils. We can scarcely over-estimate the sufferings undergone by South Wales from the incursions of these robbers, who especially attacked the churches and monasteries for the valuable altar vessels and crosses which they contained, and who seem to have taken particular pleasure in slaying the clergy or putting them to ransom. The chronicles are full of the records of the devastations of the Danes, and place-names along the coast of South Wales attest their former presence. It has even been thought that 'the Teutonic element which prevails in the topography of Lower Pembroke and Gower' is partly due to settlements of these Vikings.[1] Menevia, or St. David's, was several

[1] Clark, 'Land of Morgan,' p. 16.

times laid waste, and two of its bishops, Morgeneu[1] and Abraham,[2] were murdered. In the year of Sulien's death, 1089, St. David's was attacked for the last time, and was then utterly demolished.[3] We read also that in A.D. 987 'the Pagans devastated Llanbadarn, and Menevia, and Llanilltud (Llantwit Major), and Llancarfan, and Llandydoch.'[4] Bangor was laid waste in A.D. 1071.[5] It was at least one of the merits of the Normans that they put an end to this miserable condition of affairs.

[1] A.D. 1023 ('Brut'). [2] A.D. 1078 ('Brut').
[3] 'Brut y Tywysogion.' [4] *Ibid.* [5] *Ibid.*

CHAPTER VII.

FROM THE CONSECRATION OF BISHOP BERNARD TO THE
VISITATION OF ARCHBISHOP BALDWIN.

THE Norman conquest of South Wales was fraught with many changes for the Welsh Church. Henceforth the higher dignities were often placed in the hands of Normans—a policy which was also carried out in England, but operated there less injuriously because the Normans eventually became amalgamated with the English both in speech and language, whereas in Wales, though amalgamation went on, it was a slower process, and was never quite completed. The old Celtic monastic institutions also decayed or were destroyed, and in many cases Church lands were seized by the invading nobles. If the 'Book of Aberpergwm' is to be credited, the chief churches of the diocese of Llandaff, those of Llandaff, Llancarfan, Llanilltud (Llantwit), Llandough, St. Fagan's, Caerleon, Caerwent, and others, lost their right of sanctuary at the time of the Norman invasion, but had it restored about 1150 by Bishop Nicholas; and about the same time the churches that had been demolished were rebuilt, and new ones were founded.[1] Popes Calixtus II. and Honorius II. issued injunctions to various Norman nobles of the same diocese to restore the lands, tithes, offerings, and other dues which they had seized or were

[1] 'Book of Aberpergwm' in Arch. Camb., Third Series, x., p. 122.

withholding.[1] Among these lords were Walter Fitz-Richard, Brian Fitz-Count, William Fitz-Baderon, Robert de Chandos, Payne Fitz-John, Bernard Newmarch, Wynebald de Baalun, Milo of Gloucester, Richard de Pwns, and Robert Fitz-Martin, and the number indicates that these spoliations must have been altogether considerable. It would appear that Robert Fitz-Hamon, the conqueror of Rhys ap Tewdwr, who was not only Lord of Glamorgan, but also held the Honour of Gloucester, transferred the endowments of Llantwit and Llancarfan to Gloucestershire churches. To St. Peter's, at Gloucester, he gave the church of St. Cadoc, at Llancarfan, with Treygof and Penhon.[2] To his great foundation of Tewkesbury Abbey[3] he also made a considerable grant of Welsh ecclesiastical property, which included Llantwit. A charter exists, wherein Bishop Nicholas of Llandaff, whose tenure of the see extended from 1153 to 1183, confirmed to Tewkesbury Abbey the churches and benefices which it held in his diocese; and no better proof than this can be exhibited of the wholesale spoliation of the Welsh Church for extraneous purposes.[4] It enumerates 'the parish church of St. Mary of Kayrdif,[5] with the chapel of the castle, the chapel of St. John,[6] the chapel of St. Thomas, the chapel of Raht,[7] the chapel of St. Dionisius of Kibur, the chapel of Liffenni, the

---

[1] 'Book of Llandâv,' pp. 93, 37.
[2] Clark, 'Cartæ de Glamorgan,' i. 7-9. Treygof is now Treguff Place; Pennon is a village near Llancarfan. See also 'Cartularium S. Petri Glouc.,' Rolls Series, i. 93, 115.
[3] Originally an old Mercian foundation of A.D. 715. The new Tewkesbury Abbey was founded in 1102.
[4] 'Carta N. Land. Ep. Confirmantis S. M. Theok. Beneficia quæ Habent in Episcopatu Suo.' (Cott. MS., Cleop. A., vii. 68).; 'Cartæ et Alia Munimenta quæ ad Dominium de Glamorgan pertinent, curante G. T. Clark,' vol. i., pp. 20-22.
[5] Cardiff.
[6] 'St. John's, Cardiffe V., St. John Baptist, cap. to St. Mary's, Cardiff; but now, since St. Mary's Church was ruined, it is made the parish church.' Ecton's 'Thesaurus,' third edition, p. 506.
[7] Roath.

chapel of St. Edern,[1] the chapel of Lanbordan, with all its belongings within the borough and without, and the tithe of the lord's revenues in the county of Kairdif and of all his lordship in Wales; the church of Londoch,[2] belonging to the church of Kairdif, with the chapel of Leotwtha,[3] and the chapel of Cogan, with the lands and its remaining belongings; the church of Llandiltuit,[4] with the chapel of Liswini,[5] the chapel of St. Bartholomew, the chapel of St. Cujan of Cherleton, with its belongings of Lanbari and of Lanparan and of St. Nicholas, and with its remaining belongings; the church of St. Leonard of Newcastle,[6] with the chapel of St. Theduct,[7] the chapel of Lathelestuna,[8] the chapel in the wood on the eastern side of Leveni, the chapel of St. Thomas in the land which William, Earl of Gloucester, gave to William Fitz-Henry, between the waters of Avan and Neth; the church of St. James of Kenefeg,[9] with the chapel of St. Thomas in the same town, the chapel of Corneli,[10] which is the town of Thomas; the chapel of St. Wendun, of the town of Walter Luvel, the chapel of St. Thomas of Creitic, the chapel of St. Cunioth of Leveni, with all the rest of its belongings, as well of the church of St. Leonard, as of the church of Kenefeg, of Landbleth,[11] with the chapel of St. Donat,[12] the chapel of St. James of Landcoman, the chapel of St. Lenwara of Lathawa, with the rest of its belongings.'

It is a goodly list indeed, and the monks of Tewkesbury may well have been thankful to their munificent benefactors whose chapels and effigies still adorn their

[1] Llanedeyrn. St. Dionisius of Kibur may be Lisvane church, which is dedicated to St. Denis.
[2] Llandough.   [3] ? Leckwith.
[4] Lantwit Major, or Lllanilltyd Fawr.   [5] Llyswerni, or Lisworney.
[6] The church of Newcastle, Bridgend, is now dedicated to St. Illtyd.
[7] Tythegston, dedicated to Tudwg.   [8] Laleston.
[9] Kenefeg (i.e., Kenfig) is printed in the text 'Keneseg,' an evident mistake.
[10] Cornely, near Porthcawl.   [11] Llanblethian (Llanbleiddian).
[12] Llanddunwyd, or Welsh St. Donat's.

magnificent fane; but it is somewhat sorrowful reading for all who are familiar with the district of South Wales thus despoiled, and who can realize in some measure the wrong inflicted upon the Church therein—a wrong from which it has never recovered, for the revenues thus alienated have never been regained, and their loss has meant for many centuries the hindering of God's work in the district. All these churches were served by vicars, appointed by the monks of Tewkesbury, who were to assign them honourable sustenance. But these churches did not constitute the whole of the benefaction to Tewkesbury and plunder of the Welsh Church, for Bishop Nicholas also enumerates lands and tithes which the monks owned elsewhere.[1]

It has been said that 'on the whole the Church in the lordship' (of Glamorgan) 'had no reason to complain of the new lords,'[2] because of the new monasteries which they founded. This, however, is a weak defence, for their policy was to take from the poor and to give to the rich; to strip the native institutions and clergy of their possessions and to bestow them upon the privileged Normans. The foundation of new monasteries in Wales was no compensation to the secular clergy for the loss inflicted

[1] 'Confirmat autem eis omnes decimas quas in illo episcopatu legitime obtinuerunt, viz., duas partes decimæ dominii de Crenemarestune, duas partes decimæ dominii Rogeri de Sumeri, medietatem decimæ dominii de Sto Fagano, duas partes decimæ dominii de Sto Nicholao, duas partes decimæ dominii de Bonlemlestun, duas partes decimæ dominii de Wufa, duas partes decimæ dominii de Manwrekestun, duas partes decimæ dominii quod fuit Hugonis de Gloucestria, duas partes decimæ dominii de Treigof, medietatem decimæ dominii Willielmi de Lond. et c acras terre apud Wuggemore, duas partes decimæ dominii de Penmarc, duas partes decimæ dominii quod nunc est monachorum de Neth apud Essam, duas partes decimæ dominii de Marois, duas partes decimæ dominii de Sto Donato, duas partes decimæ dominii de Coitiff et Novocastello. Et confirmat eis terras, que in elemosinam eis datæ sunt, villulam quæ dicitur Landochan, terram quam dedit Walterus de Landbleche, terram quam dedit Robertus filius Nigelli, terram quam dedit Walkelinus, dictam Landcadhele, totum brachium aquæ de Taf ex quo exit, et etiam pratum ultra aquam juxta ecclesiam.'

[2] Clark, 'Land of Morgan,' p. 23.

on their body. But it must be acknowledged that the Normans also founded many parish churches.

This policy of spoliation was exceedingly detrimental, and often proved fatal, to the old Celtic monasteries of South Wales. Llantwit Major continued for a long time to exist as a cell, as the remains prove; and this was probably true also of Llancarfan for a time at least; but, as the legends of St. Cadoc of Llancarfan and St. Illtyd of Llantwit show, a new spirit was infused into these communities. The former legend was written by Lifris, or Leofric, who is probably the same as 'the son of a bishop, Archdeacon of Glamorgan, and Prior of St. Cadoc,' who is mentioned in the 'Book of Llandaff,'[1] and who was contemporary with Bishop Herwald, whose episcopate lasted from 1059 to 1103. The legend is Roman and anti-national in tone.[2] An appendix to the 'Life of St. Illtyd,' written apparently in the time of Robert Fitz-Hamon, records an attack of a Welsh army upon Llantwit at that period, which was repulsed by the aid of the saint, indicated by fiery signs in the sky;[3] and it is very evident that the chronicler had no sympathy with the Welsh cause.

Urban of Llandaff, though he was a nominee of the Normans, was a good Welshman and did not submit tamely to the robbery of his see, but was unremitting in his endeavours to get Church lands and property restored by the nobles who had seized them, and to secure the extension of his see so as to include the parts which are said to have been awarded it by the arbitration of Edgar, as well as to gain possession of the Teilo churches, which were thirty-seven churches in Carmarthenshire, Pembrokeshire, Brecknockshire and Radnorshire.[4] For

---

[1] 'Book of Llan Dâv,' p. 271.
[2] See 'Vita S. Cadoci,' § 23; Rees' 'C. B. S.,' p. 60.
[3] 'Vita S. Iltuti,' § 26; Rees' 'C. B. S.,' pp. 181, 182.
[4] See Grant of Rhydderch, son of Jestin, in 'Book of Llan Dâv,' pp. 253-255. They are 'nearly all churches that, if not dedicated to, at

these purposes he appealed to three successive Popes, Calixtus II., Honorius II. and Innocent II. His first appeal, addressed in 1119 to Calixtus II., gives a lamentable account of the diocese. 'It was always,' he says, 'the mistress of all other churches of Wales in dignity and in all privilege, until at length through seditions and so many wicked deeds in war, and also as my predecessor Herward had become old and therefore enfeebled, the church began to be weakened and almost deprived of its shepherd, and annihilated by the cruelty of the natives and the invasion of the Norman race. . . . Very lately in the reign of King William,[1] a great part of the clergy having already been removed, the church was yet defended by twenty-four canons, of whom at present none save two remain, and in the possession of the church, four ploughlands and four libræ. Not only by the loss of territories is the church now desolate and despoiled, but also by tithes being taken away from it, and from all the clergy of the whole diocese, both by the power of the laity and the invasion of the monks, as also by the great

---

least bore the name of the great Llandaff saint, Teilo. It must be borne in mind that the territorial name "Bishop of Llandaff" was not the ancient title of the holders of the see. The earlier name is the personal one, "Esgob Teilau." While the claim of a Bishop of Llandaff to churches outside his diocese may seem preposterous, the claim of the Bishop of Teilo to the churches of Teilo is by no means so. If the Irish mode of evangelizing the country was the one adopted in Wales — and the probabilities are that it was — then the mother monastery of Teilo sent forth bands of missionaries who obtained grants of land from the local rulers where they formed religious settlements. To use the Irish term, these colonies would form part of the possessions of "the tribe of the saint," that is, of the monastery to which the missionaries belonged; and so wherever Teilo monks went, Teilo churches, part of the possessions of the Teilo Monastery, grew up. These settlements would be considered to belong to the monastery, quite apart from any territorial division of the country that then, or afterwards, might exist. To most of the Teilo churches this view furnishes a reasonable explanation of the Bishop of Llandaff's claim, except as to that important group of them in Pembrokeshire.' — Mr. Willis Bund, in 'Arch. Camb.,' Fifth Series, x. 194, 195.

[1] Viz., Rufus, as the MS. followed in the 'Liber Landavensis' (Llandovery ed.) gives, p. 84.

invasion of our territory and diocese by our brethren, the Bishops of Hereford and of St. Dewi.'[1] In the same year as he issued this appeal Urban attended the Council of Rheims,[2] and his representations were so far successful as to obtain a Papal bull, receiving the church of Llandaff under the protection of the Apostolic See, and forbidding both clergy and laity to take away aught of its possessions.[3] Calixtus also admonished the lay plunderers of the diocese to restore their spoil,[4] and sent letters to the king[5] and the Archbishop of Canterbury, urging them to protect the See of Llandaff, ' which was so despoiled of its possessions both by bishops and laymen, that it seemed almost reduced to nothing.'[6]

Calixtus II. died in 1124, and two years afterwards an agreement was arranged between Urban and the celebrated Robert of Gloucester, the natural son of King Henry I., who by his marriage with Mabel, daughter and sole heiress of Robert Fitz-Hamon, now held the lordship of Glamorgan. The agreement was made at Woodstock in the King's presence, and in consideration of the grants and privileges conceded by the earl, the bishop on his part consented to withdraw all charges against the earl and his men.[7] The proceedings at the Papal court, however, still went on, for Urban having failed at the Council of Westminster in 1127, again appealed to the Papal See. The new Pope, Honorius II., admonished lay plunderers,[8] some of whom were among the witnesses to Earl Robert's agreement, and in 1128, and again in 1129, in the absence of Bernard of St. David's and Richard of Hereford, he adjudged the whole of the districts in dispute between the rival sees to Llandaff.[9] After this decision Bernard appeared at Rome, to plead the cause of his see, and the whole proceedings were opened again.[10] Promises were

---
[1] 'Book of Llan Dâv,' pp. 87, 88. [2] *Ibid.*, p. 89.
[3] *Ibid.*, pp. 89-92.   [4] *Ibid.*, pp. 93, 94.   [5] *Ibid.*, p. 92.
[6] *Ibid.*, pp. 92, 93.   [7] *Ibid.*, pp. 27-29.   [8] *Ibid.*, p. 37.
[9] *Ibid.*, pp. 30-33, 39-41.   [10] *Ibid.*, pp. 53, 54.

repeatedly given of a final decision, which never came until the death of Urban in 1134, when Innocent II. pronounced against the claims of Llandaff, and St. David's and Hereford finally retained possession of the districts. Thus, at last, says William of Malmesbury, 'the contention between Bernard, Bishop of Menevia, and Urban of Llandaff, concerning the right of the parishes which Urban had unlawfully usurped, was laid at rest for ever; for after so many appeals to the Roman court, so many expensive journeys, so many conflicts of lawyers, after being ventilated for many years, at length it was ended, or rather decided, by the death of Urban at Rome; for the Apostolic father, having weighed the equity of the matter, satisfied religion and the right of the Bishop of Menevia by a suitable decision.' The annalist of the Glamorganshire Abbey of Margam, who, however, copies largely from William of Malmesbury, took the same view of Urban's contention, and it may be that popular opinion generally commended the Papal decision.[1]

Urban left one memorial of his episcopate, a new cathedral church at Llandaff, portions of which still remain, including a grand Norman arch at the east end of the presbytery, one of the chief glories of the present cathedral. We are told that when he removed the relics of St. Dubricius from Bardsey to Llandaff, he determined also to build a worthy church to contain them. The old church was very small, being in length 28 feet, in breadth 15, in height 20, and with two aisles, one on each side, of very small size and height, and with a round porch of 12 feet in length and breadth;[2] an interesting

[1] The Annalist copies William of Malmesbury so closely in this, as in many other particulars, that he cannot be regarded as an independent authority. Margam Abbey was not founded until 1147. See 'Annales de Margam' (Rolls ed., p. 13) under 1131: 'Tunc etiam contentio inter Bernardum episcopum Menevensem et Urbanum Landavensem de jure parochiarum, quas idem Urbanus illicite usurpaverat, morte ejusdem Urbani apud Romam finem sortitur.'

[2] 'By which a semicircular apse is probably meant,' says Dean Conybeare. 'Arch. Camb.,' New Series, i. 26.

statement from which we may infer that Welsh churches were generally very small even down to the Norman conquest. The new church was begun on Wednesday, April 14, 1120,[1] and Urban, who in all ways seems to have been an indefatigable worker for his see, procured an indulgence from Archbishop Ralph to all contributors to the holy work,[2] and a confirmation and enlargement of the indulgence from John of Crema, the Papal legate.[3] The archbishop remitted a fourth part of the penance due from each donor, and the Papal legate remitted fourteen days besides.

Bernard, the Norman Bishop of St. David's contemporary with Urban, was as active and enterprising as his brother of Llandaff, and probably more able, but less scrupulous. He had the reputation of courtly manners, of brilliant wit and great learning, and he proved himself during his tenure of the see an ambitious and skilful ruler, but he did not scruple to secure the support of the powerful Norman barons by alienation of Church lands. He gave away in fiefs the whole cantred of Pebidiog, in which St. David's is situated, and which had been bestowed upon the see by the native princes. Fishguard was absolutely separated from the cantred and annexed to the barony of Cemaes. The clergy complained that he would assign ten, twenty, or even thirty ploughlands as a military fief, but thought one, two, or perhaps three, enough as a portion for a canon of his cathedral. He made no efforts to regain Cenarthmawr in Emlyn, Llanrian, Lawrenny, Ucceton, and the other lands which his predecessor Wilfrid had alienated, or the manors of Llanstadwell and St. Ishmael's, which had been seized by foreign intruders.[4] The introduction of the feudal tenure into the property of the see may have been a necessity of

---

[1] 'Book of Llan Dâv,' p. 86.   [2] *Ibid.*, p. 87.   [3] *Ibid.*, p. 48.
[4] 'De Jure et Statu Menevensis Ecclesiæ,' ii. ; Giraldi Camb., Op. (Rolls ed.) iii., pp. 152-154.

Bernard's position as a Lord Marcher, and he may have been forced, as Urban was, to condone alienations that he did not approve, but, so far as our evidence goes, it is impossible to acquit him altogether of the crime of dilapidation of his see. Giraldus, who is the witness against him, says that 'he alienated very many Church lands quite fruitlessly and uselessly' with a view to gaining further preferment by translation to an English see.

In other respects, however, he was an active and, on the whole, a successful bishop. He abolished the *glaswyr*,[1] *i.e.*, ecclesiastics whom, on coming to his see, he found living at St. David's without any definite rule; and he founded canonries and established canons there in their stead. He is said, also, to have procured the canonization of St. David by Pope Calixtus II.[2] He carried to a successful issue, as we have already seen, the dispute between himself and Urban, and his efforts on behalf of the Welsh Church caused the native princes to invite him to confer with them respecting Archbishop Theobald's consecration of Meurig of Bangor.[3] He also has the distinction of being praised by the Welsh chronicle as 'a man of extraordinary praise and piety and holiness,' who died 'after extreme exertions, upon sea and land, towards procuring for the church of Menevia its ancient liberty.'[4] It is strange to find such praise accorded by a Welsh author to the first alien Bishop of St. David's, who had been imposed upon that see by royal authority in opposition to the wish of the native clergy; but the cause of this praise and of the friendly attitude of the Welsh princes is to be found in the policy pursued by Bernard during the latter years of his episcopate.

Encouraged probably by his success in the contest with Urban, the Bishop of St. David's, the very next year after

---

[1] *Eglwyswyr*.
[2] Godwin, 'De Præsulibus Angliæ' (Richardson's ed.), p. 573.
[3] 'De Invectionibus,' ii. 9. Giraldi Camb., Op. iii. 59.
[4] 'Brut y Tywysogion' (Rolls ed.), p. 177.

the decision had been given, petitioned Pope Innocent II. for a pall, thereby asserting the claim of his see to be independent of Canterbury and the metropolitan See of Wales. How this claim to metropolitan authority arose is not clear, as none such can be proved to have existed in ancient times, but it probably originated or was revived during the contest with Llandaff; and Giraldus preserved a document purporting to be an assertion of this claim presented to Pope Honorius about 1125 by the chapter of St. David's. It was pleaded by Archbishop Theobald that Bernard had himself professed canonical obedience to Canterbury, and in 1148 Pope Eugenius III. decided against Bernard personally on this ground, but fixed October 18 in the following year for investigating the claims of his see;[1] but before the end of 1148 Bernard died.

The chapter of St. David's met and elected a 'discreet and honourable man,' but, we are told, when they came to Archbishop Theobald, he seduced a few of the chapter and caused them to elect David, Canon of St. David's, and Archdeacon of Cardigan, a Norman on his father's side, but Welsh on his mother's, being the son of Gerald de Windsor, castellan of Pembroke, and Nest, daughter of Rhys ap Tewdwr.[2] The election of the other candidate was quashed, and Theobald proceeded to consecrate David, under whom he hoped ' he could enjoy sleep without disturbance,'[3] and to secure this better he made David profess canonical obedience to Canterbury. David kept

[1] In a scurrilous life of David II., Bishop of St. David's, contained in Wharton's 'Anglia Sacra,' ii., pp. 652, 653, it is said that Theobald produced two false witnesses and gave the Pope 40 marks to receive them. When Bishop Bernard exposed them and alleged that witnesses of that kind ought not to be received against the bishop, 'Brother,' said the Pope, 'I don't want witnesses on your side, but on mine' (' Frater, non tibi quæro testes, sed mihi ').
[2] See the whole story in ' Vita David. II.' in ' Anglia Sacra,' also in Appendix Gir. Camb., Op., pp. 431-434.
[3] ' Sub quo securus posset carpere somnos.'

his word to Theobald; but, if his anonymous biographer is to be believed, this fidelity on his part was almost his only virtue. The cathedral was shut up during the greater part of his tenure of the see.

Giraldus Cambrensis, who was David's nephew, gives a very different account of his uncle. According to him, David was of an exceedingly modest and contented disposition, and interfered with no one and sought no unjust gains. Yet he has to confess that this quiet man was a dilapidator of his see, and alienated certain lands, as Trallwng in Brecknockshire, and others in Dugledu (now Dungleddy) and Pebidiog. The territory also of Oisterlaf was seized in his days by powerful nobles, and became lost to the see.[1]

His anonymous biographer adds particulars, and says that he distributed to his sons and nephews, and also in dowry to his daughters, the few possessions of the see left to it by his predecessor. 'He gave his daughter in marriage to Walter Fitz-Wyson, and quitclaimed the land near Llawhaden, on account of which his father had been excommunicated. He gave a fief of two soldiers to Richard Fitz-Tancard, and this Richard forthwith gave one fief to Robert, his nephew, and the bishop gave him his daughter and the fief which had belonged to Hugo de Wallingford, and gave to increase it Broghes and Trefhennan. Another fief, namely, Castelkennan, he gave to Arnold Dru, his kinsman. He gave his brother Maurice the fief of Archebold and the land of Aeyain, son of Seisill, and the land of St. Dogmael. He granted also to him the fief of Laurian, and seduced Walter Lunet to do homage to his brother Maurice for his fief which he had held of the bishops. He made also the same brother his seneschal over all his land. He gave his uncle Cadwgan a fief which is called Cadwgan's fief.'[2] The chapter of St.

[1] 'De Jure et Statu M. E.' Girald. Camb., Op. iii. 155.
[2] 'Vita Davidis II.'

David's protested, but he had stolen their seal and the register of their lands.

At length the chapter determined to prosecute their bishop before the Council of London (1176), but he met the deputation at London before they had seen the archbishop, and promised reformation and restitution. He died very soon afterwards, and in a relic chest, of which he had kept the key, there was found, says his biographer, a hoard of two hundred marks or more, which he had put by for a rainy day. If these be true particulars of David Fitzgerald, the diocese must have suffered considerably from the episcopate of this quiet and modest bishop, who, Giraldus says, impoverished it 'more sparingly and modestly' than its other bishops.

In 1171, Henry II. passed through South Wales on his way to Ireland, and went on pilgrimage to St. David's, and offered there two choral copes and about ten shillings in silver.[1] On his return in the next year, he again visited St. David's, on April 17.[2] He reached Cardiff on Low Sunday, April 23, and attended mass in St. Piran's Chapel. As he came forth and was mounting his horse to go on his journey, a man of a fair complexion with a round tonsure and meagre countenance, tall, and about forty years of age, clad in a white robe falling down to his naked feet, called out in English : 'God protect thee, O King; Christ and His holy Mother, John the Baptist, and Peter the Apostle greet thee, and command thee strictly to forbid any kind of traffic to be held throughout thy dominions on the Lord's day, or any sort of work to be done, save only in preparing necessary food ; but that Divine offices be devoutly performed and heard on that day. If thou wilt do this, all that thou shalt take in hand shall prosper, and thou shalt have a happy life.' The King turned to Philip of Marcross,[3] who was holding his

[1] 'Brut y Tywysogion' (Rolls ed.), p. 215.
[2] 'Annales Cambriæ,' p. 54.   [3] 'Philippus de Mercros.'

horse's bridle, and said in French: 'Ask the clown whether he dreamed this;' whereupon the man replied: 'Whether I dreamed this or not, mark well what day this is; for unless thou doest this, and shalt amend thy life before the end of the present year, thou shalt hear such tidings of that thou lovest best in the world, and shalt have thence so much trouble, that it shall last for all the rest of thy life.' The King then put spurs to his horse, and rode a little way, as much as eight paces, towards the town gate; but having reflected a moment on what was said, he pulled up his horse, and said: 'Call that good man.' Upon this, Philip of Marcross and a youth named William went to search for the stranger, but could not find him, and the King, leaving Cardiff and crossing the bridge at Rumney, went on his way in much vexation and lowness of spirits towards Newport. When the King's sons rebelled against him and joined Louis of France, men said that the strange prophet's words were being fulfilled. We find in the reign of John a common movement in the country for keeping the Lord's day more strictly, and it would seem from this story, which is told us by Giraldus Cambrensis, that this feeling was already at work in Wales in the time of Henry II.[1]

In 1176, the chapter of St. David's renewed the claim to metropolitanship. This was on March 14, and on May 8 Bishop David died. There ensued, as might have been expected, another dispute regarding the election of a bishop. Without waiting for the *congé d'élire*, the chapter met and nominated four candidates, their four archdeacons, with the celebrated Giraldus Cambrensis at the head of the list. The King was very angry at the slight offered to his authority, and setting aside all the nominees, held a meeting of the canons in his presence at Winchester, and forced them to choose Peter de Leia,

---

[1] 'Itin. Kam.,' i. c. 6: Op. vi. 64, 65.

Prior of Wenlock, who took the oath of canonical obedience to the English primate, and was consecrated at Canterbury, Nov. 7, 1176.[1]

Peter de Leia held the bishopric for twenty-two years, and during all this time put forward no pretensions to higher authority than was held by other suffragans of Canterbury. His canons renewed the claim of the see to metropolitanship by recording a protest at the third Lateran Council in 1179; but Peter de Leia, who was present, did nothing in support of their prayer, neither did the Bishop of St. Asaph, who also was there. Before Peter's death, Archbishop Baldwin visited St. David's in 1188, on his celebrated journey to preach the Crusade in Wales, which marks an important stage in the absorption of the Welsh dioceses into the Church of England. It will be convenient, therefore, at this point to look back for a few years and review the history of the northern dioceses of Wales, from the time of Hervé's flight from Bangor in 1109.

The attempt of Canterbury to impose its authority upon the See of Bangor was renewed in 1120, in which year Archbishop Ralph consecrated a bishop at Westminster, who formally professed canonical obedience. This was David, a Welshman by birth, and duly elected by the native clergy with the approval of the Prince of Gwynedd. Five years later, when a contest was going on between the Archbishops of Canterbury and York, a proposal was made to heal the strife, that 'the Archbishop of Canterbury should cede to the Archbishop of York three bishoprics from his great province, namely, those of Chester and Bangor, and the third lying between the two which had no bishop because of its desolation and barbarousness.' This indicates sufficiently that the See of

---

[1] 'De Rebus a se Gestis'; Gir. Camb., Op. i. 41-44; also 'De Jure et Statu,' G. C., Op. iii. 155, 156; 'Annales de Theokesberia' in 'Annales Monastici' (Rolls Series), i. 51.

Canterbury laid claim to *both* the bishoprics of North Wales, and further gives a glimpse of the terrible depression of the See of St. Asaph, on account of the border warfare. 'Melanus Lanelvensis' is said to have been consecrated by 'Bedwd,' or Bleiddud, Bishop of St. David's, who died in A.D. 1071; but this name is all we know of the bishopric from the time of Hywel Dda. Henry of Huntingdon, about A.D. 1135, gives a list of Welsh bishoprics, mentioning those of St. David's, Bangor, and Glamorgan, whose bishops were, he says, 'bishops of no cities on account of the desolation of Wales'; but he omits all mention of St. Asaph, probably because of its utter obscurity.

In 1140 the contest about the See of Bangor began anew. Meurig was elected duly by the clergy and people of Bangor, and was consecrated by the Archbishop of Canterbury, to whom he made the usual profession of obedience. He scrupled, however, at first, to take the oath of allegiance to King Stephen, saying, 'There is a man of great religiousness among us, whom I hold as my spiritual father, and who was the archdeacon of David, my predecessor, and he has forbidden me to take this oath.' But he seems to have been easily induced to waive this scruple.

Unfortunately for him, the princes of North Wales, Owen Gwynedd and Cadwalader, were more tenacious of their liberties, and they called upon Bishop Bernard of St. David's, who had shortly before applied to Pope Innocent II. for a pall, and therefore might be supposed to be a champion of the liberties of the Welsh Church, to meet them at Aberdyfi on All Saints' Day, to oppose Meurig, who 'had entered the church of St. Daniel, not by the door, but by some other way, like a thief.' The chapter of St. David's, in a statement laid before Pope Eugenius III. a few years later, complained of three consecrations of Welsh bishops by Archbishop Theobald, and asserted that Meurig had removed the staff and ring from the church by stealth.

The times were in truth very unpleasant for Canterbury nominees, for Owen Gwynedd was a very sturdy upholder of national liberties. In 1143 the See of St. Asaph succumbed to Canterbury, when Gilbert was consecrated as its bishop by Archbishop Theobald, and made the usual profession of obedience. If the letter of the chapter of St. David's can be trusted, it would seem that he was lawfully elected by the clergy of St. Asaph, to be consecrated by Bernard of St. David's, but that the captivity of King Stephen caused a delay, which gave Theobald an opportunity of advancing and enforcing his claim. But the letters of the St. David's clergy give a very one-sided account of all the events with which the claims of their see are concerned. If Gilbert were lawfully elected by the chapter of St. Asaph, it must have been with the consent of Owen Gwynedd, who at that time was in full possession of St. Asaph, and who captured the castle of Mold in the following year. In 1152 Gilbert was succeeded by the celebrated Geoffrey of Monmouth, who also was consecrated by Archbishop Theobald, but who never ventured to go to his see, and who died in 1154 at Llandaff. The next Bishop of St. Asaph was Richard, and he was followed by Bishop Godfrey, who was driven away from his diocese by 'poverty and the hostility of the Welsh,' somewhere about A.D. 1164, and finally resigned his bishopric at the Council of Westminster, in 1175. His successor, Adam, was an Englishman, a canon of Paris, and a disciple of the celebrated Peter Lombard, whose cause he pleaded at the Third Lateran Council in 1179. He died, far away from his diocese, at Oxford, in 1180, after which no bishop was appointed for about three years. After this interval, a certain John was consecrated bishop at Angers, and on his death in 1186, Reiner was appointed in his stead.

The See of Bangor was even in worse case than that of St. Asaph, for, after the death of Bishop Meurig in 1161, a controversy about the see raged for sixteen years. Owen Gwynedd would not receive a bishop consecrated by the Archbishop of Canterbury, and Archbishop Thomas (commonly called Becket), with the full approval of the Pope, refused to acknowledge any other. Owen proposed to Archbishop Thomas, about A.D. 1165, during the exile of the latter, that he should permit a bishop to be consecrated by some other than himself, on the condition that he should profess obedience to the See of Canterbury. The archbishop, however, took umbrage at the suggestion of Owen that the See of Bangor was not subject of right to Canterbury, but only of its own free will, and refused to agree to the suspicious compromise. The clergy of Bangor then took a new step, which might have been fraught with many important consequences. Having failed in their attempt to evade the archbishop's authority by a crafty compromise, and probably suspecting the foreign prelate of St. David's, they sought for a new metropolitan in the sister Church of Ireland. This was enough to provoke the anger of a milder-mannered man than Archbishop Thomas. He got the Pope to issue a mandate to the clergy of Bangor to elect a bishop within two months. The Pope also complained that in the election of an archdeacon, son had succeeded father, as if by hereditary right, and held his office without the consent of the archbishop, and in consequence thereof he formally quashed the election. But Owen and the clergy of Bangor heeded neither Pope nor archbishop, and continued their attempt to find a new metropolitan in Ireland. It would appear also, from the complaints of Archbishop Thomas, that Owen bound the clergy by an oath not to elect anyone but his nominee, a pledge from which the Pope offered to free them. Both Pope and archbishop also thundered against the rebellious Owen on account of his marriage with his cousin, which, by the Latin usages, was considered incest. When Baldwin afterwards made his progress through Wales, he found the tombs of Owen and his brother Cadwalader before the high altar of Bangor Cathedral, and admonished the bishop to seize a proper opportunity of removing Owen's body, because, on account of his marriage, ' he had died excommunicated by the blessed martyr, St. Thomas '[1]—an injunction which was secretly carried out.

Whether a Bishop of Bangor was consecrated in Ireland is not quite certain, although from one passage in a letter of the archbishop's it seems very probable; but in any case no bishop was recognised by Canterbury till some years after the death of Owen Gwynedd, when Archbishop Richard consecrated Guy to the See of Bangor, after he had made the usual profession of canonical obedience, May 22, 1177.

Thus ended a contest which recalls the days of the British Abbot Dunawd and the Irish Bishop Dagan, when all the Celtic churches were united to resist the encroachments of Canterbury and of Rome. For the defiance of Rome is virtually as emphatic as the defiance of Canterbury, and the attempted alliance with the Irish Church indicates a disposition to recur to that union of Celtic Christendom which had at one time threatened Roman supremacy in the West. But the days of David, Gildas and Cadoc, of Columba, and of Columbanus, were past, though Welsh hearts beat high at the gallant deeds done by the Welsh princes and heroes. Ivor Bach, of Senghenydd, had shown what a brave man might do, by his gallant surprise of Cardiff Castle, from which he carried off Earl William, his wife, and their son, to his mountain fastnesses.

The English King, Henry II., had thrice invaded Wales, and had been thrice repulsed. Owen Gwynedd

[1] Gir. Camb., ' Itin. Kamb.,' ii. 8 : Op. vi. 133.

had fallen upon his army at the Wood of Coleshill, and all
but destroyed it; for the Earl of Essex threw down the
royal standard, and only the personal exertions of the
King could stay the panic that ensued. The second time
he passed through South Wales as far as Pencadair; but
so little was the result that the Lord Rhys overran the
whole of Cardigan immediately on his return, 'and after
that,' adds the chronicle, 'all the Welsh combined to
expel the garrison of the French altogether.'

All Wales was then (1164) in a blaze. There were Owen
Gwynedd and his brother, Cadwalader, with the whole
force of Gwynedd; there was the Lord Rhys, son of
Gruffydd, with the forces of South Wales; there were
Owen Cyfeiliog and Iorwerth the Red, son of Maredudd,
and the sons of Madog, the son of Maredudd, with the
whole of Powys; also there were the two sons of Madog,
son of Idnerth, and their whole country with them. These
princes united their armies and encamped at Corwen. A
hotly-contested battle was fought in the Vale of Ceiriog.
Henry pressed on to Berwyn; but the storms of rain
which deluged the plains impeded his march; provisions
failed him, and he had to retire, avenging himself for his
repulse by blinding the hapless hostages. The exiled
archbishop, when the tidings came to him, exclaimed:

'His wise men are become fools; the Lord hath sent
among them a spirit of giddiness. They have made
England to reel and stagger like a drunken man.'

At a time like this foreign bishops were not likely to be
tolerated in North Wales, so Godfrey of St. Asaph was
chased away, and Bangor firmly refused to accept a
bishop from Canterbury.

When Baldwin made his progress matters were much
changed. Owen Gwynedd, the soul of the resistance to
England, had been dead for nineteen years, and Wales
was comparatively quiet. The Welsh princes, with the
exception of Owen Cyfeiliog, vied with each other in their

attentions to Baldwin. But the spirit of independence was only slumbering, and could easily be awakened. Even while Archbishop Baldwin was journeying, the young Llywelyn, son of Iorwerth, and grandson of Owen Gwynedd, was beginning to molest his uncles, who had kept his father out of his inheritance. He was only twelve years of age at the time, but he was destined to renew the contest with England more vigorously than before, and restore for awhile the liberty of his native land.

Before passing on to consider the career of the celebrated Giraldus Cambrensis and his picture of his times, it may be well to note that, even in this melancholy period of Norman conquest and Norman rule, quite a third of the bishops of the Welsh dioceses were Welshmen. The brilliant party pamphlets of Giraldus have at times been accepted with too little criticism, and his assertion that Welshmen were considered ineligible for Welsh bishoprics has been regarded as literally true. Yet Giraldus confesses that he himself was offered the bishoprics of Llandaff and Bangor, and the real reason for his exclusion from St. David's was probably not so much his Welsh blood or his connection with the Welsh princes, to which he attributes it, as his well-known ambition of erecting St. David's into a metropolitan see independent of Canterbury. His uncle, David, who was as much a Welshman as himself, and the son of Nest, had been permitted to hold the same bishopric, but then he was known to be a man of quiet disposition, who would be quite contented if he could enrich himself, and would not be likely to disturb either King or primate with visionary schemes. Undoubtedly St. David's held a peculiar position among Welsh bishoprics, for it had somehow gained the reputation of being the premier see, and so there may have been, in the case of this particular bishopric, a general fear on the part of the Crown of putting it in Welsh hands, lest it might at some time prove a snare to the ambition of its holder. But there was certainly no attempt to enforce a Norman monopoly throughout the whole of the Welsh Church.

The Norman kings and Henry II. cared little, probably, for the character of their nominees, or for the real interests of the Welsh dioceses; but they cared a great deal for the security of their authority over Wales, and their appointments were made solely in the interest of that authority. If there was a Welshman who would serve their purpose, they appointed him; if not, they appointed an alien. But they certainly did not uniformly reject Welshmen and only nominate Normans or other aliens. Though Giraldus was not allowed to hold St. David's, yet, as we have seen, another great writer and a better Welshman than he, Gruffydd ap Arthur, better known as Geoffrey of Monmouth, was consecrated by the Archbishop of Canterbury to the See of St. Asaph. The first Norman nominee to the See of Bangor, Hervé, was a Breton by race, and it is probable that his appointment was partly due to this fact, as a kinsman in race and language might be considered more acceptable to the Welsh than a Norman. We know certainly that the kinship of the Bretons was recognised at that period in Wales, for Rhys ap Tewdwr sought and received hospitality and protection in Brittany, and returned thence to Wales in 1077.

The history of the See of Llandaff proves conclusively that Welshmen were not considered ineligible for a bishopric in South Wales, where the Norman power was strongest, and where there began to be a large settlement of Normans and English. Herewald, the Welsh bishop before the Norman invasion, lived until 1104,[1] and died then at the age of a hundred years. In accordance with Welsh customs, he was a married man, and had a family.

[1] So 'Brut y Tywysogion,' p. 80; also the 'Annales de Margan' (Rolls ed. 'Annales Monastici,' i., p. 8). Godwin, 'De Præsulibus,' p. 602, says 1103. See also Browne Willis, 'Landaff,' p. 44.

Archdeacon Lifris, or Leofric, the author of 'A Life of St. Cadoc,' was his son.[1] Urban, or Worgan, his successor, and the first to be appointed by the Normans, was also a Welshman, and it would appear that he also was so far in sympathy with the Welsh Church of his time as to be a married man. He died in 1134. Uchtryd, the next bishop, was also of the same nation. He had a daughter, Angharad, who married Iorweth ap Owen ap Caradoc, Lord of Caerleon.[2] He is commended by the 'Welsh Chronicle' as 'a man of high praise, the defender of the churches, and the opposer of his enemies.'[3] He died in 1147,[4] and was succeeded by another Welshman, Nicholas, who is said by the 'Welsh Chronicle' to have been 'son of Bishop Gwrgant,'[5] by which name Urban may be intended. It was not until the see became vacant on his death[6] that the first Norman bishop was appointed in the person of William of Saltmarsh, Prior of Bristol, who was consecrated at Lambeth, August 10, 1186.[7] But even at this late period the see would not have fallen to the lot of a pure Norman if 'Gerald the Welshman' had chosen to accept it, for it was offered to him first.[8]

[1] 'Book of Llan Dâv,' p. 271. [2] Godwin, p. 604.
[3] 'Brut y Tywysogion,' p. 177.
[4] So 'Brut y Tywysogion,' p. 177; others 1148 and 1149. See Browne Willis, 'Landaff,' p. 47. 'Annales de Theokesberia' has under 1148: 'Obierunt . . . Huedredus Landavensis' ('Annales Monastici,' i. 47).
[5] 'Brut y Tywysogion,' p. 177.
[6] In 1183. So 'Annales de Margan,' p. 17: 'Obiit Nicolaus Landavensis episcopus ii non. Junii.' 'Annales de Theokesberia,' p. 53: 'Nicolaus episcopus Landavensis et . . . obierunt.'
[7] R. de Diceto, 'Ymag. Hist.' (in an. 1186) in 'H. and S.,' i. 387. There was no Bishop Geoffrey, whom Godwin inserts between Nicholas and William of Saltmarsh.
[8] The Welsh bishops of this period were: Herewald (a prior appointment), Urban, Uchtryd, and Nicholas, of Llandaff; David and Meurig, of Bangor; and Geoffrey of Monmouth, of St. Asaph. David II. of St. David's was a Norman on his father's side, and grandson of Rhys ap Tewdwr through his mother, Nest. Other bishops are: Bernard and Peter de Leia, of St. David's; Gilbert, Richard, Godfrey, Adam (called Anglus Peripateticus by John of Salisbury, but Wallensis by Hoveden), John, and Reiner, of St. Asaph; Hervé and Guy, of Bangor; and William of Saltmarsh, of Llandaff.

CHAPTER VIII.

GERALD DE BARRI AND THE CONTEST FOR ST. DAVID'S.

ARCHBISHOP BALDWIN was accompanied in his journey through Wales by one of the most notable men of the time, Giraldus Cambrensis, who thus, though professedly a champion of the metropolitanship of St. David's, became an accomplice in more surely imposing the authority of Canterbury upon the Welsh sees. By birth and position he was eminently suited to be the archbishop's companion. Though he proudly assumed the name and style of Giraldus Cambrensis, he was really Gerald de Barri, the Norman, fourth and youngest son of William de Barri, Lord of Manorbeer, and Angharad his wife. Angharad was a sister of the late Bishop David of St. David's, and daughter of Gerald de Windsor, castellan of Pembroke, and his wife, Nest, daughter of Rhys ap Tewdwr. Gerald's claim to be a Welshman, therefore, was derived wholly from his mother's mother; but the illustriousness of her birth procured him a certain amount of respect and reputation among the Welsh, which flattered his egregious vanity. As a Norman he might have ranked with other Normans of good birth, but as Gerald the Welshman he hoped to be conspicuous. Clever and restless, and with no undue bashfulness to keep him down, he rose from one position to another in the diocese of St. David's through the patronage of his uncle, and in all proved himself active, not to say fussy;

yet, though he may be credited with good intentions, he cannot be said to have effected any good. Though he posed as a Welshman, the customs of the Welsh Church were abhorrent to his soul, and he gained the Archdeaconry of Brecon at the expense of an old Welshman, upon whom he brought the anger of the Archbishop of Canterbury on the score of his being married. He, at one time the deputy of the English primate as Papal legate, to bring the Welsh to better order, at another time was the champion of the national Church against the usurpations of the See of Canterbury. Too much of a Norman to satisfy the Welsh, he was too much of a Welshman to satisfy the Normans, and so both Normans and Welsh alike mistrusted him, and he failed wholly to attain the object of his ambition, the See of St. David's. As a historian, he gives us valuable information respecting the Church history of his times, yet coloured so much by his prejudices and his personality, that we are at times uncertain how far to believe him, greatly as we may enjoy the picturesqueness of his style, and the often unconscious humour of his narrative. His statements regarding earlier ecclesiastical history are often unscrupulous and false, and he must be accounted one of the chief of those falsifiers of history who have done so much to obscure the story of the ancient Church of Wales. Yet he himself could be a most severe judge of other falsifiers, as may be seen from his story how Meilyr of Caerleon saw any number of lying devils when the 'History' of Geoffrey of Monmouth was offered to his gaze. Crafty as he thought himself, he was the easy prey of those who fooled him to the top of his bent, and when he supposed himself the duper, was often unconsciously the dupe. Had he been only Gerald de Barri the Norman, he might have lived a more useful life ; had he been only Gerald the Welshman, he might at least have made a more honest and more brilliant fight for the metropolitanship of St. David's.

As Gerald the Welsh-Norman, he is one of the most egregious and pitiful failures recorded in the pages of history, though his faults, like Boswell's, are half excused by his readers because with charming ingenuousness he reveals them all himself.

There is no question, however, that Gerald had brilliant parts, and was one of the most learned men of his day. He attempted the impossible and he failed; had he been less ambitious and more unselfish, he might have done great things both in Church and State. He was besides a consummate literary artist, one of the most brilliant that the Middle Ages produced. In public life he was a failure, absolute and complete; but in literature he touched little that he did not adorn, and details of old-world controversies, that a Dryasdust would make intolerable to modern readers, gain from him a glow and colour that give them a perennial charm. It is a mark of his real genius that he was not imposed upon by the all but universal delusion that dulness is essential to historical narrative. His prejudices often prevent him from telling the truth, but he manifests them so ingenuously, that we must be blind indeed not to deduct a certain percentage from his statements. Duller authors sometimes make us their dupes because their dulness conceals their prejudices and gains them credence. But Gerald is never dull.

There was a touch of chivalry too in his character, mean and tricky though he could be on occasion. The Welsh were weak and despised, yet Gerald the Norman (after long hesitation and much tergiversation, it is true) finally threw in his lot with them, and chose to be 'Cambrensis.' Mixed as his motives were in this as in everything else, we cannot withhold from him a certain measure of respect. For he incurred ridicule by his action; the wits of the day styled him Sylvester, 'the wild man of the woods'; he lost, too, preferment, which as a noble Norman he might have secured. If we can believe him, he was offered preferment and declined it. It is one of the most remarkable inconsistencies of his complex character, that though his personal ambition was overweening, yet in this respect he was disinterested. What was Wales to him, or he to Wales? Yet he would not rise as Gerald the Norman, if he could not reign as Gerald the Welshman. Sad it is that he who could fight on a shadowy claim, for an impracticable object with the chivalrous spirit and energy of a Don Quixote, could stoop at times to acts of meanness and self-seeking, worthy only of Sancho Panza. Marvellous, too, is it, as evincing the power of the Celtic race, that so brilliant a Norman should have been constrained to take the Welsh side, even in the hour of Welsh disaster and defeat.

The history of Gerald de Barri is connected throughout with the history of the Welsh Church. As a child, while his brothers amused themselves at Manorbeer by making camps and palaces in the sand, he used to build churches and monasteries, and his father was wont to call him his bishop, and destined him for holy orders.[1] At first, however, when he was put to his books, while his brothers were occupied with their military exercises, he was rather inclined to envy them and to regret his childish inclinations, which had brought such difficult studies upon him; but he was admonished and corrected for his laziness by his uncle the bishop, and further, as he tells us, was ridiculed by two of his uncle's chaplains, one of whom used to compare for his edification *durus, durior, durissimus*, and the other (the unkindest cut of all), *stultus, stultior, stultissimus*. Ridicule availed more than the rod; he shook off sloth, and devoted himself to his studies with zeal and success, and, after getting all the instruction he could in Wales, had a three years' course at Paris, where he obtained especial distinction in rhetoric. He returned in his twenty-fifth year, about 1172, and

[1] 'De Rebus a se Gestis,' i. 1. Gir. Camb., Op. i. 21.

speedily obtained preferment in the diocese of St. David's, where he very soon began to take part in a tithe war. The people of Pembrokeshire and Cardiganshire then, as now, were very little inclined to pay their tithes, and Gerald, chafing at the general insubordination, went to Canterbury, and obtained from Archbishop Richard, who was Papal legate, a commission to act as his legate for the coercion of the refractory farmers. The Welsh of the district submitted when he returned with these powers, but the Flemings, who had recently been settled in Rhos, were more stubborn. Retribution, however, finally fell upon them in a way they did not expect, for the obedient Welsh, who were naturally shocked at the impiety of their neighbours, attacked them and plundered the district of Rhos, carrying off not merely the wool which they had refused, but the sheep as well, so that, as Gerald reflects, the saying of Augustine was fulfilled: 'Hoc aufert fiscus, quod non accipit Christus.'

Gerald did not shrink from effective action in the discharge of his commission, as the Sheriff of Pembroke, one William Karquit, found to his cost. No prophet is honoured in his own country, and the said William Karquit was disposed to set Gerald at naught. To mark his contempt, when Gerald came to the priory of Pembroke, William Karquit drove off eight yoke of oxen. He was asked three times to restore them, but refused, and even threatened he would do worse, so Gerald determined to take severe measures. He sent the sheriff word that when he heard all the bells of the monastery sounded at triple intervals he might know for a certainty that he was excommunicated. Gerald carried out his threat—excommunicated the offender in due form, and had the bells sounded to let him know. The very next day William Karquit came with all humility before the bishop and Gerald, restored the cattle, was flogged, and absolved.[1]

[1] 'De Rebus a se Gestis.' Gir. Camb., Op. i. 26.

Another act of his legation which Gerald chronicles will, perhaps, not be so much approved by the modern reader. The Archdeacon of Brecon, an old man named Jordan, like many others of the Welsh clergy, and, it may be said, like Gerald's own uncle, the bishop, was a married man. Gerald calls his wife by a disrespectful name, but what sin there was may be found rather in the evil imaginations of those who censured clerical marriages than in the married clergy or their wives. Flushed with his victory over the Pembrokeshire farmers and William Karquit, Gerald, who did not venture to reprove his uncle for his marriage, determined to harass this old man. He first admonished him, but, finding him deaf to reproof, he threatened him with the authority of the archbishop. The old archdeacon, irritated at being tutored by a juvenile upstart, let him know in pretty plain language that he did not care a straw for him or for the archbishop either.[1] Gerald was shocked, and forthwith suspended him, and so managed to report the matter to the primate that the archdeacon was deprived and Gerald was put in his place. The poor old man, however, was provided for in some other way, as Gerald is careful to tell us.

Thus put in possession of Naboth's vineyard, Gerald, according to his own account, discharged his new duties with great assiduity and zeal. Be the weather what it might, he went out in the roughest country, if duty called, and he was wont to say that it was unmanly to wait for fine weather, at least, unless one were going to travel by sea. One evening, after he had gone out on a stormy day, his uncle, the bishop, took occasion to hold him up as an example to his suite. The storm was still raging as they were sitting at dinner, and the bishop, as he looked round the table, saw that some were drinking too much, and

[1] 'Qui non solum hoc facere renuit, sed etiam in virum tantum, personam scilicet archiepiscopi, turpia verba et contumeliosa proferre fatue nimis et temere præsumpsit' ('De Rebus a se Gestis,' i. 4: Op. i. 27).

others were talking too freely and wantonly with the ladies, so he remarked, 'He who has gone out on a journey to-day, without any regard to the weather, does not neglect *his* duty for gluttony or wantonness or sloth.'

On several occasions Gerald had need of all the firmness and resolution he could muster. Once at Elvel, after the clergy had vainly attempted by various devices to prevent him from visiting them, his suite, which he had sent on in front, was attacked with halberds and a flight of arrows, and driven back in confusion. Gerald, however, refused to turn back, and, as he could get admittance nowhere in the town, he put up in the church, and kept his horses in the churchyard, in lieu of stables. He sent for help to his kinsman, Cadwallan ap Madoc, prince of that country; and when the clergy found that he was thus supported, the six or seven clergy who, after the Welsh custom, shared the church between them, came one after another and offered their apologies and made peace with their archdeacon.[1]

Very soon after this adventure Gerald had a notable conflict with no less a person than Adam, Bishop of St. Asaph, who laid claim to the church of Keri, and had designs upon the whole district thereabout as far as the Wye—another illustration of the uncertainty of diocesan boundaries in the Celtic period of the Welsh Church. Gerald was at home when word was brought on Thursday that the bishop was going to dedicate Keri church on the following Sunday, so Gerald made up his mind to get there before him. The men who had just returned with Gerald from Elvel refused to accompany him on this new expedition, so he set out on the Friday with the few he could gather around him. Next morning, after matins and mass, he sent messengers to Cadwallan and others to despatch as many men as they could to defend with him the rights of St. David. He travelled all day, and

[1] 'De Rebus a se Gestis,' i. 5: Op. i. 30-32.

at night came to the church of Llanbist, not far from Keri.

On Sunday morning he arrived at Keri, but found an unexpected obstacle in his way. The two clergymen who shared the church had gone to meet the bishop, and had hidden the keys. At last the keys were found, and the archdeacon entered the church, had the bells rung, and began to celebrate mass. While this was going on the bishop's messengers arrived with the parson of the church, and gave orders that the church should be prepared for dedication. Gerald took no notice, and went on with the celebration. When it was finished he sent word to the bishop that he was welcome, if he came peaceably, but otherwise he would not be permitted to approach. Astonished at this message, the bishop inquired if the archdeacon were really at Keri himself, for he could not believe that he had come back there so quickly, as he had only just quitted the district. When, however, he found that Gerald had really anticipated him, he resolved to brazen it out, and replied that he had not come as a guest or a neighbour, but as the bishop of the place, in order to dedicate the church. The archdeacon's messengers protested against his claim, and appealed to the Pope; but as they could not stop the bishop, they sent messengers on the swiftest horses they had to bring word to Gerald, who accordingly, leaving men behind in the church to keep it and bolt the doors, went forth to encounter the bishop at the gate of the churchyard. Greek now met Greek, and there came the tug of war. The bishop bade Gerald to get out of the way with all speed, otherwise he would have to excommunicate him, which, he politely remarked, he would be loath to do, as they had studied at Paris together. Gerald, in reply, begged him, for the sake of their old friendship, to depart in peace; and when the bishop persisted in his attempt to enter, he charged him in the name of God, and of their lord the Pope, and of the archbishop, and of the King of England too (for the diocese was then in his custody, through the recent death of its bishop), to refrain from exercising any episcopal authority there, and from thrusting his sickle into another man's harvest. The bishop then had the archbishop's letters read, confirming to him the diocese of St. Asaph, with all its belongings, and excommunicating all trespassers thereupon. Then he formally laid claim to the church of Keri, and all the churches between Wye and Severn, and produced an ancient book in confirmation of his right, and had a passage read from it, and finished by saying that, unless the archdeacon let him pass, he would forthwith excommunicate him and his party. The archdeacon replied that the See of St. David's had held the district 300 years and more. As for his book, no doubt he could write there whatever he pleased. Had he a charter with an authentic seal or a privilegium? If so, let him show it; 'otherwise,' said he, 'if you excommunicate me, I will excommunicate you.' 'I am a bishop,' replied Adam; 'an archdeacon cannot excommunicate a bishop.' 'If you are a bishop,' retorted Gerald, 'you are not my bishop; you have no more power of excommunicating me than I have of excommunicating you. The one excommunication will be as good as the other.'

At these words the bishop drew back a little way, then suddenly slipped down from his horse, and put on his mitre, and thus on foot, with mitre on his head and pastoral staff in his hand, approached with his company. The archdeacon, not to be outdone, ordered the clergy to come in procession from the church in their white stoles and surplices, with cross and lighted candles, and to face the bishop. 'What is this?' said the bishop, 'and why are these coming?' 'If you presume,' said Gerald, 'to give sentence against us, we, no less boldly, will give sentence in return against you and yours.' 'I will spare you and those with you this time,' said the bishop, 'because we have been friends and fellow-students; and I will not give sentence against any of you by name. But I shall include in the sentence of excommunication in general terms, as the archbishop does in his letter, all who strive to take away and usurp the rights of my patron, St. Asaph.' 'Publish your general sentence from morning till evening on those mountains,' said Gerald, pointing to a range of mountains in the diocese of St. Asaph that were not far off, 'we care not a straw; it will not trouble us, who are only defending our rights. But we will not submit even to this, because the bystanders may not understand the facts, but will suppose your sentence given against us and to our hurt, whatever be the form.' After a little more wrangling, the bishop, to hide his defeat, solemnly and in a loud voice excommunicated the enemies of St. Asaph, and the archdeacon, in a louder voice, excommunicated the enemies of St. David; after which Gerald had the bells rung at triple intervals to confound his enemies and to confirm the sentence. The Welsh had a great dread of this bell-ringing when it was done against themselves, so the bishop and his people mounted their horses and rode off, and the spectators, seeing their flight, raised a shout, and pelted them with stones and clods and sticks. At Melenith the bishop met a party of clergy who were supporters of Gerald, and were well provided with good horses, halberds, and arrows. They asked him what had happened at Keri. He replied with the greatest politeness that he had no wish at all to do anything to offend the archdeacon, who was a very good friend of his, and, in point of fact, he was on his way with most peaceable intentions to visit his friend Cadwallan. Gerald afterwards sent the bishop a present, and they became good friends.[1]

[1] 'De Rebus a se Gestis,' i. 6: Op. i. 32-39.

This conflict at Keri took place in 1176, somewhere between the death of Bishop David and the election of a successor. The disputed district included the south of Montgomery and a large part of Radnorshire; and, as it was part of Powys Wenwynwyn, it is not likely that the claims of St. Asaph were well founded. St. David's still retains Keri and the deanery of Elvel.

Soon after this dispute Gerald went off to King Henry II., to Northampton, and told him the story of the bishop's attempt. The King was much amused, and repeated it to his courtiers, who appreciated it highly. But Henry had heard it already from some other source, and it does not seem to have disposed him in favour of Gerald, who was soon after nominated by the chapter of St. David's to the vacant bishopric. Abilities of this kind were not wanted in a Welsh bishop. 'It is not necessary or expedient either to me or to you,' said Henry to Archbishop Richard, 'to have too upright or too active a man in the bishopric of St. David's, otherwise either the crown of England or the chair of Canterbury may suffer loss.' He did not consider it safe to appoint as bishop a man who was of kin to the Welsh princes[1] (so Gerald says), and Gerald's election was set aside, and Peter de Leia was appointed to the vacant see.

Gerald draws a very unfavourable portrait of the new prelate. It is of course a caricature; but a caricature to be effective and artistic, must preserve some of the features of its original, and Gerald was a true artist. According to his statements, Peter de Leia was an utterly insignificant man, mean and cowardly, and of an incontinent life; a shameless dilapidator; so extortionate and grasping as to be hated by his clergy; and withal frequently non-resident, and quite inattentive to his duties. Some of these charges are scarcely compatible with known facts. Peter de Leia could not have been

---

[1] 'De Rebus a se Gestis,' i. 10: Op. i. 43.

quite so contemptible a creature as he is represented, otherwise he would hardly have been nominated by the monks of Canterbury to the metropolitan see on the death of Archbishop Richard. Neither did he quite neglect his diocese, for in 1180 he began the building of the present cathedral. The charge of incontinence, too, may be merely ornamental, for Gerald is somewhat disposed to cast the stigma upon those who offended him.[1] In many cases it merely signifies the marriage of clergy, to which Gerald was strongly opposed; but as Peter de Leia was a Cluniac monk, he cannot have been a married man.

It must be admitted that in England, away from his diocese, Peter de Leia was popular. Gervase of Canterbury, who detested the 'rebellious craft' of Gerald, has a good word for Bishop Peter, whom he calls a good and just man. The annalist of Winchester goes further, and praises him as a saint. 'Peter, Bishop of Menevia,' he says, 'a notably religious man, conspicuous for the manner of his life, and the fashion of his morals, the earthen vase of his frail body being broken, migrated therefrom, to be clothed in heaven with the robe of immortality, for which on earth he endured oft many worldly afflictions.'[2] But Peter was a monk, and monkish historians were generally partial to monkish bishops. The truth of the matter seems to be, that Peter de Leia was, 'as Gerald himself once confesses, a 'liberal man,' who kept a good table and made himself very agreeable as a companion, and could on occasion tell a good story.

---

[1] As upon Hubert Walter. 'De Invectionibus,' i. 10: Op. iii. 39: 'Denique vitium simoniæ et incontinentiæ, cujus eum accusabat archiepiscopus, in ipsum refundat, astruens eum abbatissimam quandam non procul a Londoniis prægnatam reddidisse, nec non puellam velatam deflorasse, quod fama notum est ubique in Anglia. Et ad marginem glossa addit: *Nisi forte in his et in aliis de ipso confictis fama mendax existat.*' But all libellous statements about Hubert Walter are withdrawn in the 'Retractationes,' Op. i. 426.

[2] 'Annales de Wintonia,' A.D. 1198 ('Annales Monastici,' ii. 69).

Such men are often extremely popular among those who do not know them intimately, and are accounted good-natured and excellent men; but can be at times very hard in their dealings with those whose superiors they are, and can be guilty of many unscrupulous proceedings. Bishop Peter's work at St. David's Cathedral testifies that he was more active than Gerald admits; but not that he was a better man. It must be remembered that Ralph Flambard also did much for Durham, and his life was certainly not saintly. Though Gerald's picture is false and overcharged in some respects, there can be little doubt that Peter de Leia was generally hated in his diocese as a rapacious and unscrupulous ruler.

Undoubtedly he was in a difficult position, and the Welsh were not easily to be propitiated. One incident of his bishopric shows the unruly disposition of his people, and may show also the contempt and hatred of his person which his own evil acts had occasioned. Towards the end of his life he went to the lord Rhys to beg him not to disturb the peace of the diocese by civil commotion; but his expostulations only met with abuse and contempt. Not content with thus repulsing the bishop, the following night Rhys sent his sons, who dragged the bishop out of his bed, took him out of the house, clad only in his shirt and drawers, and brought him thus through a wood to take him to their lord. The men of William de Braose rescued him, and next morning he called his archdeacons and priests together, and solemnly excommunicated the lord Rhys and his sons. Soon afterwards Rhys died. This calamity seems to have brought the guilty sons to repentance. They begged for absolution; and accordingly both they and the dead body of their father were scourged; and then both dead and living were absolved, with the full assent and authority of Hubert Walter, the primate.[1]

[1] 'Annales de Wintonia,' A.D. 1197 ('Annales Monastici,' ii. 66).

Peter de Leia seems to have followed the evil example of his predecessors, in disposing improperly of Church lands.

Gerald says that when he was first appointed the barons and soldiers who held Church lands were seized with a panic, both because he was a monk, and therefore supposed to be less open to bribes than an ordinary clergyman, and also because he was reputed to stand high in the King's favour. He augmented this fear at first by persistently refusing to receive the homage which was repeatedly tendered him. At last, when he was on his way from England, the barons who held Church fiefs came to meet him, having determined to offer him a large sum of money to listen to them, and if that failed, to give up a third of their lands. If he still proved inexorable, they were prepared to give up half their lands, with all their mills, and the patronage of the churches. But to their surprise, Peter received them very courteously, and begged them to accompany him to St. David's, and there he entertained them so well at dinner, and was so polite and good-natured in conversation, that after dinner they all rode off without waiting for his answer, and afterwards he had some difficulty in getting them to do homage at all. For as they were going away, one of them, a shrewd man named Richard, son of Tancard, said to the company, 'Be quite at ease and confident. I promise you that we need never have any fear or dread of this bishop. Therefore enjoy quiet sleep, as long as he lives.'[1]

This may possibly be gossip, though it has *vraisemblance;* but Gerald can scarcely have given a false list of alienations and grants. Peter de Leia, he says, alienated the lands of Llangadoc for oxen and cows; he gave the lands of Llanddew and Llawhaden to his English servants, and diminished the lands of the manor of Llamphey for English silver; nay, he almost wholly gave away the

[1] 'De Jure et Statu Men. Eccl.,' ii.: Op. iii. 159, 160.

lands of St. David's itself for Irish gold; proving by these and like actions too openly, that he would love his church but little, and would very rarely visit his see, and then would make so short a stay there as to appear not as a fixed star but as a wandering planet.[1]

The story of Bishop Peter's affability to his feudal tenants on first entering his diocese harmonizes very well with other statements of Gerald in a letter to the chapter of St. David's, some of which he relates from personal experience. If these are true, he cringed to the powerful and bullied the weak. One Wogan Stake and his sons plundered the churchyard of St. Michael of Talachar, and carried off two hundred sheep; but in spite of all that Gerald could do, the bishop would not excommunicate them, for he was afraid that they would lie in wait for his dues on the road to Carmarthen. All that Gerald could get from him was, 'I consider them as excommunicate.' 'But,' said Gerald, 'this is of no avail, unless publicly, with lighted candles, and with all due solemnity, you excommunicate them in the church of St. David's, or at least somewhere else, and afterwards have the sentence published, and hold firmly by it until restitution and suitable satisfaction be made.' The bishop's creature, Archdeacon Osbert, answered to this: 'If my lord were to do what you ask, he would not have a tail left of his cows and animals at St. Keven.' In like manner, according to Gerald, the bishop was afraid to interdict or excommunicate Robert Fitz-Richard, who often plundered the monastery of Whitland, or to refuse to institute his son, a child of five years old, to the churches of Haverfordwest.[2]

Peter de Leia's rapacity is the subject of much bitter comment on the part of Gerald, and apparently also of numerous scandalous stories current among the clergy. He was the first of the bishops of St. David's, says Gerald,

[1] 'De Jure et Statu M. E.,' Op. iii. 162; cf. 'Symbolum Electorum,' Ep. xxxi., Op. i. 310.
[2] 'Symbolum Electorum,' Ep. xxxi., Op. i. 315, 316.

to go wandering about seeking hospitality both in England and Wales.[1] It is one of the chief complaints made by Gerald against the bishops of St. David's of his time, that they went about their diocese on visitations, more like archdeacons than bishops, not for the sake of discharging their episcopal office, but of eating and drinking too much at other people's expense. When they were tired of their own diocese, they would make a tour through English abbeys, and among the knights templars and hospitallers for three or four months of the year. It is a sweeping charge and coarsely expressed; but it could not have been advanced unless there was a certain amount of talk bandied about among the clergy respecting the doings of their superiors, which was not without a measure of justification. Bishop Peter, too, was the first, says Gerald, to impose the heavy burden of tallages upon the clergy of his diocese every third year at least. Many stories were current of his extortionate demands. He found, it is said, that one of his clergy had a large number of fat pigs, so he sent for him, and when he came, said, 'You will give me ten pigs against next Christmas, which is not far off.' 'But, my lord,' said the clergyman, 'I have only a few pigs, and those I want for myself and my family.' 'Very well,' said the bishop, 'you will now give twenty.' 'I am glad,' replied the other, 'that your lordship pleases to joke about my pigs!' 'No,' said the bishop; 'you'll find out before you go away that it's no joking matter; you will now give thirty.' The poor parson begged for mercy, for he had not done anything wrong that he knew of. 'You will now give me forty,' said the bishop; 'and as often as you deny or delay compliance, you will have to give ten more.' By the advice of the bystanders, who knew the bishop's pleasant ways, the parson promised the forty pigs. This story Gerald

---

[1] 'De Jure et Statu M. E.,' Op. iii. 144, 145, 161.

says he had heard the bishop tell himself as a good joke.[1]

Another priest, for some trifling cause, or for none at all, was fined sixty pigs; whereupon the archdeacon, possibly Osbert, demanded his third of the spoil, and a great controversy ensued between the two rogues about the plunder

At another time, when the bishop was holding a chapter, news was brought that a certain parish priest was dead. 'God be praised,' said the bishop, who was patron of the living; 'here comes some profit to me, for the man who shall give me most shall have the living.' This he said before all the chapter. The son of the deceased came the same day, and gave the bishop twelve fine fat oxen, and got the living. But when he was coming out of the bishop's room that evening with the paper of institution in his hand, the archdeacon met him and snatched it away, and would not give it back until he, too, had the promise of six fine oxen.[2]

The dedication of a church was selected by Peter de Leia and his chaplains as an excellent opportunity of making money. Their entertainment would cost the poor incumbent three or four marks, and after the dedication the chaplains used to carry off the linen cloths, napkins, and vessels of the church, and leave the altars and the walls stripped and bare. The bishop's servants, too, required the present of a bull, and on one occasion when this was not paid as usual, the bishop interdicted

---

[1] 'De Jure et Statu,' pp. 137, 138: Op. iii. 138. The name of the bishop is not mentioned, but the context shows that Peter de Leia is meant, as another story is here told of the same bishop which elsewhere is told of Peter de Leia. Gerald tells this story again in 'Gemma Ecclesiastica,' ii.: Op. ii. 330, and adds that he heard the bishop tell it himself.

[2] 'De Jure et Statu,' Op. iii. 139. In Gerald's letter to the Chapter of St. David (Op. i. 330) he says that the parish was Llangyfelach, and that he heard the story in Ireland from a monk who had formerly been a prior in Gower, who heard the bishop say the words. The bishop is there said to be Peter de Leia. See also 'Gemma Ecclesiastica,' ii. 28 : Op. ii. 293.

the church, and forbade Divine service to be held in it, immediately after he had finished its dedication.[1]

After making all allowance for personal rancour and clerical gossip, such stories as these (for some of which Gerald produces evidence) could hardly have been put about, if the bishop had been a pattern of moderation and disinterestedness. It is to be feared that the policy of imposing alien bishops upon the Welsh dioceses was detrimental in the highest degree to the interests of the Church. The men who were sought for the purpose were not the best or the most scrupulous of the clergy, but men who would best carry out the Court policy and manage their dioceses in the interests of English rule. Such bishops as these were naturally more disposed to shear the sheep than to feed the flock, and as they cared nothing for their diocese, but only for their immediate personal gain, they scrupled not to alienate the Church lands and misappropiate its revenues.

After the election of Peter de Leia, Gerald retired for a time to Paris, to study canon law and theology; and on his return, he found that Bishop Peter had retired from Wales, alleging as the reason that he had been driven out by the people. This, at least, is Gerald's story. Gerald was appointed his commissary by the advice of Archbishop Richard. But this arrangement did not last long. The bishop, who was living in an English monastery, published a sentence of suspension upon some of the canons and archdeacons of St. David's. Gerald interceded on their behalf, and as he was not listened to, he resigned his commission, and appealed to

---

[1] This story, like the story of the pigs and that of the exclamation upon the death of the priest, is related to the clergy of Gerald's own archdeaconry in the 'Gemma Ecclesiastica,' ii. 27 : Op. ii. 294. Gerald mentions these customs in dedication as well known to his readers. As he states that he himself had heard Peter de Leia tell the story of the pigs as a good joke, and gives a certain amount of evidence for the story of Peter's impious exclamation, it may be that these stories were true, however incredible they appear.

the archbishop to reverse the bishop's sentence against the canons. The archbishop, who must have smiled to find the zealous defender of the rights of St. David's against Canterbury thus compromising his position, took off the suspension and excommunication. Finally, a synod was assembled at St. David's, and the bishop was forced to restore all the property which he had taken from the chapter, after which Gerald and the bishop were reconciled.[1]

The next important incident in the life of Gerald, which is connected with Wales, is his selection to accompany Archbishop Baldwin on his visit to Wales to preach the Crusade. Of this tour he has left a very interesting account, which furnishes us with most important information respecting the state of Wales and of the Welsh Church at the end of the twelfth century.

Archbishop Baldwin came to Radnor on Ash Wednesday in 1188, and there met the lord Rhys, son of Gruffydd, and grandson of that Rhys ap Tewdwr who had been defeated and slain by Robert Fitzhamon. 'The lord Rhys' was Prince of South Wales and a man of great ability, whom the 'Brut y Tywysogion' calls 'the head and shield and strength of the South and of all Wales, and the hope and defence of all the tribes of the Britons.' Rhys himself took the cross at Radnor, as did also the Bishop of St. David's and many others. We are told, however, that on the return of Rhys to his own territory, some of the canons of St. David's waited on him, and sought by every means to persuade him to prevent Baldwin's progress into Wales, and especially to St. David's, from a fear that the See of St. David's and the Welsh Church in general would in the future experience great prejudice, and with difficulty recover their ancient dignity and honour. But these representations failed in

---

[1] 'De Rebus a se Gestis,' ii. 6, 7 : Op. i. 54-56.

their purpose, for Rhys took no such measures as were asked.¹

From Radnor Baldwin proceeded to Hay, and thence to Llanddew, where Gerald lived, and thence by way of Abergavenny to Usk, Caerleon, and Newport. After passing 'the noble castle' of Cardiff the company reached Llandaff, where the Crusade was publicly proclaimed, the English standing on one side, and the Welsh on the other. They stayed the night with the bishop, William of Saltmarsh, and early on the morrow Baldwin celebrated mass before the high altar of the newly-built cathedral. On leaving Llandaff, they passed 'the little cell of Ewenny,' and came to the 'noble Cistercian monastery' of Margam. After fording the Avon, they came along the sandy shore of the British Channel to the River Neath (Nedd), which they crossed in a boat somewhere about the position of the present Briton Ferry, leaving Neath Abbey on their right. Here they left the bishopric of Llandaff, and entered that of St. David's. They stayed a night at Swansea Castle, and went on from thence by the castle of Cydweli (Kidwelly) to Carmarthen, and the Cistercian monastery of Alba Domus, that is, Ty Gwyn ar Dâf, or Whitland. On their arrival at Haverford, sermons were preached with great success by the archbishop and by Gerald, and the latter mentions as something wonderful and miraculous, that although he addressed the people both in the Latin and French tongues, those persons who understood neither of those languages were equally affected, and flocked in great numbers to take the cross.²

On reaching St. David's, the party were well entertained by the bishop, Peter de Leia, and in gratitude for this hospitality Gerald in his narrative permits himself to give one word of praise to his successful rival, who he confesses was 'a liberal man.' Here, too, as at Llandaff,

---

¹ 'Itin. Kamb.,' i. 1: Op. vi. 15.
² *Ibid.*, i. 11: Op. vi. 83.

Archbishop Baldwin celebrated mass before the high altar in the cathedral. The next night they stayed at the monastery of St. Dogmael, where they were entertained by Prince Rhys, who also gave them hospitality on the next day at Aberteifi (Cardigan). Gerald preached that day with such effect that John Spang, Rhys's fool, said to the prince, ' You ought to love your kinsman, the archdeacon, very much, because he has sent to-day a hundred men or more of yours to the service of Christ ; and had he only spoken in Welsh, I don't believe you would have had one man left to you of all your multitude.'[1] After preaching at Pont Stephen (Llanbedr pont Stephen or Lampeter) they came to the abbey of Stratflur, or Strata Florida, their next resting-place. On the next day, unless Gerald's memory has failed him at this point, or his memoranda became confused, they made a curious deviation from their natural route, returning to Llanddewi Brefi, and thence proceeding to Llanbadarn Fawr, where they passed the night, and where they were much scandalized by finding a lay abbot, Eden Oen, whose sons officiated at the altar. At the river Dyfi, they left the diocese of St. David's for that of Bangor, and then passed through Towyn across the Maw, or Mawddach, through Llanfair, across the Traeth Mawr and the Traeth Bychan, through Nefyn and Carnarvon to Bangor. On the next day, the archbishop celebrated mass before the high altar of the cathedral, and Guy Rufus, Bishop of Bangor, at the instance of Baldwin and others, was compelled to take the cross amid great lamentation of his people of both sexes.[2] After this they passed over to Anglesea, and returning thence to Bangor, continued their journey ' on the sea-coast, confined on one side by steep rocks, and on the other by the waves of the sea,' past Penmaenmawr to the river Conway, which they crossed under Deganwy,

---

[1] 'De Rebus a se Gestis.' ii. 19 : Op. i. 77.
[2] 'Itin. Kamb.,' ii. 6 : Op. vi. 125.

leaving the Cistercian monastery of Conway on their right hand. They came next to Rhuddlan, and to the 'poor little church of the See of Llanelwy' (St. Asaph),[1] where the archbishop celebrated mass, as before at Llandaff, St. David's and Bangor. Continuing their journey through a country rich in silver, 'where men delve into the bowels of the earth,'[2] they came to 'the little cell' of Basingwerk, and the next day traversed a long quicksand, not without some fear, leaving on their right the woody district of Coleshill, noted for the defeat of Henry II. Their way thence ran to Chester, the White Monastery (Whitchurch), Oswestry, Shrewsbury, Wenlock, 'the little cell of Bromfield,' and 'the noble castle of Ludlow,' and so through Leominster to Hereford. 'During this long and laudable legation,' says Gerald, 'about three thousand men were signed with the cross.'[3]

The most important feature of Baldwin's journey was his celebration of mass in each of the four Welsh cathedrals, which was done as a sign of his supremacy over the Welsh Church. This is noted by the chroniclers: Brompton[4] relates how 'Archbishop Baldwin, performing the legation of the cross, entered Wales, and in the whole of the cathedral churches there celebrated mass in full pontificals, a thing which up to that time had not been seen.' Gerald in like manner insists upon the same point: 'Concerning no prelate of Canterbury is it read, either after this subjection (of the Welsh Church) or before, that he entered the borders of Wales, save of this man only, who, on the occasion of this legation and in the service of the saving cross, went around a land so rough, so inaccessible and remote, with laudable devotion,

[1] 'Ad pauperculam sedis Lanelvensis ecclesiam.' 'Itin. Kamb.,' ii. 10: Op. vi. 137.
[2] 'Itum est in viscera terræ' ('Ov. Met.,' i. 138); quoted in this connection by Gir. Camb., 'Itin. Kamb.,' ii. 10: Op. vi. 137.
[3] 'Itin. Kamb.,' ii. 13: Op. vi. 147.
[4] 'Chron.' in an. 1187 ('H. and S,' i. 388).

and in each cathedral church celebrated mass as a sign of a certain investiture.'[1]

This was the chief practical outcome of Baldwin's journeyings and Gerald's eloquence, for most of the important people who took the cross, including Gerald himself, eventually evaded fulfilling their obligation. Gerald was soon afterwards offered, in succession, the bishoprics of Bangor and Llandaff, but declined both, as he had previously declined two Irish bishoprics. He seems to have been reserving himself for the chance of St. David's on the first vacancy.

About this time he withdrew awhile from the vain pursuit of promotion at Court, and devoted himself to his studies, and to this inclination of his we owe a portrait of one of the most charming characters in Welsh Church history—Wecheleu, an anchorite of Locheis in Elvel. He was a simple-minded, good old man, whom Gerald reverenced for his genuine piety, and he went to him at this time to obtain his blessing on his studies. Among other things he begged his prayers that he might know and understand the Holy Scriptures to his soul's health. Wecheleu caught his hand and, pressing it tight, exclaimed: 'Och, och! don't say "know," but "keep"; vain—vain is it to know unless you keep.' Gerald was much struck by the remark, coming, as it did, from a simple and ignorant man. He burst into tears and begged him to pray that he might not only have grace to know, but also to keep, God's Holy Scriptures.

Wecheleu spoke to Gerald in an ungrammatical Latin, in which the infinitive was made to do duty for all the moods, and there was not much heed of cases. Perhaps, although Gerald could probably speak Welsh,[2] he was not

---

[1] Giraldus Camb., 'Itin. Kamb.,' ii. 1 : Op. vi. 104.

[2] This has been doubted, but appears probable from what he says of William Wibert, who was with him in Wales as a constant companion, but had to stand dumb from his ignorance of the language, which it would appear probable from the context was used by Gerald as well as others. See 'Symbolum Electorum,' i. 1 : Op. i. 204.

very fluent in it, and the anchorite could understand his Latin better. Gerald was surprised at his acquaintance with Latin, imperfect as it was, for he knew that he had never been educated, and he asked him how he had learned it. The answer shows the simple-mindedness of the pious old man. 'I had been,' he said, 'to Jerusalem and visited the sepulchre of my Lord, and when I returned I placed myself in this prison for the love of my Lord who died for me. And I grieved sore that I could not understand Latin—either the mass or the gospel—and oftentimes I wept, and asked the Lord to grant me to understand Latin. At last one day, at my time of eating, I called at the window to my servant once and again and repeatedly, and he did not come; and through weariness and hunger I fell asleep, and when I awoke I saw a loaf of bread lying on my altar. And I approached and blessed the bread and ate, and immediately afterwards at vespers I understood the verses and the Latin words which the priest said, and in the same manner in the morning, at mass, as it seemed to me. And after mass I called the priest to my window with his missal, and asked him to read the gospel of the day. And he read and I interpreted, and the priest said I did it correctly; and afterwards I spoke Latin to the priest and he to me. And from that day I have spoken in this way, and my Lord, who gave me the Latin language, did not give it to me to speak it grammatically or with proper cases, but only so that I could be understood and could understand others.'

It is a charming story, though it teach nothing more than how God may bless prayers that are seconded by earnest attention and a retentive memory. It speaks well for Gerald that, after all his converse with Courts in that perilous age, he could retain enough simplicity of soul and humility to suffer the word of exhortation from a poor ignorant man like Wecheleu.

The anchorite loved Gerald much, and used to tell him his visions and revelations, or, if he were far distant, would send them to him in writing.[1] The sick and blind used to come to his cell and beg him to put his hand out from his window, believing that thereby they would be healed. He hesitated whether he ought to do so; some Cistercian monks had told him he should tell the people not to come, so he asked the advice of his learned friend. Gerald told him to exercise the healing power which God had given him, but to beware of spiritual pride. This veneration paid by the people was the greatest temptation of these anchorites, who could scarcely fail to believe in their own powers when everybody else was credulous, from scholarly archdeacon down to ignorant peasant. So the fame of the hermit of Locheis grew and spread abroad, until even the defeat and slaughter of three thousand Welshmen was attributed to his supernatural prescience, conveyed to the hostile English—a rumour which poor Wecheleu was at much pains to contradict.[2]

Gerald was not destined to remain long in retirement. He was soon recalled to public life, to play the chief part in one of the most exciting struggles of his time. According to his story, on the death of Peter de Leia, in 1198, the chapter of St. David's met and nominated four men: Gerald himself; Walter, Abbot of St. Dogmael's; Peter, Abbot of Whitland; and Reginald Foliot, an Englishman. These names were laid before Archbishop Hubert, the Grand Justiciary, but he somewhat plainly told the canons that the King would have no Welshman, and certainly no connection of the Welsh princes, as a bishop in Wales.[3] Gerald in return professed[4] that he had no

---

[1] Gerald paid much attention to dreams, and records thirty-one in the 'De Invectionibus,' vi. One of them is a vision of the anchorite of Locheis (Op. i. 175).

[2] 'De Rebus a se Gestis,' iii. 2: Op. i. 89-93.

[3] *Ibid.*, iii. 4: Op. i. 95.

[4] In a letter to the archbishop. 'De Rebus,' iii. 7: Op. i. 102-103; 'Symbolum Electorum,' Ep. xxvi.: Op. i. 289.

desire at all for the bishopric; a quiet life of obscurity was much more to his taste; and he would be willing to acquiesce in any suitable candidate who would not be always coveting preferment in England, and, above all, was not 'a black-hooded beast' like the last bishop. Later he took up a strongly national position, and raised the cry of 'Wales for the Welsh.' No Englishman ought to hold a Welsh see, or at any rate no Englishman who could not speak Welsh.

King Richard was away from England as usual, so the chapter was ordered to send four of their number to Normandy to elect a bishop. Archbishop Hubert, and the new justiciary, Geoffrey Fitz-Peter, offered them their choice of two men, Geoffrey de Henelawe, Prior of Llanthony, and a Cistercian monk, named Alexander. But the chapter was unwilling at present to give up the nomination of Gerald, and strongly objected to crossing the Channel. No church in Wales, they said, had ever sent to Normandy before in order to elect its bishop, and moreover they could not go, as they had no money. The latter plea decided the point, as the justiciary did not care to pay their expenses out of the public exchequer, lest he might thereby establish a precedent; so it was agreed that they should send one of their number with another clergyman to get the King's leave to hold the election in England. But before the messengers could reach the King, he had been wounded before the castle of Chaluz and was dead. They went consequently to Chinon to see John, who courteously received them, and approved the nomination of Gerald. But when John came to England and had heard the archbishop's opinion, the aspect of affairs became less favourable. Gerald and a deputation of canons waited upon the King, as he had ordered, but could get nothing but fair words. The chapter, however, met at St. David's, and plucking up courage to act for themselves, actually elected Gerald bishop, June 29, 1199. Further, they instructed him to go to Rome and seek consecration from the Pope himself, and thereby assert their independence of the See of Canterbury.

It was a bold act, and predestined to failure, but it suited well the ambitious temper of Gerald. The memory of Becket's contest and martyrdom was still fresh in men's minds, and Gerald may have hoped to rival Becket's reputation and escape his end. One martyr, he may have thought, was enough for that generation; no King could venture to add another to the noble list. He certainly knew well enough what his appeal to Rome implied; and even if his keen wit had failed him this once, he would have learned it from his friends. "'Tis a difficult and toilsome business you have in hand,' his brother, Philip de Barri, said to him, 'and withal costly and perilous; for it would seem not only to be against the Archbishop of Canterbury, but even against the King and the whole of England.'[1]

The clergy of St. David's found out before very long what the King's policy would be. Their minds were much disturbed by the receipt of a royal mandate, commanding them to appear before the archbishop and justiciary, and elect the Prior of Llanthony. If they failed to obey, they were informed that he would be consecrated without the ceremony of election. Clearly it was advisable for Gerald to act quickly, if at all. Accordingly he left Wales with haste for Rome, but had first a curious foretaste of his impending troubles, for the ungrateful Welsh, for whose sake he professed to be fighting, plundered his companion Ithenard, near Brecon, of money, horses and books, and as misfortunes rarely come singly, Ithenard himself immediately afterwards fell sick and died. Gerald, however, arrived safely at Rome, where

[1] 'De Rebus a se Gestis,' iii. 16: Op. i. 115; 'De Invectionibus,' vi. 24: Op. i. 182.

he laid the subject of his election before Pope Innocent III., and further raised the question of the status of the See of St. David's, maintaining that it was a metropolitan see, and rightfully independent of Canterbury.

The latter claim was, of course, baseless. Gerald acknowledges that the canons of St. David's used a little later on to speak of it as a crack-brained fancy of his, and of the whole story of metropolitan authority as fabulous and non-historical, and to be classed with the stories about Arthur.[1] More than this, Gerald acknowledges in his 'Retractations' that much of what he relates as the ancient history of St. David's was based upon common report and opinion, rather than upon the certitude of history.[2] His plea, as laid before the Pope, was that Caerleon was originally made the metropolis of Wales by Ffagan and Dyfan, the missionaries sent to Lucius by Pope Eleutherius; that in process of time Dubricius, Archbishop of Caerleon, retired in favour of St. David, who removed the see to Menevia, according to the prophecy of Merlin—'Menevia will put on the pall of the City of Legions'; that there were at Menevia, or St. David's, in succession twenty-five Archbishops of Caerleon, of whom St. David was first and St. Samson was last; and that St. Samson, when he crossed over to Brittany, took the pall with him, according to the sequence:

> 'Præsul ante Menevensis
> Dignitatis in Dolensis
> Transfertur fastigium.'

It would not need much historical study to upset such a travesty of history as this, and, although it was put forward in an uncritical age, it was not likely to impose

---

[1] 'De Jure et Statu M. E.,' Op. iii. 328. The comparison of Gerald's claim to the stories about Arthur, which Gerald warmly resented, originated with the Abbot of Whitland ('Speculum Ecclesiæ,' iii. 3: Op. iv. 149).
[2] 'Retractationes,' Op. i. 426.

upon the keen intellect of Pope Innocent.[1] It is, however, worth preserving here, as a specimen of the fictions whereby the perverse ingenuity of mankind has obscured the history of the early Welsh Church. The earliest known use of the term 'archbishop' for the head of the See of St. David's is found in Asser, who speaks of Archbishop Novis. As we have noticed before, the term 'archbishop' was used in ancient times in Ireland in a loose sense as a mere term of honour, without any idea of metropolitanship, and it is probably thus applied to Novis by Asser, as also by others to Elbod of Bangor, who introduced the Roman Easter into Wales. It is quite true, however, that Rhygyfarch and also the Dimetian copy of the laws of Hywel Dda claim a primacy for St. David's, but so does the 'Book of Llandaff' for Llandaff, and with equal reason. The weakness of Gerald's arguments, which he himself acknowledges, is a sufficient proof that the claim which he advanced was utterly without foundation.

Gerald had not been very long at Rome, when a courier came from Archbishop Hubert Walter with letters for the Pope and the cardinals. Some one stole them, and offered them to Gerald, in case he would like to buy them. Gerald thought it would be best to look inside one first to see whether it were worth buying. Accordingly, he opened the one directed to Peter of Piacenza, and, as he expected, found it was full of abuse of himself. To buy or not to buy was now the question, not that he hesitated from any scruples as to the propriety of the act —such do not appear to have troubled him—but he was perplexed as to what would be the more profitable course. In this difficulty he consulted John, Bishop of Alba, one

---

[1] It is to be noted that Gerald says nothing of the traditional answer of Dunawd to Augustine contained in Spelman's 'Concilia,' pp. 108, 109, which used once to obtain general credence. It is a pity it was not invented in his time, as its recognition of the primacy of 'Esgob Kaerllion ar Wysc' would have harmonized beautifully with his story.

of the cardinals whom he judged most friendly to his cause. He advised him to let the letters be, even if he could get them for nothing; for the Pope and cardinals would be offended if they ever found out that he had meddled with them; and even though they were full of abuse, it were better for him to have an adversary than to stay at Rome for ever waiting for one. Gerald recognised the wisdom of the counsel, and gave the letters back to the thief, who, disappointed of his profit from the archdeacon, sold them to the man from whom he had stolen them.[1]

The chief statement made by Hubert Walter in these letters was that Gerald had been chosen by three canons only, without the consent of the rest.[2] Hubert Walter was not at all scrupulous in this conflict with Gerald, and the archdeacon's narrative seems throughout more trustworthy than the archbishop's. But undoubtedly the election of Gerald had not been unanimous, as he had bitter enemies in the chapter who would do all they could against him. Gerald believed that the archbishop's opposition to him arose from personal malevolence, because he had previously brought about the deposition of a profligate abbot whom he calls the archbishop's friend.[3] But Hubert Walter's action is perfectly comprehensible, without supposing that he was influenced by personal motives. There is no doubt, however, that archbishop and archdeacon were antipathetic by nature. Hubert Walter was the very opposite of Giraldus Cambrensis. Quite destitute of the brilliant and showy parts of Gerald, who makes outrageous fun of his bad Latin and weak theology, he had solid statesmanlike abilities, quiet shrewdness, and plodding perseverance which made him more than a match for his adversary, for whom he seems to

---

[1] 'De Rebus a se Gestis,' iii. 18: Op. i. 119, 120.
[2] 'De Invectionibus,' i. 1: Op. iii. 14.
[3] 'De Rebus a se Gestis,' iii. 4: Op. i. 95; 'Symbolum Electorum,' i. 1-6: Op. i. 203-218.

have felt a measure of contempt. It was unlucky for Gerald that in his most ambitious undertaking he had such an opponent to contend with.

Gerald succeeded pretty well at Rome at the outset; the Pope was perfectly willing to listen to all that he had to say, and treated him at all times with courtesy and apparent kindness. One evening, indeed, he styled him 'my Lord Elect of St. David's,' and at another time used the title 'Archbishop.' Gerald was delighted at such a reception, but really the courtesy was a little too pronounced to be genuine: Innocent had found out his suitor's weak side, and was duping him with fair words. Commissions were appointed to try the questions of the validity of the election and of the metropolitan authority of St. David's, and Gerald was made in the meanwhile guardian of both spiritual and temporal matters in the diocese. With this authority he returned to St. David's A.D. 1200.

But during his absence things had been going against him. The chapter of St. David's had been cajoled or frightened by the archbishop, and had elected under his influence the Abbot of St. Dogmael's a little before Christmas, 1199. Probably they cared little about Gerald personally, for, after all, was he not a Norman, as were Peter de Leia and Archbishop Hubert? His Welsh was very possibly foreigner's Welsh, which is always offensive to the ears of a true native; besides, they did not think very much of his chance of securing their independence of Canterbury; and they would be sacrificing in his support present and certain advantages for a problematical future. So they willingly, for the most part, accepted the archbishop's suggestion of a compromise, and in electing the Abbot of St. Dogmael's congratulated themselves that they had elected a better Welshman than Gerald. True, he could not read—not even a missal written plainly in large letters—but this was not a matter which troubled them much; if he had his faults, and was aware that they knew them, he might be less careful to scrutinize theirs. Gerald had a bad reputation as a strict and fussy disciplinarian; the illiterate abbot might suit them better. Undoubtedly the crafty archbishop knew the defects of the man whose election he had permitted, and hoped that both he and Gerald would be rejected by the Pope in order to make way for his original nominee, Geoffrey de Henelawe.

The claim of the Abbot of St. Dogmael's was bolstered up by a story that after the original choice of four nominees, the canons had conferred on the archbishop the power of selecting one, because the King was out of the country; that the archbishop had accordingly, with the King's consent, chosen the Abbot of St. Dogmael's in January, 1199, six months before the election of Gerald, and consequently the subsequent election of the chapter about Christmas was merely the solemn ratification of this choice. It looks rather a weak story, but it served the archbishop's purpose as well as a better would have done.

Gerald gathered new evidence in favour of the metropolitanship of St. David's from the archives of the see, and returned with this to Rome, where he arrived in the spring of 1201. He was opposed there by one Andrew, acting as proctor of the archbishop, and by Reginald Foliot, an English canon of St. David's, who had been one of the original nominees of the chapter to the bishopric, and whom Gerald tersely calls 'the most corrupt among the corrupt, whom Peter, bishop and monk, had made canon of the church of St. David's, not by the revelation of the spirit, but of the flesh.'[1] Two months were spent uselessly at Rome, and then Gerald returned to St. David's. He found the chapter more corrupt than ever, and Archdeacon Osbert, who had been the creature

[1] 'De Jure et Statu M. E.,' iii.: Op. iii. 188.

of Peter de Leia, and the Abbot of Whitland doing all in their power against him.[1] The Papal commissioners met successively at Brackley, Bedford, and St. Alban's, and at the last place judgment was given against him. Gerald, however, appealed again to the Pope, and, in spite of a proclamation issued against him by the archbishop and the justiciary, he contrived to escape from the kingdom, and reached Rome for the third and last time on January 4, 1203.

In the final struggle of 1203 both sides did their utmost. Gerald was even accused by a Welsh monk of horse-stealing, and his horse was sequestrated by the Pope's chamberlain; but by a clever trick he recovered the horse, and filled his accuser with confusion, and the court with laughter. The Pope, who played with him to the last as a cat with a mouse, joked about the matter with Gerald in a most friendly way when they were alone together, conversing *tête-à-tête* at the Virgins' Fountain, where Innocent loved to walk; and then, after a little serious talk, asked Gerald to tell him a few more of his amusing stories of Hubert Walter's bad grammar.[2] Meanwhile, says Gerald, his adversaries were devoured by jealousy.

In the end the unfortunate archdeacon discovered the illusory nature of all these Papal favours. Innocent was a practised man of the world, and Gerald, beside him, appears like a guileless, though intelligent, child. Evidently it amused the Pope—one of the ablest that ever presided over the Western Church—to detect his artifices and to flatter his vanity. But to this amusement was united serious purpose, for from the garrulous Gerald, with all his knowledge of men and affairs in England, the subtle Italian was doubtless able by his blandishments to extract

---

[1] 'De Jure et Statu M. E.,' Op. iii. 196; 'Spec. Eccl.,' iii. 3: Op. iv. 149.
[2] *Ibid.,* iv.: Op. 249-255.

a fund of information which might be of service to him in his future dealings with that country. When the savage John offended his old tutor and drove him to the court of Rome, he little anticipated that he was thereby furnishing the Pope with intelligence which would eventually conduce to his own overthrow. Gerald knew the King well, for he had keen insight when he was not blinded by appeals to his vanity, and there was much that he could reveal in those interesting private conversations which his friend Innocent appeared to enjoy so greatly; and when the dispute respecting Canterbury arose between John and the Pope, Innocent showed that he, too, knew his man, and could deal with him effectively.

Before the final decision in the case was given, a memorial on behalf of Gerald was laid before the Pope on the part of the Welsh princes. They had done their best for Gerald during his contest, for they were quite content to use the Norman archdeacon as their tool; while he, though free from any desire for the political independence of Wales, was quite willing to accept their co-operation in his efforts for the See of St. David's. In their memorial,[1] Llywelyn ap Iorwerth, prince of North Wales; Gwenwynwyn and Madog, princes of Powys, with Gruffydd, Maelgwn, Rhys, and Maredudd, princes of South Wales, stated the grievances which the Welsh Church suffered from the English King and the English primate. The Archbishops of Canterbury (so they stated) were wont to set over them bishops wholly ignorant of the customs and language of the country, who could neither preach the Word of God to the people, nor hear confessions, except by an interpreter. These bishops were thrust upon the dioceses without election, or, if such election were held, it was a shadowy, unreal thing,

[1] 'De Jure et Statu M. E.,' iv.: Op. iii. 244-246.

held in England in one of the King's chambers, where the chapters were forced to elect most unworthy clerics. The bishops thus imposed came with an innate hatred to attack the persons of the Welsh, and not to seek the gain of souls. They exercised very little pastoral office over their flock, but whatever they could get from the country they carried away into England, and there in abbacies and lands, granted to them by the English Kings (that, as it were, by Parthian arrows shot in retreating and afar off, they might excommunicate the Welsh princes as oft as they were bidden), they spent their ill-gotten gains. The lands given by early princes to the cathedral churches they sold, gave away, and alienated—a bad example, which the authors of this document of grievances (or perhaps rather their scribe) acknowledged was followed by the Welsh princes themselves. In consequence thereof the Welsh cathedrals were reduced to extreme misery and poverty. Moreover, whenever the English attacked Wales, the Archbishops of Canterbury laid the country under an interdict, and excommunicated its princes and people, who were only fighting for their liberty; and ordered the bishops to issue the same excommunications, so that all who fell fighting for Wales died excommunicate. Wherefore the petitioners prayed the Pope to relieve them from this undeserved slavery.

The woes of Wales made little impression upon the mind of Innocent. His one great and mastering ambition was to increase the power of the Papacy, whereby he considered with all sincerity that he would likewise increase the efficiency of the Church; but, as his history makes abundantly manifest, he had no respect for the rights of nations, and, with all his keenness of intellect, never understood what justice was. In him, as in one of its highest representatives, the faults of the Papacy are writ large on the page of history. His decision was in full accordance with his policy and character. It was pronounced on April 15, 1203. Innocent quashed the election of Gerald, because the Abbot of St. Dogmael's had been previously elected by the archbishop, according to the archbishop's story, which he accepted as true; and he also quashed the abbot's election because the chapter, according to the same story, had conferred a power upon the archbishop, which in the Pope's judgment they were incompetent to confer. A fresh election would therefore have to take place. The question of the status of St. David's was left undecided, and was never raised again at Rome. Such was the futile ending of this tedious suit, which exhibits in the pages of Gerald a miserable spectacle of bribery, fraud, violence, and cowardice on the part alike of disputants, witnesses, and judges, such as is extremely discreditable to the Church of the thirteenth century, and to human nature itself.

The hands set to the Welsh memorial to Innocent are the hands of the Welsh princes; but the voice is the voice of Gerald. Yet, if it be accepted as a fair picture of the condition of the Welsh dioceses since the appointment of Bishop Bernard, and with some deductions it may, it follows that the Papacy neglected its duty to Wales at this crisis in its history, and failed in this respect, as in so many others, to justify the position it had assumed over the Churches of Christendom. Though the question of the status of St. David's was a mere chimera, and to Innocent's keen wit appeared a craze of Gerald, as it did to the chapter of St. David's, the more important matter, the right of free election to the Welsh bishoprics, deserved more serious consideration and a juster decision. But expediency, and not justice, was the ruling motive of the corrupt Roman curia, and its attitude towards the protests of Wales was one of guile and greed. The bitter rhymester, whom Gerald in his 'Mirror of the Church' quotes with professed horror, but probably with some inward appreciation, was not far wrong in his description of Rome :[1]

> 'Rome's the head of all the world, yet by filth offendeth ;
> All the body filthy is that from it dependeth.
> Rome takes men, and all their goods in its net it taketh,
> And its court a market-place for the world it maketh.
> There the votes are bought and sold ; there when all else faileth,
> He that money has at need, in his cause prevaileth.
> Whoso pleads before that court, for his wise direction
> Let him keep before his mind this discreet reflection :
> If he give no gold away, nought avails the sinner ;
> He who pays of money most, he will be the winner.
> Romans hold in secrecy every chapter meeting,
> Then, when suitors meet the court, hand with hand is greeting ;
> Give, it will be given to thee if thou dip the deepest ;
> With what measure thou dost sow, with the same thou reapest.
> When thou comest to the Pope, then remember, prithee,
> He will never hear the poor ; money carry with thee.
> *Papa*,—if you scan the word, nothing can be neater,
> For *papare* means "to eat" ; he will be the eater ;
> If you seek the root in French, it is almost better,
> *Paez, paez*, you must pay, 'tis nearly to the letter.'[2]

---

[1] The verses were written by Gerald's friend, Walter Mapes, Archdeacon of Oxford, and himself half Welsh, being the son of Blondil de Mapes, who came into Glamorgan with Robert Fitzhamon, and married Flur, daughter and heiress of Gweirydd ap Seisyllt, lord of Llancarfan. Walter built the present church of Llancarfan. Archdeacon Walter puts the verses in the mouth of his gluttonous bishop, Golias. As Gerald doubtless knew who was the author of the verses, his anger is almost certainly a pretence.

[2] I have ventured to translate as above, omitting a few lines. The passage, as it occurs in Gerald, 'Speculum Ecclesiae,' iv. : Op. iv. 292, is as follows :

> 'Roma mundi caput est sed nil capit mundum ;
> Quod pendet a capite totum est immundum.
> Trahit enim vitium primum in secundum,
> Et de fundo redolet quod est juxta fundum.
> Roma capit singulos et res singulorum.
> Romanorum curia non est nisi forum.
> Ibi sunt venalia jura senatorum,
> Et solvit contraria copia nummorum.
> In hoc consistorio siquis causam regat
> Suam vel alterius, hoc in primis legat ;
> Nisi det pecuniam Roma totum negat,
> Qui plus dat pecuniae melius allegat.
> Romani capitulum habent in secretis
> Ut petentes audiant manibus repletis ;

The rhymes, which were written by a Welshman, seem exceedingly apt, when we read the details of the Welsh suit at the court of Rome before Innocent. Gerald at first had presented the Pope with copies of his own books, saying, rather awkwardly, that 'others presented pounds, but he his publications.'[1] We are not told whether Innocent blushed at such a compliment: probably not, for the wily Italian knew how to conceal his feelings under a courteous smile. He professed to be exceedingly pleased with the present; and Gerald was happy in the belief that he took his books to bed with him, and that from one, the 'Gemma Sacerdotalis,' he could not be parted. But Gerald had to offer more than his books if he would gain a favourable hearing; and so he told the Pope that if St. David's were made independent of Canterbury and subject only to Rome, the Welsh would freely pay him Peter's pence for every house, amounting to more than 200 marks per annum; and that Rome should also receive the great tithes, amounting to more than 3,000 marks.[2] But the archbishop also bid high, and of the rival suitors, the arch-

> Dabis aut non dabitur ; petunt quando petis ;
> Qua mensura seminas et eadem metis.
> Cum ad papam veneris habe pro constanti
> Non est locus pauperi, soli favet danti ;
> Et si munus praestitum non sit aliquanti
> Respondet haec tibia non est mihi tanti.
> Papa, si rem tangimus, nomen habet a re,
> Quicquid habent alii solus vult papare.
> Vel si verbum Gallicum vis apocopare,
> Paez, Paez, dit le mot; si vis impetrare.'

Gerald adds that the author of these lines deserved not only hanging, but burning. Yet he quotes them all the same. As Mr. Henry Owen ('Gerald the Welshman,' p. 178) suggests respecting his professed ignorance of their authorship, it was 'only his fun.' The whole poem of Mapes is contained in Wright's ed. of 'Poems of Walter Mapes,' pp. 36-39.

[1] 'De Rebus a se Gestis,' iii. 18 : Op. i. 119.   'Praesentant vobis alii libras, sed nos libros.'

[2] 'De Jure et Statu M. E.,' ii. : Op. iii. 175.

bishop seemed to be more likely to be in a position to perform his promises.

With all Gerald's faults, it is impossible to withhold from him a measure of sympathy. He was duped by the Pope, betrayed by the clergy of St. David's, persecuted by the court, his revenues were seized, his friends forbidden to harbour him, yet he persisted in his suit, and journeyed to and fro, from St. David's to Rome, and from Rome to St. David's, with indomitable energy. Had there been any fairness in the Papal court, his election would have been confirmed, and the right of free election to Welsh bishoprics maintained; but as bribery and expediency prevailed, the Pope pretended to believe the plainly trumped-up story of the previous election of the Abbot of St. Dogmael's. If Gerald was not quite honest in his manner of carrying on the struggle, he is less to be blamed, because of the inconceivable corruption and venality of all with whom he had to do.

At the same time that Gerald was fighting his cause at Rome, there was another Welsh claimant at the Papal court, who had been elected to the See of Bangor. Bishop Guy died in 1191, and for some years afterwards the see had remained vacant, probably through some dispute, of which no record has been preserved. At last Alan was appointed, and professed canonical obedience to Canterbury on April 16, 1195. But a little more than a year after his appointment Alan died, and there ensued a contest between the sub-prior of Aberconway, who was the choice of the clergy, and Robert of Shrewsbury, who was foisted into the see by the indefatigable foe of Welsh nationality, Archbishop Hubert. The sub-prior, whose name is unknown, was a Welshman, and was warmly supported at Rome by Gerald, who, however, found him grievously lacking in spirit and boldness. It is not, therefore, surprising that his claims were set aside by Innocent, and that in this case also the rights of the Welsh Church were sacrificed by the Papacy.

Gerald returned from Rome a bitterly disappointed man. He found everything in confusion at his home, and at St. David's all the houses were shut against him, and no one ventured to speak to him but a poor widow.[1] The election of a Bishop of St. David's took place finally at Waltham in the presence of the archbishop, and after a long discussion the archbishop's nominee, Geoffrey de Henelawe, was elected on November 10, 1203. Gerald at first threatened to appeal, but as upon reflection he saw the futility of this course, he afterwards gave in, to the surprise of everyone. He now made his peace with the archbishop and the King, and was compensated for his losses. He retired from the archdeaconry of Brecknock in favour of his nephew, and henceforth devoted himself chiefly to his studies and literary pursuits. The date of his death is uncertain, but we know that at the age of seventy he was still busy with literary work.

[1] 'De Jure et Statu M. E.' vi.: Op. iii. 312.

CHAPTER IX.

THE CONDITION OF THE CHURCH IN THE AGE OF GERALD DE BARRI.

NEXT to the ambition of Giraldus Cambrensis to be metropolitan of the Welsh Church was his desire to be a religious reformer. The most notable evidence of this is his 'Gemma Ecclesiastica,' which is addressed to the clergy of his archdeaconry of Brecon, and contains numerous rules for their guidance in the conduct of Divine service and their other ministrations, as well as earnest denunciations of various sins and abuses that prevailed in the Welsh dioceses. It is one of the most valuable works of its author, and manifests to us what might otherwise appear doubtful, that Gerald was not animated in his actions by personal ambition only, but had also a genuine zeal for the glory of God. With much superstition, such as is to be expected from its age, it contains also much genuine common-sense and evidence of statesmanlike ability. There was little either in Church or State that could escape the keen insight of Gerald; so much we learn from his other writings, but they scarcely prepare us for the breadth of view which is often apparent in this treatise. It was written before its author was embittered by the failure of his great suit, and when he could be tolerant as well as outspoken. The precepts are supported by reasons and doctrinal remarks, interspersed with a wealth of quotations from the Holy Scriptures and the writings of the Fathers, as well as with anecdotes of all kinds gathered from all manner of sources, which combine to illustrate not only the text, but also the vast erudition of its author.[1] So rich and diversified are the contents of the book that it might well have filled the place of a clerical library to a mediæval priest. Throughout the work Gerald speaks from the standpoint of a reformer. We have already seen reason to conclude that he was no Papist; but that is in no way remarkable, for England and Wales have never been Popish; it is more noteworthy that he espied corruptions which afterwards developed further, and that he would have crushed them. For this we thank and esteem him. But the 'Gemma Ecclesiastica' is not only interesting and valuable as raising our estimate of Gerald; it gives also an insight into the mind of the thirteenth century, for which we cannot be sufficiently grateful, and it presents a picture of the Welsh Church which is unique in that age, and to which it would be difficult to find an equal in any other.

The central conception of the work is the doctrine of the Eucharist. The questions which a Welsh clergyman of the thirteenth century wished to be answered were not how he should maintain his schools against the aggressive policy of a hostile Minister of Education, or how he might best recall 'the bees' to 'the old hive,' but what he was to do if by any chance the body or blood of the Lord fell or were in any way lost; whether the host might be sent to the sick by the hands of a layman; whether the priest ought to drink of the chalice if a spider or any poison were therein; and whether any other liquor might in certain cases be substituted for the eucharistic wine. Gerald considers all these and other like questions, and answers them. Many of the rules which he lays down are of considerable interest, showing as they do the customary

[1] The quotations from the Fathers are, however, often borrowed from Peter Lombard.

usages of the day. He orders that the Eucharist should be carried to the sick through the streets with all due honour and reverence. In suitable weather the deacon was to carry a lighted candle even in broad daylight, and the priest in his surplice was to follow, carrying the host in a fair pix, covered with a stole folded in the shape of a cross. The bystanders were to pay due adoration and reverence, holding their hands before their eyes.[1] These rules, however, were laid down to guard against slovenly practices, which seem to have been rather common, for at times the host was entrusted to the hands of any layman, or even to a woman, and thereby scandals had arisen.

It is ordered also that mass should be celebrated in a consecrated church only, except in cases of necessity, and then only if a consecrated table and the other requisites could be procured. The body and blood of Christ were not to be made on board ship, because of the danger of the sacred elements being spilt; but the mass of the catechumens ending with the Gospel might be said. It was lawful for a deacon to say the mass of the catechumens, but not to proceed any further.

'The proper hour of mass,' says Gerald, 'is the third hour (9 a.m.), because at that hour the Lord was crucified, and the Holy Ghost descended on the apostles. Yet on the Nativity of the Lord it is celebrated in the night. But on festivals, when the faithful have approached, mass may be celebrated at the first or second hour, or at any hour, yet so that the mass due at the third hour be not withdrawn. In Lent and on the vigils of saints at the ninth hour (3 p.m.). On Saturdays in Ember weeks[2] about evening. On Easter Eve[3] about the beginning of the night. Private masses at any hour, that is, before the third and after the third, provided only the celebra-

---

[1] 'Gemma Eccl.,' i. 6 : Op. ii. 20.
[2] 'In sabbatis quatuor temporum.'
[3] 'In sabbato magno.'

tions be not in public, that the people be not withdrawn from the solemnities.'[1]

Gerald affirms that these were the usages sanctioned by the canons; but he admits that there were other customs also prevalent, and he does not venture to forbid them. Evidently, uniformity in ritual was not established in the Church in Wales at that day, any more than it is now. His chief desire was to obtain a celebration in all churches at nine o'clock. A priest was not to consecrate more than once a day, except that he might in case of necessity celebrate one mass of the day, and another for the dead: and on Christmas Day it was lawful for him, if he had no colleague, to celebrate three masses: one in the night, representing the time before the law: a second at dawn, representing the time under the law; and the third at nine o'clock, representing the time of grace.[2] Bishops were to celebrate, having with them deacons and sub-deacons: and priests were not to celebrate without a clerk.[3] Fasting is prescribed both for the celebrant and for the other communicants; but Gerald adds, 'if, however, anyone should celebrate after breakfast let him nevertheless consecrate, for the Lord also instituted this sacrament after the Paschal lamb, and formerly the Church on Maundy Thursday[4] celebrated after meals; but Paul first ordered that they should consecrate, and take the body of the Lord fasting.'[5]

The rule of fasting might also be relaxed when the recipient was in imminent danger of death. Gerald insists strongly that the eucharist ought to be refused to no sinner on his dying-bed, however wicked his previous life had been. Nay, even if a man became speechless

[1] 'G. E.,' i. 7: Op. ii. 24.
[2] 'Formerly,' says Gerald, 'they used to consecrate seven or more times in a day.'
[3] 'Sine responsali.'
[4] 'In cœnâ Domini.' Vide Du Cange, i. 1145.
[5] 'G. E.,' i. 7: Op. ii. 25.

before absolution and reconciliation, yet, if his friends gave their testimony that he had desired the eucharist, it was not to be denied him. So much seems to have been allowed by the common usage of the day; but in another particular Gerald impugns the ordinary custom of the Church, and indicates a desire to revert to older directions. He tells us that in his time both the eucharist and Christian burial were denied to a robber, and his body was buried underneath the gallows; but he urges that neither rite should be refused, and bases his contention upon old Canon law. Many, he tells us, were afraid that the body of Christ might be retained in the mouth of the robber and so be crucified a second time, or that the robber might keep it whole in his mouth and take it out to claim his freedom, as sometimes certainly had really happened. But he allows neither argument to weigh against the duty of the priest to save the malefactor's soul.[1]

But though the charity of Gerald would grant the eucharist to everyone at his death, he is careful to fence round the holy rites against profanation by the strong and hale, and he gives us a glimpse of the terrible prevalence of wickedness. Few of the laity received oftener than once a year, at Easter, and this because there were few who were not guilty of mortal sin.[2] He mentions the rule of reception three times a year, at Christmas, Easter, and Whitsunday, which the Church has to this day retained, and adds to these festivals Maundy Thursday as a day approved by Church usage; but he is careful to state that this applies only to those who are not guilty of mortal sin, and he most carefully refrains from any expression which might lead to more frequent communion than was usual. Rather he reproves most severely the

---

[1] 'G. E.,' i. 40: Op. ii. 116.
[2] 'Quoniam rari sunt hodie seculares qui aliquo mortali non involvantur' ('G. E.,' i. 141: Op. ii. 117).

parochial clergy for receiving not only on the Lord's day, as the more perfect, not only thrice in the year or once as the less perfect, but even every day, or twice in the day as the most perfect of all. Such frequency seemed to him to savour of the grossest presumption.[1]

That there was much slovenliness on the part of the clergy with respect to the accessories of Divine service is indicated by the rules which Gerald lays down on this point. He orders that if the chalice cannot be of gold or silver, on account of the poverty of the church, it should be at least of pure and solid tin, and that a fair and seemly pix and a piscina be everywhere provided. He points out that the clergy could easily procure what was necessary, if only they would refrain from superfluity in eating and drinking, and in riding, and clothing themselves and their households. Gerald aims here at what he seems to consider the root of all clerical evils, the marriage of the clergy; but possibly the spoliation of parochial revenues by the founders and benefactors of the new monasteries may have had much to do with the miserable condition of the churches to which he refers. Some churches even appear to have lacked office books, for a custom prevailed whereby the incumbent left the church books at his death to his sons or daughters, his nephews or his nieces. Gerald forbids this, except in cases where the church had more than one set of books, when the clergyman might dispose of all but the best set, which must be retained for the service of the church. He orders also that if on the decease of an incumbent the church were found without books or with a defective supply, or if the roof of the church were ruinated, and especially the roof of the chancel, the expense of buying fresh books, and making the needful repairs, should be paid out of the late incumbent's estate. 'For it is unworthy,' he adds, 'that we should at our death leave

[1] 'G. E.,' i. 41: Op. ii. 117: and *ibid.*, i. 9: Op. ii. 29.

those churches which have supplied us so long with all the necessities, and even some of the luxuries, of life naked and without ornaments or covering, behaving as ungrateful sons who pay not due honour to their mother, to the grievous scandal of our Order, and to the great peril also of souls.'[1] Such rules and admonitions as these point to a lamentable state of things in the Welsh dioceses in his time.

From the subject of the eucharist, Gerald turns to baptism and other points of clerical duty. The clergy are ordered to be careful to instruct their people in the correct formula of baptism, so that they may be able in case of necessity to perform the rite themselves. They were also to warn them that marriage between godparents was unlawful, on account of the spiritual relationship which the godfather and godmother of a child had contracted with each other. To prevent the danger of such unlawful unions, no male child was to have more than two godfathers and one godmother, and no female child more than two godmothers and one godfather. If many people came to a baptism from respect to the child's parents, they were not to be admitted as godparents, but only as witnesses. No clergyman was to charge or receive aught for baptism, burial, extreme unction, marriage, or any sacrament, though Gerald adds somewhat inconsistently that if anyone made a voluntary offering at these rites, but not on account thereof, such might be received: but the greatest caution was to be used, lest any evasion of the rule might thereby be permitted.[2]

Though not a rigorist for uniformity, Gerald was evidently anxious to establish decency of ritual in his archdeaconry, and we may infer that had he attained the chief object of his ambition, the metropolitanship of Wales, he would not have been slack in pursuing the

[1] 'G. E.,' i. 10: Op. ii. 38.
[2] Ibid., i. 13: Op. ii. 46.

same end throughout his province. The very caution with which he states many of his rules, and the number of exceptions and evasions which he allows, prove more conclusively than the severest censure could prove how far the customs of the Welsh dioceses differed from the established rules of Western Christendom. It is unfortunate that he has left no indication which may help us to decide whether the ritual variations to which he alludes were survivals of ancient Celtic usage, or merely instances of local laxity or ignorance. He speaks throughout as an educated and orthodox Latin churchman, broadminded and tolerant, anxious to remove scandals, and desirous, on the ground of culture, to improve away local peculiarities.

It is pretty evident that there was little of what Gerald would consider culture to be found among the Welsh clergy. He apologizes in the 'Gemma Ecclesiastica' for the plainness of his style and the triteness of his remarks on the ground that he was addressing the clergy of his archdeaconry of Brecon; and he justifies his copious quotations from the 'Legends of the Saints' by the plea that they were little known in Wales, as very few copies existed there.[1] The Welsh clergy were noted rather for their breeding of cattle and pigs and for the care of their 'housekeepers' and children than for their attention to literature. We may remember that a dignitary like the Abbot of St. Dogmael's was unable to read his missal. Doubtless they were attached to their own customs, which had been handed down to them by their forefathers, and were little inclined to welcome the enlightenment which Gerald, as a scholar of the University of Paris and a Norman possessed of Norman refinement, was desirous of bestowing. But though illiterate in his eyes, they may perhaps have had a culture of their own, to which he was almost a stranger.

[1] 'Præmium in Gemmam Ecclesiasticam.' Op. ii. 6.

Though he speaks of Wales as a 'barbarous district,'[1] it was in possession, at the time when he wrote, of a rich and varied literature. In the age of Llywelyn ab Iorwerth, who reigned from 1194 to 1240, that literature attained its acme. There was a feud between the monks and the bards, but the secular clergy, who loved not the monks, may have enjoyed the intricate and elaborate muse of Kynddelw, the bold imagery and martial vigour of Llywarch, and the varied store of odes, elegies, englynion, and simple rhymes which the other poets of the age, Davydd Benvras, Seisyll Bryffwrch, Gwgan Brydydd, Gwilym Ryvel, Einion Wann, Phylip Brydydd, Gwynvardd Brycheiniog, and others produced. But all this in the eyes of Gerald would have scarcely merited the name of literature. Yet it may be inferred that the Welsh clergy can scarcely have been very ignorant of Latin, as otherwise it would have been quite useless to address to them in that tongue the admonitions of the 'Gemma Ecclesiastica.' Illiterateness is a charge which Gerald brings against others than the clergy of Wales, and against archbishops and abbots, as well as against the inferior clergy. Its prevalence may be estimated by the number of good stories to which it gave rise, as of the priest who, when preaching on St. Barnabas' Day, confused the saint with Barabbas, and stated that 'he was a good man and a saint, but yet had once been a robber': or of his brother ignoramus who, on announcing the feast of St. John *ante portam Latinam*, explained, for the benefit of his congregation, that 'this John first brought the Latin language into England,' expounding thus: '*ante*, first: *portam*, he carried: *Latinam*, the Latin language.' Such were the stories which the wits of the day loved to repeat, and with many of which Gerald enlivens the pages of his archidiaconal charge.[2] One

[1] 'In barbaris regionibus.' 'G. E.,' ii. 27 : Op. ii. 293.
[2] 'G. E.,' ii. 35, 36. Gerald attributes the decay of the knowledge of Latin to the increasing attention paid to logic.

only, or at most two, may be supposed to refer to Wales. The more likely is that of the unfortunate priest whom his bishop taxed with the heinous crime of being a 'Catholic.' The ignorant fellow, who knew not the meaning of the word, denied the charge on oath, whereupon the bishop proved it by witnesses. and condemned him to a heavy fine.[1] Another story, which may be intended to apply to Wales, is of the priest who by a blunder promised his bishop 200 sheep (*ducentas oves*). What he meant to say was 200 eggs (*ducenta ova*): but the bishop insisted on having the sheep, and fat ones too, and the priest was forced to comply.[2] Gerald's stories, however mythical they may be, indicate a low state of education among the clergy in general, in England as much as in Wales. Wales, too, had at that time a superior native literature to that of England, so that the average intelligence of its clergy may have been greater than that of the English.[3] However this may be, it would certainly appear probable that there were many among the ranks of the Welsh clergy who were ill-qualified for their sacred office, and this indeed was but the natural result of the plunder of the Welsh Church, for a pauper clergy could scarcely be well educated. Ignorance and slovenliness go together, so that it is not marvellous that the Archdeacon of Brecon has to notice so many instances of clerical laxity and neglect.

But ignorance and slovenliness are by no means all the charges that Gerald brings against the clergy in general, and against the clergy of Wales in particular. Half of the 'Gemma Ecclesiastica' consists of censures and admonitions provoked by grievous scandals as well as by what Gerald considered the greatest scandal of all

[1] 'G. E.,' ii. 34: Op. ii. 331. [2] Op. ii. 332.
[3] Gerald's opinion of the English as a race is by no means favourable. as expressed in reply to Master Andrew, his opponent at Rome, who, however, it must be acknowledged. had provoked such a retort by abuse of the Welsh.

—clerical marriage; and other of the works of our author deal with the same matters, and at times with even greater severity. The picture which he draws of the Church is dark indeed. He himself speaks as an orthodox churchman of his age, who acquiesces in the grossest expression of the doctrine of Transubstantiation, and who had gazed with awe-struck veneration upon a blood-stained host.[1] But Flanders, where he witnessed this portent, was overrun, as he confesses, with the foul heresy of the Patari, or Cathari, who made a mock of the most sacred rites of the Church. While heretics were jeering outside, saints within the Church were weeping at their inability to accept a dogma which outraged their understanding and destroyed the nature of a sacrament. Such was Richard de Aubrey, whom Gerald knew at Paris, and who is interesting to us because he was not improbably of kin to Sir Reginald Aubrey, the companion of Bernard Newmarch, who, on the conquest of Breconshire, received the lands of Abercynrig and Slwch as his portion of the spoil, and founded a family which, from constant intermarriage with their Welsh neighbours, became at last thoroughly Welsh.[2] This Richard de Aubrey was learned in the liberal arts, and lectured to a large audience on the Fourth Book of the Sentences respecting the Holy Eucharist. He seemed, too, to be a mirror of religion and morality among the clergy, afflicting his body with fastings and vigils, with much abstinence and earnest prayers, and spending all his substance in almsgiving. Yet, when he was seized with his last illness, and the

---

[1] 'G. E.,' i. 11: Op. ii. 40. A woman, to whom a consecrated wafer had been entrusted to carry it to the sick, had wrapped it up and put it away. 'Inventa est hostia quasi per medium carne existente cruenta, altera medietate sub specie panis permanente, literis quoque hostiæ impressis, ad miraculi majoris et evidentioris ostensionem, tam in carne quam in panis specie legibiliter extantibus.'

[2] The celebrated John Aubrey, author of the 'Miscellanies,' was of this family. So, too, was William Awbrey, Principal of New Inn Hall, Oxford, and Regius Professor of Civil Law in the reign of Elizabeth; also father-in-law of the poet Donne.

body of the Lord was brought to him, he could not receive it. Nay, he even turned away his face, as unwilling to receive, saying that this had happened to him through the just judgment of God, because he had never been able to hold this article of the faith. And so he went the way of all flesh without the viaticum.[1]

Sad as this picture is, there is one yet sadder, that of the wretched priest whom reaction from superstition had driven to infidelity. 'That many persons enter the priesthood unworthily in this day,' says our author, ' I will make plain by one solitary example. There was a priest in our time who knew that another celebrated Divine service and made the Lord's body with less devotion and reverence than was seemly, and so he came to him in the zeal of charity to reprove him. And when he had rebuked him in private for many faults, last of all he reproved him for this especially, that he celebrated so great a sacrament of the Lord's body and blood indecorously, for he used for this sacrifice neither clean and white wafers as was seemly, nor even fresh and fit ones, but those that were musty and broken. But to all this the wretched man replied: "What is it that you say? You and your religion are hateful. Do you think that this bread is made flesh and this wine blood? Nay, do you think that God, the Creator of all things, took flesh of a woman?—that He willed to suffer? Do you think that a virgin could conceive, or after conception remain a virgin? Do you think that our bodies will rise again after they are turned into dust? All these things are fictions. Men of old time, forsooth, invented such things as safeguards to strike terror into men and bridle their unruly passions." Oh! how many are there like this man,' adds Gerald, 'at this day lurking secretly among us! Though not by their words, yet by their deeds many are manifestly adversaries of the faith.'[2]

[1] ' G. E.,' i. 9: Op. ii. 33.   [2] Ibid., ii. 24: Op. ii. 285.

Pictures such as these drawn from the life contrast curiously with the imaginative sketches which we sometimes see of the untroubled peace of the ages of faith. The descriptions of Gerald are as dark as those of his fellow-countryman, Gildas. The See of Rome, which should have been the protector of Western Christendom, was its tyrant, and set an example of fraud and greed which many of the higher ecclesiastics only too faithfully copied, shearing, or rather flaying, the sheep they should have fed. The inferior clergy were frequently ignorant, and lax in the performance of their duties; too often they led immoral lives,[1] and prostituted the sacred mysteries of the eucharist to the basest purposes for gain. The great religious corporations of the monasteries plundered the clergy, and imposed upon the laity, whom yet they scandalized by their worldliness, their luxury, and not unfrequently their licentiousness; and of the secular laity few indeed were not living in mortal sin. To heighten the gloom, heresy of the deadliest and foulest description was rampant in certain parts of the Continent, while among those who seemed to be orthodox sons of the Church some of the most saintly were bewailing in secret their inability to receive a dogma which shocked alike their faith and their reason; and many an unholy priest was laughing in his sleeve at the rites he celebrated and the doctrines he taught.

Such is the impression which a first reading of the works of Gerald leaves upon the mind. Further study reveals brighter spots in the picture, and, as with Gildas also, teaches us to make allowance for exaggeration due to the prejudice and temperament of our author. Gerald wished to be a religious reformer, and believed this to be his mission, so he speaks with the fervour of 'a prophet new inspired' in denunciation of the enormities of his age.

[1] If their neglect of the rule of celibacy be regarded as fornication, as Gerald regarded it.

When he wrote the 'Gemma Ecclesiastica' he could still be tolerant, but when in later life he wrote his history of the struggle for St. David's and his 'Speculum Ecclesiæ,' he had thrown moderation to the winds, had allowed *sæva indignatio* to tear his heart, and indulged without stint his bent for invective. Bluff Harry, when he 'broke into the spence and turned the cowls adrift,' would have had a warm sympathizer in Gerald had he lived in the sixteenth century, for no one has lashed the monastic orders with a more unsparing hand. Latimer and he might have applauded each other's pungent criticisms of vice, and Luther in his denunciation of indulgences probably would have found the great Welshman on his side.[1] His keen intellect detected abuses around him which were destined to be fruitful and multiply after he was dead, and his plain common-sense swept away the evasions whereby they were excused. His picture of the Church is perhaps over-dark, but there was substantial justification for most of his strictures.

If we exclude the heresy of the Cathari, the rest of Gerald's picture of the Church will apply to the Welsh dioceses. Nearly the whole can be found in the 'Gemma Ecclesiastica,' and, although the author has gathered his anecdotes and illustrations from all sources, they were gathered for the especial behoof of the Welsh clergy, and some points which particularly concern Wales are there especially emphasized. The charges which Gerald in his various writings brings against the Church in Wales may be best considered under their three natural divisions, as relating to the three classes—the alien dignitaries, the native clergy, and the new monasteries.

Gerald's condemnation of alien bishops is exceedingly severe. We have already had occasion to notice his

---

[1] 'Sin,' he says, 'is remitted in seven ways: by the sacrament, martyrdom, faith, mercy, charity, prayer. *and perhaps by pontifical indulgence*' (G. E., i. 5: Op. ii. 17).

criticisms of Bishop Bernard and his wholesale condemnation of Peter de Leia, whom he evidently regarded as the worst of all the Norman prelates, and who, indeed, f half the stories we read of him in the pages of Gerald are true, must have richly merited the title he gives him of 'wild beast.'[1] But though Bishop Peter was the worst, all alike without exception were bad. 'The English plantation of Wales,' says Gerald, 'was not one of nature, or adoption, but of violence alone. Wherefore in the episcopal office it had to all appearance no watering of Divine grace, nor did it receive growth and increase from above. All the bishops I have seen in my days transferred from England into Wales have been covetous, rapacious, yet always pretending the greatest poverty, perpetually begging among the abbeys in England, ever haunting the exchequer to obtain greater emoluments by translation or addition: and to make their canvass the more effectual, they have played the part of buffoons between England and Wales, to the utter neglect of their pastoral duties, and for this cause frequently, not to say always, have thrust themselves forward at court. Consequently all their authority and the authority of their Church is becoming contemptible among the great, the honest, and the discreet.'[2]

Non-residence and general neglect of their dioceses, alienation of the episcopal lands, simony and abuse of patronage, and extortionate oppression of their clergy, are the main charges against the alien bishops. 'Scarcely once in seven years do they visit their church,' says Gerald, 'either in person or by deputy,' and the result was that youths died by thousands without the grace of confirmation, and in many places people grew to adult or to old age, and even then died before the grace was imparted.[3] It must be remembered, however, that in

---

[1] '*Belua.*' See 'G. E.,' ii. 27: Op. ii. 294, *et passim.*
[2] 'G. E.,' ii. 34: Op. ii. 330, 331.
[3] *Ibid.*, ii. 27: Op. ii. 301.

some cases the non-residence was not voluntary, but was enforced by the opposition of the flock to their alien pastor.

We have already related the dilapidations of Bishops Bernard, David Fitzgerald, and Peter de Leia, of St. David's, and it would appear that Geoffrey de Henelawe followed in the steps of his predecessors. He made grants of the lands of Landegoph, of the prebend of Brawdy, of the manor of Llanddewi in Gower, and of the church of Llangyfelach; gave away half of the manor of Trallwng to a powerful man of the district for oxen and cows; alienated Llangadoc and Llandygwydd, and lost by his carelessness other lands in the vale of Towy, which were seized by neighbouring barons.[1] We have seen that the spoliation of the neighbouring diocese of Llandaff was due to the powerful Norman nobles, and not to its bishops, who were at least Welshmen. Probably many of the alienations charged against the Bishops of St. David's were in like manner rather the acts of the nobles than of the bishops themselves, whose complicity was involuntary and caused by fear and not by favour; but Gerald allows no excuse for their conduct. Yet if we make certain deductions on this ground from his specification of alienations, it seems impossible to acquit the Bishops of St. David's altogether from the charge of shameless dilapidation. It is worthy of remark that Gerald makes no such charge against the bishops of other dioceses.

In all ages of the Church complaints have arisen of the abuse of patronage, and at the end of the twelfth century these seem to have been exceedingly rife. In the 'Gemma Ecclesiastica' our author gives us numerous anecdotes of such offences, some quite unfit for repetition, and some ludicrous, but all alike scandalous. Peter de Leia's joy at the death of the priest of Llangyfelach, and

[1] 'De Jure et Statu M. E.,' 7 : Op. iii. 349, 350.

subsequent sale of the benefice is, of course, mentioned; but it is impossible to identify other bishops who are referred to, or to say which had Welsh bishoprics. though in many of the anecdotes Gerald appears to be hitting at men who would be recognised by his readers.[1]

One bishop used to promote his stupid and ignorant nephews, and neglect the good and worthy, and excused his policy on the ground that the latter could help themselves, whereas the stupid ones would starve unless he helped them—a plea, as Gerald observes, founded on the Apostolic maxim that 'those members which we think to be less honourable, upon these we bestow more abundant honour.' Another bishop, on hearing that a man had bet his steward a hundred marks that his son would not get a vacant prebend, gave it the son, and received the money. Others gave canonries and churches to the sons of men who had lent them money, or presented to benefices while their incumbents were still living. All these and many other abuses of patronage are mentioned in Gerald's scandalous chronicle; and although it would not be fair to conclude that the stories generally refer to Wales, it would certainly appear that the readers of the 'Gemma' were expected to be familiar with such a condition of affairs as is depicted. The era of the Angevin Kings was not distinguished for virtue, and if some of the stories of Gerald be true, the prevalent corruption of morals must have led to scarce utterable enormities, even in the ranks of the episcopate.[2]

Episcopal avarice was displayed no less in extortions from the clergy than in simoniacal disposal of patronage. Peter de Leia and Geoffrey de Henelawe had an evil reputation among Welsh bishops for their oppressions. Such prelates sent forth their subordinates, in strange

---

[1] *E.g.*, **Longchamp, Bishop of Ely**, in ii. 27: Op. ii. 302; cf. Preface, lviii.

[2] 'G. E.,' ii. 27: Op. ii. 295.

contrast to the Apostolic mission, 'as wolves in the midst of lambs,' to pillage and devour the flock. An archdeacon one day refused a present of a ram, hoping to get something greater. 'Strange it is,' said a bystander, 'that a wolf should refuse a sheep.'[1]

The clergy looked upon archdeacon and archdevil as synonymous terms, so degraded was the office, in which no Laurence or Vincent was to be found in that degenerate age. The bishop's seneschal, 'unmerciful in all his ways,' was equally detested. One day a clergyman who had lost all he had at dice, except five shillings, began in his despair to curse and swear, and promise those five shillings to anyone who would teach him how to offend God the more. 'Get some bishop to make you his seneschal,' one suggested, and all the company agreed that he had earned the money.[2]

'From the crown of the head to the sole of the foot,' from the lowest to the highest office in the Church, 'there was no soundness in her'; but the whole body was tainted with the plague of avarice. The inferior clergy had to take an oath to their bishops that they would carry all causes from which money could be made to the bishop's court, and would hush up none, even when they could easily bring about a peaceable settlement by themselves. Every device was adopted which would bring gain to the bishop: one notable means being the granting of dispensations to marry and divorces, which were used as nets to catch money. 'Whom we will we join,' says Gerald; 'and when we will we separate them. But if we stood by the limits and boundaries placed by the Lord, we should not so dispense at our will, contrary to the sacrament of matrimony.'

Excuses were, of course, pleaded for episcopal rapacity, and it is amusing to see what short work the critic makes of them. 'The workman is worthy of his hire.' Aye, if

[1] 'G. E.,' ii., xxxiii.: Op. ii. 325. [2] Ibid., ii., xxxii: Op. ii. 322.

he works; but there is much virtue in that 'if.' 'Thou shalt not muzzle the mouth of the ox that treadeth out the corn.'[1] Oh that someone would muzzle the mouths of our modern preachers, not to prevent their eating, but their tearing and devouring! The devil could quote Scripture for his purpose in the days of Gerald de Barri, as always. But sometimes the tone adopted was more apologetic. 'The times are so expensive: so much has to be spent on kings and princes, on the court of Rome, and the cardinals, and their nephews, and on legates sent to us from Rome, and again on the maintenance of our households; on horses and carriages, and in keeping up a table suitable to our dignity, that when you count up all, you will find that all our income is scarcely sufficient for our requirements.'[2] The plea itself was their condemnation; but the mention of the court of Rome hints that above the rapacious bishops was a power more rapacious still, and that possibly in his remark about the unsoundness of the 'crown of the head' the archdeacon may allude to the Supreme Pontiff himself.

One abuse of episcopal power which was very keenly felt in Wales, and which was even aggravated a little later by the policy of the Papacy, was the constant employment of excommunication. The petition of the Welsh princes to Pope Innocent III. set this forward as one of their chief complaints against the alien bishops; but when the same Pope took John under his protection, the Papacy attempted to crush all national movements for independence by the same weapon. In the 'Gemma Ecclesiastica,' Gerald mentions that the Welsh, who formerly had a greater dread of excommunication than any other nation, had grown more indifferent to it than any other, for their bishops fulminated sentence of excommunication too frequently, rashly, and without sufficient cause, and then often unwisely took it off without exacting satisfac-

[1] 'G. E.' ii., xxxiii.: Op. ii. 328.   [2] Ibid., ii., xxxiv.: Op. ii. 332.

tion.[1] It was natural that what was so lightly imposed and removed, should be lightly accounted of.

As were the bishops, so were the native clergy. It could scarcely be otherwise, for the bishops took no care to choose fit persons; any illiterate fool could get ordained; and when he was ordained there was no one to set him a good example of life and morals. Many men sought orders merely for a livelihood, and such found no difficulty with the bishops. Gerald recommends to the prelates of his day the example of a bishop of Amiens, who, when his dean presented to him certain candidates, saying, 'You can do a good act here, for they have no other means of subsistence,' rejected them forthwith, because they sought ordination for that reason.[2] But the bishops were generally men who had been thrust into their sees by royal violence, against the will of the chapters, and so were careless of their flocks, and passed their time as hangers-on at Court, and in like manner their clergy set themselves to court the favour of soldiers and patrons, to the grievous scandal of the laity. From the highest to the lowest, all the clergy were tainted with worldliness and greed, and the sacred mysteries of the Eucharist were prostituted to purposes of gain. Mass was celebrated with what, in Gerald's opinion, was indecent and presumptuous frequency. St. John in the desert, he says, though he was sanctified from his mother's womb, did not dare, even at our Lord's invitation, to touch the sacred head at which angels trembled; yet these unworthy clergy dared to receive whole Christ, both God and man, in the prison of their polluted bodies.[3] St. Mark, rather than consecrate the Eucharist, cut off his thumb, to prevent his ordination to the priesthood; but these presumptuous ones consecrated the body

[1] 'G. E.,' i., liii.: Op. ii. 159.
[2] *Ibid.*, i., xlix.: Op. ii. 136.
[3] *Ibid.*, i., li.: Op. ii. 145.

of Christ as their daily banquet; nay, even twice a day.[1] The canons permitted clergymen in rural districts to consecrate three times on Christmas Day; but by the new fashion of multiplying masses, Christmas was now kept all the year round. The sacrament became contemptible from its constant celebration; for as the Word of the Lord was precious in the days when it was rare, so the consecration of the Eucharist was more venerated when it was less frequent. 'If,' he says, 'one sacrifice of a lamb in one house, at one time, was offered to the Lord at the Passover, and was eaten whole and with haste, how darest thou, O sinner, irreverently and constantly duplicate, triplicate, multiply the very truth of the figure, especially under the brand and appearance of venality?'[2]

That these strictures were not undeserved is proved by the abuses which Gerald reveals. It might have been thought that the doctrine of Transubstantiation would tend to augment reverence for the Eucharist; but in that age, at any rate, the outcome was widespread practical infidelity. One of the chief abuses was connected with trentals, which were celebrations of thirty masses for the dead on thirty several days.[3] It was the custom for confessors to urge their penitents to have trentals celebrated, in order that thereby they might make gain. Gerald stigmatizes such profits as simony. 'Judas sold Christ,' he exclaims, 'for thirty pieces of silver; these men sell Him for a penny. He sold Him, thinking He was a mere man, and at a time when his family was in need; these sell Him, knowing Him to be very God and man. He repented, though not with true penitence, and brought the thirty pieces back and cast

---

[1] 'G. E.,' i., xlix.: Op. ii. 130.
[2] *Ibid.*, ii., xxiv.: Op. ii. 284.
[3] 'Tricenarium, Tricennale, Trentenarium, Trigintale. Officium 30 Missarum, quod totidem diebus peragitur pro defunctis.' Du Cange, 'Glossarium,' 1316.

them away; but in the Church there is no one who renounces his ill-gotten gain. Then the money was not put into the treasury, because it was the price of blood; now, altars and churches are raised with it. Then Christ was sold once for all; now He is sold every day.'[1]

The result of this practice of compelling the laity to have trentals celebrated was that almost daily a mass for the faithful had to be tacked on to the mass for the day. A synod in France had a little while previously tried to put a stop to this evil. Some contended that if one trental were completed it would hold good for two or three others, or, indeed, for any number whatever that had been undertaken, a suggestion in favour of which Gerald recalls our Lord's prohibition of 'vain repetitions' and censure of those 'who for a pretence make long prayers'; but he would only allow this remedy to be adopted by those who had taken on themselves the burden of too many trentals from indiscretion and in all simplicity of heart, not by those who had erred from avarice. The laity, too, objected to the 'aggregation' of trentals. To the question, 'What should a priest do, when asked by one and another to celebrate trentals, if he were not able to get through them all?' he answers: 'Let him say to his petitioners, "I will remember your dear ones in so many masses," not "I will perform a trental for them," unless he intend a special one.'[2]

Another abuse was the celebration of 'anniversaries' for people who were still alive; but worst of all was the practice whereby some used the Eucharist for magical purposes, and celebrated masses over waxen images to bring down curses on others, singing the Mass of the Faithful ten or more times in order that those they wished to curse might die within ten days.[3]

[1] 'G. E.,' ii., xxiv.: Op. ii. 282. I have somewhat abridged the passage.
[2] *Ibid.*, i., xlix.: Op. ii. 133.   [3] Op. ii. 137.

The clergy had numerous devices for getting money out of their people, and by no means confined themselves to trentals. Some would repeat the Mass of the Holy Innocents, or some other commemorative of the slain in order to attract the offerings of those who had lost friends in war; or they tacked on to the proper mass of the day what were considered by the people lucky masses, as of the Holy Spirit, of the Trinity, of the Angels, or of the Epiphany. The last seems to have been especially popular, as the clergy gave their flocks the notion that if they heard it devoutly and made their offerings, they would get rich—this idea being founded upon the gospel which told about the kings and their gold. Gerald complains that some priests would sing the Mass of the Epiphany every day, even on Easter Day, in defiance of all propriety of season.

Frequently, however, instead of adding a lucky mass, the clergy multiplied gospels. In France this custom had been prohibited by synods and bishops, and had been put down; but in England (and it would seem in Wales also) it was flourishing, because soldiers and the laity in general were wont to make offerings at their favourite gospels. In France the usage had been to multiply gospels and introits before the mass; in England it was done after mass. Gerald tells some curious stories of scandals which had happened in France in connection with this abuse before it was abolished. 'Once,' he says, 'a priest began the service and proceeded as far as the offertory,[1] and when a soldier who was present had made his offering, forthwith he began another mass, and continued that as far as the offertory, when the soldier made a second offering. The priest then began another, but when five masses had thus been begun, the soldier got tired and told the priest, " You won't beat

---

[1] *I.e.*, the hymn during which the offerings are made. See Du Cange, iii. 46, *s. v.* 'Offertorium.'

me this way; I have more pennies than you have gospels, and if you go on till evening I shan't leave off offering until you have consecrated the Eucharist."' The people laughed at this, and the priest, in much confusion, proceeded to complete the service.[1]

At another time a priest, seeing a great number of people in the church, began three masses in succession, bringing each down to the offertory. But as none of the people made an offering either time, he took off his vestments and so ended the service.

A third priest, after beginning a mass and continuing it to the offertory, received the offerings of the soldiers at whose request he was celebrating, and then turning to them, informed them that he had already that day celebrated two Masses of the Virgin, and so could not say a third. This clever trick was, however, surpassed by a subdeacon, who happened to be present when a woman came to be churched. As the priest was away, she asked him to read at least a gospel, and take her offerings. As he was only a subdeacon he read her instead two epistles, and told her that two epistles were always thought as good as one gospel.

Lucky gospels and masses were sometimes sought for curious reasons.[2] If anyone reproved the crafty priests who cheated the laity with such gospels, they used to say, ' It is good medicine, and drives away ghosts, especially the beginning of John.' Gerald sarcastically compares the priests who multiplied gospels in the hope of attracting offerings from those with whom they were favourites, to singers of fables and gests, who, when they saw the song of Landeric did not please their

[1] 'G. E.,' i., xlviii.: Op. ii. 127.
[2] 'Tempore quoque Anglorum regis Henrici primi, puella nobilis . . . de rege concipere magnopere desiderabat; quæ suggestione capellani sui, cum singulis diebus anni unius, Missam de Dominica in Adventu cujus introitus "Rorate cœli desuper" devote audisset et obtulisset,' etc. ' G. E.,' i., xlviii.: Op. ii. 128.

hearers, changed it for the song of Wacherius, and if this failed, changed it again for some other. In France the fashion had been to multiply faces to the mass, but in England they multiplied tails; and when so many wrong gospels were introduced the old proverb was applicable, 'This tail does not belong to that calf.'[1] But although Gerald censures and sneers at this multiplication of gospels, it is significant that he cannot venture to forbid it. He says, 'I neither approve nor forbid, but I await the prohibition of greater persons.' In the meanwhile he sought, by various suggestions, to mitigate the evil.

In truth, our author seems to have been in utter despair about the corruption of the age. Perhaps he erred on the side of strictness; he would seem to condemn all payments, of whatever nature, for spiritual work. Many things that are considered harmless at the present day would have come under his lash; it would be interesting, for example, to know what he would have thought and said about bazaars and fancy fairs for religious purposes. Paid choirs, we know, he abhorred. 'Those who play and sing in church for money are idolaters, adoring money more than God, and only sing to God for money.'[2] They were, in his opinion, like the hired mourners of the Lombards. A certain bishop whom he had heard of wanted his choir to keep the Feast of St. Stephen with special honour, but he could not prevail on them till he promised them an annual dinner and double pay for the occasion, so that, as Gerald remarks, they kept the 'feast of double pay,' rather than the Feast of St. Stephen. Such things are sometimes heard of even in our enlightened age.

The sentiment of the thirteenth century is not the sentiment of the nineteenth, and though Gerald speaks

---

[1] 'G. E.,' ii., xxvi.: Op. ii. 290.
[2] *Ibid.*, ii., xxv.: Op. ii. 289.

at times like a modern, his ways of thought are not ours, and here and there in the middle of his most modern passages, an unfamiliar note is sounded which reminds us of the essential difference which the gap of centuries puts between us. All reverent souls can sympathize with the indignation which stirred him as he saw the Church wholly given up to the idolatry of wealth, and the most sacred rite of the Christian religion profaned for greed. But the remedy which he suggests is almost as startling to a modern reader as the abominations he reveals. It is perhaps even more calculated to impress his mind with the depth and extent of these evils than the bitterest denunciation. 'To expel from the Church,' he says, 'this manifold disease, I believe that there can be no other remedy than this: if there were few churches, few altars in them, few and select candidates for orders, a selection, too, of those admitted to orders, above all especially a proper choice of bishops, and of their subordinates as deans. And the greatest remedy of all, which Gregory VIII. thought of, would be the abolition of all offerings, except three times a year, at Christmas, Easter, and Pentecost, and besides on the feast of the patron saint, and at a burial, and on the day of each anniversary or of a churching. See how in the whole of Jerusalem there was only one temple, only one tabernacle, only one altar of offering in the open air in the court of the temple. In the Holy Place, indeed, there was an altar of incense, but nothing was offered thereon except a little incense. Hosea, in detestation of a multitude of altars, said: "Because my people have made many altars to sin, altars shall be made unto them to sin; they sacrificed victims, but the Lord has not accepted them." Therefore, after the example of the one temple, in each city there ought to be one church only; or, if the city be populous, a few, and so that |they be under one greater church. For the number of chapels has caused unlawful gifts, and many other enormities, and many extraordinary abuses. It would be better, far better, that churches should be fewer, and service be held in them less frequently, and then should be conducted and listened to with more devotion.'[1]

Such an opinion as this, coming from an orthodox and enlightened Churchman who had remarkably keen powers of insight and a statesmanlike grasp of ecclesiastical problems, is an exceedingly significant indication of what kind of influence the numerous chapels and their needy clergy had upon the Church and nation. If the times demanded such a remedy as this 300 years before the Reformation, it is not wonderful that when the crisis came, some of the reformers forgot the claims of archæology and architecture in a ruthless extirpation of mediæval abuses by which rookeries suffered as well as 'rooks.'

The difference in sentiment between the thirteenth century and our own is perhaps nowhere more evident than in Gerald's remarks upon the vices of gluttony and drunkenness, which were not unknown among the clergy. He says that it were better for the reputation of the clergy if they put a stop to the feastings and drinkings which they were accustomed to hold every year, at which laymen and women were present, with results that were well known to all,[2] but at the same time he allows the clergy to get drunk in giving hospitality. Such a slip he considers not only excusable, but even praiseworthy,[3] sanctioned as it was by the example of several saints. Once upon a time, he says, St. Philibert had been entertaining friends, and had indulged too freely, and as he

[1] 'G. E.,' i., xlix.: Op. ii. 137, 138.
[2] *Ibid.*, ii., xix.: Op. ii. 258. Such a meeting was called 'fraternitas,' says Gerald, which may mean a guild-meeting. Probably he alludes to the annual festival still held on the day of the patron saint (Old Style generally) in many Welsh parishes, and called Mabsant *Anglicè*, wake).
[3] 'Non solum est excusabile, verum etiam non illaudabile.'

was lying down intoxicated, the devil came to him and, patting him on the offending part, said, 'Philibert has done very well to-day.' The saint replied, 'He will do badly to-morrow,' and the next day fasted on bread and water. If, remarks Gerald, the enemy thus mocked an excusable excess, and the saint thus atoned for it by penance, how much more must our inexcusable offences be an object of derision to the evil one, and ought to be a source of contrition to ourselves?[1] But on the whole the clergy of Wales do not appear to have been notable offenders in this matter, as were the clergy of Ireland, who fasted every day, and got drunk every night.

The fault which Gerald most largely dwells upon, and which he was most anxious to correct, was the marriage of the clergy. In the heyday of his youth, when all the world was before him, and he felt himself sufficient to conquer it all, he removed the Archdeacon of Brecon for this fault and got the post for himself. As he grew older, he estimated his strength better, and no longer attempted to deprive the stubborn clergy who adhered to their national customs; he rather in the 'Gemma Ecclesiastica' sought to cure the custom by advice and exhortation. But in old age, when his ambitions were over and he had nothing to gain or lose, when, moreover, he was soured by disappointment, he liberated his full soul in bitter invective. But neither the decisive action of his youth, the admonitions of his mature manhood, nor the invective of his age made any impression upon the prevalent custom; it was too much for him; vice or virtue, it outlived Gerald, yet the protest of the baffled archdeacon is still vociferous over the gulf of centuries.

Roman canon law required that priests should not marry. The Welsh and English clergy[2] alike utterly

[1] 'G. E.,' Op. ii. 260.
[2] 'Filius autem *more sacerdotum parochialium Anglie fere cunctorum*, damnabili quidem et detestabili, publicam secum habebat

ignored that law. We have already seen that in Gerald's
own time there were Bishops of Llandaff and St. David's
who were married men. Such marriages were generally
recognised by clergy and laity alike as real marriages,
although the stricter sort, like Gerald, regarded such
wedlock as concubinage. Yet Gerald himself, in common with other thinkers of his day, was aghast at the
utter breakdown of discipline, and longed for the intervention of some higher authority to free the clergy from
their restriction. His master, Peter Manducator, in
presence of his whole lecture-room of erudite scholars,
once asserted that the devil had never invented so clever
a device against the Church as the rule of celibacy, and
Gerald evidently agreed with this opinion. He admits
that 'neither in the Old nor the New Testament,
whether in the writings of evangelists or apostles,' was
the marriage of priests forbidden; and although he main-
tains that the rule of celibacy was expedient in times of
fervent charity, yet in 'that evening of the world,' the
thirteenth century, other times demanded other manners.[1] Even the Papal See itself, he says, had been
shaken in its advocacy of the unpopular rule, and
Alexander III. had proposed to abolish it, but was opposed by his chancellor, who afterwards was Gregory IV.
'On account of the opposition of this one man so useful
a proposal of so great and so discreet a father was not
carried into effect, though our sins required it.' Gerald
holds out no hope of a remedy for priests, except from a
general council. He asserts, however, that for clergy in
minor orders, who held churches, some high authorities
had suggested that they should hold their churches as
married men, provided only that they should have

---

comitem individuam, et in foco focariam, et in cubiculo concubinam.'
'Spec. Eccl.,' iii. 8: Op. iv. 170.   See also Wright's 'Poems of William
Mapes.'

[1] 'G. E.,' ii. vi.: Op. ii. 187.

'honest and discreet vicars, to whom a moderate salary should be paid out of the altar dues and smaller tithes.' Some rigid folk urged that marriage could never be allowed in any case, because a man ought not to have two wives, and the Church was his first bride; but Gerald, with his usual common-sense, puts this fallacy aside with the remark that the Church was the Bride of Christ, not the bride of the clergyman. He had heard that even some subdeacons had obtained from the Pope dispensations to marry, and he advises clergy in minor orders to apply for dispensations in like manner.[1]

It must not be inferred, however, that Gerald regarded marriage as honourable either in clergy or laity. His regret that the strict rule of prohibition remained in force flowed merely from the impression that marriage would be a less evil than what he termed concubinage, and some of his remarks in the 'Gemma Ecclesiastica' concerning the sacrament itself, savour of the most offensive form of 'niceness.' His picture of the life of a married priest is eminently hard and unsympathetic.

'The priest,' he says, 'who has chosen to live a secular life, to his own destruction and perpetual damnation, and who has in his house a housekeeper suffocating and maltreating all his virtues, and has his miserable house crammed full of infants and cradles, midwives and nurses —how can he, among all these inconveniences, practise moderation or avoid the sin of covetousness? For to say nothing of dainty suppers and dishes, the woman will extort from him every market day a skirt with a long tail draggling in the dust and sweeping the ground, and costly robes to please many others besides himself—a pretty nag withal, that walks gently and softly, adorned with trappings and a saddle gilt with pictures and sculptures for her pleasure. I will tell you of a priest who sat behind his domestic (I will not call her his lady,

[1] 'G. E.,' ii., v.: Op ii. 186.

or even his mistress), as she rode to market dressed out for show, for they go to see and to be seen; and this priest sat on the same horse behind her, and was holding her up with both arms lest she might sway or totter ever so little on either side.' Then he tells of another priest who followed his wife on foot, and did for her the work of a groom or footman, and whom she afterwards jilted.

'See,' exclaims Gerald in conclusion, 'how precious and worthy a thing is she for whom miserable man, nay, the most miserable of all things, who yet ought to be worthier than all other creatures under heaven, in condition as in rank, thinks fit to lose reputation, honour, substance, his own soul, and God Himself, and to give himself over to the devil and his angels, to be tortured everlastingly.'[1]

In a later work he abuses the canons of St. David's, who were nearly all married, for what he regarded as their incontinence. They attended more to their boys than to their books, to their families than to their folios, to the rearing of children than to the reading of books.[2] 'What,' he says, 'is fouler and more disgraceful and indecent than around the mother Church, erst metropolitan—where holy men once lived, where their sacred relics still repose, where good angels often came—to find the dwellings of nurses and midwives, nay, of harlots, and many noisy cradles of new-born babes and crying boys, the witnesses to incontinence? Why should I say more?'[3] Why indeed! Yet he does say more, and that in a style of abuse unfit for transcription in these pages, and probably, in the opinion of most of his modern readers, far 'fouler, more disgraceful and indecent' than the spectacle which evoked from him such violent language. There can be no better proof how utterly Roman canon law was dis-

---

[1] 'G. E.,' ii., xxii.: Op. ii. 277, 278.
[2] 'Non ergo libris intencurt sed liberis, non foliis sed filiis, non librorum lectioni sed liberorum dilectioni pariter et promotioni.' 'De Jure et Statu M. E.,' vii.: Op. iii. 329.
[3] 'De Jure et Statu M. E.,' Op. iii. 362.

regarded in Wales than these diatribes of Gerald. Strange it is, too, that in the midst of an easy-going and somewhat secular-minded clergy, with no Puritanical leanings, there should have arisen at different epochs of the history of the Welsh Church such contemners of the flesh and its snares as Gildas, Gerald, and Rowlands of Llangeitho.

Closely connected with clerical marriage was the succession system which prevailed in Wales, and which, in early times, was common to all the Celtic churches. The custom of dividing benefices by gavel-kind greatly aggravated this evil. We have seen that Keri had two rectors; another church in Radnorshire had six or seven; and the rectory of Hay in Breconshire was divided between two brothers, one of whom was a layman. 'The churches,' says Gerald, 'have almost as many parsons and sharers as there are families of principal men in the parish. Sons obtain churches also by succession and after their fathers, not by election; possessing and polluting by inheritance the sanctuary of God. And if a prelate should by chance presume to appoint or institute any other person, the family would certainly revenge the injury upon the institutor and the instituted.'[1] The same feeling had also some influence in the election of bishops, as may be seen in the history of the two southern dioceses. Gerald himself was not unwilling to avail himself of it as the nephew of Bishop David Fitzgerald, and he managed to secure that his nephew, William de Barri, should succeed him in the archdeaconry of Brecon.

In various places in his works Gerald affords a useful insight into the religious customs and morals of the Welsh laity. He inclines to praise them for their religiousness, but to censure their morals. He attests their orthodoxy since the time of German and Lupus.

[1] 'Descriptio Kambriae,' ii. 6: Op. vi. 214.

Since that time, he says, nothing heretical or contrary to the true faith was to be found among them.[1]

Some of their peculiar religious customs were popularly supposed to be derived from the teaching of the two saints.[2] For example, Gerald says : ' They give the first piece broken off from every loaf of bread to the poor; they sit down to dinner by threes, in honour of the Trinity. With extended arms and bowed heads they ask a blessing of every monk or clergyman, or of every person wearing a religious habit. But they desire above all other nations, episcopal confirmation and the unction of chrism by which the grace of the Spirit is given. They give a tenth of all their property, animals, cattle and sheep, either when they marry, or go on a pilgrimage, or, by the counsel of the Church, make some amendment of life. This partition of their effects they call the great tithe, two parts of which they give to their baptismal church, and the third to the bishop of the diocese. But of all pilgrimages preferring that to Rome, they adore more zealously with devout minds the thresholds of the Apostles.'

Gerald also notices, in various places of his 'Itinerary' and his 'Description,' as also in the 'Gemma Ecclesiastica,' the curious superstitions regarding bells, books, and pastoral staves, which are so characteristic of Celtic Christianity. 'We observe,' he says, 'that they show a greater respect than other nations to churches and ecclesiastical persons, to the relics of saints, staves, portable bells, books of the gospels,[3] and the cross, which they devoutly revere ; and hence their churches enjoy far greater peace than elsewhere. For peace is not only preserved towards all animals feeding in churchyards, but

---

[1] 'Nihil hæreticum, nihil rectæ fidei articulis contrarium sensere.' 'Descriptio Kamb.,' i. 18: Op. vi. 202.
[2] Bohn's translation, which is that of Sir R. C. Hoare, is here singularly misleading.
[3] 'Libris textis.' See Du Cange, *s. v.* 'Textus' (iii. 1230).

at a great distance beyond them, where certain boundaries and ditches have been appointed by the bishops, for the sake of the peace. But the principal churches to which antiquity has shown the greater reverence extend their protection to the herds as far as they can go to feed in the morning and return in the evening. If, therefore, any person have incurred the deadly enmity of his prince, if he seek the refuge of the church, he and his will continue to live unmolested; but many persons abuse this indemnity, far exceeding the indulgence of the canons, which in such cases grant only safety to life and limb, and from these places of refuge even make hostile irruptions, and harass the whole country on all sides as well as the prince.'[1]

Unquestionably pagan survivals had something to do with some of these superstitions which Gerald mentions. He says that the people of Scotland, Ireland, and Wales were alike in holding in veneration portable bells, and crooked staves, and similar relics, and were much more afraid of swearing falsely by these than by the gospels.[2] The staff of St. Curig at St. Harmon's, near Rhayadr, in Radnorshire, the portable bell Bangu at Glascwm, a stone at Llanvaes, the collar of St. Cynawg, the celebrated Lechlavar, or talking stone, and a miraculous stone of Anglesey, are all mentioned in the 'Itinerary' for their wonderful properties. But the most curious of all the superstitious usages recorded are those connected with the festival of St. Elined, which evidently astonished Gerald himself, and which probably are of pagan origin.[3]

Gerald accounts as the chief faults of the Welsh nation[4] their inconstancy and instability and want of

[1] Gir. Camb., 'Des. Kamb.,' i. 18 : Op. vi. 202-204.
[2] 'Itin. Kamb.,' i. 2 : Op. vi. 27. See also 'G. E.,' i., lii : Op. ii. 158; 'Top. Hib.,' iii. 33.
[3] 'Itin. Kamb.,' i. c. 2 : Op. vi. 32. Gerald calls her Ælivedha. She is also known as Elevetha, Aled, Almedha. She was a daughter of Brychan.
[4] 'Des. Kamb.,' ii. : Op. vi. 206-218.

reverence for good faith and oaths; their living by plunder, and disregard of the bonds of peace and friendship; their sudden panics in battle at the first repulse; their ambitious seizure of lands and dissension between brothers; their great exaction and want of moderation; the abuse of churches by succession and participation, and the crime of incest. Of the last he says that it prevailed among all orders of the people, high and low alike.[1] Some of the marriages censured, as that of Owen Gwynedd, and those contracted between godparents, are such as would not be condemned by the present ecclesiastical or civil laws of England and Wales; but there are records in the 'Chronicle' which prove that Gerald had good cause for his remarks. 'In 1173,' says the 'Brut y Tywysogion,'[2] 'was born Meurig, son of the lord Rhys, son of Gruffydd, of the daughter of Maredydd, son of Gruffydd, his niece, the daughter of his brother.' There is, indeed, no room for doubt that such sins of the flesh and perjury were exceedingly rife in Wales.[3] Gerald, in the 'Gemma Ecclesiastica,' urges upon the clergy to reprove their flocks for their proneness to perjury, and elsewhere he lays it to the charge of the nation in very explicit terms. 'They have,' he says, 'no oath, no reverence for faith or truth; for so lightly are they wont to esteem the covenant of faith, inviolable by other nations, that they are accustomed to sacrifice their faith for nothing, by giving the usual sign, not only in serious and important concerns, but even on every trifling occasion, and for the confirmation of almost every common assertion. They never scruple

---

[1] 'Des Kamb.,' c. 6: Op. vi. 213.
[2] P. 221.
[3] Gerald also says: 'Matrimoniorum autem onera, nisi expertis antea cohabitatione, commixtione, morum qualitate, et præcipue fecunditate, subire non solent. Proinde et puellas, sub certo parentibus pecuniæ pretio, et resipiscendi pœna statuta, non ducere quidem in primis sed quasi conducere, antiquus in hac gente mos obtinuit.'— 'Des. Kamb.,' ii. 6: Op. vi. 213.

at taking a false oath for the sake of any temporary emolument or advantage, so that in civil and ecclesiastical causes each party, being ready to swear whatever seems expedient to its purpose, endeavours both to prove and defend, although the venerable laws, by which oaths are deemed sacred and truth is honoured and respected, by favouring the accused and throwing an odium upon the accuser, impose the burden of bringing proofs upon the latter. But to a people so cunning and crafty this yoke is pleasant, and this burden is light.'[1]

'Rare to-day are the secular laity who are not involved in some mortal sin.' Such are the few pregnant words in which Gerald sums up the moral condition of the laity of Wales and England. Let us hope that his temperament had led him here, as often elsewhere, into involuntary exaggeration. It is the peculiarity of some minds to be so deeply impressed with the sinfulness of the sins and follies of their age, that they are incapable of recognising the goodness that nevertheless exists. Other prophets beside Elijah have exclaimed, 'I, even I only, am left!' and, perhaps, even in the days of Giraldus Cambrensis there were the 'seven thousand' untainted by the prevalent vices. Good men often live quietly in 'secure repose,' and are unnoticed, while loud-voiced hypocrisy flaunts itself in the public gaze, and the world knows nothing of its silent saviours who are the salt that keeps it from corruption. Still, as in the earlier ages of the Welsh Church, Wales was noted for its hermits, of one of whom, his friend Wechelen, Gerald has already drawn for us the picture. Of another, the hermit Caradog, who died at St. Ismael, in Ros, in 1124, he wrote a life, which has perished, and he endeavoured to procure his canonization from the Pope. 'Hermits and anchorites,' he says, 'more strictly abstinent, and more spiritual, cannot be found elsewhere; for this

[1] 'Des. Kamb.,' ii. 1: Op. vi. 206, 207.

nation is earnest in all its pursuits, and neither worse men than the bad, nor better than the good, can be met with.'[1] Doubtless, among the laity, and even in the ranks of the married clergy, whom he abhorred, many a one lived the life and served the Master.

But at the same time the existence of two moral codes in the country could not but be detrimental to its morality. There was the ancient Scriptural rule of the Welsh Church, that marriage was honourable for all men, and there was the new Papal rule that clerical marriage was no marriage at all, but fornication. It could not have been beneficial to the laity to be assured on high authority that their clergy were living in deadly sin; it must have tended to lower the tone of the clergy in course of time to be assured by the leaders of orthodoxy and culture that the women they loved were concubines or harlots. It was not the least of the evils which the Papacy inflicted upon Wales, that by the imposition of the rule of celibacy upon the clergy it attacked and weakened the national morality.

[1] 'Des. Kamb.,' i. 18; Op. vi. 204.

CHAPTER X.

THE NEW MONASTERIES.

THE olden zeal which in the sixth century drove forth into the wilderness so many of the noblest sons of Wales, to live there the life of monks or of hermits, was not extinct in the age of Gerald de Barri. Still, in the little island of Priestholm,[1] off the coast of Anglesey, there dwelt hermits who, after the ancient fashion, supported themselves by the labour of their hands and suffered no woman to approach their secure retreat. Yet, for all that, so went the story, discord sometimes arose among them, and on such occasions they were visited with a plague of mice, who devoured their food and so punished them for their infirmity. Bardsey, too, the ancient isle of saints, was not forsaken, but was still inhabited by 'very religious monks, called Cœlibes, or Colidei,'[2] and thither in their last hours Welsh patriots turned their thoughts and desired to be buried in its solitude. Thus prays the twelfth-century poet, Meilyr, in his 'Death-bed of the Bard':

> 'On that appointed day, when there shall rise up
> Those who are in the grave, I will then look forward,
>   When I am in my allotted rest,
>   There waiting for the call,
>   To strive and win the goal
>   In time of need—

---

[1] Called then Enislannach (Ynys Glanach), 'the ecclesiastical island.' 'Itin. Kamb.,' ii. 7 : Op. vi. 131.
[2] *Ibid.*, ii. 6: Op. vi. 124.

> ' And let that be a solitude, by passengers not trodden,
> And around its walls the bosom of the briny sea;
> > The fair isle of Mary,
> > The holy isle of saints,
> > The type of renovation,
> > > There to rest in happiness.
>
> ' Christ, the predicted Cross,
> > Will recognise me there.
> And guard me from the rage of hell,
> > A place of exiled beings ;
> The Creator who formed me, will give me room among
> The community of the inhabitants of Enlli !'[1]

The old monasteries and the old monastic customs were still dear to the hearts of patriotic Welshmen.

There was another old monastery too, so Gerald tells us, at the foot of Snowdon, probably at Beddgelert, which in his days had to fight for its very existence with the Cistercian monks of Aberconway, who sought to annex it as a farm or a subordinate cell, and with this view did their utmost to procure its destruction or to force its inhabitants to accept the rule of their order. Eventually, however, after much trouble and expense the Snowdon monks obtained letters of protection from the Pope.

---

[1] Stephens, ' Literature of the Kymry,' p. 23.

> ' Prid y bo cyvnod yn cyvodi
> Ysawl y sy 'met, armäa vi,
> > As bwyv yn adev
> > Yn aros y llev
> > Y lloc a achev,
> > > Aches wrthi :—
>
> ' Ac yssi didryv, didraul ebri
> Ac am i mynwent mynwes heli:
> > Ynys Vair Virain,
> > Ynys glân y glain
> > Gwrthrych dadwyrain—
> > > Ys cain yndi.
>
> ' Crist, croes darogan
> > A'm gwyr, a'm gwarthan,
> > Rac ufern afan
> > > Wahan westi
> Creawdyr a'm crewys a'm cynnwys ym plith
> Plwyv gwirin gwerin Ennlli.'

These monks were also Cœlibes, or Culdees,[1] and are described as 'clergy, devoted servants of God, living in common in a holy assembly, and after the apostolic custom, having nothing of their own, and bound to no special monastic or canonical rule, given to chastity and abstinence, and especially conspicuous for works of charity and for hospitality,' after the manner of other holy communities which existed before St. Benedict framed his rule.

So far Gerald has nothing but praise for those monastic communities of the ancient type which still survived. But in others of the old monasteries he found corruptions which moved his indignation. The most conspicuous of these was Llanbadarn Fawr, which in the reign of Henry I. was granted to the monks of St. Peter's, Gloucester, but afterwards was recovered by the Welsh, and resumed its ancient customs. Gerald tells a story how in the reign of Stephen a Breton knight came in his travels to Llanbadarn. 'On a certain feast-day, whilst both the clergy and people were waiting for the arrival of the abbot to celebrate mass, he went at last with others to meet the abbot; he saw a body of young men approaching, about twenty in number, lightly equipped, according to the custom of their people, and armed; and on inquiring which of them was the abbot, they pointed out to him a man walking foremost, with a long spear in his hand. Gazing on him with amazement, he asked, "Has not your abbot another habit, or a different staff, from that which he now carries before him?" On their answering, "No!" he replied, "I have seen, indeed, and heard this day enough of novelty and marvel," and from that hour he returned home and finished his labours and researches.'[2] According to Gerald there were other

[1] 'Tamquam cœlibes sive colidei, hoc est deum colentes, dicti.' 'Speculum Ecclesiæ,' iii. 8: Op. iv. 167.
[2] Gir. Camb., 'Itin. Kamb.,' ii. 4: Op. vi. 121.

churches in Wales with lay abbots, for a custom had prevailed among the clergy of appointing the most powerful people of a parish stewards or patrons of their churches. These in process of time, from a desire of gain, usurped the whole right, appropriating to their own use the possession of all the lands, leaving only to the clergy their altars, with their tenths and oblations, and assigning even these to their sons and relations in the Church. When Gerald and Archbishop Baldwin visited Llanbadarn they found 'a certain old man, waxen old in iniquity, whose name was Eden Oen, son of Gwaithwod,'[1] there as abbot, and his sons were officiating at the altar. Every great Irish monastery was similarly connected with some family, either of founder or patron, and in many cases, at least during the ninth and following centuries, there was a lineal succession of abbots.[2]

But the main part of Gerald's criticisms and the whole of his work entitled 'Speculum Ecclesiæ'—'The Mirror of the Church'—are devoted to the Latin monastic orders, which were entirely distinct from the Celtic communities, and did not obtain a footing in Wales until the coming of the Normans. When a Norman noble conquered a district, and began to settle his military colony, his first step was to raise a castle for his protection, and his second was to set apart a share of the plunder for some Norman or English abbey. This house, in sign of acceptance of the gift, sent out a few monks with a prior, who occupied the land given, and founded a cell, which might be large and beautiful like Brecon Priory, or small and insignificant like Llangenith, according as the lands given, or the parochial tithes appropriated, were considerable or the reverse. Each new party of monks that came brought with it its Norman or English

---

[1] 'Ethenoweyn filius Withfoit.' Op. vi. 121.
[2] Reeves' 'Columba,' 'Hist. of Scot.,' vi., ci. The abbacy of Hy was, with one or two exceptions, strictly limited to a branch of the Tir-Conallian family.

speech and its Latin ritual, and so introduced more and more of the new leaven that was to work in the old Celtic lump. In South Wales all but three of the new monasteries belonged thus to what Gerald calls 'the English plantation,' and were at first anti-national in character and influence, a fact which goes far to explain the intense hatred felt by many of the bards for 'the false, luxurious, and gluttonous monks'—a sentiment which the monks, for their part, seem to have fully reciprocated.[1] But after a little time, when the Cistercian Order took Europe by storm, the Welsh princes followed the prevailing fashion, and themselves came forward as founders and benefactors of the new monasteries; and it would seem also that many of the foundations which were at first alien in origin, race, language, and feeling, became so affected by their Celtic surroundings that they, too, were Celticized. For such has ever been the wondrous glamour of the Celtic race, that those who have been planted in its midst have often lost their nationality and been absorbed. The Cistercian Order, which from its lack of revenues had to fight its way for itself, and was forced more or less to adapt itself to the people among whom it lived, became to a considerable extent identified with Welsh national feeling.

The secular clergy were generally hostile to the monks, for very good and substantial reasons, and Gerald de Barri shared the antipathy of his class. In two of his works he relates with evident appreciation the bitter sarcasm which Richard I. levelled at them when a holy man, named Fulke, reproved him for his vices. 'You have three daughters,' said Fulke, 'Pride, Licentiousness, and Avarice; and as long as they shall remain with you, you can never expect to be in favour with God.' Quoth

---

[1] 'Myneich geuawg, gwydawg, gwydus.' — 'Avallaneu.' See Stephens' 'Literature of the Kymry,' 223, 110-111. Stephens, however, confounds monks and friars together.

Richard: 'I have already given away those daughters in marriage; Pride to the Templars, Licentiousness to the black monks, and Avarice to the white.'[1] Holy men were very plain-spoken in those days, but they met their match in the early Angevins.

Gerald fully endorses the language of King Richard, though, according to him, the Cluniac or black monks were far worse on the Continent than in England or Wales. The reverse, however, he says, was true of the Cistercians.[2] It must not be forgotten, in judging the value of Gerald's estimate of the monastic orders, that his chief aversion, Peter de Leia, was a 'black-hooded beast,' or, in other words, a monk of the Cluniac Order; that the seducer of the St. David's chapter from his side during his contest with King and primate was another monk, the Cistercian Abbot of Whitland; and that he had suffered much from the treachery of the infamous William Wibert, the Cistercian Abbot of Bitlesden. The monks of Strata Florida, too, another Cistercian foundation, had compelled him to sell his books to them when he wanted money for a journey to Rome. He had put his whole library, which he had been collecting from his boyhood, under their care, and they had voluntarily offered to lend him money upon it, but when the time came for him to start, and he asked for the loan to be paid, they pleaded that their 'Book of Uses' suffered them to buy, but not to lend on security; and so the unfortunate archdeacon had, as he expresses it, to part with his very bowels, and felt himself overreached as well.[3] Gerald was not the man to put these personal injuries on one side, and form an impartial judgment upon the general conduct of the monastic orders. He admits that the conduct of the Abbot of Bitlesden had

---

[1] 'Itin. Kamb.,' i. 3: Op. vi. 44; 'Speculum Eccl.,' ii. 12: Op. iv. 54.
[2] 'Spec. Eccl.,' ii. 6: Op. iv. 45.   [3] *Ibid.*, iii. 5: Op. iv. 154, 155.

so affected him that as often as he repeated the Litany he added a new clause, which he recommended to all his friends : ' From the malice of the monks, and especially of the Cistercians, good Lord, deliver us.'[1] We get, therefore, little but the darker traits of the monastic orders in Gerald's picture, and those painted with all the skill and vigour of a consummate artist.

The grosser abominations which we hear of seem to have been especially rife in the cells. There was much luxury in eating and drinking in the larger houses, as Gerald found at Canterbury, where he was entertained by the Prior of Christchurch at a dinner of sixteen courses, with wines and various kinds of strong drink. Beer, for which Kent was even then noted, was not thought worthy of a place at so sumptuous a feast.[2] Winebibbing was a common reproach against the monks; 'Golias the Bishop' speaks of the abbots who 'joyously chant *Wesheil* over and over again with their intimate friends';[3] and Gerald tells a scandalous and probably fictitious story of some nameless abbot who, all unwitting of the quality of his royal guest, kept it up with Henry II. with *Pril* and *Wril* into the small hours of the morning. For in that particular abbey, which was Cistercian (and Gerald hated the Cistercians), it was the custom to say *Pril* and *Wril*, instead of the usual *Wesheil* and *Drincheil*.[4] Stories like these doubtless had a certain amount of basis in fact, for the original rule of St. Benedict put no great restrictions upon food and drink, except in the matter of flesh meat ; and the number of reformers who appeared one after another to start modifications of his order with stricter rules, proves that the tendency of each order in turn was to grow laxer and laxer, and to become more

---

[1] 'Spec. Eccl.,' iii. 6: Op. iv. 160. 'A monachorum malitia, maxime vero Cisterciensium, libera nos, Domine.'
[2] 'De Rebus a se Gestis,' ii. 5 ; 'Spec. Eccl.,' ii. 4 : Op. iv. 41.
[3] 'Goliæ Versus de Prælatis'; 'Poems of Walter Mapes,' p. 45.
[4] 'Spec. Eccl.,' iii. 13: Op. iv. 213.

and more conformed to the wicked world around. But in the larger houses there was some semblance of discipline observed, and cases of general and flagrant immorality, such as was charged against the Cistercian Abbey of Strata Marcella by Edward III.,[1] were comparatively rare. Matters were worse in the cells, which were dependent upon some mother abbey, and as most of the monastic foundations in Wales were merely cells, and some of them very small cells, it is not surprising that Gerald finds much material for censure. Not unfrequently two or three monks only would be sent out to a cell, and even in some cases one only, with the natural result that, as they were without any supervision, they did as they pleased, and, mixing more or less with the secular world around them, lived as their neighbours did, or even, as Gerald does not scruple to say, 'lived as beasts.'[2] Scandals consequently arose such as we read of in connection with Llangenith, a little cell of some two or three monks in Gower.[3] In some of the more remote cells the poor monks were forced to subsist on the very meanest fare, very different from the plenty they had enjoyed in their abbey; and yet, for all this, so sweet was the liberty they enjoyed, that there was the greatest desire on their part to be chosen to garrison these outposts, and the greatest reluctance to quit them. Men were wont to jeer at them on account of this reluctance, and put some such words as these in their mouths: 'This I will never do; I would rather go down alive into hell; nay, sooner and more readily would I go back again to the prison of my cloister.'[4] But these lawless monks at times not only brought down disgrace upon themselves and their order, and upon the very name of monk, but proved a pest and a danger to their neighbourhood. Gerald tells us of a small party of this kind, some three

---

[1] In letters addressed to the Abbots of Clairvaux and Citeaux.
[2] Bestialiter. 'Spec. Eccl.,' ii. 1 : Op. iv. 35.
[3] 'Spec. Eccl.,' ii. 1 : Op. iv. 33. [4] *Ibid.*, p. 37.

or four in number, whom Prince Rhys ap Gruffydd was forced to eject and banish because of the frequent complaints brought to him by his people of outrages done to their wives and daughters. So grievous and so frequent were the wrongs they inflicted, that Rhys asserted to Gerald that his townsmen had threatened to leave the place altogether and retire into England if the plague were not abated.[1] Abominations such as these explain the mediæval play upon the words 'monk' and 'demoniac,'[2] and go far to excuse the bitter speech of Walter Mapes—'There is no greater devil than a monk.'[3] For though people might perhaps consider these as exceptional acts of wickedness, if they were confined to the occupants of small cells, there were at times other cases which gave their numerous enemies occasion for hinting that all was not right in the larger houses, and that gluttony and drunkenness were not the only sins which they harboured. Recently public confidence had received a severe shock through the grievous sin of Enoc, the Cistercian Abbot of Strata Marcella, a man of good report among the people for discretion, strictness of life, and religious zeal. He had been especially active in founding nunneries in the various provinces of Wales, until a scandal, which arose in connection with one of these communities at Llansantfraed, in Elvaen, drove him to throw aside the religious habit altogether, and return to the world to live in sin.[4]

When the Cistercian Order was founded, early in the twelfth century, men hoped that a better and purer era of monasticism was dawning, and contemplated with respect

---

[1] 'Spec. Eccl.,' ii. 32: Op. iv. 100, 101.
[2] 'Quisque de monacho fit dæmoniacus.' 'Poems of Walter Mapes,' p. 18. See also *note*.
[3] *Ibid.*, p. 19. 'Est nullum monacho majus dæmonium.'
[4] 'Spec. Eccl.,' iii. 8: Op. iv. 169; 'Gemma Eccl.,' Op. ii. 248. He repented afterwards and returned to his monastery, according to 'Itin. Kamb.,' i. 5: Op. vi. 59.

and veneration the simplicity and austerity of these new monks. And in very truth, as their enemies allowed, for some space of time before the fire of their love had grown feeble, this respect and veneration were not misplaced. Gerald, who loved them not as he saw them a hundred years after their first establishment, draws a candid and a pleasing picture of their early manners. They avoided all superfluity in dress, shunned coloured garments, and wore nothing but woollen. In cold weather they put on them no furs or skins of any kind, and made no use of fires or hot water. As was their clothing, so was their food, plain and simple in the extreme, and they never ate meat either in public or in private, except under pressure of serious illness. They were conspicuous in charity and given to hospitality; their gate was shut against no one, but stood open at morning, noon, and evening; so that in almsgiving they surpassed all other religious orders. Moreover, seeking out the desert places of the wilderness and shunning the haunts and noise of crowds, earning their daily bread by the labour of their hands, and tilling the waste solitudes, they brought before men's eyes the primitive life and ancient rule of monastic religion—its poverty, its spare diet, the meanness and roughness of its dress, its abstinence and austerity in all things.[1]

Unfortunately this ideal was not long maintained, and the distinctive vice of the order, its proverbial avarice, brought it many enemies. How sharp was the contrast between Cistercian profession and Cistercian practice may be inferred from the bitter satire of 'a disciple of Bishop Golias.' 'Rise,' he exclaims, 'my muse, from sleep and silence and from the ease of torpor, and be brief.' Then solemnly he draws, in much the same way as Gerald, an ideal picture of Cistercian virtue. 'The glorious order adorns the world, it has come down from heaven to overthrow utterly Babel and Wi of the Cha -

---

[1] 'Spec. Eccl.,' ii. 34: Op. iv. 113.

dæans, and to destroy all slavery to idols. They are of wondrous continence, of wondrous abstinence, enemies of vainglory, enemies of vanity; with cold and hunger they afflict themselves, if so be they may thus enjoy the sight of the Deity. Their outer dress is rude and mean: their food austere; their bed neglected; they are sparing of their speech; no order is more holy, none so perfect. They despise things terrestrial for the sake of the future; they receive a hundredfold for their contempt of this world; they take by violence the kingdom of heaven; the joys of Paradise alone have savour for them. Good Jesu, ruler of such monks, who art the judge of quick and dead, make me, I pray Thee, their companion; join me with them in the festival of all saints.'

Then, suddenly changing his tone, he places another picture side by side with the ideal. They are a race deservedly hated by all mankind; wolves in sheep's clothing, full of deceit and given to plunder, exceeding rapacious and avaricious. studying in the basest manner to get gain; they are false prophets whose spare diet and mean garments denote an avaricious heart; they thirst for nothing but the present world; they reap where they have not sown; they have enriched themselves with the penury of the poor; they are Satan's bond-slaves, and ever will be; they ravage the world like a fell disease; their lusts are not checked by any laws of chastity, and among all men there are none worse.[1]

> [1] 'Continentes minime possunt appellari,
>   sed rapaces maxime et nimis avari,
>   nam student nequissime capere præclari,
>   et horto rectissime possunt comparari.
>
> 'Tenuis refectio pseudo-prophetarum,
>   et vestis abjectio notat cor avarum;
>   gerunt sub silentio animum amarum,
>   fucata religio nil valet aut parum.
>
> 'Nil nisi præsentia sitiunt aut quærunt,
>   farsiunt marsupia, metunt quæ non serunt,
>   pauperum penuria sese ditaverunt;
>   Satanæ mancipia sunt et semper erunt.
>
> * * * *

The bitterness of the satire is excessive; but its truth, so far as the charge of avarice is concerned, is undeniable. Perhaps its author, like his exemplar, Walter Mapes, and like Gerald himself, had suffered from the rapacity of the order. The other charges may perhaps be dismissed as rash generalizations from occasional instances. The number of monks was large; and it cannot be held strange if here and there one monk, or even one abbey, was tainted with the moral corruptions of an age in which, be it remembered, few indeed of the secular laity were not involved in the guilt of mortal sin. But the Cistercians had no cells—each abbey was a separate community—so that they escaped the dangers which from this cause beset the other branches of the order of St. Benedict. Neither were they generally wealthy, as were the Benedictines, and consequently they had less temptations than that order to gluttony, wine-bibbing, and the sins of luxury. Gerald complains that they indulged themselves in eating and drinking in private, but he gives little evidence in support of his accusation,[1] and there is no reason to believe that it was generally applicable. Even 'the disciple of Bishop Golias' admits that their diet was spare and their garments were mean, and censures them only for avarice and unchastity. But the poverty which protected them against the sins of luxury rendered economy necessary in their monasteries, and almost forced them to drive hard bargains and prac-

> ' Pestis animalium, quæ *shuta* vocatur,
>   et Cisterciensium quæ sic dilatatur :
>   duplex hoc contagium orbem populatur,
>   quod sit magis noxium prorsus ignoratur.
>
> ' Carent femoralibus partes turpiores,
>   Veneris ut usibus sint paratiores,
>   castitatis legibus absolutiores ;
>   in cunctis hominibus nulli sunt pejores.'
>   'Poems of William Mapes,' pp. 55-57.

[1] 'Spec. Eccl.,' iii. 13 : Op. iv. 208-219.

tise little dishonest tricks such as that whereby the monks of Strata Florida annexed Gerald's books. The common proverb of the countryside attested their current reputation: 'They are bad neighbours, like the white monks.'[1] Undoubtedly they had their good qualities, and these in no mean degree; they loved the beautiful in art and nature; they abounded in deeds of charity and hospitality even beyond all other monks; the poor never went away hungry from their gates, and the weary stranger was never refused hospitality. The monks of all orders were generally good landlords and popular with their tenants; they were liked by the common people and beloved by the poor; they were the benefactors of genius, and many a clever son of a poor man rose by their patronage to a position of power and influence; they operated as a democratic check upon a dominant aristocracy; and in an age of brute force and stupid oppression they kept alive arts, science, and literature, and handed on the torches of learning and of liberty to succeeding generations. But they were hated by two classes—the clergy, whom they robbed, and the landlords, who wanted to rob *them*. These noted their vices, and longed for their fall: but when they fell the landlords took the spoil, whereas the clergy were worse off than before, and as for the poor —their lot was hard indeed.

One thing which eventually contributed to the fall of the monasteries, but which at the time was the object of their ambition, was their frequent exemption from episcopal control and subjection to Rome only. This made them in a way the first English Roman Catholics, and the only communities that can be considered in any way the precursors of the modern Italian schism. In Wales, however, the only houses which claimed such exemption were those of the Cistercians. Of all the orders the Cistercian was the most favoured at Rome,

---

[1] 'Spec. Eccl.,' iii. 12: Op. iv. 207.

partly because of its austerity, and partly, as Gerald plainly says, because of the money which it expended in promoting its causes before the curia. Whatever privileges it sought, it was for these reasons sure to obtain. Pope Alexander III. was reported to have said that there were three orders more beloved than the rest, which he wished especially to protect and guard with privileges: the Templars, the Hospitallers, and the Cistercians.[1] As such privileges were generally to the prejudice of the secular clergy, the Cistercians had to bear a greater burden of ill-will on the part of the clergy than the other orders. But avarice was their besetting sin. Not only did the Cistercians add field to field and oppress the less powerful landowners around them, but they were especially noted in Wales for seizing upon parish churches and, if they saw fit, destroying the sacred buildings and profaning the churchyards.[2] Actions such as these can scarcely be excused by the plea which Gerald condescends to consider, that as they had no revenues like other monks, but lived only by the labour of their hands and by prudent economy, it was needful for them to add to their estates as much as possible, in order to have wherewith to feed poor men and travellers.[3]

Gerald gives numerous instances of oppressive and avaricious acts of Cistercian abbeys in Wales, some of which will have to be noticed later on, and several of which were practised towards other smaller houses. But the great blot upon all the religious orders in Wales (as indeed in England, but perhaps in a somewhat less degree) was that which has been just indicated—the oppression of the parochial clergy, whose tithes were seized for their maintenance. How Tewkesbury Abbey was founded out of the spoils of the parishes in the Vale

---

[1] 'Spec. Eccl.,' iii. 12 : Op. iv. 205.
[2] *Ibid.*, iii. 1 : Op. iv. 136, 137.
[3] *Ibid.*, iii., Introd. : Op. iv. 120.

of Glamorgan has been already stated. Gerald, in one brief but trenchant chapter of his 'Speculum Ecclesiæ,' indicates the various ways in which the parochial clergy of Wales were defrauded of their just dues.

'The whole of the Welsh monasteries,' he says, 'are in common involved in one and the same vice, which proceeds from the root of wicked covetousness. For as they were wont to seize the parishes of mother and baptismal churches, and either wickedly mutilate them of the greater part, or even wholly appropriate them, the parishioners being expelled and the churches being empty, deserted, or even thrown down and destroyed; so also, to the great loss and prejudice of churches and parsons, they presume to carry off the bodies of the dead either by stealth or by open violence, and to remove them for burial in their own graveyards, without any respect, but rather with utter contempt, for the rights of the churches whereof they had been parishioners. For they send monks or brethren through the parishes, whether distant or close at hand, as spies, and wherever they find men of noble birth, or even mean men, if only they have numerous herds and other possessions (for they take no heed of the poor), forthwith they enter their houses and preach to them, and promise them the kingdom of heaven as by a sure pledge, however great and grievous be the sins they have committed. They never afterwards leave the house, but lie day and night among the servants and the young women, without regard to their order or to decency, until they carry the masters away with them alive or dead. And what is more dreadful and abominable, they bury without delay and with all due rites in their graveyards men who have been excommunicated by name by their bishops and laid under an interdict for plunder, and who have never been absolved, in spite of the prohibitions and appeals of the clergy and deans of the province.'[1]

[1] 'Spec. Eccl.,' iii. 10: Op. iv. 177, 178.

The first of all the new orders to obtain a settlement in Wales were the Benedictines, whose founder had consecrated labour and taught the world that work was worship, a strange and startling lesson to his age and to subsequent ages. In making manual labour a principal part of his discipline, Benedict agreed with Paulinus and Illtyd and their fellows, but his rule in other respects was far less austere than that of the Celtic monks. Its concessions to the weakness of human nature and its general suitability to the age in which it was inaugurated caused it to spread and wholly to supersede on the Continent the Celtic rule of Columbanus. But the Celtic customs still held their ground in Wales even down to the time of the Norman invasion, although the older asceticism had for the most part been forgotten, and perhaps not unfrequently the salt had altogether lost its savour. It was in the reign of William the Conqueror, and somewhere before 1071,[1] that William Fitzosberne, who held the most southerly of the three border earldoms, that of Hereford,[2] gave to his Norman foundation of Cormeilles a grant of land at Strigul, now called Chepstow, which he had recently conquered from the Welsh, and where he built himself a castle. This was the origin of the Benedictine Priory of Chepstow, which survived various vicissitudes and was finally suppressed at the dissolution, when it had three inmates and was valued at £32 per annum. In Leland's time it was a cell to Bermondsey Abbey.[3]

Another early Benedictine priory in Monmouthshire was Abergavenny. This owed its foundation to the Norman, Hamelyn Baladun, who occupied the district and ousted its native owners. He gave lands at Aber-

---

[1] Earl William was killed in that year.
[2] The others were Cheshire and Shropshire.
[3] Leland, 'Itin.,' v. 5 (2nd edition). 'The Celle of a Blake Monke or two of Bermundsey by London was lately there suppressed.' Also v. 12.

gavenny to the Abbey of St. Vincent at Le Mans, and, dying in the reign of William Rufus, was buried in the priory which he had founded. William de Braose, a treacherous monster, whose cruelty was only equalled by his superstition, endowed the priory further a little later with the tithes of his castle of Abergavenny, of bread, wine, beer, and all manner of drink, and of flesh, fish, salt, honey, wax, and tallow, etc., on condition that the abbot and convent of the mother house of St. Vincent should pray daily for the soul of King Henry, and also for the souls of him, William, and of Matilda his wife.[1] The present fine parish church of Abergavenny was the chapel of the old priory.

The alien Priory of Monmouth was founded by Wihenoc de Monmouth, who obtained the surrounding district after the forfeiture of the estates of Roger, Earl of Hereford, son and heir of Earl William, the founder of Chepstow. Roger had taken a prominent part in the rebellion of 1074, and lost his estates in consequence. Wihenoc founded the priory about 1095,[2] and built its church in his castle of Monmouth, and gave it for ever to the monks of St. Florence of Saumur, a Benedictine abbey in the diocese of Angers.

Other Benedictine houses in Monmouthshire were Goldcliff, at the mouth of the Usk; Bassaleg, also near the town of Newport on the west, and a nunnery at Usk. The first of these was founded about 1113 by Robert de Chandos, and was a cell to the illustrious Abbey of Bec, in Normandy.[3] It was eventually seized by the Crown as an alien priory, and given to Eton College.[4] Bassaleg was a cell to Glastonbury, founded about 1110 by Robert de Haya and his wife Gundreda, and was probably soon

---

[1] Dugdale, 'Monasticon,' pp. 556-558; Leland, 'Itin.,' v. 12.
[2] Charter in Dugdale, 'Monasticon,' p. 600.
[3] Charter of Edward I. reciting the gift of Robert de Chandos, in Dugdale's 'Monasticon,' p. 590.
[4] Leland, 'Itin.,' v. 7.

abandoned.[1] Usk was a nunnery of five nuns, founded by the De Clares.[2]

Close to the Welsh border in Herefordshire, and anciently within the diocese of St. David's, was founded, about 1100, the Benedictine cell of Ewias Harold, which was affiliated to the great Abbey of St. Peter's, Gloucester. Its founder was Harold, Lord of Ewias, and son of Ralph, Earl of Hereford. Ewias took its name of Ewias Harold from him, and was thus distinguished from Ewias Lacy. In 1358 it was found advisable, on account of poverty, to remove the monks from this cell to the mother abbey at Gloucester.

All the monasteries hitherto enumerated were founded, as we have seen, by Normans, and were cells to some English or foreign abbey. If we turn our glance away from the border further westward in South Wales, we shall find the same process going on. After the overthrow of Rhys ap Tewdwr, and the ensuing conquest of South Wales by the Normans, similar cells were everywhere planted in the subdued districts. It is unnecessary to suppose that this was part of a deep-laid plan to deprive the Welsh of their language and their national ritual; it was the fashion of the Normans so to do, and they considered it to be part of their religious obligations. So Bernard Newmarch, a little before 1100, founded at Brecon a cell to the Abbey of Battle;[3] Arnulph de Montgomery founded Monkton Priory, and affiliated it to St. Martin's Abbey at Séez, in Normandy; Maurice de Londres founded what Gerald calls 'the little cell of Ewenith,' or Ewenny, the fine church of which still holds his tomb in a perfect state of preservation;[4] Roger, Bishop of Salisbury, about 1130, founded Kidwelly Priory, a cell to the Abbey of Sherborne; Robert, Earl of Gloucester,

---

[1] Charter in Clark's 'Cartæ de Glamorgan,' i. 2.
[2] 'On the River side a flite shot from the Castel.' 'Itin.,' v. 12.
[3] Charter in Dugdale, 'Monasticon,' p. 320.
[4] Charter in Clark's 'Cartæ,' i. 14.

in 1147, established at Cardiff a cell to the grand foundation of Tewkesbury, which drew so much of its endowments from his estates; Roger de Bellomont, Earl of Warwick, founded in the reign of Stephen Llangenith Priory[1] in Gower, as a cell to the Abbey of St. Taurinus at Evreux in Normandy; a cell to St. Benoit-sur-Loire was established at Llangwyn in 1183; and at an uncertain date, but certainly before 1291, a cell to Chertsey was established at Cardigan. These complete the long list of Benedictine cells in South Wales, which contrasts in this respect with North Wales, where there were scarcely any foundations of this order, a circumstance due to the longer duration of the power of the native princes. Bardsey, which in the time of Gerald's journey in company with Baldwin was inhabited by Culdees, became afterwards the seat of a Benedictine foundation. The earliest known deed in favour of this priory is dated 1252, but the name of Laurence, 'an eloquent man, prior of the Island of Saints,' is found as early as 1202. Glannach, or Penmon, in Anglesey, was richly endowed and perhaps founded in 1221 by Llywelyn ap Iorwerth. But the native princes, as a rule, were more favourable to the Cistercians than to the Benedictines.

The Benedictines have left behind them in their churches permanent memorials of their work in South Wales. They were pretty generally used both for parochial and monastic purposes, and, as a result, many survived the dissolution, and have been handed down to the present time. Among the most noticeable are Brecon and Ewenny; the former as the grandest and most important of all; the latter as 'the most perfect specimen of an early Norman semi-ecclesiastical, semi-defensive structure to be found throughout the princi-

---

[1] It was seized as an alien priory, and was afterwards given by Henry VI. to All Souls' College, Oxford. Tanner's 'Notitia Monastica' (1744), p. 714.

pality.' Little Ewenny contrasts greatly with the noble pile of Brecon, yet, standing as it does on a slight elevation above the little river, it attracts attention by its embattled tower and its military peculiarities, which show that it was originally raised in the midst of a hostile population as much to be a castle as a church. Some portions have been destroyed, but what remains has undergone little alteration since its original construction; and the wall, which from the beginning has separated the parochial and monastic churches, still exists, a somewhat unsightly object, blocking up the western arch under the central tower. There are few windows; 'all is dark, solemn, almost cavernous; it is, indeed, a shrine for men who doubtless performed their most solemn rites with fear and trembling, amid constant expectation of hostile inroads.'[1]

St. John's Priory Church at Brecon, on the other hand, is the glory of the fair town, which, for the picturesque beauty of the surrounding scenery, is unsurpassed in Wales. Among Welsh churches, excluding those in ruins, it comes third, if not second, for although it must yield to the superior beauty of St. David's, its grandeur is, at least to some minds, more impressive than the loveliness of parts of Llandaff.[2] The priory was largely endowed, for Bernard Newmarch's followers co-operated with him in making gifts to it, and afterwards it received gifts and charters from Roger, Earl of Hereford, Mahel, Earl of Hereford, William de Braose, Reginald de Braose, the Herberts, and Humphrey de Bohun, Earl of Hereford.[3] It owned some ten churches in Breconshire, with Patingham in Staffordshire; Bodenham, Burchell, and the tithe of Bruneshope in Hereford-

---

[1] See Mr. Freeman's paper in 'Archæologia Cambrensis,' 1857; also 'Arch. Camb.,' 1888, pp. 397-399.
[2] It is fully described by Mr. Freeman in 'Arch. Camb.,' 1854, pp. 150, 151, 164-179.
[3] Dugdale, ' Monasticon,' pp. 321-323.

shire, and Hardington in Somerset. It had also an interest in some other churches, but some of these gifts were lost. Its connection with Battle was due to Bernard Newmarch's confessor, Roger, who was a monk of that abbey. Two priors of Brecon became abbots of Battle in 1261 and in 1503 respectively.

The next order after the Benedictines to obtain a footing in Wales was that of the Augustinian canons, which was constituted in 1061 by Pope Alexander II. A settlement of these canons was made at Llanthony, in the unrivalled cloister[1] of the Black Mountains, and was endowed by Hugh de Laci. But, like Walter Savage Landor in later times, the canons found Llanthony a very unpleasant and unsafe residence, although Gerald, in his love of asceticism, praises it as 'a situation truly calculated for religion, and more adapted to canonical discipline than all the monasteries of the British isle.' Even at the present day it is rather inaccessible, and except in sunny weather 'the deep vale of Ewias,' grand and romantic as it is, is calculated to inspire the visitor with a feeling of awe. Here a few might live the hermit's life, as St. David is said to have done in this valley, and as two companions, William and Ernicius, were living when Hugh de Laci founded the large Augustinian house. But it was difficult for forty canons to get subsistence in so wild and rough a country, and consequently many of them after a few years were removed to Hereford, of which see their former prior, Robert de Betun, was bishop, from whence afterwards they removed in 1136 to another Llanthony, which was founded near Gloucester. But the original house was not forsaken, and about 1200[2] there rose another magnificent church, the ruins of which still add loveliness to the romantic vale. It was proposed in the reign of Edward IV. to

[1] So termed by Roger, Bishop of Salisbury. 'Itin. Kamb.,' i. 3.
[2] See Mr. Freeman's paper in 'Arch. Camb.' for 1855, pp. 82-109.

reduce the number of inmates to a prior and four canons, and to make the house a cell of the Gloucestershire Llanthony; but it is doubtful whether this arrangement was ever carried out.

There were other houses of this order in Wales at Haverfordwest, Carmarthen, and Beddgelert. The first of these was endowed largely by Robert de Haverford, who may have been its founder. Ruins of it still exist. The Carmarthen house received gifts from Bishop Bernard and Peter de Leia. It was burned down in 1435. The Priory of Beddgelert seems to have succeeded an older Celtic foundation, and was accounted, next to Bardsey, 'the oldest religious house in all Wales.' It received benefactions from Llywelyn ap Iorwerth, Llywelyn ap Gruffydd, and other Welsh princes.[1]

In 1120 Norbert, Archbishop of Magdeburg, founded a reformed order of canons, who were called Premonstratensian, from their first home Premonstré, in Picardy, or sometimes White Canons, from their habit, which was white, and distinguished them from the older Augustinians, who wore black. Their dress was a white cassock, a rochet, a long white cloak, and a white cap. From Premonstré they came to Liskes, a house in Normandy, and thence, in 1143, they came to Newhouse, in Lincolnshire. Subsequently Welbeck, in Nottinghamshire, was founded in 1153 by a colony from Newhouse, and this became the chief house in the island. In Wales, Talley in Carmarthenshire belonged to this order,[2] and was founded by Rhys ap Gruffydd some time before 1196. The Premonstratensians, like the

---

[1] Grant of Indulgence to the Convent of Beddgelert in 'H. and S.,' i. 584.
[2] This is the statement of Leland, to which Tanner assents. Dugdale thought it was Benedictine, and it is called Cistercian in a Cambridge MS. But existing documents and the statements of Gerald prove it was Premonstratensian. See an excellent history of Talley Abbey by Mr. Edward Owen. 'Arch. Camb.' for 1893, pp. 29-47, 120-128, 226-237, 309-325.

Cistercians, in accordance with the preference of their founder, St. Norbert, sought out wild and lonely spots away from towns and near water, and Talley is situated in just such a spot at the extremity of two connected lakes, from which it gets its name, Tal-y-llychau (the head of the lakes). The gifts to the abbey, which were numerous, were confirmed by a charter of Edward III., which is extant, and sets forth *in extenso* an earlier charter of Edward II.

Soon after its foundation, Talley suffered from the greed of the Cistercians of Whitland. According to the story told by Gerald, there was at that time at the head of Whitland a young and raw abbot, who wished to signalize himself, and to enlarge the possessions of his abbey. Talley was then a poor and meanly endowed house, and he marked it as his prey. Accordingly he enticed to Whitland its abbot, with some of his canons and brethren, and by various and artful flatteries and bland and deceitful words he persuaded them to lay aside their canonical habit and assume the cowl of the monk. Then, going to the principal man of the province and patron of Talley (by whom Gerald seems to mean Prince Rhys ap Gruffydd, or his son), he by petition and by bribery gained from him that he should expel the canons, and establish there the Cistercian monks. Accordingly the convent, with the brethren and servants, were driven out one night by a band of armed men, and the Abbot of Whitland and his monks took possession, and sang *Salve Regina* with a loud voice to a lively and joyful tune. The unfortunate canons went to England and laid their complaint before Archbishop Hubert, who took up their cause, and restored them to their house and their possessions. A long and vexatious lawsuit followed, and after proceedings at Rome, and before appointed judges in England, Whitland retained a rich grange called Buthelan (or Ruthelan), which it had seized, and gave the canons of Talley in compensation some other lands, together with a sum of money.[1] 'With what measure ye mete, it shall be measured to you again,' remarks Gerald at the conclusion of this narrative, a moral which monastic ruins emphatically endorse.

In 1215, Talley gave a bishop to St. David's in the person of its abbot, Gervase, or Iorwerth, who may perhaps have recommended himself for promotion by zeal and ability in the contest with Whitland. His election was regarded as a triumph of the national party in the Church, as he was a pure Welshman by blood and language, a fact which shows how the houses which were founded by native princes and fostered by native support threw in their lot with the national party. Gervase did not forget his abbey, but during his episcopacy appropriated to it the churches of Llandeilo Fawr and Llanegwad. In after years Talley declined in morals, as so many of the Welsh monasteries did. The Abbot of Premonstré wrote to Edward I. to complain that the 'church of Thaleshen had, by the malice of its inmates, been so turned into the brine of barrenness and dishonesty, that there was no likelihood of its recovery to the fruit of religion, unless the corrupt weeds' were first plucked out. He had commissioned the Abbots of Newhouse and Halesowen to disperse the wicked, and gather them into other churches of the order, and to let the vineyard to other husbandmen.

We find that in 1285 Edward I., by a charter, placed Talley under the jurisdiction of Welbeck, in order that the various irregularities therein might be amended. Still later, in 1391, a charter of Richard II. shows that the revenues of the abbey had been much impaired, and that

---

[1] 'Spec. Eccl.' iii. 2: Op. iv. 143-145. Buthelan in the text ought probably to be Ruthelan, *i.e.*, Rhyddlan. Lampeter is divided between the townships of Rhyddlan Ucha and Rhyddlan Issa.

matters were generally in a bad state, partly from bad management on the part of the abbots, and partly from the lawless condition of the neighbourhood. At the dissolution the number of canons was eight only, including the abbot, Roderick Jones.

We have seen that houses of canons were but few in Wales, whereas the houses belonging to the lay monastic orders were exceedingly numerous. Besides those of the Benedictines, which have been already enumerated, there were many others belonging to the different orders which sprang from the Benedictine stock; for a desire for greater austerity of life, and for more devotion to religion than was shown by the Benedictines, led to the institution of various reformed orders, which aimed higher, though they did not always reach the mark. There were the Cluniacs, founded by Odo, Abbot of Cluny, about A.D. 912; there were the Grandmontines, who took their name from Grandmont in the Limousin, and were founded about 1076 by Stephen d'Auvergne: there were the Tironians, the foundation of Bernard d'Albeville, who established them first at Tiron, in the diocese of Chartres, in 1113; and there were the White Monks, or Cistercians, who owed their origin to the zeal of the Englishman, Stephen Harding, and who were originally divided into Bernardins and the Grey Brothers of Sauvigny. All these had houses in the Welsh dioceses.

The Cluniacs were not loved in England, and though Gerald admits that they were better here than on the Continent, he plainly shows that this was very slight praise indeed, for, if his picture of the Continental Cluniacs be at all accurate, it seems remarkable that they were even tolerated. Much allowance, however, must be made for his animus—Peter de Leia was a Cluniac—and for his love of scandal. But the fact that the Cluniacs were under the supervision of French houses, to which they paid an annual rent, was not likely to commend them to the nation at large. It was not until 1332 that Cluniac monks were even naturalized in this country. Their first house in England was at Lewes, in Sussex, and was established in 1078. In Wales they had cells at Malpas, near Newport, in Monmouthshire, and at St. Clears, in Carmarthenshire. There was also a cell in the Marches at Clifford. Malpas was founded in the twelfth century by Winewald de Badon, as a cell to Montacute, in Somersetshire. It had two monks only. St. Clears is not mentioned until 1291. It was a cell to St. Martin des Champs, Paris, and had a prior and two monks.[1] A report of a visitation of Cluniac houses in 1279 states that 'the Prior and his companion' lived dishonourably and incontinently, that the buildings were in an exceedingly bad state, and the revenues of the priory wasted. In 1412 the house was reported to be in decent order so far as was permitted by the condition of the country, which was very bad. As an alien priory, St. Clears was suppressed by Henry V., and in 1441 its revenues were given to All Souls' College, Oxford.[2]

The only house of the Grandmontines was a cell at Craswall, near Hay, within the ancient diocese of St. David's. It was founded about 1216 by Walter de Lacy for a prior and ten monks. It suffered the lot of the other alien priories, and was given to Christ's College, Cambridge. Gerald speaks favourably of this order in his 'Mirror of the Church.'

The Tironian Benedictines had in Wales Llandudoch, or St. Dogmael's, Pill, and Caldey, all in Pembrokeshire. These were the only monasteries of the order in England and Wales. St. Dogmael's, which got its name from the older monastery near which it stood, was founded by Martin de Turribus, and completed by his son Robert. Pill was founded by Adam de la Roche, and was at first a cell to St. Dogmael's, but afterwards became independent.

[1] Dugdale, 'Monasticon,' p. 1026.   [2] Leland, 'Itin.,' v. 13.

Caldey also became a cell to St. Dogmael's. But all these monasteries seem afterwards to have forsaken the Tironian order and to have become ordinary Benedictine houses.

The first Cistercians to come to Wales were the Grey Brothers of Sauvigny, a colony from which abbey was planted near Neath in 1130 by Richard de Granville and his wife Constance.[1] In the next year Walter de Clare established at Tintern[2] a body of Cistercians from L'Aumone. A few years later, in 1143, Bishop Bernard of St. David's performed one of the chief acts of his notable episcopate by bringing Cistercians to Trêfgarn, in Daugleddau,[3] whence they soon removed to Whitland, of which house nearly all the later Welsh Cistercian abbeys were daughters.[4]

Up to this date the native population of Wales had remained wholly uninfluenced by the plantation of foreign orders, except in so far as they may have aroused feelings of antipathy as the allies of their invaders. But Bernard's foundation of Whitland seems to have attracted their interest, and before long their admiration. Here, on the site of one of their ancient monasteries, they beheld men who by their ascetic life recalled the memories of their ancient saints, and by their deeds of charity, done alike to Welshman and Norman, showed in a practical manner their belief in the precepts of the Divine Master. These men seemed to them very different from the monks of Benedictine cells, who lived an easy and somewhat self-indulgent life, secure in their distance from the dis-

[1] 'Annales Cambriæ,' p. 39, under 1130: 'Fundata est abbatia de Neth.' See also Foundation Charter and two charters of confirmation by King John (A.D. 1207-8) in Francis, 'Charters, etc., of Neath.' Dugdale, 'Monasticon,' p. 719.
[2] Dugdale, 'Monasticon,' p. 731, which contains a charter of William, Earl Marshal, junior.
[3] 'Annales Menevenses,' in Wharton's 'Anglia Sacra,' ii. 649.
[4] 'Quæ duo quidem sola matrici domui de Albalonda cæterarumque fere cunctarum ordinis hujus matri per Walliam totam non subjiciuntur.' 'Spec. Eccl,' iii. 1: Op. iv. 129. Charter of King John is given by Dugdale, 'Monasticon,' p. 884.

ciplinary control of the abbot of the mother house in
England or France. The Benedictines, too, lived in the
towns where the English garrisons dwelt, and beneath the
protection of the Norman castles, and mixed but little
with the native population, whereas the Cistercians lived
remote from garrisons and castles, and in the wildest
parts of the country beside the rivers, raised the lofty
fanes which even in desolation and decay excite the
wonder and admiration of later ages by their loveliness,
and in their fresh beauty doubtless stirred the feelings of
a race that has ever loved the beautiful. Whitland, the
home of Paulinus and David; Tintern, where Tewdrig
the martyr had lived as a hermit and died a patriot; the
vale of Neath, the sacred retreat of Cadoc; Margam, an
ancient home of Celtic piety, were already hallowed to
the Celtic race by old associations, and the order that
inhabited anew these ancient sanctuaries, that put not its
trust in princes or foreign conquerors, but ministered to
the poor Welsh rustics among whom it dwelt, enlisted in
its favour the sympathies of the native population and the
patronage of the native princes.

Cwmhir, in Radnorshire, situated in a lovely and lonely
valley, was founded, very soon after the establishment of
Whitland, by Cadwallon ap Madoc, the owner of the
district, and settled by a colony from Whitland.[1] It
received also at a later date large endowments from his
son Howel, and grandson Meredith ap Maelgwn, and
from his brother Einion Clyd, as well as from the
Norman, Roger Mortimer. A few years later, in 1164, as
the Welsh Chronicle relates, 'by the permission of God
and the inspiration of the Holy Spirit, a convent of
monks came first to Ystrad Fflur,[2] which is better known
by its Latin name of Strata Florida. This was 'first

---

[1] Dugdale, 'Monasticon,' p. 825 (with charters from Llywelyn ap
Iorwerth and Henry III.).
[2] 'Brut y Tywysogion,' p. 202.

founded,' according to Gerald, ' by a noble man, Robert Fitz-Stephen,' and afterwards richly endowed by the Welsh prince, Rhys ap Gruffydd,[1] who, as we have seen, was the founder of the Premonstratensian Abbey of Talley, and who was also a benefactor to Whitland and founder of a Cistercian nunnery. It is worthy of notice that Talley was an abbey, not a cell, and therefore under stricter discipline than the Welsh Benedictine priories, and that it belonged to a reformed and austere order, and one that chose out the desolate places of the wilderness to be its homes. In all these respects Talley resembled the Cistercian houses, and it is easy, therefore, to infer what were the particular monastic features that attracted the Welsh. The movement was now fast becoming a national one, for in 1170 we find the patriotic prince and bard, Owain Cyfeiliog, founding and endowing the Montgomeryshire abbey of Ystrad Marchell, or Strata Marcella. In 1186 a colony from Strata Florida was settled at Aberconway,[2] an abbey which was largely endowed by Llywelyn ap Iorwerth, who was buried there; Cymmer

[1] 'Spec. Eccl.,' iii. 5: Op. iv. 152 : ' Erat autem domus monialium pauperum in dextralis Walliae parte superiori sita, a Reso Griffini filio principe regionis illius suis nostrisque diebus egregio fundata, et praediis ac pascuis, quibus vivere juxta modulum suum Deoque servire poterant, caritative dotata. *Erat et domus Cisterciensis ordinis opima sub montanis Elennith, a nobili viro Roberto Stephani filio in pascuis pinguibus et amplis primum fundata*, nec propinqua tamen priori quinimmo remota. Sed postmodum a dicto principe terris fertilibus et grangiis plurimis abunde ditata, adeo quidem ut tempore procedente, cunctis domibus ordinis ejusdem Walliae totius armentis et equitiis, pecoribus ac pecudibus, et opulentiis ex his provenientibus, longe copiosius esset locupletata.' This Cistercian house is the same as that to which Gerald pledged his books, and must be Strata Florida. If his statement be accepted, this settles the question as to who was the founder of Strata Florida, and disposes alike of the claims of Rhys ap Tewdwr and Rhys ap Gruffydd. For other opinions see Mr. Stephen W. Williams' valuable monograph on ' The Cistercian Abbey of Strata Florida,' and papers by Mr. S. W. Williams and Mr. Willis-Bund in ' Arch. Camb.' for 1889, pp. 5-23. The Charter of Rhys ap Gruffydd (Dugdale, ' Monasticon,' p. 893) states that he began to build the abbey, loved and cherished it when built, increased its property and augmented its estates.

[2] Charter of Llywelyn ap Iorwerth in Dugdale's 'Monasticon,' p. 918.

was settled by a colony from Cwmhir in 1198; and in 1200 the lovely valley of the Dee received the added loveliness which its rivals, Conway and Mawddach, had worn before, for in that year, as the Welsh Chronicle relates, ' Madoc, the son of Gruffydd Maelor, founded the monastery of Llanegwestl near the old cross in Iâl,'[1] or, to use the more familiar names, the monastery of Valle Crucis near Eliseg's pillar. There was also a Cistercian nunnery in North Wales, at Llanllugan in Montgomeryshire, which received a grant of tithes in 1239 from a Bishop of St. Asaph, and in Leland's time was ' a very poor little nunnery.' Leland tells us also that Clynog Fawr, the old seat of St. Beuno's monastery, was made a monastery of White Monks, which, however, was suppressed ' many yeres ' before his time.

Meanwhile, in South Wales the Cistercian movement had been progressing under Norman auspices. Robert of Gloucester, in 1147, founded what Gerald calls ' the noble Cistercian monastery ' of Margam, which he admired both for its beauty and for the renown of its charitable deeds. Another abbey was founded in the same year at Dore, in Herefordshire, by Robert, youngest son of Harold, the Lord of Ewias.[2] In 1226 John of Monmouth founded the Abbey of Grace Dieu.[3] It was utterly destroyed by the Welsh in a very short time, but was refounded by the same benefactor in 1236 in a different place.[4] A few ruins still remain about two miles from Monmouth, and a farm called Parker's Due preserves a distorted reminiscence of the name. Caerleon and Llantarnam in the same county were also Cistercian houses. Llanllyr in Cardiganshire was a Cistercian nunnery and a cell of Strata Florida. One monastery in North Wales, that of Basingwerk, must

---

[1] ' Brut y Tywysogion,' p. 256. Charter of Madoc in Dugdale, ' Monasticon,' p. 895, where it is confused with Strata Marcella.
[2] Dugdale, ' Monasticon,' p. 862.
[3] ' Annales de Waverleia,' A.D. 1226 ('Annales Monastici,' ii. 302).
[4] *Ibid.*, A.D. 1236 ('Annales Monastici,' ii. 317).

be added to the list of Norman foundations. About 1131 Ralph, second Earl of Chester, who is sometimes accounted the founder,[1] gave benefactions to Basingwerk, but when Archbishop Baldwin and Gerald lodged here in 1188 it was still merely 'a little cell.' The position of the abbey on rising ground in the immediate vicinity of a castle seems to indicate that it was not originally a Cistercian settlement, and it is not improbable that the order came here very early in the thirteenth century, at which date, as is indicated by the architecture of its ruins, the present Cistercian abbey was raised, not by Welshmen, but by the English.[2]

Though some of the Cistercian abbeys of Wales must have been exceedingly beautiful in themselves, as well as in their surroundings of hills, valleys, and streams, neither they nor any other of the Welsh monasteries can be compared to the great English monasteries in wealth or extent of buildings. Two only, Tintern and Valle Crucis, possessed at the dissolution a yearly income of over £200, and even these are doubtful. Their estates in some cases were extensive, but the land was frequently poor and unproductive. This comparative poverty of the Welsh houses offered temptations to the vice of avarice, to which they were so generally subject. Gerald relates other cases besides the oppression of Talley by Whitland, and of the Snowdon house by Aberconway. Two neighbouring Cistercian houses near the coast of South Wales, possibly Margam and Neath, had a very long and bitter dispute about their boundaries, for the richer was ever seeking to rob and harass its poorer sister. Finally, however, a monk of the poorer house gathered a band of Welshmen, and organized a raid upon the lands of the oppressors, and having

---

[1] 'Dugdale, 'Monasticon' (p. 720), gives a charter of Henry II., confirming the grants of Ralph, Earl of Chester. There are charters also of Llywelyn ap Iorwerth and David to this abbey.

[2] 'Arch. Camb.' for 1891, pp. 126-134.

thoroughly routed them and their allies (for they also had hired a party of Welshmen), he carried off a quantity of spoil to the mountains. This exercise of what Gerald calls 'Welsh law,' wonderful to relate, restored peace between the rival houses, and thenceforward they managed to live in tolerable concord.[1] Cwmhir and Strata Marcella had a similar dispute respecting rights of pasturage, but in this case 'Welsh law' does not appear to have been called into requisition, for the matter was settled in 1226 by a compromise. Gerald mentions also a case in which a Welsh nunnery, founded in South Wales by Rhys ap Gruffydd, was oppressed by Strata Florida.[2]

In spite, however, of the comparative poverty of Welsh abbeys, the Cistercians had some very fine churches. That which was planned on the largest scale, Cwmhir, was never finished. Leland says of it that no Welsh church 'is scene of such lenght, as the fundation of walles ther begon doth show; but the third part of this worke was never finischid.' Only the nave was completed, and this was 242 feet in length, the longest in Wales; the next, the nave of Strata Marcella, being only 201 feet. Strata Florida comes third with $132\frac{1}{2}$ feet. The total length of Strata Marcella was 273 feet, and of Strata Florida 213. The length of the nave of Neath, which Leland considered 'the fairest abbay of al Wales,'[3] and the beauty of which is celebrated by Lewis Morganwg, the bard, was 110 feet.

[1] 'Spec. Eccl.,' iii. 1 : Op. iv. 129-133.
[2] *Ibid.*, iii. 5 : Op. iv. 153.
[3] 'Itin.,' v. 13.

CHAPTER XI.

THE AGE OF THE TWO LLYWELYNS.

THE period of Welsh history which comprises the reigns of the two Llywelyns (1194-1282) is one of national glory and of literary brilliancy, but of grievous trouble to the Welsh Church. This was in part due to the opposing elements of which that Church was now composed. There was the old Welsh stock, generally conservative of old customs and even abuses, and there was 'the English plantation,' which had great power in the southern dioceses, and was favourable to modern usages and reforms. There were, again, the Benedictines, who were generally English in nationality and sympathies, and there were their rivals the Cistercians, who, in no small degree, leaned upon the support of the native princes, and threw in their lot with the native population. Both of these orders were objects of dislike to the secular clergy, whether native or English; yet clergy and monks were united in a common jealousy of the new missionary organizations of the friars. The Church, therefore, was a house divided against itself, and, so far as by its leaders it mixed in the life-and-death struggle of Welsh independence, it played an inglorious part. But even had it been united it could have done little, since it was under the yoke of the Papal See, which first encouraged and then repressed the assertors of Welsh freedom, gambling away for its own selfish ends the lives and liberties of Welshmen. But though the Church at this time did little for Wales, or for the general weal of either nation (so far, at least, as concerned their political condition), it suffered grievously alike from English and Welsh, according to the fortune of war.

King John had attempted to propitiate Llywelyn ap Iorwerth by giving him his daughter in marriage; but this had but little influence upon the conduct and policy of that ambitious and able prince, who, although recognised by the English as 'Prince of Aberffraw, and Lord of Snowdon only,' aspired to the higher dignity of Prince of an united and independent Wales. Gwenwynwyn of Powys, who at first resisted his power, was forced to submit, and all the princes of Wales, hitherto so restive and jealous of any semblance of superior authority, found it expedient to acknowledge Llywelyn as their lord paramount. John soon discovered that his son-in-law would not be a very obedient vassal, and was provoked to reprisals. In 1211[1] he made an attack upon Wales, in consequence of what the Welsh Chronicle calls Llywelyn's 'cruel attacks upon the English.' He laid siege to Deganwy Castle, at the mouth of the Conway; but his army was reduced to great straits for lack of provisions, so that 'an egg was sold for a penny halfpenny, and it was a delicious feast to them to get horseflesh.' In consequence of this John retired, but returned in August and burned Bangor, and 'Robert, Bishop of Bangor, was seized in his church, and was afterwards ransomed for two hundred hawks.' Llywelyn made peace, and gave hostages and cattle and horses, and gave also 'the midland district[2] to the King for ever.' But the next year Llywelyn reconquered all that he had

---

[1] A.D. 1210 in 'Brut y Tywysogion,' pp. 266-271. But 'Annales Cambriæ,' p. 67, gives 1211 as the date.
[2] Perfeddwlad, the country between Dee and Conway.

lost, and, as the Chronicle records, Pope Innocent removed the interdict from the dominions of Llywelyn ap Iorwerth, and Gwenwynwyn, and Maelgwn ap Rhys, and 'commanded them for the pardon of their sins to give a sincere pledge of warring against the iniquity of the King,' an order which forthwith they joyfully obeyed. In 1215 the Welsh princes combined with the barons and overran South Wales, capturing the castles of Senghenydd, Kidwelly, Carmarthen, Llanstephan, St. Clears, Llaugharne, Newport (Pembrokeshire), Cardigan, and Cilgerran.[1] It is not strange that at a time of such confusion the chapter of St. David's declined to accept Hugh Foliot, John's nominee, as their bishop, and elected a thorough Welshman, Iorwerth, Abbot of Talley, whom the King ultimately accepted.[2] But the canons attended at London, and again at Rochester, for the election, and the Abbot of Talley was consecrated by the Archbishop of Canterbury, June 21, 1215.[3] At the same time was consecrated also Cadwgan, Abbot of Whitland, whom John had nominated to the See of Bangor, as the see was vacant through the death of Robert. It is rather curious that Llywelyn should have permitted this nomination, but perhaps, as the Pope had now taken John under his protection, he did not care to bring down the wrath of Rome too severely upon his head. It is noticeable also that John could not venture to nominate an Englishman.

The tyranny of English kings was now succeeded by

[1] 'Brut y Tywysogion' (Rolls ed.), p. 288.
[2] Geoffrey had died in the previous year. 'Annales Cambriæ,' p. 72. 'Galfridus Menevensis episcopus obiit. cui successit Gervasius : consecratus est Gervasius Menevensis episcopus.' So MS. C. under 1214. But Gervase, or Iorwerth, was really consecrated in 1215 ('Brut y Tywysogion,' p. 284).
[3] Bishop Iorwerth mediated in 1216 or 1217 between Llywelyn ap Iorwerth and the people of Ros. 'Brut y Tywysogion,' A.D. 1217, p. 301 ; 'Annales Camb.' A.D. 1216, p. 72. The latter authority is angry with Iorwerth, or Gervasius, as it calls him : ' Wallensibus magis nocuit quam profuit.'

Papal tyranny. In 1215 Llywelyn was excommunicated. In the following year Wales was placed under an interdict by the Papal Legate Gualo, 'for holding with the barons' against the young King Henry, but this was taken off in 1217 or 1218.[1] However, in 1219 Pandulph, the Papal Legate, invaded the privileges of the Welsh Church by issuing a 'provision' for the See of Llandaff, on the death of Henry, its bishop. William, Prior of Goldcliff, was the clergyman thus appointed.[2] In 1223 Pope Honorius III. ordered the Archbishop of York to excommunicate Llywelyn and place his lands under an interdict. The Bull enumerates five occasions on which Llywelyn, 'styled Prince of North Wales,' had sworn to be faithful to the crown of England, and orders that, inasmuch as he was accustomed to prevarication and ready to deceive, the archbishop and his suffragans should place the lands of the prince and his supporters under the strictest interdict, 'so that besides baptism, penance, and extreme unction, all the sacraments of the Church should be there denied, and the bodies of the dead should not receive Church burial.' If this punishment did not bring the offenders to their senses, the archbishop and his suffragans were further ordered, at the expiration of six months from the publication of this interdict, to absolve Llywelyn's subjects from their allegiance.[3] Again, in 1231, a council was held at Oxford, to which the bishops of the province of Canterbury, and among them the Bishops of St. David's and Llandaff, were summoned, and by this Llywelyn was excommunicated as 'a violator of churches.'

'One thousand, two hundred and forty was the year of Christ,' says the Welsh chronicler, 'when Llywelyn ap Iorwerth, Prince of Wales, died—the man whose good

[1] 'Brut y Tywysogion.'
[2] Browne Willis, 'Landaff,' Appendix, pp. 113, 114.
[3] Rymer, 'Fœdera,' i. 1, 180 (ed. of 1816), where it is placed under 1225; H. and S., i. 459-461, where the date is corrected.

works it would be difficult to enumerate—and was buried at Aberconway, after taking the habit of religion.'[1] Rarely has Wales had such a leader as Llywelyn, who has been worthily styled 'the Great.' Disunion is the besetting sin of the Celtic race, and Wales has not been without its share of this quality. But Llywelyn, by his force of character and his prowess in arms, united for once the hitherto divided and weakened forces of Wales into one powerful body, and thereby exposed English supremacy to imminent danger of extinction. 'Destroy England and plunder its multitudes,' is the exhortation which one of his bards[2] addresses to him, and the advice was followed so far as the English towns of South Wales were concerned, for there were few, or none, that felt not the power of the allied armies under his command. But his abilities were not confined to leadership or to war. Not only 'did he rule his foes with shield and spear,' and extend his boundaries by warlike achievements, he also 'gave food and clothing to Christ's poor,' he 'bestowed justice on all according to their merits, with the love and fear of God;' he 'bound all men to himself by love,' and he 'kept peace for the monks.'[3] The bards who thronged his court and flourished under his protection extolled him not only as the protector of his country, the generous maintainer of bards, the joy of armies, and a lion in danger, but withal as 'a tender-hearted prince, wise, witty, and ingenious.'[4] His wisdom was especially manifested by his willingness to receive under his care and foster by his protection all the movements and agencies of his day which seemed most to make for righteousness. He gave large endowments to the Cistercian Abbey of Aberconway, though a narrow-minded Welshman might have organized the total expulsion of the Latin orders, and he chose this abbey as his burial-

---

[1] 'Brut y Tywysogion,' p. 327. [2] Elidir Sais.
[3] 'Annales Cambriæ,' pp. 82, 83. [4] Eineon ap Gwgan.

place, where he was laid in his grave in the habit of a monk. He was also a patron of the friars, for he founded the friary of Llanfaes in Anglesey in memory of his wife, Joan. But this was not all; he endowed the Benedictines of Penmon, although, as a general rule, the Benedictine Order was more closely attached to his opponents, for most of the English monastic houses in South Wales were Benedictine. Owain Glyndwr would not have done the like. As a good Welshman and a good Churchman he strongly supported Gerald de Barri in his attempt to maintain the cause of the chapter of St. David's, offering to give double to any of the clergy who suffered losses from the English in the patriotic cause, and a settlement in his dominions to any who were exiled. The Welsh element in the National Church of Wales undoubtedly derived great support from his victories, and the English element was correspondingly depressed; but it is certainly noteworthy that so gallant a supporter of the Welsh cause was so broad-minded in his sympathies. The interests of the Welsh Church might have been safely left in the hands of so enlightened a ruler as Llywelyn the Great.

His favourite son, David, who inherited his dominions, was a very inferior man in abilities and character, and Wales under his rule very speedily lost the position that Llywelyn had gained for it. He was the younger son, and, in defiance of a solemn compact, kept his elder brother, Gruffydd, in prison. Richard, Bishop of Bangor, interfered on behalf of Gruffydd, and excommunicated David, and in consequence found it advisable to quit Wales. Gruffydd was wholly a Welshman, by both parents, whereas David had Angevin blood on the side of his mother, who was Joan, the daughter of King John: but this relationship to the English royal family did not prevent the interference of Henry III., who demanded that David should give up his brother into his hands. In 1241, says the 'Annals,' 'the King of England subdued all the Welsh to himself.'[1] David was forced to surrender Gruffydd, and to acknowledge the supremacy of the King of England. His submission was guaranteed by the Bishops of Bangor and St. Asaph, who bound themselves to carry out to the full any sentence of excommunication or interdict which might be published in the event of David's failure to keep to his obligations.[2] The unfortunate Gruffydd soon after perished in an attempt to escape from the Tower of London by letting himself down by a rope. 'The rope breaking, he fell and broke his neck.'[3] As for David, he found the English yoke so oppressive that he attempted, in 1244, to secure the protection of Rome, by offering Pope Innocent IV. to hold his principality in immediate dependence upon the Papal See, a desperate proposal, which clearly indicates the prince's utter incapacity for government. He sent messengers to the Pope for this object, and promised to pay him annually five hundred marks. David's arguments, backed up by the expenditure of a large sum of money, procured the appointment by the Pope of the Abbots of Aberconway and Cymmer to investigate the matter.

Armed with the Pope's mandate, the two abbots summoned King Henry to appear before them at Caerwys, on January 20, 1245, that they might carry out the prescribed inquiry. This, however, enraged the King and his barons, and they refused compliance with the impudent order, and only hurried on the more their preparations against Wales. Innocent soon found it expedient to recall his commission, and issued a somewhat apologetic mandate to the Bishops of Ely and Carlisle to reverse the abbots' proceedings;[4] but, as Matthew Paris sarcastically notices, he kept David's

[1] 'Annales Cambriæ,' p. 83.
[2] Rymer, 'Fœdera,' i. 1, 242, 243. (Caley and Holbrooke.)
[3] 'Brut y Tywysogion,' p. 330, under A.D. 1244.
[4] Rymer, 'Fœdera,' i. 1, 255. Dated April 8, 1244.

money, nevertheless. David was excommunicated at the end of the year;[1] and, in March 1246, he died at Aber, and was buried with his father at Aberconway.[2]

A graphic picture of the state of Wales and its Church at this disastrous time is presented to us in the pages of Matthew Paris. 'Wales,' he says, 'was hard pressed in these days; for tillage, commerce, and the pastoral care of flocks ceased; and they began to be consumed by hunger, and were (all unwillingly) bowed beneath the laws of the English. Their ancient, proud nobility withered away, and even the harp of the men of the Church was turned to mourning and lamentation. So the Bishop of Menevia, that is, of St. David's, died, wasting away from grief. William, Bishop of Llandaff, is stricken with blindness. The Bishop of St. Asaph, and the Bishop of Bangor, their sees destroyed by fire and sword, were compelled to beg, so as to live on alms.'

Gerald has given us copious materials respecting the Bishops of St. David's who held the see during his lifetime, but we know comparatively little of the bishops of other sees during the period we have been considering, so that the glimpse which Matthew Paris affords us of the Welsh bishops in 1247 is full of interest. The unfortunate Bishop of St. David's whose death he mentions at that date was Anselm, surnamed Le Gras,[3] who had succeeded Iorwerth after a short interval. William of Llandaff was William de Burgh, who died in 1253, after having suffered blindness for seven years, which cover nearly all the period of his episcopacy, for he was consecrated in February, 1245. Immediately after his appointment he was excused attendance at the Council of Lyons by Pope Innocent IV. on the ground that he was 'stripped of all the property of his bishopric by the

---

[1] Rymer, 'Fœdera,' i. 1, 258; H. and S., i. 472.
[2] 'Annales Cambriæ,' p. 85; 'Brut y Tywysogion,' p. 332.
[3] 'Anseul Vras.' 'Brut y Tywysogion,' p. 332.

King's enemies.'[1] He had previously been chaplain to Henry III.

There had been three bishops between him and William of Saltmarsh, the first Norman Bishop of Llandaff. These were Henry, Prior of Abergavenny, William, Prior of Goldcliff, and Elias de Radnor. The first-named divided the lands of the bishop and chapter, which had never been divided before, and assigned prebends to fourteen canons.[2] He died in 1218.[3] In the next year the Prior of Goldcliff was consecrated at Canterbury.[4] The troubled condition of the diocese in his time may be inferred from the short and scanty notices of the Annalist of the Glamorganshire Abbey of Margam, who relates ravages committed by the Welsh on the possessions of his abbey, and the neighbouring abbey of Neath, and the burning in the year 1226 of the Glamorganshire towns of St. Nicholas, Newcastle and Laleston.[5] The bishop died in 1229.[6] Elias de Radnor, treasurer of Hereford, was elected in the next year,[7] and was consecrated on Advent Sunday at Merton, in spite of the opposition of the monks of Canterbury, who asserted that he ought to have been consecrated at Canterbury.[8] The Annalist of Margam relates various disasters suffered by South Wales about this time, especially how, in 1231, Llywelyn captured Brecon and burned it, but could not

---

[1] Rymer, ' Fœdera,' i. 1, 259.
[2] 'Ad illius usque tempora præsulatus, Episcopalia, et Capitularia prædia indiscreta permansere. Quatuordecim Canonicis hic primus præbendas assignavit : et Capitulo elargitus quæ nunc possidet ; cætera sibi successoribusque retinuit.' Godwin, 'De Præsulibus,' p. 605 (Richardson's ed.).
[3] 'Annales de Margan' ('Annales Monastici,' i. 33).
[4] Ibid., i. 33 ; 'Annales de Theokesberia,' in 'Annales Monastici,' i. 64.
[5] 'Annales de Margan' ('Annales Monastici,' i. 34, 35).
[6] 'Hoc anno obiit Willelmus Landavensis episcopus v. kal. Februarii "Annales de Margan" (" A. M.," i. 37), "Annales de Theokesberia" ("A. M.," i. 73).'
[7] 'Annales de Margan' ('A. M.,' i. 38).
[8] 'Annales de Theokesberia' ('A. M.,' i. 77).

take the castle; afterwards, coming farther south, he burned Caerleon and its church, but there also failed to take the castle. He succeeded, however, in capturing Neath Castle, and forced the Abbey of Margam to pay him sixty marks of silver.[1] The Annalist of Tewkesbury relates a curious and instructive story respecting the church of Llanblethian, near Cowlridge, which illustrates the unsettled character of the times. The Abbey of Tewkesbury claimed the church, and Bishop Elias, in 1231, allowed the claim, whereupon a monk was sent to take seisin. However, when he came, he found that Ralph Mailok, who held the church and had withstood the claim of the abbey, had caused the key to be carried off to the mountains. The monk consequently 'took what seisin he could, namely, the door of the church,' and appealed on behalf of the privileges of his monastery, whereupon he was himself carried off to the mountains, and kept a prisoner for three days. Bishop Elias interfered, and excommunicated the offenders, and sent his sentence up to Hubert de Burgh, the justiciary; and Abbot Peter, of Tewkesbury, also excommunicated the leader of the outrage, one John Grant.[2]

Squabbles of this kind between the abbey and the Welsh were not unfrequent; only the year before there had been a difficulty about Llantwit Major, where, according to the Welsh custom, the people desired the appointment of the brother of the late holder of the benefice.[3] After the death of Elias de Radnor in 1240,[4] the see remained vacant for some years, in consequence of a dispute between the King and the chapter. The latter elected Maurice, Archdeacon of Llandaff,[5] but the

---

[1] 'Annales de Margan' ('A. M.,' i. 38, 39).
[2] 'Annales de Theokesberia' ('A. M.,' i. 80, 81).
[3] *Ibid.*, p. 75. Landirwit is the name mentioned, supposed by the editor, with good reason, to be Llantwit Major.
[4] *Ibid.*, p. 114.
[5] *Ibid.*, p. 116, under date A.D. 1140.

King quashed the election, probably becaus˙ he was a Welshman.¹ During this vacancy, difficulties again arose about Llanblethian. The Archdeacon of Llandaff nominated one Thomas of Penarth as vicar, but the Abbot of Tewkesbury forced him to resign, and receive a fresh appointment from himself.² One Roger Meylok also, who was probably of the same family as Ralph Mailok before-mentioned, gave trouble about the church, carrying off the corn, and threatening to ravage the possessions of Tewkesbury, both in England and Wales, so that the abbot found it advisable to buy him off by paying him twelve marks annually, until he could provide him with some benefice either in England or Wales.³

The troublous nature of the times in Wales and the borders is further indicated by the statement that, in 1231, the Prior of Leominster paid a large sum of money to Llywelyn to buy peace from him.⁴ The confusion in the diocese of Llandaff was further augmented at times by the conflicting claims of the Crown and of the De Clares as lords of Glamorgan. During the vacancy of the see after the death of Elias de Radnor, Maurice, the Archdeacon of Llandaff, died, and Richard de Clare appointed in his stead one Ralph of Newcastle. The chapter was divided in opinion as to the appointment, which had been made when the King was away from England, and finally another archdeacon was appointed by royal authority, and Ralph was forced to yield—' being unwilling to open a controversy on account of his lord,

---

[1] Maurice probably is Meurig. Browne Willis ('Survey of Landaff, p. 49) inserts a William de Christchurch between Elias de Radnor and William de Burgh. His name is not mentioned in the list in the ' Book of Llan Dâv,' and the 'Annales de Theokesberia' speaks of the see as vacant. Yet he seems to have been elected, but there is no record of his consecration. See also H. and S., i. 467.
[2] 'Annales de Theokesberia' ('A. M.,' i. 125).
[3] *Ibid*, p. 126.
[4] *Ibid.*, p. 80.

the said Richard de Clare, who had not yet received seisin of his lands in England.'¹

Brief and scanty as are the notices of the Annalists, they are in their way as valuable to the student as the finished portraits of Giraldus; for, although we can form very little idea respecting the personal qualities of the bishops of Llandaff during the time of Llywelyn ap Iorwerth and David, we can judge pretty accurately what was the state of the diocese. Llandaff was the only one of the four Welsh dioceses in which the English or Norman episcopate was still maintained. All its bishops seem to have been English by descent, though three of the four latest were connected with Wales by family or position prior to their election. The influence of the De Clares, and the extent of the English 'plantation' of Glamorganshire, would account for this in part. Yet even here the chapter sought to appoint a Welshman in 1240, for Maurice, then elected, was probably Meurig, and another Maurice, son of Rely Wrgan, whom he appointed to Llandough, is stated to have been his nephew.²

In North Wales the English episcopate had broken down, and it would seem that both Richard of Bangor and Howel ap Ednyfed, whose miserable exile is described by Matthew Paris, were native-born Welshmen. Richard had, in 1237, succeeded Cadwgan of Whitland, for, as the Welsh Chronicle relates, in the previous year, Pope Gregory IX. released Cadwgan from his diocese, and ' he was honourably received into the white religious society in the monastery of Dor, and there he died and was buried.' Between Reiner of St. Asaph, who held the see at the time of Baldwin's itinerary, and Howel ap Ednyfed there had been two Bishops of St. Asaph of whom little is known; the first, Abraham, who

---

[1] 'Annales de Theokesberia' ("A. M.,' i. 131, under date 1243). Browne Willis ('Landaff,' p. 79) says that the King appointed Thomas, his chaplain, in place of Ralph.

[2] 'Annales de Theokesberia' ('A. M.,' i. 128, 129).

was consecrated in 1225 and died in or about 1234, and the other, Hugo, or Howel I. The unfortunate Howel ap Ednyfed died in 1247 at Oxford, and was there buried.[1]

The glory of Wales, which had suffered eclipse by the death of Llywelyn ap Iorwerth, was revived again by his grandson and namesake, Llywelyn, the son of the unfortunate Gruffydd, who on the death of his uncle David succeeded to a share of his principality. At first his brother, Owain the Red, held half of the inheritance, but after his overthrow Llywelyn became the acknowledged head of the people against the English, and by his conquest of Perfeddwlad and other successes, aroused the national spirit. During the Barons' War he was the undisputed master of Wales, and after its close he obtained from England, as the price of his allegiance, an acknowledgment of his authority as Prince of Wales—a title which had never been conceded to his illustrious grandfather.[2] Courtly bards sang his achievements, as a few years before they or their predecessors had sung those of his grandfather, and old predictions were revived and new ones invented to animate the race with the hope of throwing off for good and all the hated yoke of the false Saxon. Had Henry III.'s son been as weak as himself the reign of Llywelyn ap Gruffydd might have been the most glorious in the annals of Wales, and no melancholy pity would be blended with the pride which the mention of his name awakens in the heart of every Welshman.

Unfortunately the Welsh Church suffered even from Welsh successes, and stood in utmost need of a cessation of their constant warfare. Yet it produced, in these troubled times, at least one or two bishops of decided ability and character. Most of the bishops of the period were either Welsh by blood and place of birth, or at least had some connection with Wales and its Church prior to their election. Thomas Wallensis, who was elected in

[1] 'Brut y Tywysogion,' p. 332. [2] Rymer, 'Fœdera,' i. 1, 474.

1247 to the See of St. David's on the death of Anselm,
was a Welshman by descent, as his name implies. He
had been Archdeacon of Lincoln before his appointment,
and is praised by Roger Bacon, in his 'De Utilitate
Scientiarum,' together with Bishop Grosseteste and Adam
Marsh, for his earnest study of languages and science.
The bishopric was considered unworthy of the acceptance
of so distinguished a man, for, as Matthew Paris tells us,
it was 'very poor' and 'slender,'[1] but he was led to
accept it by various motives, among which were a natural
love for his country and a desire to be of use to it.
During his tenure of the see a controversy arose with the
royal courts, which sought to deprive the bishop of his
right of jurisdiction regarding questions of patronage, and
Thomas Wallensis appealed to the Pope against the
royal interference, and obtained a Bull from Innocent IV.
in his favour.[2] This good bishop died in 1255,[3] and was
succeeded in the next year by Richard de Carew, or De
Caron, whom the 'Welsh Chronicle' calls Rhys of Caer
Rhiw,[4] and who was elected by the chapter, and consecrated at Rome by Pope Alexander IV., independently of
the Crown.[5] The reason of this consecration is unknown.
Richard seems, from his name, to have been a native of
Pembrokeshire, and when elected was a canon of St.
David's. As he was appointed one of the arbitrators who
settled the Dictum of Kenilworth, he must have been a
man of some weight and character. In the same year as
Richard's consecration, William of Radnor was elected
Bishop of Llandaff on the death of John de la Ware,[6] who
had been bishop since the death of the blind William de

---

[1] Pauperrimus, exilis.
[2] Rymer. 'Fœdera,' i. 1, 283.
[3] 'Brut y Tywysogion' (p. 341) gives 1254, but the 'Annales Cambriæ' (p. 90) 1255, which is right.
[4] 'Brut y Tywysogion,' p. 342, under 1255.
[5] Documents in H. and S., i. 481-484.
[6] Formerly Abbot of Margam.

Burgh in 1253. William of Radnor's election was carried out in opposition to the King's will,[1] but the royal consent was given notwithstanding, and he was duly consecrated by Archbishop Boniface, 1257. At this time the Welsh were in arms under Llywelyn and were successful, and the King had also troubles nearer home, so that it was scarcely a convenient season to undertake a quarrel with the clergy of Llandaff. An indication of the disturbed state of South Wales is given by a letter of Richard de Carew to the King, written in 1265, wherein he asks him to allow his bailiff of Carmarthen to signify the royal assent to the election of a prior of St. John's, Carmarthen, in order to spare the canons a second journey to the King, as the roads were unsafe and they had not sufficient money, on account of the destruction of their house.[2] Richard de Carew died in 1280, and was buried in his cathedral. He was succeeded by Thomas Beck, of whom more will be said hereafter. William of Radnor, Bishop of Llandaff, died in 1265, and was succeeded by William de Breuse. It is evident from the history of the southern dioceses that even in these the royal authority had little power, and the chapters seem to have executed their right of election to vacancies without the King's interference. All the three bishops of Llandaff after William de Burgh were closely connected with the diocese: John de la Ware had been abbot of Margam; William of Radnor had been treasurer of the diocese, and William de Breuse had held a cathedral prebend. Thus, though these bishops were Englishmen, this was not due to the action of the Crown but to the power of the English element in the diocese itself, strengthened as it was by the influence of the De Clares.

In North Wales Llywelyn had to confront a consider-

---

[1] Browne Willis, 'Landaff,' App., 113, 114; H. and S., i. 484, 485. He had previously been treasurer of Llandaff.
[2] Letter in H. and S., i. 493, 494.

able amount of opposition from the clergy. Richard, Bishop of Bangor, after staying for some time at St. Alban's Abbey, had returned to his diocese; but he seems to have been a man of a restless and discontented spirit, for Anian of St. Asaph and certain other arbiters were called upon in 1261 to make an agreement between him and Llywelyn respecting a number of civil rights which were in dispute between them.[1] Again we find later on that he had laid an interdict on Llywelyn's chapel, not for any ecclesiastical grievances, but for purely civil matters in which he fancied himself wronged, and in 1265 a royal order was issued commanding him to withdraw this interdict.[2] Two years later, just before his death, the same bishop described his position with most piteous rhetoric in a petition to the Pope to allow him to resign his see. He was placed in desolation and beset on every hand with snares, days of affliction possessed him, and, besides the natural troubles of old age and infirmity, he was distressed by the malice of his people, who were continually agitated by blasts of sedition and insolence. He cried, wailed, shouted, and beat at the doors of his patron that he might loose that marriage tie whereby he was bound to his Church, which had now become the chains and fetters of a prison-house.[3] It is a melancholy document, but there is some reason to think that the shepherd was no less blameworthy than his flock. Bishop Richard died in the same year, and was succeeded by Anian, Archdeacon of Anglesey.

Another Anian had succeeded Howel ap Ednyfed in 1249 as Bishop of St. Asaph. It was he who, as we have seen, arbitrated between Llywelyn and Richard of Bangor. He died in 1266, and was succeeded by John, who was consecrated in the following year by the Archbishop of Canterbury. He did not hold the see long, for

[1] H. and S., i. 489-493.   [2] *Ibid.*, i. 494.
[3] *Ibid.*, i. 496, 497.

in 1268 Anian II., known as Y brawd du o Nannen, 'the black brother of Nannen,' was consecrated to the bishopric in the church of St. Mary Overies, Southwark, now known as St. Saviour's, by London Bridge. He was a Dominican, and was a prelate of a bold temper and vigorous in action, but quarrelsome and fond of litigation. He carried on three lawsuits, the first with the Abbot of Shrewsbury respecting the patronage of the vicarage of Whitchurch, which was long contested at Rome; another with the Abbot of Valle Crucis respecting the vicarages of Llangollen, Wrexham, Ruabon, Chirk, Llansaintffraid, and Llandegla; and a third with Thomas de Cantelupe, Bishop of Hereford, respecting the jurisdiction of the territory of Horddor. In the first two suits he was in the main successful, but the last was decided against him.[1]

Anian also had a struggle with Llywelyn ap Gruffydd, in which he gained his point, although the seven Cistercian abbots of Whitland, Strata Florida, Cwmhir, Strata Marcella, Aberconway, Cymmer, and Valle Crucis, who disliked this quarrelsome friar, protested to the Pope that he lied in his assertions that Llywelyn had wronged any monks or monasteries. In 1276 Anian and his chapter drew up a formidable list of twenty-nine grievances. They stated that Llywelyn did not allow the Bishops of St. Asaph to make wills, and, if they made them, treated them as void and seized their goods on their death; that any gifts made by them during their last illness were likewise appropriated; that the episcopal manors were wasted during vacancies of the see; that the canons were not allowed on a vacancy to elect without the prince's license; that bailiffs held courts in the churchyards, and sometimes even in the churches, on Sundays and festivals; that fines due to the Church were withheld and appropriated by the prince to his own use;

[1] Godwin, 'De Præsulibus,' pp. 636, 637.

that the vassals of the Church were in various ways ill-treated; that matters belonging to the Church courts were taken away from their jurisdiction; that certain procurations were violently exacted from clergy and the vassals of the Church; and that Llanrwst had been appropriated by the prince, though it had been Church property from time immemorial. These encroachments they confessed had in some degree decreased at the time of their manifesto, but they feared that Llywelyn was only waiting a suitable opportunity to renew his tyranny in its full extent.[1] Soon afterwards, however, Llywelyn ceded all the points demanded in a charter of liberties granted to the bishop and chapter. Engaged as he was in a struggle with the most powerful foe that Wales had yet encountered, he was glad almost at any price to buy off or to mitigate the enmity of the Church. But the Bishop and Chapter of St. Asaph, who took advantage of his difficulties, did not profit much otherwise by the operations of the English armies. Archbishop Kilwardby admonished the Earl of Warwick and the other captains of the English forces at Chester to respect Church property. 'The men of your army,' he said, 'setting aside the fear of God, spare not churches, churchyards, or ecclesiastical possessions and goods; hostilely attacking places and things of this kind. Some of them lately burned a certain manor of the Bishop of St. Asaph, killing one of his men there, and in different ways in other places they have committed sacrilege and rapine.'[2] This was probably written in 1277. It would seem that both in the war referred to by Kilwardby and in that of 1282 great atrocities were perpetrated on both sides. 'The Welsh are more cruel than Saracens,' wrote Archbishop Peckham to Llywelyn in 1282, when, in defiance of the

---

[1] H. and S., i. 511-516.
[2] Letter in H. and S., i. 522, 523: Browne Willis, 'St. Asaph,' App. x., vol. ii., pp. 32, 33 (Edwards' edition).

King's wishes, he came into Wales to promote the cause of peace.[1] But Llywelyn replied with a lengthy list of grievances, among which were enumerated 'the robbery and burning of churches, the slaughter of ecclesiastics—priests, monks and nuns, and others—the slaughter, too, of women, of infants at the breast and in the womb; the burning of hospitals and other religious houses; murders in churchyards, churches, and on the altars, and other crimes and deeds of sacrilege which even pagans would shudder to hear,' and in support of these general charges he added a schedule of particulars, respecting which the archbishop could make inquiry for himself. At Llangadoc, for example, the English troops had turned the church into a stable, and stripped it of its goods, and wounded the priest before the high altar. Other churches, as those of Dyngad and Llantredaff, had been despoiled of chalices, books and ornaments. We find, too, that in 1282 the English troops burned down St. Asaph's Cathedral, and the resolute Bishop Anian threatened the offenders with excommunication.

For a time Anian was under the displeasure of Edward I., who seems to have considered him too favourable to Llywelyn in the war, and he was consequently removed from his diocese. He showed considerable obstinacy in refusing to agree to the proposed transference of the monastery of Aberconway to Maenan, which the King had at heart,[2] and this somewhat delayed his restoration. He was also in disfavour for a time with Archbishop Peckham, because he alone of the suffragan bishops had delayed publishing the sentence of excom-

---

[1] See also description of the ravages of the Welsh in 1282 in 'Annales de Waverleia' ('Ann. Mon.,' ii. 398).

[2] Letters of Edward I. in Dugdale's 'Monasticon,' p. 921. This transference was accomplished. The old abbey of Aberconway stood on the site now occupied by the Castle Hotel at Conway. Maenan was a short distance up the river, nearly opposite the pretty spa of Trefriw.

munication against the Welsh who were in arms. But after the death of Llywelyn at Cilmery in December, 1282, Archbishop Peckham set himself to bring about as far as he could a general amnesty, and through his mediation Anian was enabled to make his peace with the King.

During Anian's tenure of his bishopric, and apparently about 1281, before the burning of the cathedral, an attempt was made by him, with the support of Edward I., to get the cathedral transferred from St. Asaph to Rhuddlan, as a safer place. Somehow this proposal fell through, and the cathedral was rebuilt after its destruction on its old site. Even before the war of 1282 the diocese had been so reduced that certain clergy were sent round to solicit alms for their church and exhibit the famous St. Asaph copy of the Gospels, commonly called 'Ereuegilthes,' or 'Euaggultheu,' and this device was again employed in 1284.

With the gallant Llywelyn fell the independence of Wales. The independence of the Welsh Church may perhaps be considered as having ended a hundred years before, when Archbishop Baldwin and Gerald de Barri went on their celebrated itinerary; but after Llywelyn's death even the most sanguine patriot must have abandoned all hope of reviving it, at least until many years were past. Many a Welsh clergyman doubtless sorrowed with the bard[1] who lamented the fall of 'the golden-handed prince, the hero of the red-stained spear':

'A lord I have lost, well may I mourn;
A lord righteous and truthful, listen to me!
A lord victorious until the eighteen were slain:
A lord who was gentle, whose possession is now the silent earth;
A lord who was like a lion, ruling the elements.
Lord Christ, how bitterly I grieve for him!
Lord of truth, grant him salvation.'[2]

[1] Gruffydd ab Yr Ynad Coch.
[2] Stephens, 'Literature of the Kymry,' p. 388.

The great and bitter wrong inflicted upon Llywelyn by the Church was his excommunication. But this was the fault of England, rather than of Wales, and, at least, Anian of St. Asaph would not promulgate the sentence. It is also to the credit of the Papal See that in 1274 the Pope inhibited an interdict. But it would seem, from a Bull of Pope Martin IV.,[1] that but little regard was paid by the clergy to these political excommunications, and it is said that the dying Llywelyn received the last offices of the Church from a White Friar. We know, too, from the statements of Archbishop Peckham and of Edward I., that, although some of the Welsh clergy sided with the King against Llywelyn, others, and it would appear far the greater number, took the part of their native prince, so thoroughly, indeed, that many were not content with stirring up their people to the war, but bore arms themselves.[2]

It is to the credit of the conquerors that when once Llywelyn was slain, and the Welsh resistance crushed, they showed themselves anxious to act fairly and justly towards the Welsh people, and especially to the Welsh Church. Ruthless as Edward I. was to those who opposed him, he was wise and politic in his measures for consolidating his kingdom. To conciliate Welsh sentiment, and to prove his devotion to the Welsh Church, he and his Queen Eleanor went on pilgrimage to St. David's.[3] His archbishop, the bold and honest 'Friar John,' was indefatigable in his exertions for the Welsh Church, which, in spite of the loss of its independence, he still regarded as the veritable Church of Wales (Ecclesia Walliæ), and wished to maintain with all its

[1] Rymer. 'Fœdera,' i. 2, 641.
[2] *Ibid.*, i. 2. 642, 643.
[3] 'Annales Ecclesiæ Menevensis' in Wharton's 'Anglia Sacra' (1691), ii. 651, under 1284: 'Dominus Rex Edwardus venit causâ peregrinationis apud Sanctum David una cum Dominâ Reginâ Angliæ nomine Elianorâ die Dominicâ in crastino B. Katerinæ Virginis.'

ancient rights and liberties. He was instant in season and out of season in pressing its claims upon the King; and one of his letters is so notable that it deserves to be quoted in full :

'To the perpetual honour and glory of your realm, by His ordinance, who is King of kings and Lord of lords, you have subdued the unconquered race of Wales to your authority by your victorious hand, for which God be praised. But it cannot be without wrong and offence to the Majesty of God Himself, if the victory which He has granted be turned to the shame of His Church. And although certain ecclesiastics were disloyal to you, as is said, in this gracious triumph, yet others assisted your rule with all their might. And, besides, the honour and reverence due to holy Mother Church ought never to be diminished or disturbed on account of degenerate sons; especially because the disturbers and violators of ecclesiastical liberty (both that which is general throughout the breadth of the world and that which is special and varies in innumerable places through custom and privileges) are undoubtedly involved in the sentence of excommunication. Wherefore, with humility and with all the affection we may, we supplicate your Excellency, that you may foster in its ancient liberties and rights the Church of Wales (*Ecclesiam Walliæ*), which has been happily transferred to your immediate dominion, so that the prosperity which heaven has given you may not be used to the injury of heaven. For there is one glorious city of God, whereof part is in pilgrimage on earth, and another part of its fellow-citizens rules, crowned, in heaven. We write this to your royal Majesty for this reason, because the new lords and bailiffs, to whom you have committed the government of Wales, are wise carnally, but spiritually foolish, and so divide the aforesaid liberty, that whatever things contrary to English custom seem to be for their own advantage, these they claim for themselves with all their power; but whatever things for the relief of the Church differ from English usages, these they destroy and overthrow, not without peril to their own souls, and the chain of anathema in which they by the very act entangle themselves. Therefore may your royal Piety deign so far in this respect, that the increase of your honour (which God augment) may not turn to the mourning of the Church; for know assuredly how greatly an embittered clergy can easily in process of time stir up the people to bitterness, which may the Highest avert. May the Lord keep your royal Excellency in prosperity and joy for longer time. At Tywyn, July 3, A.D. 1284.'[1]

This wise and honest letter may give us some idea of the spirit in which Archbishop Peckham set to work to repair the waste places of that which he regarded as being still 'the Church of Wales,' as well as four dioceses of his own province of Canterbury. By a letter written from Bangor, on June 15, 1284, he had already urged upon the King the necessity of making good the damage which had been done to the churches by the English troops. He pointed out with outspoken candour that, although such injuries had been inflicted contrary to the King's express will, yet he could not for that reason be altogether excused, because 'if at the beginning of the war evildoers had been restrained by the terrors of royal severity and by penal decisions, the greater part of the Church's grievances which afterwards followed would not have happened.' Everywhere, as he was passing through Wales on his visitation, he heard, both from secular clergy and from monks, of churches and sacred buildings despoiled and burned; while laymen complained that their goods had been sacrilegiously carried off from the

[1] Original is in H. and S., i. 569, 570.

sanctuary of churches and churchyards where they had placed them for safety.[1]

Edward, for his part, was quite willing to co-operate with the archbishop. Ten days before Peckham wrote this letter he had already issued a writ ordering restitution to be made. A commission was to be appointed to inquire about depredations, and if they found that ecclesiastical property, such as books, chalices, and general ornaments had been carried off from the churches, the spoilers were to make full restitution, which the King would see to strictly; or, in case they were unable to do so from lack of means, the King himself would make good the loss inflicted. And 'because many ecclesiastics had borne arms against their lord the King, and had conducted themselves as enemies against him, if any property had been taken from these, no restitution was to be made in their case': but such clergy as had suffered, although they were innocent, should receive restitution, and special inquiry was to be made both in the case of the innocent and of the guilty. If any churches or chapels or religious houses had been burned, in a case where the King had ordered the destruction of any place for military reasons, they were to be restored from the royal property, and the same was to be done in the case of the houses of the bishops or of anyone who had been of the King's party. Intercession was to be made to the Pope for absolution from excommunications incurred by the spoilers and incendiaries, for by none other than the Supreme Pontiff could such absolution be granted.[2] A commission was issued immediately afterwards by Archbishop Peckham to the Prior of Rhuddlan, the Warden of Llanfaes, and Ralph de Brocton, to make inquiry into the damage done.[3] Eventually a hundred pounds sterling was paid to the

---

[1] Rymer, 'Fœdera,' i. 2, 643. [2] *Ibid.*, i. 2, 642.
[3] *Ibid.*, i. 2, 644.

Archdeacon, Dean and Chapter of St. Asaph; two hundred and fifty to the Bishop of Bangor; seventy-eight to the monastery of Strata Florida; and seventeen pounds ten shillings to the Dominican Friars of Rhuddlan.[1]

Archbishop Peckham, as has been mentioned, went round Wales in 1284 on a visitation of the four Welsh dioceses. When he came in turn to St. David's, Bishop Beck of that diocese formally protested that he would receive Peckham as primate, but not as archbishop. Peckham, however, rejected the protest on penalty of excommunication. This was the last echo of the old claim. Thomas Beck, who thus endeavoured to pose as a new Gerald, was a native of Lincolnshire, and was appointed to his diocese in 1280. He was the first of an illustrious line of bishops of St. David's, and before his appointment had held the offices of Lord Treasurer, and Chancellor of the University of Oxford. He had also had the custody of the Great Seal, while Edward I. was away from England in 1279. His episcopate was notable by his foundation of the two collegiate churches of Abergwili in 1283, and Llanddewi Brefi in 1287. The former was first placed at Llangadoc. Beck also founded a hospital at Llawhaden, dedicated to the blessed Virgin, St. Thomas, and St. Edward.

Archbishop Peckham was much impressed as he passed through Wales by what he considered the uncivilized condition of the people. They are 'trop sauvages,' he wrote to the King, and to improve their manners he urged that a similar policy should be adopted to that which the emperors had used towards the Burgundians, that is, to make them live together in towns. As for their 'Wysshanbighan' (Gweison Bychain), or young lads, they ought, he thought, to be sent to England to be educated, for the Welsh clergy were quite

[1] See receipts in Rymer's 'Fœdera,' i. 2, 650, 648.

unable to teach them, as they knew scarcely more than the lay people themselves.[1] During his visitation of the Welsh dioceses he issued injunctions respecting the matters which seemed to him chiefly to need attention: Clerical dress and behaviour, the performance of the proper services of the Church, the reservation of the Host, tithes of dower and mortuaries, and procurations of rural deans and officials, were among the points noticed. The faults which he found most prevalent and deemed gravest, were the incontinence of the clergy, the custom of dividing livings into portions, an inclination to resort to dreamers of dreams and seers of visions, and idleness. 'The vice of incontinence,' he says, 'is known to have stained your clergy enormously beyond all bounds from ancient times.' No doubt the archbishop was referring to the prevalence of marriage among the clergy, which was the ancient custom of the Welsh Church, and we must not too hastily assume that concubinage prevailed to any large extent. He blames the bishops of former times for negligence in enforcing ecclesiastical canons on this matter, and orders that beneficed clergy should be deprived, unless they sent away their concubines on admonition, and that unbeneficed clergy should be repelled from benefices, unless they were of approved chastity. In fixing punishment for this offence, the bishop was to choose such a one as was most objectionable to the guilty person.

As regards the division of benefices, the archbishop states that the portions were often so small that the portionaries could not reside, neither had the vicars enough stipend for them to bear the parochial burdens. He quotes in this connection 'the maxim of the Saviour: "Every kingdom divided against itself is brought to desolation."' He orders this evil custom to be wholly abolished, and adequate provision to be made for vicars

[1] See letter written from Newport, July 8, 1284.

where the rectors were non-resident, so that they might sustain properly their parochial burdens, and maintain due hospitality, and celebrate the worship of God in their churches with proper assistance.

Welsh superstition comes under the lash of this censor in a curious passage of his 'Injunctions for the Diocese of St. Asaph.' He had heard with grief that the people were too much given up to dreams and fantastic visions, following in the track of Brutus, who, coming as a fugitive from the shame of Troy, having perpetrated the crime of idolatry through the advice received in a dream by the whisper of Diana, or rather of a devil, entered the island of Britain, which formerly was called Albion, and inhabited by a German race, from which race the Saxons were believed to spring. Idleness also was to be blamed; "it is the life of robbers, not of Christians, to eat the bread of idleness." Never before had he met clergy so illiterate, wherefore he ordered that Friars Preachers, and Minors, 'among whom almost solely in those parts the doctrine of truth resided,' should be received and cared for when they went round preaching the Word of God. He complained that many rectors and priests were unwilling to receive them, and he censured such as being rather wolves than shepherds.[1]

The preaching of the friars was already a power for good in Wales, even before Archbishop Peckham, himself a friar, urged its acceptance upon the Welsh people. As has been already said, Llywelyn the Great was one of the patrons of this great religious movement, and the Dominican house at Rhuddlan had given a bishop to the diocese of St. Asaph in the person of the bold and restless Anian. Nearly fifty years before the visitation of Peckham, a certain Friar Anian had preached a Crusade in West Wales. The movement spread all over the country, and we have evidence of settlements of the

[1] See 'Injunctions' in H. and S., i. 562-567, 571-574.

various orders in all parts. The Franciscans, or Grey Friars, were established at Carmarthen as early as 1209; and the Dominicans, or Black Friars, were at Haverfordwest in 1215. There were Dominicans also in the same diocese of St. David's, at Brecon and Rhayader; Carmelites at Tenby; and Austin Friars at Newport in Pembrokeshire. In Newport, Monmouthshire, there was in Leland's time 'a house of religion by the key, beneth the bridge,' which seems to have been a friary. There were settlements also both of Franciscans and Dominicans at Cardiff, and the remains of the latter house have recently been excavated.[1] The Dominicans had houses in North Wales, at Bangor and Rhuddlan, the Franciscans at Llanfaes, and the Carmelites at Denbigh and Ruthin.

The criticisms of Archbishop Peckham, taken in connection with the description given above of the destitution of the Church from civil turmoil, and of its division of feeling due to internal jealousies, may perhaps produce an impression that there was a lack of deep religious feeling and of spiritual power in the Church of Wales during the thirteenth century. But this would probably be an utter misconception of the true state of the case. The deeper aspirations of man are not on the surface, and the pages of history which record conflicts and dissensions find nothing to chronicle in the little acts of piety and beneficence which chiefly make up a good man's life. If the Welsh Church of the days of the two Llywelyns failed, from its rival jealousies, to do what it might have done for the Welsh nation, it at least kept the whole of the country united in allegiance to a common creed, and thereby did much to mitigate the results of bitter animosities of race. If the monastic orders erred from the strictness of their ideal, and at times fell into sins of self-indulgence, they set an example of

[1] 'Archaeologia Cambrensis' (1889), pp. 97-105.

charity and benevolence which should, in our eyes at least, cover a multitude of sins, and which may well put modern religious bodies to the blush. If the world and its snares led men of religion astray then, they do so at least as often now. Wales at the present day might well rejoice were it as united or as abounding in the deeds of charity as it was even in the thirteenth century.

Considerations of this kind may well correct modern arrogance in judgment; but it is possible also to refer to writings which breathe a deeply devotional spirit, and which were produced in this season of the Church's tribulation. Such were unknown altogether to Archbishop Peckham, who judged of the education of Wales from a false standard. The popular vehicle of Welsh thought was the Welsh language, and in this, then as now, the Welsh people loved especially to utter forth their sentiments of devotion. The Welsh literature of this age is not solely martial, but is also, strange to say, largely devotional. Students of the bardic literature are surprised at this fact:[1] but the Welshman is naturally a religious being, and his national literature bears witness to the needs of his nature, and gives expression thereto. Many of the religious poems doubtless are conventional compositions on sacred subjects; but even these show how deeply religion entered into the common life of the people. The same fact is attested by the common invocations of God at the beginning of poems on ordinary subjects and by the conventional endings. Would Llywarch ab Llywelyn praise Rhys Grug for his victories over the English, he must begin by invoking 'Christ Creator, Emperor, who owns us, Christ the Mysterious,

---

[1] 'I was not a little surprised in perusing these to find the bards, almost to a man, exercising their talents in the composition of a species of literature which seemed so inconsistent with their practices and professions, but, on examination, it soon appeared that they had been judged both harshly and unfairly.'—Stephens, 'Literature of the Kymry,' p. 392.

pillar of peace,' to watch over him; and he concludes with a prayer that the prince may have a 'permanent abiding-place and a summer dwelling in heaven,' and be 'a prince of the kingdom of God above.' These things are little enough in themselves; but some of the bards strike a fuller note. The same bard who wrote the Elegy on Llywelyn ap Gruffydd, already quoted, Gruffydd ab Yr Ynad Coch, has written some passages of much religious feeling:

> 'The blood is as fresh
>   As the day He was crucified.
> And His hands were spread out
>   When the deed was done.
> And the blood was in streams
> About His breast,
> And His wounds
>   Are unhealed.
> And the crown of thorns,
> And His lifeless body,
> And His head encircled
>   With the thorny ring.
> And the mark on His side
> Of the scourge
> Which took away His life,
>   And gave Him pain.
> And all to purchase the son of man
> From the everlasting fire,
> By the enemy
>   In whose hands he was.'

This would be difficult to render adequately in English verse, but even in bald prose it is full of beauty, and is plainly animated by religious feeling. Those who know how the Welsh are inspired by the hymns of their own language can form an idea of what it would be to a Welshman. Or take the following lyric, simple as one of Herrick's and as beautiful, from the Friar Madawc ab Gwallter:

> 'A son has been given us,
> A kind son is born
>   With great privileges,
> A son of glory,
> A son to save us,
>   The best of sons.
>   *   *   *

> A God, a man,
> And the God a man,
> > With the same faculties;
> A great little giant,
> A strong puny potentate
> > Of pale cheeks.
> Richly poor
> Our father and brother,
> > Author of being,
> Jesus, He whom
> We expect,
> > King of kings;
> Exalted, lowly,
> Emmanuel,
> > Honey of minds;
> With the ox and ass,
> The Lord of life,
> > Lies in a manger;
> And a heap of straw
> As a chair,
> > Clothed in tatters;
> Velvet He wants not,
> Nor white ermine
> > To cover Him;
> Around His couch
> Rags were seen,
> > Instead of fine linen.[1]

The age which produced poems like these may yet rise in the judgment and condemn us.

It will make matters clearer if we understand, before passing on, what henceforth were the English King's possessions in Wales. First, there was his 'Principality,' which had been Llywelyn's; viz., Anglesey, Carnarvon, and nearly all Merioneth. Next, there was his 'Dominion,' including Flint, and most of Cardigan and Carmarthen. The rest of Wales with an adjacent strip of land in England formed the Marches, under Lordship Marchers, of whom the King claimed to be over-lord. Pembroke and Glamorgan were added later to his 'Dominion;' the rest was not annexed till 1536.[2]

---

[1] I take the translations from Stephens, 'Literature of the Kymry,' pp. 401, 402, 406, 407.
[2] See Nevins' 'Wales during the Tudor Period,' pp. 68-89.

CHAPTER XII.

FROM THE CONQUEST OF WALES TO THE DEATH OF OWAIN GLYNDWR.

The strong hand of Edward I., which crushed the independence of Wales, dealt also a blow at the great power of the lords of Glamorgan. The 'land of Morgan' had passed under the authority of the house of Clare in 1226, and continued under them until 1314. But the quarrel which broke out in 1289 between the Earl of Gloucester, Gilbert de Clare, and his neighbour, the Earl of Hereford, gave Edward an opportunity of carrying out his policy of unifying the kingdom. The two earls had a dispute concerning a castle which Gloucester had built, and they were carrying on a petty warfare with each other. Edward intervened, and, as they did not cease their hostilities, imprisoned them both. Eventually the lands of both parties were forfeited, but the forfeiture was limited to the period of their lives.

About the same time a question arose, or, rather, an old dispute was renewed, respecting the custody of the temporalities of Llandaff during the vacancy of the see. The claim of the Crown had been previously put forward in 1240, during the long period of the vacancy between the death of Bishop Elias and the election of William de Burgh. The King had then put in an official to administer.

In March, 1287, William de Braose, Bishop of Llandaff, died. The Chapter of Llandaff met, and elected Philip de Staunton, precentor, of Wells, and the election was notified to the King, who signified his approval. The letter to the King, informing him of the election, was not sealed with the common seal, which had been withheld by the chancellor of the diocese, who was a De Clare, and eventually, owing probably to the opposition of the De Clares, the election fell through, and Philip de Staunton was not consecrated. The see consequently remained vacant for a considerable time, and the Earl of Gloucester and the other lords of the Marches took possession of the temporalities during the vacancy. But in 1290 objection was made to this on behalf of the King, and the previous action of the Crown in 1240 was adduced as an argument in favour of the royal claim. At that time, on the death of Bishop Elias, Henry III., it was stated, 'committed the custody of the temporalities to 'Walerandus Teutonicus Miles,' who, when his administration was ended, rendered an account to the Treasury. . . . And in the same vacancy he conferred one vacant prebend on Master William de Burgh, at that time treasurer of his wardrobe, and another prebend on Alfred de Fescamp, then sub-treasurer of the same wardrobe; and the archdeaconry of Llandaff on a certain Thomas, then chaplain of Eleanor,' the Queen. It was claimed, also, on the King's behalf, that the Bishops of Llandaff held their barony, lands, and possessions from the Kings of England, and not from the Earl of Gloucester and his progenitors, and that, on a vacancy in the bishopric, the canons sought liberty of election from the Kings, and not from the earls. It was proposed, therefore, that Gilbert, Earl of Gloucester, should accept a life-interest in the temporalities, but acknowledge absolutely the King's right therein.[1]

[1] See document in Rymer, Fœdera, i. 2, 742 ; H. and S., i. 590, 591.

The other lords gave way, but the Earl of Gloucester held out for what he deemed to be his rights, but he was non-suited. In 1293, a new case arose in the diocese of St. Asaph, of which John de Warenne, Earl of Surrey and Sussex, claimed the temporalities. The case of De Clare and the other claimants of the temporalities of Llandaff was cited against him, and he failed to obtain his petition. In the same year Humphrey de Bohun, Earl of Hereford and Essex, petitioned for the custody of the temporalities of St. David's on the death of Bishop Beck, but was assured that they belonged to the Crown alone. In the cases of Llandaff and St. David's, the custody of the temporalities during vacancies was eventually leased by the Crown to the chapter at an annual rent.[1] As regards Bangor, there was a claim put forward in 1327 by the dean and chapter to receive half the profits of the see during a vacancy, and the King's Escheator in North Wales was ordered to investigate into the claim, and to satisfy it, if it were rightly made.

The petition in the case of St. Asaph arose through the death of the resolute and somewhat quarrelsome Anian, who was succeeded by Llywelyn of Bromfield, whose election was confirmed by the Prior and Chapter of Canterbury, the archbishopric being then vacant.

The See of Llandaff remained vacant for several years. Probably the chapter were unwilling to elect another clergyman, as their nominee, Philip de Staunton, had failed to obtain consecration, in spite of the royal approval. Some time in 1294 or 1295 Philip de Staunton died, and in October, 1294, Pope Celestine intervened, and issued a 'provision,' appointing John de Monmouth to the See of Llandaff. Celestine abdicated before the end of the year, and consequently a still further delay was caused until the Papal provision was confirmed by

[1] This was fixed in the case of St. David's at £190 7s. 6¾d., by a royal order, dated May 1, 1377.—Rymer, 'Fœdera,' iii. 2, 1076, 1077.

Pope Boniface VIII. Finally, John de Monmouth was consecrated February 10, 1296. Gilbert de Clare handed over the temporalities to the new bishop, and admitted that he and his wife held only a life-interest in them during a vacancy. The serious diminution of power and prestige which the Earl had suffered from the resolute action of Edward in enforcing at all times the royal authority, may be inferred from the fact that the Prior of Goldcliff ventured to summon him before his court at Newport to answer a charge of trespass.

South Wales had suffered grievously during the troublous reign of Henry III., and Glamorgan had not been spared. 'The land was wasted, the houses burned, the cattle driven off, the borough towns and religious houses sorely bested. The clergy were in arrears with their tithes, the bishops and monastic bodies with their dues, and the landlords of all ranks with their rents and the produce of their demesnes. Treaties and truces between the English and the Welsh were of no avail. Each party broke them at pleasure. The King's writ did not run in the Marches, and would have been but little respected, if it had had legal sanction; and the chief lords, though strong enough to be a thorn in the King's side, were often unable to preserve peace.'[1]

In considering the history of Wales and of its Church, we must bear in mind that since the Norman conquest of South Wales there had ever been a large Norman and English population there. Wherever the Norman knight built a castle and garrisoned it, thither came, in the train of the soldiers, a body of English artificers and workmen, who settled down in the neighbourhood; wherever he founded a monastery, there he introduced Norman and English monks. In Glamorgan itself there were at least thirty castles, and in the whole of Wales nearly one hundred and fifty, and, as the Norman monasteries were

[1] Clark, 'Land of Morgan,' p. 132.

also numerous, it may be inferred how large a power the English element was in Wales, and in its Church, even before the overthrow of Llywelyn.

The indisposition of the Welsh to manual labour, of which Archbishop Peckham complained, also aided the English immigration, for the Welsh themselves seem to have got their servants and workmen from England. The English 'are the meanest nation under heaven,' said Gerald de Barri, with a fine contempt, in which the pride of his Norman and of his Welsh ancestry was equally mingled. ' In their own land they are the slaves of the Normans, and the vilest slaves. In our land we have none but Englishmen as herdsmen, shepherds, shoemakers, furriers, mechanical artificers of our drains also, that I may not say, cleaners of our sewers.'[1]

Probably English was nearly as commonly spoken in the plain of South Wales in the reign of Henry III. as it is now. At Haverfordwest there was, of course, a Flemish colony. It was the object of the Welsh leaders in the wars of independence not merely to harass and subdue, but in some cases to drive out these alien settlements. In 1217, we are told, Rhys Grug, or the Hoarse, 'destroyed the castle of Senghenydd, and all the castles of Gower and their strength. And he expelled the English population that were in that county entirely, so that they had no hope ever to return back, taking as much property as he chose, and placing Welshmen to dwell in the lands.'[2] Llywarch ab Llywelyn, in recording the exploits of the same hero, says that

> ' His hand taught the bloody-stained blades
> To make the Germans move to exile,'

and mentions among the settlements of the foreigners which he captured, 'the barren courts of Rhos;' 'Haverford of the surge;' Pembroke, 'the castle of Gwys,' and

---

[1] ' De Invectionibus,' i. 4: Op. iii. 27.
[2] ' Brut y Tywysogion,' p. 303.

'Arberth[1] of the light gossamer;' 'Carmarthen and its hosts from France;' 'St. Clears with its bright white lands,' and 'Swansea, the strong key of Lloegria.' Long after the time of Rhys Grug, English settlements were still marked off from Welsh possession by their divergent customs. An old document[2] of the age of Elizabeth thus describes these settlements and their condition in the time in which it was written:

'The said lords espying out the best and most fertile parts in each county, builded them castles for themselves, and towns for their own soldiers and countrymen, which came with them to remain near about them as their guard, and to be always ready to keep under such of the country inhabitants as would offer to rebel. Where the lords parted the Englishmen that came with them and gave them lands, the Welsh customs were not used, but they held all their lands according to the laws of England, and the eldest son had the whole inheritance, and for this cause in many lordships there is a Welsh court for the Welshmen by themselves, where their Welsh customs were observed, and the Englishmen had another court, in part for themselves, and in common speech among them. The one part is yet to this day called Englisherie, and the other part the Welsherie:' as examples of which the writer mentions Gower, Coyty Anglicana and Coyty Wallicana, Avon Anglicana and Avon Wallicana, English Talgarth and Welsh Talgarth, 'and in Pembrokeshire is the like;' also Kydwely Anglicana and Commota Kydwely Wallicana; and in Llanstephan, Dominium Anglicanum and Dominium Wallicanum, etc.

It may be imagined how gladly the English settlements would welcome the fall of the national cause, and rejoice at the prospect of settled peace presented to them by the

---

[1] Viz., Narberth.
[2] 'Harleian MS. 1220,' quoted by Mr. Ivor James ('Welsh Language in the Sixteenth and Seventeenth Centuries,' pp. 35, 36).

strong rule of Edward I., who crushed native princes and restrained lords marchers by the central authority of the English Court. Glamorgan, Brecon, Carmarthen, and Pembroke in the south, and Flint, Montgomery and part of Denbigh in the north, were the parts of Wales chiefly affected by English colonization and English influence.

Thus the conquest of Wales, which to one part of the Welsh Church was a cause of lamentation and mourning, to another was rather suggestive of exultation and thanksgiving. Doubtless, too, as the previous history has suggested, there was some diversity of ecclesiastical usage between the English section and the Welsh section; but the union in a common creed prevented the rise of any religious feud, such as has existed for centuries in Ireland between the native population and 'the English garrison.'

Though Llywelyn and David were dead, Wales was not quieted immediately. In 1295, Madoc was in insurrection in North Wales, and the Archbishop of Canterbury ordered the Bishop of St. Asaph to excommunicate the insurgents, unless they laid down arms within eight days. All the land of Wales that adhered to their party was to be laid under an interdict. The letter was received by the Bishop of St. Asaph on Quinquagesima Sunday, and duly obeyed.[1]

In the same year Pembroke and Carmarthen were exposed to the incursions of another Madoc, and Glamorgan was occupied by the forces of Morgan of Avan. Edward I. acted with his usual promptitude. He left Aberconway in April and went to Anglesea, and on May 7 came to Bangor. Thence he passed to Cymmer Abbey, near Dolgelly, and on the 14th and 15th was at Talybont, near Towyn. He passed through Llanbadarn Fawr, Aberystwith, and Llanddewi Brefi,

[1] H. and S., i. 606-609.

and reached Cardigan about June 2, and proceeded by Drysllwyn Castle to Merthyr Tydfil and Morlais. Afterwards he returned to Aberconway by Brecon, Builth, Clun, Welshpool, and Whitchurch. 'All the Welsh of the dominion of the Earl of Gloucester,' we are told, 'the King received to his peace, contrary to the will of the said earl; and the King gave them a guardian, namely, the lord Walter Hacklut.'[1] The rule of the De Clares over Glamorgan was practically at an end. Earl Gilbert died the same year, December 7, 1295: his son, also named Gilbert, died in 1314, and with him ended the main line of the House of Clare. John of Monmouth, the contemporary Bishop of Llandaff, who had been appointed by a Papal provision after the long vacancy, was a somewhat notable figure in his time. He was one of the Lords Ordainers in 1310, and in the latter part of the reign of Edward II. is found taking the King's side in time of civil war. He died in 1323. The bishopric during his occupancy cannot have been very valuable pecuniarily, for, on account of its poverty,[2] the Church of All Saints, Newland, was granted to it as an augmentation in 1308. In 1315 there was a brief insurrection under Llywelyn Bren, who owned land by the river Taff in the highland district.

The premier see in Wales at this period was unquestionably the See of St. David's, which had recovered somewhat from its state of poverty. The period of its history, from 1280 to 1414, has been called the 'Period of Illustrious Bishops.'[3] 'Of the ten prelates included in it, one is said to have been a cardinal,[4] two became archbishops, two, perhaps three, held the office of Lord Chancellor, three that of Lord Treasurer—two of them

---

[1] Continuator of Florence of Worcester. See further Clark, 'Land of Morgan,' pp. 145, 146.
[2] 'Nimis exilis esse dinoscitur.'
[3] Bevan, 'St. David's,' p. 120. See Jones and Freeman, p. 298.
[4] This, however, is on somewhat doubtful authority.

more than once—three were keepers of the privy seal, one was Master of the Rolls, three were Chancellors of the University of Oxford.'[1] It is clear that the bishopric from some cause or other had completely changed its reputation since the time when Matthew Paris had described it as 'a meagre bishopric' (*exilis Episcopatus*). One bishop, Gilbert, appointed in 1389, had previously filled the Sees of Bangor and Hereford. Seven of the ten bishops retained possession of the see until their deaths. Brian was translated in 1352 to Worcester; Thoresby, in 1349, to Worcester, and in 1352 to the Archbishopric of York; and Chicheley, in 1414, to Canterbury. During the period of the great depression of the see from 1215 to 1280, three of the four bishops, Iorwerth, Anselm le Gros, and Thomas Wallensis, had been Welshmen, and the fourth, Richard de Carew, or de Caron, had probably a connection with Pembrokeshire. Of the 'illustrious bishops,' only one, David Martyn, was of Welsh descent, being a grandson, through his mother, of the lord Rhys; but Houghton and Gower had a connection with Wales.

The first of these bishops, Thomas Beck, has been already mentioned as the founder of the collegiate churches of Abergwili and Llanddewi Brefi, and the assertor of the privileges of his see against Archbishop Peckham. Upon his death, David Martyn was elected in May, 1193, and his temporalities were restored to him by a writ dated October 11. But an appeal was entered against his election 'on behalf, apparently, of one David of St. Edmund's, who was also elected and confirmed to the see in 1293.'[2] The matter remained pending for about three years. On January 1, 1295, David Martyn was again elected, and on August 16

---

[1] Jones and Freeman, p. 305.
[2] So H. and S., i. 617. Jones and Freeman, p. 302, identify David Martyn with David of St. Edmund's.

Edward I. wrote on his behalf to Pope Boniface VIII. and asked him to favour his candidature.[1] In December of the next year the Pope consecrated David Martyn at Rome, and on January 24, 1297, his temporalities were again restored to him, the writ granting them stating that the Pope had 'provided' him to the See of St. David's. David Martyn was a descendant of Martin de Tours, the conqueror of Cemmaes, and on his mother's side, as has already been stated, was descended from the lord Rhys. During his episcopate the present Lady Chapel was added to St. David's Cathedral.

Henry Gower succeeded in 1328. In various letters written to the Pope and cardinals, notifying his election, the King mentions that he had already been Chancellor of the University of Oxford, and Archdeacon of St. David's, and praises him for his experience in civil as well as ecclesiastical affairs, and for his acquaintance with various languages which, he says, made him 'especially necessary to us and the kingdom.' The See of St. David's was regarded as 'being placed in greater danger than the other sees of Wales,' and its people as 'unsubdued, wayward, and silly,'[2] English and Welsh alike.[3] Complaints of the 'restless fickleness' of the people of Wales are very common in the State papers of the time; 'levitas' was evidently regarded as their besetting sin.[4]

It has been said that Gower 'has left on the whole more extensive traces of his mind at St. David's than any bishop who has occupied the see either before or since.'[5] He founded the beautiful episcopal palace of St. David's, which calls forth the enthusiastic praise

---

[1] See document in H. and S., i. 617.
[2] 'Indomitos, devios et deliros.'
[3] Rymer, 'Fœdera,' ii. 2, 747-749.
[4] *Ibid.*, ii. 2, 748, levitas; 749, levitas cervicosa; 913, effrœnata levitas; 1218, levitas.
[5] Jones and Freeman, p. 302.

and admiration of the historians of the diocese, and which is a fine example of the Decorated style. He also carried out extensive alterations in the cathedral. At Swansea he founded a hospital, which he endowed with lands.[1] It has been suggested that the chancel of Swansea Church, and also Carew Church, near the episcopal residence at Lamphey, may have been his work.[2] He appears, from what he has left to posterity, to have been a consummate architect. His buildings, say the historians of St. David's, 'are the more remarkable and valuable, because the trembling claim of Decorated architecture to be admitted as a definite style nowhere finds a nearer approach to a standing place than in his erections. Gower's buildings are most eminently neither Early English nor Perpendicular; not only is their actual detail quite distinct from both, but there is not the slightest approach to the character of either. We miss alike the distinctness of the one, and the continuity of the other. But the result is that we are presented with purely negative characteristics, we miss the positive marks of the earlier and later styles, and find no others in their stead. There is the marked impress of an individual mind, but not, as before and after, the expression of an architectural idea.'[3]

Thoresby, who succeeded Gower in 1347, did not hold the bishopric long, being transferred to Worcester in 1349. He was made Lord Chancellor during his tenure of the See of St. David's; he was noted for his learning, and was a vigorous opponent of the friars, against whom he wrote a treatise. In 1352 he was advanced to the archbishopric of York, when Reginald Brian, his successor at St. David's, succeeded him also in the See of Worcester. Neither Brian nor his suc-

[1] Foundation charter (date 1332) in Clarke's 'Cartæ de Glamorgan,' iv. 146.
[2] Jones and Freeman, p. 206.
[3] *Ibid.*, p. 204.

cessor, Fastolfe, were bishops of any particular note; but Adam Houghton, who comes next on the list, was made Lord Chancellor in 1377, and held the office for about two years. This bishop, with John of Gaunt, founded the college, or chantry, of St. Mary close to the cathedral. Its members were a master, seven chaplains, and two choristers. The ruins of the beautiful chapel still add a charm to the cathedral precincts.

Adam Houghton died in 1388, and Richard Mitford was duly elected to the see. But the Pope interfered, and set aside the nomination, and, finally, John Gilbert, a Dominican friar, who had previously held the bishoprics of Bangor and Hereford, and had also been lord treasurer, was appointed and consecrated. The Pope's action was not the first instance of Papal tyranny in connection with this diocese; both Brian and Falstolfe had previously been appointed by Papal 'provision.'

Gilbert was first appointed treasurer at the troublous period in the reign of Richard II., when Thomas, Duke of Gloucester, was leading an attack on the King's ministers and favourites. At that time the King dismissed his ministers, gave the seals to the Bishop of Ely, and made Gilbert, then Bishop of Hereford, the treasurer. Soon afterwards he was appointed one of the commissioners to govern the realm during the suspension of the royal power. When Richard, by a bold stroke, resumed his authority and asserted his right to be no longer 'under the control of tutors,' it was from Gilbert that he required the keys of the exchequer. Gilbert's chief work at St. David's, so far as is known, was the reformation of the cathedral statutes. Though an active politician, he probably resided for some time in his diocese, for he was buried in the church of the Dominican friars in Haverfordwest.

The next bishop, Guy de Mone, who succeeded in 1397, seems to have had little to do with his diocese.

He was much engaged in political life, and was at various times keeper of the privy seal and lord treasurer. He also was one of the representatives of the Church of England at the Council of Pisa. He seems to have usually resided in Kent, and was buried at Leeds in that county. He lived occasionally at Llanddew, near Brecon.[1]

The history of Chicheley, who succeeded Guy Mone in 1408, belongs rather to the general history of the Church of England than to that of the See of St. David's. He was 'provided' and consecrated by the Pope in spite of the pretensions of Adam of Usk, who held a prebend in the collegiate church of Abergwili, but whose local claims were passed over. Chicheley, as Bishop of St. David's, succeeded Guy de Mone in his capacity of representative at the Council of Pisa, which had been summoned with the purpose of reforming the Church and reuniting it under one Pope, and which deposed the two rival Popes and elected another in their place. As the two deposed Popes refused to obey the Council, the result was that there were now three instead of two. Chicheley did not visit his diocese of St. David's until 1411. He brought about the suppression of the alien priories, and the revenues of St. Clears and Llangenith were eventually transferred to his foundation of All Souls College, Oxford. In 1414 he was translated to the archbishopric of Canterbury.

But although several of the Bishops of St. David's during this period must have been much occupied outside their diocese, we have seen that on the whole very much was effected for the diocese itself. Only three of the bishops were promoted to other sees, so that the post was not selected as merely a stepping-stone to other preferment. It was otherwise with the neighbouring diocese of Llandaff during the latter part of the same

[1] Bevan, 'St. David's,' p. 137.

period. From 1383 to 1407 there were no less than seven Bishops of Llandaff. Of these Thomas Rushooke (who in 1383 had succeeded Roger Cradock, formerly Bishop of Waterford and Lismore) was translated in 1385 to the English Bishopric of Chichester. William de Bottisham, his successor, was translated in 1389 to Rochester. The next bishop, Edmund Bromfield, died during his occupancy of the see, after a very short episcopate, in 1391; but the next, Tydeman de Winchcombe, was translated in 1395 to Worcester. Andrew Barret, who succeeded him, probably missed translation by his speedy death, for he died in 1396; but John Burghill was translated in 1398 to Lichfield, and Thomas Peverell, his successor, was preferred to Worcester in 1407. Such constant change must have been very prejudicial to the interests of the diocese, for bishops who were ever seeking for preferment, were not likely to pay much attention to the charge of which they hoped soon to be relieved.

It does not appear, however, that England played the tyrant in these appointments; it was generally Rome that was in fault. On the death of John of Monmouth in 1323, Alexander de Monmouth, Archdeacon of Llandaff, was duly elected and approved by the King,[1] but the Pope interfered, and gave the bishopric to John de Eclescliff, a Dominican, Bishop of Connor in Ireland. He died in 1346, and was buried in the Dominican church in Cardiff. The chapter then met, and elected John Coventry, Archdeacon of Llandaff; but he also was set aside by the Pope in favour of his nominee, John Pascal, who is said to have been a very learned and eloquent man.[2] Cradock, who had been Bishop of Waterford and Lismore, Rushooke, William de Bottisham, Bromfield, and John de la Zouche, were all imposed upon the

[1] Browne Willis, 'Survey of Landaff,' p. 53.
[2] Godwin, 'De Præsulibus Angliæ,' p. 607.

see by Papal authority. The last-named bishop succeeded Thomas Peverell in 1408.

The case of Bromfield was peculiar, and he has the distinction among the Welsh bishops of evoking from Parliament a second Statute of Provisors. According to Godwin,[1] who relates the story with some graphic force, he was a very learned man, a monk of St. Edmund's, Suffolk, who was envied by his fellow-monks for his superior qualities. They called him a factious person and a disturber of the common peace, and, to get rid of him, they sent him on an honourable mission to Rome; but before he started, they made him swear that he would not get himself made abbot. But when the abbot was dead, Bromfield preferred to forget his oath, and obtained the Pope's nomination. The monks were highly disgusted, and elected their sub-prior. Bromfield returned to England, and claimed the abbacy, but the King apprehended him under the Statute of Provisors passed in the previous reign, and committed him to the Tower. The Pope was now in a dilemma;[2] he did not like to desert his nominee, but he dared not offend Richard II., who might in that case espouse the cause of the anti-Pope. Accordingly he sought to promote Bromfield to an Irish bishopric, but, on Rochester falling vacant, he got out of the difficulty by translating William de Bottisham, Bishop of Llandaff, to Rochester, and presenting Bromfield to Llandaff, after he had lain in the Tower several years. Browne Willis calls Bromfield 'a very learned man, though of a pragmatical humour.'[3] He received the temporalities of his see on December 17, 1389. He held the bishopric a very short time, for he died in 1391, and was buried in his cathedral.

In North Wales something was done in the interval

[1] Godwin, 'De Præsulibus Angliæ,' p. 608. See also Lingard, 'History of England,' sixth edition, iii. 171.
[2] 'Lupum jam Pontifex auribus tenebat,' says Godwin.
[3] Browne Willis, 'Survey of Llandaff,' pp. 55, 56.

between the annexation and Glyndwr's rising to repair the damage that had been wrought during the wars of independence. The canons of St. Asaph were fairly successful in their begging expedition, and seem to have collected annually about £30, or, in the nine years which they devoted to this purpose, about £9,000 of our present money. The cathedral was completed about the end of 1295, and the services were reorganized according to the injunctions of Archbishop Peckham. It was ordered in 1296 that 'the Dean and the Prebendaries of Vaenol and Llannefydd (the precentor and the chancellor) should each find a priest, skilled in music, to serve their cures and attend the daily services with the vicar-choral; that the archdeacon should find a priest or a layman, skilled in vocal or instrumental music; the Prebendaries of Meliden (treasurer) and Llanfair (2) should find four singing boys or choristers, and the Prebendary of Meifod (sacristan) should contribute ten shillings per annum in augmentation of the salary of the waterbearer to secure his attendance with the other ministers in the daily services. All the minor clergy (beneficed in Gwyddelwern) were required to be present at the daily services at all the canonical hours under penalty of a penny fine for each absence.'[1]

In the neighbouring diocese of Bangor a diocesan synod was held on July 14, 1291, and the following days in the Church of St. Mary of Garthbranan, which at that time was the parish church of Bangor. The constitutions drawn up by this synod have not been preserved, but it is clear that the peace consequent upon the conquest and the admonitions of Archbishop Peckham were productive in this diocese also of an effort to reorganize matters. Anian was Bishop of Bangor at this time. Edward I. had intervened between the unfortunate Llywelyn and Anian in 1278, professing

[1] Archdeacon Thomas, 'St. Asaph' (S.P.C.K.), pp. 52, 53.

to advocate the just claims of the latter, and in the same year had made a grant of liberties to the Diocese of Bangor.[1] In 1280 a grant was made to the same Anian of Bangor House, in Shoe Lane, in the parish of St. Andrew's, Holborn, London. In 1284 a grant was made by the King to the Bishops of Bangor of certain civil privileges within their own episcopal lands, such as that no viscount, bailiff, or servant of the King's should enter the bishops' lands to exercise any office in them except on defect of the bishops' bailiffs. In 1286 a grant was issued confirming to the Bishops of Bangor a third part of the tithes of the King's demesnes, mills, and lead mines in 'Englesend,' and in 1288 Bishop Anian petitioned that the Justiciary of Chester should be compelled to obey this grant.[2]

There is in existence a record of a curious grant of indulgence on the part of this Bishop Anian of Bangor to those who should help the Augustinian Priory of Black Canons, situated in the lovely vale of Beddgelert. The bishop relates that he had inspected various charters granted to the Prior and Convent of the Valley of Blessed Mary of Snowdon, namely, a charter of Llywelyn the Great, three of Llywelyn, the son of Gruffydd, one of the lord Owen, and another of the lord David. He had also seen Papal letters, not cancelled, or in any respect made void. Therefore, he lets all men know that 'the said house of blessed Mary is the senior religious house in all Wales, except Bardsey, the Island of Saints, and of better and more common hospitality to needy English and Welsh travellers, passing from England and West Wales to North Wales, and going from Ireland and North Wales into England.' The priory, having been accidentally destroyed by fire, had been restored by King Edward. To those who aided it

---

[1] Documents in H. and S., i. 525, 526.
[2] H. and S., pp. 580, 581.

further by their alms Anian granted an indulgence of forty days.[1]

Anian is termed by Browne Willis 'a most excellent bishop,' praise which is somewhat qualified in the eyes of sympathizers with the Welsh national movements by the further statement that he was 'in great favour with Edward I.'[2] He was the bishop who christened Edward II. He is notable also for drawing up a Missal or Pontifical for his church and diocese. This book was lost in the troubles of Henry IV.'s reign, but restored in 1485 by Bishop Richard Ednam, or Evyden, and again was recovered to the see by Bishop Humphrey, after it had passed into private hands during the Great Rebellion.[3] Anian is mentioned as still alive in 1305, but probably died in that year or the next. He had held the see since 1268, in a very troublous period, and seems to have been an able and conscientious prelate.

Both of the northern sees suffered from Papal encroachments during this period. Llywelyn was succeeded as Bishop of St. Asaph, in 1314, by Dafydd ap Bleddyn; but the next bishop, John Trevor, was nominated by the Pope, first in 1344, to the next vacant canonry or sinecure in the diocese, and afterwards to the bishopric as soon as it should fall vacant. Consequently he succeeded Dafydd in 1352. The first instance in this diocese of Papal provision was the appointment by Pope Clement V. of John Toppan to a canonry in the cathedral, and to the Rectory of Llanwyllin[4]—probably Llanuwchllyn, at the far more beautiful, but less frequented, end of Bala Lake. Bishop Llywelyn ap Madoc, the successor to John Trevor I., was provided to the see, and consecrated by the Pope at Avignon.

---

[1] Rymer, 'Fœdera,' i. 2, p. 664; H. and S., i. 584, 585.
[2] Browne Willis, 'Survey of Bangor,' p. 67.
[3] It is described by Browne Willis, 'Bangor,' pp. 70-72, 192-199.
[4] Thomas, 'St. Asaph' (S.P.C.K), p. 55.

He had been dean, and on his appointment to the bishopric a dispute arose as to whether he, the new bishop, or the Prince of Wales, the custodian of the temporalities of the see during a vacancy, had the right of presentation to the deanery. Eventually the bishop was allowed to nominate a friend of the Prince's, William de Spridlington, who succeeded to the bishopric afterwards, in 1376. Spridlington was succeeded in 1382 by Lawrence Child, and he in 1390 by Alexander Bache, and in 1395 John Trevor II. became bishop, whose episcopate will require somewhat fuller notice later on.

Bangor seems to have had Welsh bishops for some years after the death of Anian. In 1306 Gruffydd ap Iorwerth was consecrated at Carlisle to the vacant see, and in 1309 he was succeeded by Anian Seys, formerly Canon and Dean of Bangor, and Archdeacon of Anglesey. This bishop had a difficulty, in 1316, with William Trumwyn, the King's justice in Carnarvon, because of the escape of two of the bishop's tenants from prison; but on an appeal to the King the bishop was discharged from any liability, and the grant of Edward I. to the see, that it should retain all its ancient rights, liberties, possessions, and customs, was acknowledged as valid and binding.[1] Anian died in 1327, and was buried at Bangor. Matthew de Englefeild ap Kirid, otherwise called Madoc ap Iorwerth ap Kirid, was the next bishop. He had been formerly Canon of Bangor and Archdeacon of Anglesey, and as Welsh Englynion were written in his favour, may be considered as popular among his people.

The next bishops, Thomas Ringstede and Gervase de Castro, were Dominicans, and were provided by the Pope. Ringstede's will proves his dislike of the Welsh people.[2] Gervase has been supposed[3] to have received his education at the Dominican house in Bangor, but

[1] Rymer, 'Fœdera,' ii. 1, 284.
[2] Browne Willis, 'Bangor,' pp. 217-219.   [3] *Ibid.*, p. 78.

the Welsh character of the next bishop, Howel, is much more certain. He was a Canon of Bangor, and on the death of Gervase was duly elected by the chapter. Pope Gregory XI., however, was offended by this, which he regarded as an infringement of his prerogative, for he had determined to keep the appointment in his own hands, and, accordingly, he quashed Howel's election as null and void; but after a short interval appointed him of his own authority.[1] John Gilbert, the next bishop, was also provided by the Pope. He was translated to Hereford, and thence to St. David's. John Swaffham, a Carmelite, was next advanced from the Irish Bishopric of Cloyne by a Papal provision, dated July 2, 1376.[2] He obtained his promotion by his book against Lollardism, and is described as 'a great stickler'[3] against the doctrines of Wickliffe. He was present at a synod in London, held in 1387, against the Lollards.

In 1399, Richard Young succeeded to the bishopric of Bangor. The bishopric was now falling wholly into the hands of Englishmen. Henry IV. sent Young on a mission into Germany in 1401, and he does not appear ever to have returned to his diocese. Godwin states that he spent the time of his episcopate in chains, but acknowledges that he knew not the cause or place of his captivity.[4] Browne Willis denies the statement altogether. In 1404, Young was translated to Rochester, for his see was quite uninhabitable by a bishop of English race and sympathies. Owain Glyndwr had raised the cry of Welsh independence, and all Wales was in arms.

[1] Bull in Rymer's 'Fœdera,' iii. 2, 912, 913, dated xi. Kal. Maii, 1371.
[2] Writ ordering that the temporalities of the see should be surrendered to him, dated October 28, 1376, in Rymer's 'Fœdera,' iii. 2, 1063.
[3] Browne Willis, 'Bangor,' p. 81.
[4] Godwin, 'De Præsulibus Angliæ' (Camb., 1743), p. 623: 'Agens in vinculis (captivitatis vel causam vel locum non intellexi).'

Whatever opinion may be entertained of Glyndwr's character, or of the purpose which he had in view, it is impossible to approve the wisdom of his enterprise or to justify his methods. No one probably, whether Welshman, Dane, Norman, or Englishman, had previously inflicted so much injury upon the Church in Wales as was done by Owain Glyndwr. He damaged the Church directly by the devastations which he wrought, and indirectly both by the poverty and desolation which he left behind as his legacy to subsequent generations, and by the warlike and legal retaliations which his outbreak provoked. For no other reason, as is stated, than that John Trevor II. of St. Asaph had pronounced sentence of deposition upon his patron, Richard II., he burned down the cathedral of St. Asaph and the canon's houses, as well as the bishop's houses at St. Asaph, Meliden, and St. Martin's. Bangor Cathedral suffered the same fate as St. Asaph's, and the monastery of Cwmhir in Radnorshire was also destroyed. Henry IV., on his part, plundered the Friary of Llanfaes, and either slew or carried off the friars, and placed Englishmen therein. He also, in 1401, destroyed Strata Florida. In 1402 Glyndwr burst into Glamorgan, destroying as he went. Then, as one of the Iolo manuscripts relates, 'he won the Castle of Cardiff and many more; he also demolished the castles of Penlline, Landough, Flemingston, Dunraven of the Butlers, Tal-y-van, Llanblethian, Llanguian, Malefant, and that of Penmark, and burned many of the villages and churches about them. He burned also the villages of Llanfrynach and Aberthin, and many houses at Llantwit Major and other places, the men of which would not join him. But many of the country people collected round him with one accord, and they demolished castles and houses innumerable, laid waste and quite fenceless the lands, and gave them in common to all. They took away from the powerful and rich and distributed the plunder among the weak and poor. Many of the higher order and chieftains were obliged to flee to England under the protection and support of the King.'[1] It was a revolution, and as such might have justified itself, had it been successful and permanent; but the destruction of cathedrals and churches leaves a stain upon its leader, and would have laid a burden upon the restored principality, if Owen had succeeded in perpetuating his princedom. When Cardiff was destroyed, the Benedictine priory and the house of the Black Friars were destroyed with it, but Glyndwr is said to have spared Crokerton Street,[2] outside the town, in which the house of the Franciscans was situated. Glyndwr also destroyed the bishop's castle and the archdeacon's house at Llandaff, but spared the cathedral. We find that some of the Pembrokeshire churches were saved from destruction by payments of money. 'Great Glendower,' 'the light of Powys,' the hero of Sycharth, the friend of Iolo Goch, would have left a brighter name behind him, had he not sullied his gallant struggle on behalf of the liberties of his country by ill deeds done to the Church.

The English Parliament retaliated on the Welsh by a series of unjust and oppressive laws. They were rendered incapable of purchasing lands or holding office in any town; disputes between Englishmen and Welshmen were to be decided by English judges and juries; and an Englishman who married a Welsh woman was disfranchised. By these and other severe enactments the Welsh were put in a much worse position than before.

Bishop Trevor of St. Asaph would seem to have been a man of a very inconstant temper. He received from Richard II. permission to hold *in commendam* with his bishopric the church of Meifod and the chapels of Pole

---

[1] 'Iolo MSS.,' pp. 98, 493.
[2] Afterwards Crockherbtown, now swallowed up in Queen Street, Cardiff.

and Guldeford or Guildsfield, but he afterwards turned against his benefactor. The Parliament which was summoned to consider the claim of Bolingbroke and the crimes of the unfortunate Richard appointed seven commissioners: 'the Byshop of Seint Assa for Ershbishoppes and Byshoppes; the Abbot of Glastenbury for Abbotes and Priours, and all other men of holy Chirche seculers and Rewelers; the Erle of Gloucestre for Dukes and Erles; the Lord of Berkeley for Barones and Banerettes; Sir Thomas Irpyngham, Chaumberleyn, for all the Bachilers and Commons of this Lond be south; Sir Thomas Grey for all the Bachilers and Commons by north';[1] and William Thirnyng, the Justiciar. It fell to Bishop Trevor, as the head of this commission, to pronounce the sentence of deposition.

Most men would deem one such change of allegiance enough, and would be constrained by shame, if by nothing else, to adhere to a cause chosen with such decision. But Bishop Trevor acted as if determined to exemplify in his person the 'fickleness' charged in those days against his race. At the beginning of the war he suffered grievously, as we have seen, from Owain Glyndwr and the insurgents, and was, on the other hand, supported by the authority of the King, who issued a writ on his behalf in 1401,[2] because of the trouble caused him by the wars, and in the next year confirmed the permission previously granted him to hold *in commendam* Meifod, Pole and Guildsfield.[3] But very soon afterwards he joined Glyndwr—a remarkable change, which is attributed to his disgust at English tyranny. It is said that when he remonstrated with the English lords respecting the unwisdom of their Welsh policy, they replied that

---

[1] Thus specified by William Thirnyng in announcing the sentence to Richard, and renouncing homage and fealty. 'Rotuli Parliamentorum,' iii. 424, etc.
[2] Rymer, 'Fœdera' (first edition), viii. 222.
[3] *Ibid.*, p. 246.

'they cared not for the anger of such a pack of barefooted blackguards.'[1] In a royal document, dated May 16, 1409, 'John, the pretended Bishop of St. Asaph,' is mentioned among 'traitors and rebels.'[2] He was sent on an embassy to Paris by Glyndwr, and died there, and was buried at St. Victor's Abbey. Robert de Lancaster succeeded him as bishop in 1411. Possibly Trevor had been partly influenced in his change of sides by the general feeling of his clergy, which was certainly favourable to the revolution. In 1404 the Archbishop of Canterbury issued a writ to William Memborough, Archdeacon of Chester, ordering him to certify to him the names of those who preached rebellion in the diocese of St. Asaph.

Glyndwr had got rid of the Englishman, Young, from the diocese of Bangor, and he persuaded the Pope to acknowledge as Young's successor in the see a nominee of his own, Llywelyn[3] Bifort, or Byforde. Neither Henry IV. nor the Archbishop of Canterbury would acknowledge this bishop. His name in found in a list of outlaws, in 1406, as 'Lewelinus Bifort, vocat. Episcopus Bangor.' According to Walsingham, he was taken prisoner in a battle fought in Yorkshire on February 19, 1408. His life was spared because he had no weapon on him, but he was deprived of his bishopric. The Pope provided to the see in his stead one Benedict Nicholls, who was translated to St. David's in 1417. Owain Glyndwr himself died in 1415, a defeated and disappointed man. He was not without noble ideals—a university of Wales, an independent Parliament, and a Church free from the thraldom of England, with an archbishopric of its own—but his measures were detestable. As old Fuller has said, 'being angry with the King, his

---

[1] 'Se de illis scurris nudipedibus non curare.'
[2] Rymer, 'Fœdera,' viii. 588.
[3] So Browne Willis, 'Bangor,' p. 85. Godwin ('De Præsulibus,' p. 623) calls him 'Ludovicus.'

revenge fell upon God, burning down the fair cathedrals of Bangor and St. Asaph. His destructive nature delighted in doing mischief to others, though no good to himself.'[1]

[1] 'Worthies of Wales' (edition of 1662), p. 39.

CHAPTER XIII.

FROM THE DEATH OF OWAIN GLYNDWR TO THE DISSOLUTION OF THE MONASTERIES.

'THE light of Powys' proved to be the scourge of Wales. Never since the age of its primitive barbarism was the general condition of the country so gloomy; the North was indeed nearly a desert. Wherever Glyndwr moved, he left desolation and destruction in his wake; and the Wars of the Roses which followed seemed likely to extinguish altogether the expiring civilization. But for the beneficence of the monks, and the useful labours of the parish priests, anarchy and barbarism would have been universal in the north of the principality. Sir John Wynn, of Gwydir, who is one of our chief authorities for this obscure period of our history, has depicted the state of the country in the darkest colours :

'All the whole country' (of Nantconway), he says, ' then was but a forest, rough and spacious, as it is still, but then waste of inhabitants, and all overgrowne with woods ; for Owen Glyndwr's warres beginning in 1400, continued fifteen yeares, which brought such a desolation that greene grasse grew on the market-place in Llanrwst, called Bryn y botten, and the deere fled into the churchyard, as it is reported. This desolation arose from Owen Glyndwr's policie to bring all things to waste, that the English should find no strength nor resting place. The countrey being brought to such a desolation, could not be replanted in haste;

and the warres of York and Lancaster happening some fifteen yeares after, this countrey being the chiefest fastness of North Wales, was kept by David ap Jenkin, a captaine of the Lancastrian faction, fifteen yeares in Edward the Fourth his time, who sent diverse captaines to besiege him, who wasted the countrey while he kept his rocke of Carreg y Walch; and lastly, by the Earle Herbert, who brought it to utter desolation. Now you are to understand that in those dayes the countrey of Nantconway was not onely wooded, but alsoe all Carnarvon, Merioneth, and Denbigh shires seemed to be but one forrest haveing few inhabitants, though of all others Nantconway had the fewest, being the worst then, and the seat of the warres, to whome the countrey about paid contribution. From the towne of Conway to Bala, and from Nantconway to Denbigh (when warres did happen to cease in Hirwethog, the countrey adjoining to Nantconway), there was continually fostered a wasp's nest, which troubled the whole countrey, I mean a lordship belonging to St. John's of Jerusalem, called Spytty Jevan, a large thing, which had privilege of sanctuary. This peculiar jurisdiction, not governed by the King's lawes, became a receptacle of thieves and murtherers, who safely being warranted there by law, made the place thoroughly peopled. Noe spot within twenty miles was safe from their incursions and robories, and what they got within their limits was their owne. They had to their backstay friends and receptors in all the county of Merioneth and Powisland. These helping the former desolations of Nantconway, and preying upon that countrey, as their next neighbours, kept most part of that countrey all waste and without inhabitants.'[1]

Such was Nantconway at the beginning of the reign of Henry VII.; yet other districts of North Wales were in little better case. Meredith Wynn, Sir John's uncle, who

[1] 'History of the Gwydir Family' (ed. Askew Roberts), pp. 74-76.

lived in Nantconway, and who built the new church of Dolwyddelan in 1512, 'durst not goe to church on a Sunday from his house of Penanmen, but he must leave the same guarded with men, and have the doores sure barred and boulted, and a watchman to stand at the Garreg big, during divine service. . . . He durst not, although he were guarded with twenty tall archers, make knowne when he went to church or elsewhere, or goe or come the same way through the woodes and narrow places, lest he should be layed for.' He told his nephew also that the reason he demolished the old church, 'which stood in a thicket,' and built the new one stronger and greater than before, was 'because the countrey was wild, and he might be oppressed by his enemies on the suddaine, in that woodie countrey; it therefore stood him in a policie to have diverse places of reatreat.'[1] Yet even so disturbed a district as Nantconway, which was a veritable den of robbers, was to Meredith, honest man though he was, a haven of refuge. For when asked why he had left his home in Carnarvonshire to dwell there, he replied 'that he should find elbowe roome in that vast countrey among the bondmen, and that he had rather fight with outlawes and thieves than with his owne blood and kindred; for if I live in mine house in Evioneth, I must either kill mine owne kinsmen or be killed by them.' 'Wherein,' adds Sir John Wynn, 'he said very truly, as the people were such in those days there.' For family feuds prevailed through the district, and men were constantly killed 'for noe other quarrel, but for the mastery of the countrey, and for the first good-morrow.'[2] Murderers, who were called in Welsh 'Llawrudds,' that is, *red hands*, were used to 'resort to the most powerful of the gentry, where they were kept very choisely.'[3] There was an incessant feud in Chirkeland and Oswaldstreland

---

[1] 'History of the Gwydir Family,' p. 82. [2] *Ibid.*, p. 76.
[3] *Ibid.*, p. 65.

between the Kyffins and the Trevors. 'These had their alliance, partisans, and friends in all the countreys round thereabouts, to whome, as the manner of the time was, they sent such of their followers as committed murther or manslaughter, which were safely kept as very precious jewells; and they received the like from their friends.'[1]

One anecdote of these wild times incidentally illustrates the benevolent hospitality of the parish priests, which tended to soften the prevalent brutality of manners. It happened, we are told, 'that the parson of Llanvrothen tooke a child of Jevan ap Robert's to foster, which sore grieved Howell Vaughan's wife, her husband having then more land in that parish than Jevan ap Robert had. In revenge thereof she plotted the death of the said parson in this manner. She sent a woman to aske lodgeing of the parson, *who used not to deny any*. The woman being in bed, after midnight began to strike and to rave; whereupon the parson, thinking that she had been distracted, awakeing out of his sleepe, and wondering at soe suddaine a crie in the night, made towards her, and his household also. Then she said that he would have ravished her, and soe got out of doores, threatening revenge to the parson. This woman had her bretheren three notable rogues of the damn'd crew fit for any mischiefe, being followers of Howell ap Rys. In a morning these bretheren watched the parson, as he went to looke to his cattle, in a place in that parish called Gogo yr Llechwin, being now a tenement of mine, and there murthered him; and two of them fled to Chirkeland in Denbighshire, to some of the Trevors, who were friends, or of a kinne to Howell ap Rys, or his wife.'[2]

When to murders such as these, to the 'dayly bickerings' between 'near and hateful neighbours,' of which Sir John Wynn's short history is full, and to the desolations which the rising of Glyndwr and the Wars of the

---

[1] 'History of the Gwydir Family,' p. 61.   [2] *Ibid.*, p. 60.

Roses had caused, is added the terrible visitation of 'the plague, which commonly followeth warre and desolation,' this awful picture of the condition of North Wales receives its finishing touch.

It is not surprising that amid such conflicts and desolations no bishop could live in the country. It is to the credit of the northern bishops that they ventured to do as much as they did in their dioceses. Their cathedrals and palaces were destroyed, their revenues almost annihilated, and their dioceses turned into a wilderness. It was impossible for a bishop to hold his see without having some other benefice *in commendam*. That the bishops were generally Englishmen may be matter for regret, but scarcely for astonishment, seeing that so many of the Welsh ecclesiastics had recently supported Glyndwr, and whatever blame is due for these appointments should be mainly apportioned to the See of Rome, which had now altogether usurped the patronage. It was, be it remembered, the age in which Archbishop Chicheley was oppressed by the Pope, and the Papacy crushed for a time the liberties of the Church of England.

Of the two dioceses, that of Bangor was in the worse condition, with respect to its episcopate. For a long time, says Godwin, until the reign of Henry VII., 'it gave its bishop for the most part a mere empty title, while ambitious men, already enriched with ecclesiastical promotion, took this bishopric as their title, retaining by Papal dispensation their former possessions, and content with the name of bishop, they lived in England, utterly neglecting the episcopal estates, which were left to the depredation of the neighbours.'[1] Yet at least one of the bishops so censured, John Cliderow, showed in various ways a certain regard for his see. St. Asaph had, probably, two Welshmen as its bishops before the accession of the House of Tudor, Robert de Lancaster

---

[1] 'De Præsulibus,' p. 132.

and the celebrated Reginald Pecock, and had several
bishops who did good work for their see. Though the
Wars of the Roses, by rendering confusion still more
confounded, postponed the rebuilding of the cathedral
for many years, English bishops had previously done
what they could to prepare the way for this important
work, and had been seconded by the support of the English
King. This is proved by a grant of Henry VI., issued
in 1442, which, as showing the desolation of the diocese,
and the efforts of its English bishops for its welfare,
deserves to be quoted in full:

'Henri by the grace of God Kyng of Englande and of
Fraunce, and Lord of Irland. To the worshipfull Fadre
in God the Bishop of Bath our Chauncellour greeting.
We late you wite that we havying Consideration howe
the Chirch Cathedrall of Saint Assaph, with the Steple,
Bells, Quere, Porch, and Vestiary, with all other Con-
tentis, Bokes, Chaliz, Vestimentis, and other Ornaments,
as the Bokes, Stalles, Deskes, Altres, and all the aparaill
longying to the same Church, was brent and utterly
destroyed, and in likewys the Byshop's Palays and all
his other three Mannoirs no Styk laft in the last werre
tyme of Wales, as we bene enformed by a Supplication
presented unto us in the behalve of the Reverend Fadre
in God our right trusty and well beloved Johan Lowe
now Bishop of the sayd Cathedral Chirche; and it is so
as it is saide, that both for the exilitee of the endowing
of the sayd Cathedral Chirch, with the indisposition of
the Cuntree there, and also for lack and scarcetee of
Stuffee in all the coste both of free Stone and Tymber,
the sayd Palays and Manoirs be not like to be belded
again withouten grete Costes and Laysence, the which
may not well be borne, withouten our Grace be shewed
in that Partie, notwithstanding that Robert, late Bishop
of the said Chirche Cathedrall and the saide Johan nowe

Bishop, have putte their great peyne and diligence to amend suche Parcels of the saide Palays and Manoirs as be now reparelled. Wherefore we havyng Consideration unto the Premisses, have of our grace especiale graunted unto the sayde Johan now Byshop of the sayde Cathedral Chirche that he from hensforth be quite and fully discharged ageinst us and our Heirs of all manour dismes and quinzismes, and parcells of dismes and quinzismes that have been and shall be granted unto us or our Heirs by the Clergie of this our Royaume, and of paying unto us or our said Heires the saide dismes or quinzismes, or parcels of dismes and quinzismes of the which the saide Johan hath, be, or shall be grauntez, with other Prelates of this our Royaume. Wherefore we woll and charge you, that hereupon ye do make Lettres Patentes under our grete Seal in due Forme. Geven under oure privie Seal, at oure Castell of Wyndesore the XXIII. Day Julyy, the Yere of our Regne XXI."[1]

The bishops mentioned in this royal grant are Robert de Lancaster, Abbot of Valle Crucis,[2] who was consecrated at Lincoln by Archbishop Arundel, in 1411, to succeed the inconstant John Trevor, and John Lowe, his successor, an Augustinian canon, of some celebrity for his learning, who was appointed by Papal provision in 1433. Both of these bishops would appear to have made at least some efforts for the improvement of their diocese; but in the general history of the Church their fame is small compared with that of the next bishop, the celebrated Reginald Pecock, who has been exalted

---

[1] A.D. 1442. Browne Willis, 'St. Asaph,' ii. 116, App. 51, where this note is added: 'N.B.—This writ was delivered August the 3rd to the Chancellor to be executed. It is called in the Record remaining in the White Tower, London. a Privy Seal.'
[2] He held the abbacy *in commendam* with the bishopric.

by some writers to the rank of a Protestant confessor—a curious fate for so zealous a Papist.

Pecock was a Welshman, according to the statements of Leland and others. He seems, in early life, to have been connected with the southern division of the principality, for he is styled in a Papal instrument, 'priest of the diocese of St. David's.' He was educated at Oriel College, Oxford, and was elected a Fellow in 1417. His learning gained him a considerable reputation, and when the See of St. Asaph became vacant by the transference of Bishop Lowe to Rochester, Pecock was appointed by a Papal provision of the date April 22, 1444.

Pecock's intellect appears to have been of the kind that delights in paradoxes, and his ambition inclined him to produce sensational effects. At the same time he was, undoubtedly, a bold and independent thinker. He was a stanch and uncompromising opponent of the Lollards, whom as a class he despised, but he was not willing to cast in his lot wholly with the conventionally orthodox party of his time. At first he appeared as an advocate of the most extreme Papal claims, such as the great bulk of the English clergy detested. In a sermon preached at St. Paul's Cross, in 1447, he justified Papal Bulls of provisions, by one of which indeed he had been himself promoted, maintained the right of the Popes to exact annates from the clergy, and in all respects adopted what would now be called an Ultramontane position. In the same sermon he further boldly met the criticisms which the Lollard party had levelled at the bishops, said that preaching was not a necessary episcopal function, and defended non-residence. So bold and outspoken a pronouncement provoked antagonism from all quarters, as Pecock doubtless anticipated, and for some time the sermon formed the subject of lively discussion, and the bishop gained to the full the notoriety which he desired. It does not appear, however, that Pecock was at all negligent of his own diocese; his very love of paradox made the advocate of non-preaching bishops a zealous preacher at home.

About 1440 Pecock wrote 'Donet,' an introduction to the chief truths of Christianity, and in 1449 he produced one of his greatest works, 'The Repressor of Overmuch Blaming the Clergy.' This latter was directed against the 'Bible-men,' or Lollards. Despite some blunders and peculiarities, such as are common in mediæval literature, it is a great and powerful work. Though a defender of the orthodox position, according to the standard of orthodoxy of that age, and also an advocate of Papal supremacy, the weapons which he used in the conflict were not orthodox weapons; but the Papacy was not inclined to quarrel with its champion, though others were. Eventually Pecock's political connections caused his ruin. In 1450 he was translated to Chichester by his favourite method of Papal provision; but the appointment was due in some measure to the influence of the unpopular Duke of Suffolk. Suffolk fell soon afterwards, and Pecock somewhat later fell too. Some passages in his 'Treatise on Faith,' published in 1456, were deemed to savour of heresy, and, indeed, were hard to reconcile with conventional orthodoxy, and the great Welshman was condemned and deprived. In spite of faults of character which we need not harshly blame, the intellectual qualities of Pecock claim for him a conspicuous niche in the fabric of Welsh greatness. It has been said of him by an admirer that, 'as the expositor of the province of reason in matters of religion in opposition to the absolute dogmatism of the one party, and the narrow scripturalism of the other, Pecock stands out prominently as the one great Englishman of his age, and as the precursor of a still greater Englishman in the age following, viz., Richard Hooker.'[1] We must not forget that this great Englishman was also a Welshman.

But though intellectually great as a thinker and a divine, Pecock lacked the physical courage and perhaps, also, the moral conviction of a martyr. He broke down utterly under the fear of being burned at the stake, and made a most abject confession, submitting himself as 'a very contrite and penitent sinner to the correction of the Church' and of the Archbishop of Canterbury, and exhorting that no man hereafter should give credence to his 'perilous doctrines, heresies, and errors.'[2] But the malice of his enemies, whom he had provoked perhaps as much by the superiority of his genius as by the restlessness of his ambition, was not satisfied by this pitiful submission; he was committed to the care of the Abbot of Thorney, and by him kept in rigorous seclusion until his death. The instructions given to the abbot by the Archbishop of Canterbury breathe all the malignity of petty spite. He was to have 'a secret closed chamber,' where he might have a sight of some altar, to hear mass; one person only, 'that is sad and well-disposed,' was to attend upon him, 'to make his bedde and to make his Fyr'; he could have no book to look on, 'but only a Portuos and a Masse Book, a Saulter or Legend, and a Bible'; worse still, he was to 'have nothing to write with, no stuff to write upon'; finally, he was to have competent fuel and meat and drink, according to the discretion of the abbot. Forty pounds were assigned to the abbot for his maintenance.[3] In this close imprisonment the 'ample spirit' of Reginald Pecock pined until his death. Such was the fate of perhaps the greatest thinker that has filled a Welsh bishopric. The ill-luck

---

[1] Pecock's 'Repressor' (Rolls Series), Introd. xxv.
[2] Confession in Collier's 'Eccl. Hist.,' i. 676.
[3] Browne Willis, 'St. Asaph,' i. p. 83, etc., where the instructions are given in full.

that waits upon genius has rarely forsaken the great men of Wales.

Pecock was succeeded in the See of St. Asaph by Thomas Knight, who held the Priory of Daventry in conjunction with the bishopric. He was forced to surrender his bishopric and sue for pardon in 1471, on account of his political action in opposition to Edward IV. Richard Redman, who was appointed in his place, held the see between 1471 and 1495, and did very much for his diocese, though he, like so many others, held another benefice *in commendam*, being also Abbot of Shap, in Westmoreland. He was the rebuilder of the cathedral, which for eighty years had lain in ruins. Though it might have been supposed that the charge of a diocese with that of an abbey was enough for one man, Redman found time for political life as an ardent Yorkist, and served both Edward IV. and Richard III. on embassies. On the accession of Henry VII. he viewed the triumph of the Lancastrian party with dislike, and took part in the imposture of Lambert Simnel, but afterwards made his peace with the King, and was again employed on embassies.

The Bishops of Bangor during the same period seem to have had very little connection with their diocese, which was indeed more a wilderness than the neighbouring diocese of St. Asaph. Benedict Nicholls was translated to St. David's in 1417, and was succeeded by William Barrow, who was 'provided' by the Pope. He had previously been Chancellor of the University of Oxford, and, after a short episcopate, was translated to Carlisle. John Cliderow, his successor, is said to have been a man of influence at court, and he obtained a confirmation of all charters and privileges of his church.[1] He died in 1435, far away from his diocese, in London. He left to his cathedral his white mitre, a sacerdotal vestment, three

[1] Browne Willis, 'Bangor,' App. xx., p. 224. It is dated 1425.

copes, and some tunicles, besides other benefactions.[1] The next bishop, Thomas Cheryton, was a Dominican. John Stanbery, his successor, was 'provided' by the Pope in 1448. He was a Carmelite, and is said by Browne Willis to have been 'reputed the learnedest man of his order, if not of the age wherein he lived.' He was translated to Hereford, and was succeeded by James Blakedon, who had previously held an Irish bishopric. In 1468 Richard Evyndon, or Ednam, who was then bishop, represented to the Pope the great poverty of his see, and that its income was not worth more than £100 per annum, and he obtained leave for himself and his successors to hold some other benefice *in commendam*.

With the end of the Wars of the Roses, and with the accession of the House of Tudor, there was at first promise of much improvement in the condition of the four Welsh dioceses, especially of Bangor and St. Asaph. Law and order began to gain ground and anarchy to recede. The old waste places were repaired—we have already seen how Redman restored the Cathedral of St. Asaph—and the close of the century was marked also in the same diocese by the restoration of the churches of Wrexham, Mold, Northop, Holywell, Ruthin, Holt, and Llangollen. Henry Dean, who succeeded Ednam in the bishopric of Bangor in 1496, is notable as the rebuilder of the choir of his cathedral, and as taking vigorous measures for asserting the claims of his see to possessions which had become alienated, owing to the carelessness, or more probably the powerlessness, of former bishops. Dean had been Prior of the Monmouthshire Llanthony, so that he had a previous connection with Wales, and he continued to hold the priory *in commendam* after his appointment as bishop. He was a man of much political note and ability, and received the bishopric of Bangor as a reward for his services as

[1] Browne Willis, 'Bangor,' App. xxi. Will of Bishop John Cliderow.

chancellor in Ireland, where he put down the movement in favour of Perkin Warbeck.[1] The same activity and vigour which he had shown in Ireland were apparent also in the measures which he adopted for enforcing his rights in the anarchical condition of North Wales. As he was unable by peaceful means to gain possession of the Isle of Seals, off Anglesey, he used what Gerald would have called 'Welsh law,' and at the head of an armed force drove out the illegal occupants.[2] Dean was promoted to Salisbury, and eventually, on the death of Morton, was made Archbishop of Canterbury. He showed attachment to his Welsh diocese, on his translation, by leaving his crozier and mitre, which were of considerable value, to his successor, on condition that he would finish his work at the cathedral.[3] Thomas Pigott (1500-1504), the next Bishop of Bangor, was Abbot of Chertsey, in Surrey, and seems to have lived there. He is said by Wood to have been 'a Denbighshire man born.'[4] After his death, in 1504, on the visitation of Archbishop Warham, forty-four priests in this diocese were found to be keeping 'concubines' publicly, that is, very probably, were found to be living as the majority of the clergy had lived in the days of Giraldus Cambrensis, for the Welsh Church never altogether recognised as binding the arbitrary decrees of the Papal See respecting clerical celibacy.

John Penny (1505-1508), the next Bishop of Bangor, held the Abbey of Leicester *in commendam*, and after a short tenure of the see was translated to Carlisle. He had the reputation of being an eminent canonist.[5] Thomas Pace, *alias* Skeffington, who was provided by the Pope in 1508, and was consecrated in 1509, held the Abbey of Beaulieu *in commendam*, and usually resided

---

[1] Wood, 'Athenæ Oxonienses' (ed. 1691), p. 551.
[2] Godwin, 'De Præsulibus,' p. 132.
[3] Browne Willis, 'Bangor,' p. 95.
[4] 'Athenæ Oxonienses,' i. 553.
[5] *Ibid.*, p. 561.

there. But it must be mentioned, to his credit, that he built the steeple and the entire body of the cathedral of his see, from the choir westward, and also rebuilt a great part of the episcopal palace. His divided affections may be argued from the fact that his body was buried at Beaulieu and his heart at Bangor. Of the next bishop, John Salcot, or Capon (1534-1539), we know little, either bad or good, so far as his see was concerned. He was one of Henry VIII.'s bishops, and was elected in 1533 for his subserviency to that tyrant, whose divorce from Queen Catherine he did his best to promote. He was translated to Salisbury in 1539.

Two of the first three bishops appointed to St. Asaph during the Tudor Period were Welshmen. Redman was succeeded in 1495 by Michael Diacon, and he in 1500 by a Welshman, Dafydd ap Iorwerth, Abbot of Valle Crucis, who probably lived at his abbey within the diocese. The other Welshman, Dafydd ap Owen, who succeeded Dafydd ap Iorwerth in 1503, was also an abbot of a Welsh monastery—but whether of Strata Marcella or Valle Crucis is uncertain—and afterwards Abbot of Aberconway. His episcopacy was rendered notable by the rebuilding of the Episcopal Palace, destroyed by Glyndwr; and by the erection, in 1507, of what used to be reckoned as one of 'the seven wonders of Wales,' the fine tower of Wrexham church. The building of this church was greatly forwarded by Dafydd ap Owen's successor, Edward Birkhead, who was appointed by Papal provision in 1513. On the death of Birkhead, Henry Standish was provided to the see by a Bull of Pope Leo, dated May 28, 1518, and was consecrated at the Franciscan Church at Oxford.

Standish, who occupied the see from 1518 to 1535, was a noted controversialist. He was a Lancashire man, a Franciscan, and provincial of his order, and shortly before his appointment had been proceeded against for the part he took in an ecclesiastical controversy. He was a stanch opponent of the Reformation, and wrote against Dean Colet and against Erasmus's translation of the New Testament. He also assisted Queen Catherine against Henry VIII. during the divorce suit. But, as regards his work for his diocese, very little can be said; perhaps his other occupations left him but little time. He left, however, a sum of money to pave the choir of his cathedral, and it is said that with this the organ was bought. His executors were sued, because they had not carried out his will in this respect to the letter.[1]

Standish died on July 9, 1535, and on the 16th of the following January a man of very different views was elected in his place. This was William Barlow, an Augustinian canon, who had been at St. Osyth, in Essex, and had been thence preferred by the favour of Anne Boleyn to the priory of Haverfordwest. Barlow was one of those men, common enough in times of religious reform or revolution, who, to a genuine conviction of the iniquity of use and wont, unite a total disregard of the rights of property and a lack of comprehension of the very meaning of sacrilege, and who, if any part of the tithe and offering of which God has been robbed come by any chance into their possession, consider it to be a providential dispensation in their favour. Such men were the spots and blemishes of the English Reformation, though they are sometimes accounted among the ornaments of the Puritan Revolution. Fortunately for the See of St. Asaph, it escaped from his authority very soon after his appointment, and before he had time to work any of the evil to which his disposition inclined him, for on April 21 he was translated to St. David's. It is even doubtful whether he was consecrated to St. Asaph. His confirmation was on February 23,[2] and, according to

[1] Browne Willis, 'St. Asaph,' i. 92, 93.
[2] Godwin ('De Præsulibus,' p. 642) says, 'Consecratus est vicesimo

the Act of 1534, consecration should have taken place within twenty days after this date. It also appears that he received the possession of the see, as he appointed to the Rectory of Whitford and the sixth cursal canonry. This would seem to establish the fact of his consecration. But, on the other hand, he was on his way to Scotland on an embassy on February 1, and remained there during March; so that it is difficult to find a date for his consecration, which could hardly have taken place in Scotland, and also he is called 'Bishop-elect of St. Asaph' after he vacated that see. On the whole, it would seem most probable that he was not consecrated until after his appointment to St. David's. The Roman theory that he was never consecrated at all is sufficiently refuted by the fact that during his lifetime he was recognised as bishop not merely by the Reformers, but by leading men on the other side, as Gardiner and Lee. That no record of his consecration exists is no disproof of his consecration, as the same is true of various other contemporary bishops of both parties.

Barlow was not long at St. David's before he raised up to himself enemies there, on account of his extreme and heterodox opinions. In the January following his appointment articles[1] were exhibited against him by one Roger Lewis, bachelor of law, before the Lord President of Wales. One Talley, preaching before him, had said 'that in times past there was none that did preach or

---

secundo Februarii, 1535,' viz., February 22, 1536, as we now reckon. Wharton ('Anglia Sacra') says he was consecrated on February 23. These statements seem to have arisen from confusion with his confirmation. The commission to confirm is dated February 22, the certificate of confirmation February 23.

[1] See the articles in Collier's 'Eccl. Hist.,' ii. 135 (ed. A.D. 1708-1714). Bevan ('St. David's,' p. 168) seems to consider this accusation as prior to his appointment to St. David's, and puts it in January, 1536. The date given by Collier is January 11, 1536. But the year began then on March 25, and January 11, 1536, would be January 11, 1537, as we now reckon.

declare the Word of God truly, nor the Truth was never known till now of late.' Bishop Barlow himself was charged, not only with denying the existence of purgatory and the advantage of auricular confession, but also with the following statements: 'that wheresoever two or three simple persons, as two Coblers or Weavers, were in Company, and elected in the Name of God, that there was the true Church of God,' and 'that if the King's grace, being Supreme Head of the Church of England, did chuse, denominate, and elect any Layman' (being learned) 'to be a Bishop, that he, so chosen' (without mention made of any orders) 'shou'd be as good a Bishop as he is, or the best in England.' These accusations seem to have been true, and not malicious distortions of innocent speeches; for Barlow afterwards, in his answers to certain questions put to various bishops and divines touching the sacraments, asserted that no consecration of bishops and priests was required by the New Testament, but only appointing to the office; and maintained, further, that at the beginning bishops and priests were all one; that laymen have sometimes made priests; and that 'bishops have no authority to make priests unless they be authorized of the Christian Prince.'[1] Evidently Barlow, whom even the zealous Burnet censures as 'not very discreet,'[2] had much of the Puritan in his composition. But the charges of Roger Lewis incidentally establish also the fact of his consecration, wherever it may have taken place, for had he not been consecrated, the words attributed to him respecting his own title to be bishop would have been absolutely void of meaning. That he had the Puritan taste for spoliation is evident from the subsequent history of his episcopate, which lies beyond our present view. His successor at St. Asaph,

[1] 'Resolutions of several bishops and divines,' in Burnet's 'History of the Reformation,' Book iii., App. xxi., vol. i., pp. 225, 228, 230 (ed. A.D. 1679).
[2] 'Hist.,' i., p. 255.

Robert Parfew, or Warton, Abbot of Bermondsey, who was allowed to hold his abbacy *in commendam* until the dissolution of the monasteries, has been accused of despoiling his see, but apparently without sufficient grounds.

South Wales had suffered grievously from the incursions of Owain Glyndwr, but both its cathedrals had escaped destruction, and it was not left at the end of the war a waste, howling wilderness, as was part, at least, of the north. The gate-house of the old Episcopal Palace of the Bishops of Llandaff still stands on the rising ground to the south-east of the cathedral, recalling the devastations of the ruthless Prince of Wales, who in some parts of Pembrokeshire exacted money payments as the price of his sparing the churches. Not far away from Llandaff, near Cardiff Castle, may be seen the site of the priory and church of the Black Friars, which were burned down in 1404 by the same prince as a sacrifice to the cause of Welsh liberty. The English King, on his part, in 1401 used the church and choir of the monastery of Strata Florida as a stable, even up to the high altar, and plundered the whole building. But it would appear that in the very next year compunction seized him, and he sought to make reparation by the following order:

'Whereas the Abbey of Strata Florida, by the frequent aggressions of Welsh rebels, and also by raids of the King's lieges for the castigation of the same rebels, is greatly impoverished, and its lands devastated, so that the dispersion of the Abbot and monks is to be feared, the King has taken the Abbey and its appurtenances, with all annuities, pensions, leases, etc., granted by its abbots, into his hand, and has committed the custody of the Abbey and its lands, etc., to Thomas de Percy, Earl of Worcester, and John Belyng, clerk, to dispose thereof to the Abbey's best advantage, and for its relief; all issues to be devoted to the support of the abbots and monks, for the succour and relief of the said place ; and until this is effected, all annuities, pensions, etc., are to cease: none of its corn, cattle, etc., are to be taken by purveyors for the household of the King or of the Prince of Wales. Dated Westminster, April 1, A.D. 1402. By the Council.'[1]

Spoilers of Church and monastic revenues had frequently in those days the grace to confess their fault, and in some degree to make amends, and Henry IV., though he lacked the politic skill of Edward I., did not desire that the Church of Wales should suffer injury at his hands.

South Wales suffered in some degree in the ensuing reign from the suppression of alien priories, a measure which, however justifiable in itself, set an example of confiscation which subsequent generations copied. But the possessions of these priories were not diverted, as by subsequent legislators, to secular purposes, but were used for good and religious objects. Wales, however, had good ground of complaint, as the revenues of the Welsh priories were bestowed upon colleges and other institutions in England, and so were lost to the principality. The revenues of Llangenith, which were derived from the churches of Llangenith and Pennard, were transferred to Archbishop Chicheley's foundation of All Souls' College, Oxford, as were also those of St. Clears, Carmarthenshire.

Those of Craswall, near Hay, in the same diocese of St. David's, were given to Christ's College, Cambridge. Monkton, near Pembroke, had been previously confiscated for a time by Edward III., and Henry VI. afterwards gave it to Humphrey, Duke of Gloucester, who, however, transferred it to St. Alban's Abbey, so that it escaped suppression. Goldcliff, in the diocese of Llandaff, was granted by Henry VI. to Eton College, which

[1] 'Arch. Camb.,' A.D. 1889, p. 48.

grant, after a transfer to Tewkesbury, was again restored to Eton by Edward IV. Llankywan, or Llangwin, near Gresmond, was bestowed upon Shene, in Surrey.

One of the most noticeable features of the literature of this period is the extinction of the old feud between bard and monk, and the growing feeling of amity between the two classes. Gytto'r Glynn writes to Tryhaearn of Waunllwg a complimentary poem begging him to lend 'the goodly Greal—the Book of the Blood, the Book of the Heroes, where they fell in the court of Arthur,' to his friend, Abbot Dafydd of Valle Crucis, whom he likewise extols in high terms. Perhaps friendship between a bard and a North Wales abbot, whose sentiments might be presumed to be national, is not unnatural, though it did not universally exist in earlier days; but it is certainly a new feature both in the history of the mediæval monasticism of Wales and of Welsh literature, to find Neath and its abbots extolled by Welsh bards. Yet Black Ieuan of the Billhook, in the fifteenth century, writes in somewhat grandiose style a poem to Abbot Lewis, of Neath, extolling him in no measured terms, and begging of him the same Welsh book that Gytto'r Glynn had begged of Tryhaearn. The extravagance of the laudation bestowed upon the abbot may suggest that the bard expected to receive a liberal return in the shape of benefactions:

> 'Grammar, he is as firm in the faith,
> With the strength of forty grammarians;
> In Art, he is fully matured;
> In Civil Law, he is a perfect surety;
> In Sophistry, he brightly effervesces;
> In Music, he has no limit.
> There is no one scholar, nor even two,
> In the world of equal knowledge.
> Learning is in his possession.
> He is also, if required, a mirror to distant countries.
> He would determine every disputation.
> Precious in his judgment, solid is his sentence,
> In purity like the Pope's, of ancient pure descent,
> Superior to Oxford and its devices.'[1]

[1] Translation in 'Iolo MSS.,' p. 707.

This is nonsense undoubtedly, but it is very significant nonsense. The abbots filled now the position towards the bards that the Welsh princes had formerly occupied; they were the patrons, and the bards gave them flattery without stint. They sang no longer the olden strains of liberty and freedom. Dafydd ap Gwilym, Rhys Goch, and their tuneful brotherhood, had already, in the fourteenth century, tuned the Cambrian lyre to softer strains, and carolled lightly of love and beauty; of Gwen reclining mid the trefoils; or of the thrush pouring forth an englyn in the woodland vale; or of summer in lovely Glamorgan. But Dafydd enjoyed the patronage of Ivor the Liberal, of Maesaleg, and probably had little to do with monasteries and monks, except for occasional intercourse, until he came to be laid in his grave at Talley Abbey. Others, smaller bards than he, were glad to purchase favours of the abbots by paying court to them, and towards the end of the fifteenth century such a practice would seem not to have been rare. Guttyn Owain passed his time at the abbeys of Basingwerk and of Strata Florida alternately.

Occasionally, however, mercenary bards were disappointed. One, Deio ab Ieuan Ddu, visited Bardsey, carrying with him a poem in praise of Madoc, the abbot, which he hoped would procure for him a favourable reception and lavish hospitality. But, unfortunately for the bard's anticipations, the abbot lived as an ascetic in rigorous mortification of the body, and had either no means or no inclination to provide sumptuous feasts for itinerant bards. Deio was entertained with musty bread, maggoty cheese, and sour buttermilk, and in revenge burned his ode of praise, and indicted a satire upon his niggardly host.[1]

Neath Abbey seems, in the fifteenth and sixteenth centuries until its dissolution, to have been entirely Welsh in sentiment, a remarkable change from the time of

[1] Wilkins, 'Literature of Wales,' pp. 96, 97.

Richard de Grenville, its founder. Abbot Lewis, whom
Black Ieuan celebrated, is said to have been the son of
Dafydd Ddu Offeiriad of Glyn Neath, who translated
the Service of the Virgin into Welsh.[1] As the poem
of Black Ieuan contains an implied sneer at the Saxons,
and an assertion that the abbot was not of their stock,
it may be taken for granted that Abbot Lewis considered himself a thorough Welshman *o waed cochcyfan*.
How this transformation of a South Wales abbey had
been effected is not easy to trace, but it probably merely
illustrates a change which had become pretty general
by the beginning of the sixteenth century. In the period
of depression after Glyndwr's rising, Englishmen and
Welshmen in South Wales seem to have drawn closer
together, and the Celtic race had in great measure
absorbed the Saxon. Undoubtedly the process had been
going on ever since the conquest of Wales by Edward I.,
nay, it had commenced even earlier, for was not it the
proudest boast of Gerald de Barri, the Norman, that he
was above all Gerald the Welshman? It has ever been
the peculiar power of the Celtic race that it absorbs
alien elements, and infuses into them a double portion
of its Celtic spirit. The original English plantation in
Ireland eventually became more Irish than the Irish,
and Abbot Lewis of Neath, notwithstanding his boast
of Welsh descent, and his love of the Welsh language,
may very probably have had in his veins a goodly intermixture of English or Norman blood.

Those who regard the mediæval monasteries of Wales
as centres of English influence, and who would maintain that it was to a large extent the mission of monk
and priest to teach English, have much to justify their
position, at least, with regard to the monks, in the
history of the twelfth and thirteenth centuries. But
although connection with culture, such as the monasteries

---

[1] 'Iolo MSS.' p. 706, *note*.

enjoyed, would go far to modify narrowness, and we need scarcely look to a South Wales monastery to provide advocates of the policy of Glyndwr, the most important of the Norman foundations seem to have been imbued, in the fifteenth century at least, with a strong feeling of true Welsh patriotism, and a keen sympathy with Welsh literature. The northern monasteries, which were generally the creation of Welsh princes, and the Abbey of Talley (and perhaps that of Whitland), seem to have been Welsh in feeling almost from the first. It would be interesting to discover whether the Benedictines, who lived in the English towns, were similarly affected by Celtic influence as was the Cistercian Abbey of Neath, which evidently found the neighbourhood of the town, only about a mile away, no check upon its Welsh proclivities. By the end of the fifteenth century, however, even the townsmen of English extraction had probably more than half forgotten their difference of race from their Welsh neighbours, and wholly forgotten their ancient enmity. Some Norman families, we know, as the Aubreys, had altogether identified themselves with the race among which they had settled.[1]

Margam, another Cistercian abbey within a few miles of Neath, and also situate in the plain of Glamorgan, within the most especial sphere of English influence, had also in the fifteenth century a bard of its own, named Iorwerth. But, judging from the poems extant, Neath would seem to have been by far the most notable abbey in South Wales for the nationality of its sentiments and its patronage of Welsh literature. The poem of a second-rate bard like Black Ieuan might by itself be

[1] Jones, 'History of Breconshire,' ii. pp. 563-568, and 603-608. Saunders de Alberico came over with the Conqueror. Reginald was one of the chief companions of Bernard Newmarch. Thomas, grandson of Reginald, married Joan, daughter of Trahaern ap Einon ; and his son, Thomas Awbrey Goch, married Nest, daughter of Owen Gethin.

thought to supply but scanty evidence of such a position, containing, as it does, much gross flattery, which suggests that the appetite of Abbot Lewis for such tributes must have been of the coarsest. But a much more important poet, Lewis Morganwg, at a slightly later date, lauds Abbot Lleision of Neath in a more polished strain, though with flattery not much more delicate. He is 'a true son of Nonn,' which is as much as to say that he is a second St. David; he is 'the chief of every abbot, fruit of heavenly culture, fragrant as Jerome, of the sweetness of Augustine; a goodly churchman of Divine mission: an apostle of the race of Iestyn; a second Daniel of the blood of Einion, the key of learning, another blessed Lleuddad'; 'another paternal Dunawd,' 'a Bernard,' 'the shepherd of the faith, the support and staff of the pastoral office, and the rod of Aaron; like balm to this palace of Mary, as when the fulfilment of Simeon's blessing came to the Virgin's abode.' Neath, over which he presided, is styled 'the sanctuary of our language.' 'The university of Neath,' says the bard, carried away, surely, by his enthusiasm— 'lo! it is the admiration of England: the lamp of France and Ireland; a school greatly resorted to by scholars, for every science, as if it were Sion itself.'[1] If it be true, as has been stated, that this ode was composed for an Eisteddfod, held at Neath Abbey under the patronage and presidency of Abbot Lleision, the identification of the Norman abbey with Welsh national sentiment is complete.

We have, then, abundant reason to conclude that the Church in Wales was completely Welsh in sentiment at the end of the fifteenth century as much in the southern dioceses as in the northern. The bishops, indeed, were Englishmen, until the accession of a Welsh-

---

[1] Translation in Francis's 'Charters of Neath.' See, further, the Appendix to this chapter.

man to the throne of England caused a pleasant variation to be made from the monotony of constant English appointments, for two Welsh bishops were soon afterwards appointed to St. David's. But as the English bishops were frequently non-resident, they had far less influence upon the tone of their dioceses than might have been expected, except in so far as deterioration must have set in through their neglect. Bishops, too, do not by themselves make up a church—a fact which has been frequently forgotten—for the appointment of English bishops constitutes the chief basis for the common ignorant reproach as to the alien character of the Welsh Church. The paucity of known facts respecting the ordinary work of the Welsh clergy causes of necessity a disproportionate space to be given to the history of the Welsh episcopate, just as in English history the social condition of the people has often been ignored or lightly treated of in comparison with the records of battles and treaties. Yet we know that even in the past ages of conflict men did something else besides fighting, and so in Wales the inferior clergy and the godly laity had a religious life of their own, which is little known, and is, therefore, difficult to pourtray.

It is, of course, possible to regard the religious life of the fifteenth and sixteenth centuries from opposite points of view. The zealous, but 'not very discreet,' Barlow, whose zeal for God was compatible with an overweening regard for self, considered the state of the diocese of St. David's, when he became its bishop, exceedingly lamentable. According to his statements, the clergy were 'all utter enemyes' to God's Word; and 'Welsch rudenesse,' 'ydolatrous infidelytie and papisticall practyses' prevailed. At Haverfordwest there was a holy taper, much reverenced, and at Cardigan an image of the Virgin with a taper in her hand, which was believed to have burned nine years, until, one forswearing himself upon it, it went out. The cathedral and all about it he found so full of superstition, that his only hope of amending matters was to remove the see from St. David's to Carmarthen.[1] That there was much superstition in Wales cannot be disputed. There were various holy places to which pilgrimages were made by those in search of healing, whether of body or soul. St. Winifred's Well was in much requisition, and from thence to Bardsey there are holy wells on the pilgrims' road, where devotions might be paid. Bardsey itself, the 'Isle of Saints,' where the bodies of twenty thousand holy men were buried, was a place which every devout man in North Wales sought to visit, although the passage from Aberdaron is at times rough enough to deter any but earnest pilgrims; and, if Deio's satire is to be credited, the hospitality therein afforded was not such as would tempt anyone who was in search of creature comforts. But piety lingered long about the place, even to the last century, for when Pennant crossed from Aberdaron, the rowers offered a prayer upon the way. The Parish Church of Aberdaron[2] on the shore was a customary place of devotion for the pilgrims.

At Llandderfel, near Bala, was the celebrated image of Derfel Gadarn, or Derfel the Mighty, which was famed to possess wondrous power. Ellis Price, the visitor of the diocese of St. Asaph, reported concerning it on April 6, 1538, that the people came daily on pilgrimage, 'some withe kyne, other with oxen or horsis, and the reste with money,' so that the day before he wrote there were five or six hundred pilgrims. There was a saying among them 'that whosoever will offer

---

[1] 'Letters relating to the Suppression,' pp. 77-80, 183-189.

[2] Leland's 'Itin.,' v. 51 (I quote here Hearne's, the third edition, as I have not the second by me): 'The paroche chirch is above almoste a mile on the shor, as the salt water cumpasith aboute with a hedde. The chirche is caullid in Walsch Llanengan Brening, id est, Fanum Niniani Reguli, where was of late a great pilgrimage.',

anie thinge to the saide image of Darvellgadarn, he hathe power to fatche hym or them that so offers oute of hell when they be dampned.'[1] Concerning this image, we are told that the story went that it would one day burn down a forest, a tradition which was supposed to be fulfilled when it was brought to London and used to feed the fire in which honest Friar Forrest was burned.

Then, again, the good people of North Wales had their favourite saints, and as we read in a poem of Lewis Glyn Cothi, the friars would carry about with them the images of such saints, and exchange them for cheese, bacon, and corn among their simple devotees. The images of Seiriol and of Curig were found the most acceptable, for Seiriol was held in reverence as a healer of certain disorders, and the image of Curig drove away evil spirits from farm-houses. All over Wales were the holy wells, some of which, like Ffynnon Elian, the well of cursing, were put to exceedingly wicked uses, and at none of which the devotions paid savoured of the truly religious. Such customs as these were essentially Pagan, however much they may have been interpreted in Christian fashion by the clergy. But this worship of wells and streams, which Gildas had deemed extinct in his day, survived the Reformation, as it had survived the establishment of Christianity, and may not be altogether extinct at the present day; nay, even now we hear of the miracles wrought at the wondrous well of St. Winifred. In South Wales men went on pilgrimage to the shrine of St. David's, and so great was the efficacy attributed to this devotion, that it was considered that two pilgrimages to St. David's were fully equivalent to one pilgrimage to Rome, and three to a pilgrimage to the Holy Sepulchre[2]—a belief which was not likely to die away as long as English Kings approved

[1] 'Letters relating to the Suppression.' pp. 190, 191.
[2] 'Llyma Cywydd Dewi Sant,' by Thomas ap Ieuan, 'Iolo MSS.,' p. 300.

it by their practice, as did Henry II. and Edward I., with his wife, Eleanor. There was also the shrine of the Virgin at Penrhys, in Glamorgan, where was the image which Latimer called 'the Devyl's instrument,' but of which Lewis Morganwg sang with much devotion: 'There are nine heavens in one island, this grace is at Penrhys. Here are men who are drawn over land and sea by thy miracle, O Mary! Hither didst thou come, bestowing great blessings to this place, from heaven to earth. Thine image, which they see every day, was received of yore alive from heaven. Great is the number in writing, great is the number of thy miracles, holy Mary.' Again, 'If the cry of the humble blind come to thee, the blind shall see the light of day. . . . Should a deaf man come in addition to another, he will hear a cry from the wound of that other. Were a sick man to visit it upon crutches, he would not thus be brought from the Church of Mary. Thine is the image to heal sickness: thou dost heal aches and pains.'

Much of this, no doubt, is utterly bad, nearly as bad in its way, perhaps, as nineteenth-century agnosticism, which is itself false worship of another kind. There was, probably, little Lollardism in Wales, although in the south Sir John Oldcastle must have been pretty well known. Walter Brute, the Lollard, avowed himself a Welshman, having his 'offspring of the Britons, both by father's and mother's side,'[1] and Thomas ap Ieuan, the bard, was imprisoned in Kenfig Castle for his Lollard opinions. Lollardism, too, has been detected in the poems of Sion Cent, but little indeed is known about the personality of that poet. Certainly, when the Reformation began, Wales was far from ripe for it. It had at first very few supporters, and was thrust generally by English bishops upon an unwilling people, who seem to have resented the acts of their superiors, if we may

[1] Fuller, 'Worthies of Wales,' p. 8.

judge from the stories, some quite untrue, which were spread abroad to the discredit of such bishops. But though there was little Lollardism, there may have been genuine piety nevertheless. The people of those days had the sun as well as we; we have but added the glare of gas and the cold electric light. Though the Bible had not been translated into Welsh, passages of Scripture were undoubtedly contained in popular manuals, such as the Welsh translation of an Office of the Blessed Virgin Mary, which may be found in the 'Myvyrian Archæology,' and which is attributed to Davydd Ddu Hirraddug, a Vicar of Tremeirchion in the middle of the fourteenth century. Here and there, too, we find in the poetical literature of the age a strong, full note, as in Sion Cent's death-song of penitence and prayer; but it must be confessed that the favourite devotional tribute of the bards, a *cywydd* to some popular saint, such as David, Illtyd, or Teilo, does not commend itself to modern taste as any evidence of religious earnestness. Such poems were generally mere versifications of the current legends of the saints, and are chiefly remarkable for their extravagance. Superstition, gross, absurd, and abominable, undoubtedly abounded in Wales; but though it obscured, it did not necessarily destroy genuine piety. The faults of men and of churches vary in different ages, and each age is inclined to judge leniently its own weaknesses, and to magnify those of others. If we ourselves are inclined to regard with scorn the false beliefs of the Christians of the fifteenth century, we may be well assured that they would recoil in horror from the spectacle presented by Christian Wales at the present day.

Undoubtedly, however, there was much sin in Wales then, as now. The wild and lawless condition of North Wales during the period has been made clearly apparent; life and property were held on the most uncertain tenure, and deeds of violence were of daily occurrence. Yet the picture we have seen, exhibited at least one spot of brightness in the priest who was 'given to hospitality,' and whose virtues caused his death. However false beliefs obscured the true faith, and however human failings weakened the ministerial power, priest and monk showed forth a light that illuminated the darkness around, and the Church and the monastery sheltered the kindlier and gentler virtues that might otherwise have taken flight from a realm of violence and anarchy. There are indeed indications which may be taken to signify that the light which was in that dark world was itself darkness. We have noticed already that forty-four priests in the diocese of Bangor were found, in 1504, to be keeping 'concubines' publicly. We are told also that in the diocese of St. David's, during the episcopate of John de la Bere, between the years 1447 and 1460, certain of the clergy petitioned him for leave to put away their 'concubines,' alleging that they feared the vengeance of the relations of these women if they acted without his orders. The bishop rejected the petition, because the licences granted to the clergy to keep these women brought him in a considerable revenue. Statements such as these might lead to the conclusion that corruption of morals was widely prevalent in the ranks of the clergy themselves. But it would probably be rash to infer this. The clergy of Wales had never generally accepted the Papal and unscriptural rule of celibacy as binding. Whether we ought to consider these women concubines, or, in point of fact, wives, is a doubtful matter. It would task a skilful casuist to determine the amount of moral culpability involved in these unions, which were licensed by the bishops, if not blessed by the Church, and which were recognised by the laity as binding and indissoluble, if not acknowledged by the law. Where the boundary-line between right and wrong was so doubtfully marked, it is not surprising that men interpreted it as suited their own inclinations, and even at times ventured far into forbidden ground. Such is ever the result of artificial rules of morality which are not grounded upon the law of God.

It is to be feared that the clergy of St. David's would not receive much aid or godly admonition from the majority of the bishops of this period, though few, if any, were so utterly bad as was John de la Bere. The see had a succession of 'small' bishops, and suffered, as Llandaff had previously suffered, from constant translations. John Catterick, or Keterich, Archdeacon of Surrey, appointed by Papal provision to succeed Chicheley in April, 1414, and consecrated at the end of June, was translated by the Pope to the See of Coventry and Lichfield in February of the next year.[1] Stephen Patrington, his successor, who is styled 'a very learned man,' can have done little to enlighten his diocese by his scholarship. In 1417 he was away at the Council of Constance, and before the end of the year the Pope promoted him to Chichester; but he seems to have died before he entered upon his new see.[2] The next bishop was Benedict Nicholls, formerly of Bangor, appointed by Papal provision in December, 1417, who seems to have paid some attention to his diocese, for he was the author of a code of statutes regulating the services of the cathedral. He was one of the judges who condemned Lord Cobham to death. He held the see till his death in 1433. Thomas Rodburne, his successor, is styled 'a great theologian and a distinguished mathematician.' He had been Chancellor of the University of Oxford and Provost of Merton, of which college he built the gate-tower. For his diocese, however, he did nothing, as he

---

[1] Richardson's Godwin, 'De Præsulibus,' pp. 322, 582.
[2] Godwin, pp. 509, 582. J. and F.. p. 307. Bevan (p. 143) says that he was translated to *Chester*, possibly a misprint.

lived in Wiltshire during his episcopate, and left his
duties to be discharged by David Cherbury, who, one
would think, had sufficient on his hands already, for,
besides being Bishop of Dromore, in Ireland, he held
also the archdeaconry of Brecon. Rodburne was succeeded, in 1442, by one of the most distinguished of the
bishops of this period, the canonist, William Lyndwood.
John Langton, the next bishop, provided by the Pope in
1447, died on the fifth day after his consecration. His
successor was the 'bishop of abominable fame,'[1] De la
Bere, who, 'notwithstanding he was made Bishop of St.
David's, never saw it, but committed the care of his
bishopric to one Griffin Nicolas, son[2] to Richard Fitz-
Thomas, a stout knight.'[3] Possibly De la Bere was unable to fulfil his duties, from physical weakness, for we
find that in 1458 he was excused from attending Parliament, as he was 'detained by divers infirmities of body
and by old age.' He had been previously heavily fined
for non-attendance.[4] There is some reason to suspect
that the See of St. David's was not only used as a
stepping-stone to richer and more dignified preferment,
but also as a post for old or decrepit clergy, whose failing
powers were unequal to the discharge of its duties.
John Langton was not the only bishop who died very
soon after consecration. As all these appointments were
made by Papal provision, they are to be reckoned among
the many wrongs inflicted by the See of Rome upon the
Church of Wales.

De la Bere was provided by Pope Nicholas, on
September 15, 1447. He had previously, in 1446, been
provided by Pope Eugenius to the deanery of Wells, but
was never installed. As he had been deposed from the
position of King's Almoner, it is possible that his failure

[1] So Gascoigne calls him.
[2] Really *father*, as J. and F. point out, p. 307.
[3] Browne Willis, 'St. David's,' p. 113, quoting Leland.
[4] Rymer, 'Fœdera' (first edition), xi. 386.

to secure the deanery of Wells was in some way due to his evil reputation. If this be so, the guilt of appointing such a man to a bishopric is all the greater. The one good deed recorded of him is his building of Dorchester bridge, in Oxfordshire, in which county he seems to have spent the years of his episcopate. He was finally deposed from his see, and imprisoned, the reason being, probably, that he had obtained Bulls from Rome, and so violated the statutes of præmunire and provisors. His pardon is dated February 5, 1460,[1] and he is therein styled 'John, *late* Bishop of St. David's, otherwise called John de la Beare, late Bishop of St. David's.'[2]

Robert Tully, appointed in 1460, was a man of much superior type to his predecessor. He is said to have been deprived of the temporalities of his see by Edward IV., probably for Lancastrian proclivities; but, nevertheless, he did good work for the cathedral, contributing from his own means to its completion. The stalls and the desks were erected by him, and the roof of the choir and the upper east window contain his arms and those of his successor, Richard Martyn, which, in conjunction with other evidence, points to the conclusion that they were put up from funds partially derived from legacies left by these bishops.

Richard Martyn's episcopate was one of the briefest. Provided by the Pope by a Bull dated April 26, 1482,[3] he died in a few months.

His successor, Thomas Langton, was an able and distinguished man, who afterwards, at Winchester, showed himself, according to Anthony Wood, a 'Mecænas of learning,'[4] but, unfortunately, he was not long enough in possession of St. David's to benefit that see. He was

---

[1] 1461, new style.
[2] Rymer, 'Fœdera' (first edition), xi. 469.
[3] Temporalities were restored to him July 1, 1482. Rymer, 'Fœdera' (first edition), xii. 159.
[4] 'Athenæ Oxonienses' (ed. 1691), p. 549.

appointed by the Pope in July, 1483, and was translated to Salisbury by the same authority in February, 1485.

The next two bishops, Hugh Pavy (1485-1496[1]) and John Morgan, alias Young (1496-1504[2]), though neither held the bishopric for a very long period, seem to have paid attention to their diocese. The former urged his clergy to admonish all persons to visit St. David's once a year, or at least to give something to the proctors who went round yearly with relics. Morgan was a native of Wales, and had been for some years before his appointment Archdeacon of Carmarthen, in addition to which office he held the deanery of Windsor and various other rich English benefices; for, with the accession of the Tudors, there was a movement of Welshmen into England, where they rapidly gained preferment. Morgan made provision for the support of the choristers of St. David's, and raised their number from four to six.

Robert Sherborne, appointed to succeed Morgan in 1505, was preferred to Chichester in 1508. He was succeeded by Edward Vaughan, another Welshman, who built the chapel in the cathedral which bears his name, and the roof of the Lady Chapel and its ante-chapel.[3] To him, also, Leland ascribes St. Justinian's Chapel, the chapel of Llawhaden Castle, with general repairs at the same place, and a great barn at Lamphey. The chapel at Lamphey also, from internal evidence, has been supposed to be his work. The historians of the cathedral assign to him 'the most prominent place among the prelates who occupied the See of St. David's during the closing days of the ante-Reformation era.'

[1] Temporalities restored to him September 19, 1485. Rymer, 'Foedera' (first edition), xii. 275.
[2] Temporalities restored November 23. Rymer, 'Foedera,' xii. 646.
[3] J. and F., pp. 164-168, 309. The roof of the nave also is thought by these writers to belong to his period. 'Perhaps the porch' (as it appears at present) 'and the upper stage of the tower may be attributed to him, though neither would confer immortality on his taste in architecture' (p. 309).

The appointments of Morgan and of Vaughan mark also a new era in the episcopate of St. David's, inasmuch as Morgan was the first bishop of Welsh blood appointed to that see since at least the time of Thomas Wallensis.

The next two bishops, Richard Rawlins (1523-1536) and William Barlow, were no particular credit to the see. The former had a reputation as a learned man, and had filled various important positions in England. He enjoyed the favour of Henry VIII., and accompanied him on his expedition into France, and afterwards succeeded Wolsey as King's almoner. But, in 1521, he was deprived by the Archbishop of Canterbury of his Wardenship of Merton College, Oxford, which he had held for thirteen years, as he was found guilty of 'many unworthy misdemeanours'; and 'soon after, because he should not be a looser, had the Bishoprick of St. David confer'd upon him';[1] surely the most extraordinary reason for preferment that was ever given, and one that shows how low the bishopric had fallen in public estimation since it was filled by Beck, Thoresby, and Chicheley.

The causes of the sudden rise and of the sudden decline of the fortunes of the see are alike undiscovered, but it is extremely probable that in some way the insurrection of Glyndwr was responsible for the decline. Never before had Wales been so prostrated, and it was natural that the premier see should share the low estate of the principality. It may be that its previous exaltation was due in some measure to the policy of the first Edward, who, though the conqueror of Wales, behaved wisely and justly towards his conquest, and spared the submissive, while he crushed the proud.

Of the See of Llandaff and its bishops during this period there is nothing of importance to chronicle. The bishopric seems to have been considered rich,[2] and although in the

[1] 'Athenæ Oxonienses,' p. 573.   [2] *Ibid.*, p. 560.

previous period five bishops had been translated from it, none was so translated in this period, for Holgate's advancement to York falls a few years later. But the bishops were generally undistinguished men, and did little that might serve to perpetuate their memory.

John de la Zouche (1407-1423) was succeeded by John Fulford, a man so insignificant that Godwin omits his name altogether. The next bishops were John Wells, a Friar Minor (1425-1440), Nicholas Assheby, Prior of Westminster (1441-1458), and John Hunden, a Minorite, Prior of King's Langley, who probably became involved in the political troubles of the day, for he was pardoned by Edward IV. in 1473.[1] He resigned the see in 1476, and John Smith (1476-1478) succeeded. The next bishop, John Marshall (1478-1496), is a man of some little note as a benefactor to his cathedral, in which his fine monument still stands. John Ingleby, Prior of Shene, succeeded, but held the see for a very short time, for in 1500 Miles Salley, who had been Almoner of Abingdon Abbey, and afterwards Abbot of Eynsham, was appointed. By his will he directed that his heart and bowels should be buried 'at the high altar of the church at Matherne before the image of St. Theodorick,' and his body on the north side of our Lady's chapel before the image of St. Andrew in St. Mark's Church, Bristol.[2] According to tradition he was a great benefactor to the episcopal palace at Matherne, and built the chapel, hall, dining-room, an adjoining tower, and the kitchen.[3] He left by his will twenty pounds to Matherne and his mitre to his cathedral, and directed that a solemn Mass and a dirige should be kept up for his soul at his Abbey of Eynsham, which he had continued to hold *in commendam* with his bishopric.

[1] Rymer, 'Fœdera,' xi. 734.
[2] 'Athenæ Oxonienses,' p. 560. Browne Willis, 'Landaff,' p. 61.
[3] So Godwin had heard from old men (p. 611).

The next appointment to the bishopric was a rather extraordinary one. Pope Leo thought so little of the claims of Welsh nationality that he chose as the fittest man to fill the see a certain Spanish Dominican, George de Attica, or Athegua, the chaplain of Katherine of Arragon. The Bull appointing him bore date February 11, 1517. He was succeeded in 1537 by Robert Holgate, a Yorkshireman, and Prior of Walton, in Yorkshire, which appointment he held *in commendam* with his bishopric. Holgate's services at the time of the dissolution of the monasteries gained him further, in 1544, the Archbishopric of York.

APPENDIX TO CHAPTER XIII.

TRANSLATION OF
AN ODE BY LEWIS MORGANWG,
TO LLEISION, ABBOT OF NEATH, CIRCA A.D. 1500.

(*From* '*Original Charters, etc., of Neath and its Abbey,*'
by G. G. Francis, F.S.A., Swansea, 1835.)

Everlasting courts of Lleision, Abbot of Neath : famed insulated retreats ! May a golden crown adorn his head —true son of Nonn.[1]

An Abbot, the chief of every Abbot : fruit of heavenly culture ; fragrant as Jerome ; of the sweetness of Augustine.

A goodly churchman of divine mission :[2] an apostle of the race of Iestyn ; a second Daniel of the blood of Einion ; the key of learning ; another blessed Lleuddad.[3]

---

[1] Nonn, the mother of St. David.
[2] Leision is a name of the divinity, and appears to be a contraction of Kyrie-eleeson. It is found in this meaning in the Awdl Fraith, and elsewhere.
[3] St. Lleuddad, an ancient British saint.

The temple of Neath, with its many new-built dwellings: God is glorified in this temple. He [Lleision] is another paternal Dunawd.[1] An Abbot of ready answers, a Bernard,[2] the arbitrator of religionists.

The shepherd of the faith, the support and staff of the pastoral office, and the rod of Aaron: like balm to this palace of Mary, as when the fulfilment of Simeon's blessing came to the Virgin's abode.[3]

We now present to the Virgin a petition, that the one God above, for the blood that flowed from his breast, intercede for a long life to Lleision; that there may be here sages of eminence, ardent men of learning, men of piety, humble and beneficent. May the protection of God be over this sanctuary of our language, holy and venerable amidst its verdant meadows.

Like the sky of the vale of Ebron[4] is the covering of this monastery: weighty is the lead that roofs this abode—the dark blue canopy of the dwellings of the godly.

Every colour is seen in the crystal windows, every fair and high-wrought form beams forth through them like the rays of the sun.—Portals of radiant guardians!

Pure and empyreal, here is every dignified language and every well-skilled preceptor. Here are seen the graceful robes of prelates, here may be found gold and jewels, the tribute of the wealthy.

Here also is the gold-adorned choir, the nave, the gilded tabernacle work, the pinnacles, worthy of the Three Fountains.[5] Distinctly may be seen on the glass, imperial arms; a ceiling resplendent with kingly bearings, and on

---

[1] St. Dunawd, an ancient British saint.
[2] St. Bernard.
[3] The abbey was dedicated to the Virgin Mary.
[4] The Vale of Ebron is celebrated as the scene of Adam's creation. 'Ar lawr Glyn Ebron.' etc.—Awdl Fraith.
[5] The three mystical fountains are described by Taliesin, 'Tair ffynnon y sydd,' etc., and also in Merlin's Prophecy.

the surrounding border the shields of princes; the arms of Neath of a hundred ages; there is the white freestone and the arms of the best men under the crown of Harry; and the church walls of gray marble.

The vast and lofty roof is like the sparkling heavens on high; above are seen archangels' forms; the floor beneath is for the people of earth, all the tribes of Babel, for them it is wrought of variegated stone. The bells, the benedictions, and the peaceful songs of praise, proclaim the frequent thanksgivings of the white monks.[1]

Here, on the banks of the river, is a court resembling the temple of Solomon, or the edifices of Rome; this monastery and court of Lleision is equal to those, and its priests[2] more exalted than the Patriarch of India.[3]

Never was there such a fabric of mortal erection, nor roofed walls, nor vast habitation: never was there such a foundation, nor splendid palace, nor oak of earthly growth; never was there, and never will there be, such workmanship in wood as this, which will not perish whilst the day and the wave continue.

Here are the flowing streams of the grape; the animation of the multitudes; the three colours of wine, and the ready service; the abode of evening conviviality, as in the dwellings of Kings, for the congregated hosts. A temple of masterly construction, through gracious co-operation from the heavenly mansions. A building of regular construction through skilful workmanship, a house of piety for the fathers.

Chief of schools; heaven-arrayed benefactor; noble founder of honours; the gentle occupier has been to St. Mary, the dedicator of gracious votaries. Golden ceilings are over their heads; goodly canopies, in these splendid

---

[1] The abbey being Cistercian, the monks were robed in white.
[2] The original word is *phreutur*, but whether it is the plural of *frater*, a friar, or *pretre*, a priest, is not quite clear.
[3] Prester John, of the Indies. Presbyter Johannes.

dwellings; also masses, together with writings in books; all dignified and complete.

Sacred is this dwelling by the cheerful sea.

Such are the benefits conferred by Lleision.

In this compact retreat will be found the warmth of hospitality and welcome banquets, and deer from the parks of yonder hill above,[1] and salmon from the ocean, and wheat and every kind of wine—these from the bounteous land and sea.

The university of Neath,[2] lo! it is the admiration of England; the lamp of France and Ireland; a school greatly resorted to by scholars, for every science, as if it were Sion itself. With organs for the men attired in white, and great applause of contending disputants; arithmetic, music, logic, rhetoric, civil and canon law.

As the Bernard of courts let Lleision decide; the palace of Asa[3] be to the Abbot Lleision, as that of St. Beuno,[4] chief of the venerable sages, be the speech of Lleision; long be the life of Abbot Lleision.

May he receive a gift to his satisfaction in this Caerbaddon[5] of Wales—be it from the hand of Jesus to the Abbot Lleision.

[1] *Fron* literally signifies a hillside, but is often a proper name of a hilly slope.

[2] It is said that the Abbot Lleision had obtained from Jaspar Tudor, Lord of Glamorgan, a charter for founding a university at Neath, but that the death of that nobleman took place before it was signed. The Reformation occurring soon after, the abbey lands were confiscated, and the whole design frustrated. See 'Cyfrinach y Beirdd.'

[3] St. Asav, an ancient British saint.

[4] St. Beuno, an ancient British saint.

[5] Badon Mount was the scene of one of Arthur's victories. As Caerbaddon is the British name of Bath, was that city at this time celebrated enough to be here intended?

N.B.—I quote the notes to the above, as found in Francis' 'Charters of Neath,' but I do not necessarily endorse them.—E. J. N.

CHAPTER XIV.

THE DISSOLUTION OF THE MONASTERIES.

THE accession of the House of Tudor raised Wales to some extent from the depression which had been caused by the insurrection of Glyndwr. Welshmen were no longer content to mumble the dry bones of an effete and false nationalism, or to abide in sullen resentment at oppression within the gloomy barrier of their mountains; the nobler spirits had risen to the broader conception of a true nationalism, which found nothing in the love of country inimical to the love of one's fellow-men, and which shared in the hopes and ambitions of the kingdom at large. They had given a King of their own 'red blood' to the land of the Saxons, and for a time they hoped that his successor would be an Arthur, in whom the old dim traditions about the return of their ancient hero, and the revival of the glories of their race, would have their fulfilment. Though Arthur died ere his time, and another Henry succeeded, who united to the Tudor shrewdness and tact a double portion of the licentiousness of his Plantagenet grandfather, yet neither in his reign nor in those of his children did Welshmen find themselves forgotten by their sovereigns. Henry VIII.'s Act of Union[1] showed that he was not unmindful of the land of his fathers, but bore towards his subjects therein

[1] 27 Henry VIII., c. xxvi.

'a singular zeal, love, and favour.'[1] The Welsh, for their part, flocked into England and asserted their right to take their place in the government and in the various institutions of the kingdom to which they belonged, and soon won by the natural force of the brilliant Celtic genius, no longer cribbed, cabined, and confined by native prejudice or alien oppression, distinguished places in the ranks of statesmen, scholars, lawyers, and divines. To trace in detail this Welsh renascence is beyond our present scope, and beyond the limits of our period. It had begun, however, before the dissolution of the monasteries, and the pages of the 'Athenæ Oxonienses,' to mention but one work in illustration, bear witness to the celebrity of many of the sons of Wales.

In general, however, the Welsh leaders, as well as the commonalty, were opposed to the great movement of the Reformation. Its pioneers in Wales were, for the most part, Englishmen, and frequently men not qualified by their moral equipment for such a work. During the reigns of Henry VIII. and Edward VI., the new movement made no progress among the Welsh people. One cause of this, perhaps, was the ruthless and wicked policy of Henry VIII. in carrying out the dissolution of the monasteries—a measure of spoliation, from the effects of which the Church of Wales has not yet recovered.

That all monks were saintly and devout men cannot be affirmed; that greed, worldliness, and even at times unchastity, were present within the pale of the cloister cannot be denied. Such sins are not peculiar to the monastic system, nor even to the pre-Reformation period. Gerald de Barri's description of the monastic orders

---

[1] 'His Highness, therefore, of a singular zeal, love and favour, that he beareth to his subjects of the said "Dominion" of Wales, minding to extirp all the sinister usages, and to bring his subjects to an amicable unity, hath enacted that his said Dominion of Wales shall be for ever hereafter incorporated and annexed to this his Realm of England.'

may be overcharged, but must have had a substantial basis of truth; the literature of the Middle Ages teems with jest and satire respecting monkish gluttony and monkish greed, and it would be rash to dismiss all this as mere unfounded slander. As regards Wales, we know enough of Strata Marcella and Talley to assure us that the monasteries were not always untainted by the licentiousness of the times. But popular gossip multiplied such evils and magnified them tenfold, and many stories were current that we cannot now test. The landowners envied abbots who lived in more luxury and with more pomp and show than themselves, who had the management of broader lands, and who (greatest crimes of all) were better landlords, and gave alms liberally to the poor. The parochial clergy, starving on their paltry pittances, credited the monks, who took the greater tithes of their parishes, with all manner of luxury, and while they prided themselves on their apostolic poverty, sighed for the pleasures of the cloister. Earnest men, who grieved over the superstitions by which the people were bound, blamed the monks as the main fosterers of such delusions, and contrasted what seemed to them the careless indolence of their lives with their own restless desire of action. Few men, indeed, were the friends of the monks save the peasantry, and the peasantry then were scarcely reckoned as a political force. If they felt strongly on a question, they might indeed rise in insurrection, but they were soon put down by force, and the machinery of the State went on as usual, unchecked by the temporary resistance.

The day of retribution for the monks' plunder of the parochial clergy, for their worldliness and greed, for all their sins and all their unfashionable virtues, had now come. The King, to whom virtue and chastity were but empty names, sent out visitors (one of them, Ap Rice, being a Welshman) to investigate into the lives and morals of the monks, and was shocked by the record of abominations which they laid before him. It is not worth while to discuss the credibility of this report; the commissioners were sent to discover wickedness, and it would have gone hard with them if they had blessed and not cursed; they were men worthy of their mission, and of the master they served; they brought back what they knew would please him, and they had their reward.[1] One in particular, Dr. London, was, as Fuller says truly, 'no saint,' and was afterwards convicted of perjury.

In 1536 the measure for the suppression of the smaller monasteries, 'not above the clear yearly value of two hundred pounds,' was carried through Parliament, the King stimulating the Commons by the remark: 'I will have it passed, or I will have some of your heads.' The preamble states that 'manifest sin, vicious, and abominable living is daily used and committed commonly in such littel and small abbayes and priories of monks, chanons, and nonns, where the congregation of such religious persons is under the number of twelve persons, whereby the governours of such religious houses, and their convents, spoil, destroy, consume, and utterly waste as well these churches, monasteries, priories, principal houses, ferms, granges, lands, tenements, hereditaments, as the ornament of their churches, as their goods and cattalls, to the high displeasure of Almighty God, slander of good religion, and the great infamy of the King's highness, and the realm, if redress should not be had thereof.' But while the smaller houses are thus censured, and ordered to be utterly suppressed for their 'unthriftey, carnal, and abominable living,' the preamble expressly states that in the 'great solemn monasteries' of this realm 'religion is well kept and observed.' As Gerald

[1] Richard, Bishop of Dover, visited the Welsh monasteries. He sent Cromwell the holiest relic in North Wales, which with another image was worth to the friars in Bangor 'xx markes by yere.' 'Letters,' p. 212.

de Barri testified in the thirteenth century, it was in the smaller houses, and especially in the cells, that disorders were most rife, and that discipline was of necessity less strictly enforced, and from these chiefly arose those scandals which brought discredit upon the monastic communities. It was ordered, therefore, by this act, which in profession was a measure of temperate reform, brought forward for the improvement of the monastic life, that the monks of the smaller houses should be 'commytted to great and honourable monasteries of religion in this realm, where they may be compelled to live religiously, for reformation of their lyves.' However, even among the smaller monasteries there were some found of sufficient virtue, or sufficient wealth, to escape suppression for a while. No less than fifty-two monasteries were immediately refounded in perpetuity under a new charter. Among these we find the three Welsh monasteries, Alba Landa, Nethe, and Strathfloure, or Whitland, Neath, and Strata Florida. The first received its grant on April 25, 1537, and paid for it no less a sum than £400, the highest amount given, only equalled by Pollesloe in Devon, and equivalent to nearly three times its annual revenue. Neath and Strata Florida received their grants on the same day, January 30, 1537, the former paying £150, and the latter £66 13s. 4d.[1] But when the King and his favourites had once begun to taste the sweets of plunder, they were hard to satisfy, and so 'the great solemn monasteries' were likewise discovered to be guilty of divers abominations, and both they and the fifty-two smaller monasteries that had been refounded 'in perpetuity' were swept away in a common destruction by the Act of 1539. Honest Latimer, earnest reformer as he was, begged that some houses might be allowed to stand, two or

[1] Gasquet, 'Henry VIII. and the English Monasteries,' ii.; App., pp. 529, 530.

three in every shire, 'not in monkery, but so as to be converted to preaching, study, and prayer'; but the King and his creatures were too eager for the prey, and, as usually happens in measures of disendowment, the revenues were wasted, and the 'porealty' were robbed. 'A great part of this treasure,' says one earnest reformer, 'was turned to the upholding of dice-playing, masking, and banqueting; yea (I would I could not by just occasion speak), bribing, whoring, and swearing.'

By far the greater part of the monastic property was alienated from religious uses, and fell into the hands of laymen. At times the monastic church was spared, and thenceforth was used wholly for parochial purposes, as happened in Wales, at Brecon, Usk, Abergavenny, Kidwelly, Ewenny, and Penmon. But some of the fairest churches and buildings in Wales were destroyed or suffered to fall into ruin and decay, and some became eventually profaned in a manner repulsive to all devout persons. At Abergavenny, the people interposed to save the three bells of the priory from falling into private hands, saying that the money for these bells had been collected by their ancestors, and that they had always been regarded as parochial property.[1]

The Welsh monasteries were not generally rich foundations. Tintern, Valle Crucis, Margam, Slebach, Maenan, Basingwerk, Carmarthen, Talley, Whitland, and Neath, were the only houses that exceeded one hundred and fifty pounds in annual value. But though comparatively poor, they were numerous, and the Church and principality of Wales suffered grievously in after years from the manner of their suppression. Had the parochial tithes, which had been appropriated to the monasteries, been restored to the parishes from which they were derived, the parochial clergy might ever afterwards have held the name of Henry VIII. in grateful and honoured remembrance,

[1] Gasquet, ii. 430.

and posterity might generally have excused and palliated the hardships inflicted by a measure, the main results of which had been so eminently beneficial. But as these tithes fell into private hands, the parochial clergy were benefited no whit, and various circumstances combined to make their position even worse than it was before. The lay impropriators, into whose hands the tithes came, merely continued to the curates of the parishes thus robbed the exact sum that used to be paid by the monasteries without any regard to the decreasing value of money, and no appeals or remonstrances were of any avail in stimulating them to do their duty.

Again, where the income of prebendal churches was leased out, if there was no vicarage, the curate was paid by the lessee, who gave the smallest pittance possible. The results of this lay oppression were consequently more serious even than those of monastic oppression, and the poor parochial clergy found that new impropriator was but old abbot writ large.

The whole matter constitutes a valuable object-lesson in disendowment, which it would be well for the present age to note and lay to heart. The subsequent depression of the Welsh Church, from which it is only now recovering, was more largely due to this cause than to the Anglicizing policy of prime ministers, or to the sloth and neglect of the parochial clergy, to which it has been fashionable to ascribe it. Those who, in positions of ease and comfort, carelessly deal wholesale censure to the struggling Welsh clergy of the eighteenth century, or invite their present successors, in an inhospitable age and a northern clime, to seek in Apostolic poverty a stimulus to Apostolic zeal, cannot do better than ponder the moral of the disendowment of the monasteries. The bounty of Queen Anne, and the labours of the Ecclesiastical Commissioners have, in great measure, repaired the injuries inflicted, and have caused their memory to pass out of the minds of men. But in the eighteenth century, when they were plain for all men to see, they were thus described in the preface to his 'Thesaurus Rerum Ecclesiasticarum,' by John Ecton, who had been receiver-general of the tenths of the clergy, and who had studied the subject and knew it in all its bearings :—

'What abundantly adds to the hardship of the case of many incumbents of impropriate cures, is that the discretionary power, which before the Reformation was lodged in the bishops, of augmenting (as they should see occasion) the incomes of vicars and curates; this power, I say, which in the Popish times though in many cases put in execution with very good effect, yet (by some means or other) after the Reformation became of little effect. The lay impropriators of many large cures became empowered to receive and enjoy £300 or £400 per annum in tithes and other spiritual revenues, which were torn from the clergy without any manner of default or forfeiture committed, or possible to be committed, by them, or on their part; and their new proprietors have ever since contented themselves to this very day with paying only the poor pecuniary stipend or pittance that was antiently allowed to the vicar or curate before the Reformation. This makes the case of such poor vicars and curates worse (now) than it was even in the times of Popery, when money was of such a value, as that £10 or £12 were reckoned a competency equal to £90 or £100 now; and the power of augmenting the income of such vicarage or curacy out of the spiritual revenues of one place having been disused, that stipend is now all that the poor incumbent can legally claim.

'Besides, in many cases the officiating clergy hold their benefices upon such a precarious tenure, that the incumbent is obliged to be satisfied with any small arbitrary allowance that shall be made him by his impropriator, otherwise he will displace his poor minister, and put another, who will come into a more servile compliance, in his room. In such a case it is not hard to guess what a poor, necessitous curate must do, who has no other choice but to comply or starve. This grievance arises chiefly from such places as are exempt from all jurisdiction of the ordinary, and subject only to the visitation of the impropriator or donor himself. Of this sort are many livings formerly held, and now claimed, under a title derived from the Priory of St. John of Jerusalem; and many others there are that claim exemption of the like kind, which in some parts of the kingdom are so numerous, that it is needless to give examples of them.

'Can it otherwise be expected than that (as the case now stands) there should be diverse mean and stipendiary preachers in many places entertained to serve the cures and officiate there, who, depending for their necessary maintenance upon the goodwill and liking of their hearers, should be under the temptation of suiting their doctrines and teaching to the humours, rather than the good of their hearers?... Can we suppose doctrines and instruction, though ever so faithfully delivered or zealously urged, to have their due influence in such a case?

'But when a man is to appear as a teacher and instructor of multitudes, if, besides other qualifications, he makes a suitable figure and appearance; if in his habit and mien he appears grave and decent, without the marks of meanness and poverty; if he lives among his neighbours with credit, free from the pressure of debts and other manifold misfortunes—the constant attendants upon want and narrowness of circumstances—his admonitions will certainly have the greater weight, his doctrines make the deeper impressions, and all his labours may, in a great measure, have their desired effect. On the contrary, what fruit is to be expected from the labours of a pastor, who (we will suppose) is willing to do all the good he can, is contented to drudge on with his little allowance, in hopes of seeing some good effect from his labours among his parishioners, but, notwithstanding his best endeavours, falls into contempt of the meanest of them, which his poverty alone, without any personal demerit of his own to add to it, is sufficient to bring upon him? In such a case it is no wonder that all his endeavours to do good in his profession are rendered vain and ineffectual.

'Instances of this kind are (God knows) too many in this kingdom, no country being free from some examples of them, and in some countries, as *Wales*, Yorkshire, and many others, they are very numerous.'[1]

Particular instances may be adduced in plenty to prove these general statements. The evil, as will be seen from the words of Ecton, began at the epoch of the dissolution of the monasteries, and increased as years went on, and the value of money became more and more depreciated, until at the beginning of the eighteenth century the Church in Wales was in large measure a disendowed Church, and was suffering from all the proverbial evils of the voluntary system. In order for the clergy to have a decent subsistence, it became absolutely necessary for one priest to have charge of several parishes, as their combined incomes only made up a decent stipend, and many of the poorer sort were scarcely able to keep body and soul together upon the scanty pittances that they received. Even of the money which was devoted to church purposes, Wales received very little; the bishopric of Gloucester received the tithes formerly appropriated to St. Peter's Abbey, Gloucester, and the bishopric of Chester those appropriated to St. Mary's Nunnery, Chester. Thus the tithes of the important parish of St.

---

[1] Preface to Ecton's 'Thesaurus,' iv., v., third edition, with additions by Browne Willis, 1763.

Woolos, Newport, Monmouthshire, of Glasbury, Radnorshire,[1] with part of those of Defynock and its chapel of Ystradfellte, in Breconshire, and Ewias Harold in Herefordshire, were appropriated to the bishopric of Gloucester. The living of St. Woolos in Ecton's time was among those discharged from paying firstfruits and tenths on account of the smallness of their income, and is stated by him to have been of the clear yearly value of £20.[2]

In the diocese of St. David's the whole amount of the tithes held by the monasteries is represented in the present day by about £35,000 tithe-rent charge. None of this was restored to the diocese on the dissolution, though part was granted to the Church in English dioceses. 'Some of the tithes appropriated to St. John's Priory, Carmarthen, fell into the possession of the See of Lincoln and the Royal Chapel of Windsor, and the latter also acquired the tithes of Talgarth from Brecon Priory. Altogether, about £3,300 of tithe-rent charge, as commuted, was by these grants secured to the Church, and has in part reverted to the diocese under the arrangements of the Ecclesiastical Commissioners. The vicarages (about sixty), whence the £35,000 is drawn, have retained only £9,000 a year of tithe-rent charge, an average of £150 each.'[3]

One special loss to this diocese occurred through the appropriation of Llanbadarn Fawr to the monastery of Vale Royal in Cheshire, which had taken place in 1360. 'The parish was of very large area (about 125,000 acres) and contained at that time, in addition to the mother-church, three chapelries, described under the names Castel Walter (now Llanvihangel Geneu'r Glyn), Llanilar, and Gelyndrod (now Llanvihangel y Creuddin). It is now broken up into seventeen ecclesiastical dis-

---

[1] The church has been since rebuilt across the river in Brecknockshire.
[2] 'Thesaurus,' p. 514.
[3] Bevan, 'St. David's,' pp. 163, 164.

tricts, with twenty churches; but the whole of the tithe, to the present value of about £5,000 a year, has been alienated, and only some trifling pensions are paid out of it to the incumbents of the mother-church, and a few of the dependent churches."[1] Inasmuch as the Welsh Church had first been plundered largely for the benefit of English institutions, and afterwards was in great measure further disendowed by the dissolution of the monasteries, it is not wonderful that many even of the benefices in important towns had mere starvation salaries; that small county chapelries frequently had stipends of less than ten pounds attached to them; and that not a few churches were deserted, and fell altogether into ruins.

In the diocese of St. David's, which we have been just considering, we find the following given by Ecton as the clear yearly values of the churches and chapels which had formerly belonged to the Priory of Haverfordwest: Camrose Vicarage, £40; Llanstadwell, £30; St. Mary's, Haverfordwest, £19 10s.; Ros-Market, £15; Dale Curacy, £6; East-Haroldston Curacy, £5; Lambston Curacy, £5; St. Martin's in Haverfordwest Curacy, £6. The following are the values of churches and chapels in the same diocese, which formerly belonged to the Priory of Llanthony: Cwmyoy Curacy, £11; Llanthony Curacy, £5; Old Castle Curacy, £3; Llanwenno Chapel, £6 10s.; Longtown Chapel, £16; Dulas Curacy, £4; Llancilloe Curacy, £3; St. Margaret's Curacy, £6; Michael Church Eskley Curacy, £7; Rowlston Curacy, £4; Walterstone Curacy, £3.

The Church in the Vale of Glamorgan still suffers from the benefactions which Fitzhamon bestowed on his foundation of Tewkesbury. Though much has been done of recent years to improve matters, the enormous increase of population which has taken place in some parts

---

[1] Bevan, 'St. David's,' p. 103.

makes the contrast between the meanness of the endowments and the stupendous amount of work to be accomplished remarkable. The population of St. Margaret's Roath, from which St. German's is now severed, according to the latest return, is 23,096. It is at the present time served by eight clergy. Its patron is the Marquis of Bute, and the particulars of its revenue are as follows, according to Crockford's 'Clerical Directory': Tithe-Rent Charge—Impropriated, £212 ; Vicarial, £100 ; average £76 with glebe, value £25 ; fees, £35 ; Queen Anne's Bounty, £80 ; gross income, £216; net, £193. In Ecton's 'Thesaurus' it is classed among the smallest livings, those not in charge, and its value was so small that it is not specified. This was one of the churches belonging to the Abbey of Tewkesbury, the revenues of which, at the dissolution, were not restored to the Church in Wales, but were appropriated to the Dean and Chapter of Gloucester. Llantrisant, Penmark, St. John's and St. Mary's, Cardiff, Llysfaen, Llanishen, Llanblethian, with its Chapel of Cowbridge, Llantwit Major, and Lisworney, were churches and chapels so appropriated. The clear yearly value of St. John's, Cardiff, in Ecton's 'List,' was £30, and of St. Mary's, Cardiff, £28. It is not surprising to find that the latter church, which had become ruined, was not rebuilt. Ystradyfodwg, which has now a population of 35,523, is still subordinate to Llantrisant, and is entered by Ecton as a chapel of the certified value of £10. If the tithes, of which the Welsh Church was robbed, first by Fitzhamon, and afterwards by Henry VIII., had remained in its possession, or had been restored, it might in these latter days have been better able to do its duty to the vast population which has recently settled in these despoiled districts. Other churches of the diocese of Llandaff had been appropriated to the monasteries of Margam, Ewenny, Neath, Abergavenny, Monmouth,

Llanthony, Tintern, Chepstow, Goldcliff, Usk, and St. Kinemark; one to the Knights Templars; one to the Order of St. John of Jerusalem; and five, Penarth, Marshfield, St. Melons, Rumney, Peterston-Wentlog, to the Abbey of St. Augustine's, Bristol. Most of the last-named passed at the dissolution to the Dean and Chapter of Bristol. The result of all these appropriations was that the clergy in this diocese were, as a rule, miserably paid, and that even in the present day the endowments are utterly inadequate.

There was some show made at the dissolution of a desire for justice in the distribution of the revenues, even of those derived from Wales, but little indeed was really done. The new bishoprics founded had nothing to do with Wales, except that Wales had to contribute towards two of them, the bishoprics of Chester and Gloucester. At first the income of Brecon Priory was granted to the bishopric of St. David's. A year afterwards, however, it was diverted to John ap Rice. The College of Abergwili was removed to Brecon in 1542, and the buildings of the Black Friars were given to it. It was called Christ's College, and provision was made for a school under a master, an usher, and a lecturer in theology. The Friary at Bangor also was changed into a free school.

Such was the scanty atonement made to Wales for the policy of robbery, which was inaugurated by Henry VIII., and was not wholly abandoned by his children. The hardship inflicted upon the monks by their dispersion was but a small matter compared to that under which a large part of the parochial clergy laboured for many generations. But the robbery of Christ's Church involved also then, as always, the robbery of Christ's poor, who suffered not merely from the lack of the monastic alms, but also from the spiritual destitution caused by the inadequate number of clergy. For the scanty funds would not support a large body of clergy, and of those who were content to starve on paltry salaries, many unfortunately sprang from the class of 'mechanics,' who were ignorant, and not qualified to discharge their sacred office. The poor could not support their pastors themselves, and in many districts had few opportunities of receiving the ministry of the Word and the Sacraments. This evil of the policy of disendowment continued until recently, nay, is not yet wholly ended. 'Within my own recollection,' says a recent writer, 'the vicar of a parish in South Wales, in which for a time my family was residing, held three "livings" at the same time. They were twenty miles apart, and the only means of going from one to another was on horseback across mountain roads—if the weather or the floods would permit of this —and the total value of the three was £80 a year.'[1]

* * * * *

We have now traced the history of the Church of Wales from its first small and obscure beginnings in the second century to the great act of wrong done to it in the sixteenth. The story has been one of much sore tribulation, yet lighted up by gleams of supernatural glory. The Roman tried to destroy the Church, and the heroes of Caerleon signalized their faithfulness to the cause of the Crucified, and won the starry crown of martyrdom. The pagan English assaulted it next, and from the very valley of destruction rose up the exceeding great army of its saints, whose holy lives and labours not only consecrated the whole of Wales, but also restored the declining Christianity of Ireland, and lit the flame that was carried by Columba to Iona, and by Columba's successors from Iona to Northumbria. Enriched by the piety of its sons with the endowments necessary, under

---

[1] 'Picture of Wales during the Tudor Period,' by J. Birkbeck Nevins (1893), p. 31, *note*.

mundane conditions, to carry on its sacred mission, it was plundered by Norman invaders, who strove to denationalize it, and who planted on the borders and in the heart of the Principality an alien population. But the Celtic genius conquered by its spell the hearts of the conquerors, and the Norman strongholds became the educational centres of Celtic freedom. English oppression, native strife, and Papal tyranny could not crush the Church, nor quench its fire of devotion and love to its Lord, which burnt bright even amid the mists of mediæval superstition. The great measure of disendowment, carried out in the sixteenth century by a King of the Welsh House of Tudor, crippled it just at the moment when it bade fair to rise to new heights of glory and usefulness, and for three centuries hindered it in its beneficent career. How this prostration was intensified by the Puritan oppression of the seventeenth century may, perhaps, be told in a future volume. Yet even the days of greatest gloom for Wales have not been without their gleams of splendour, as in its own mountain districts, though the day may be dark and stormy, it happens now and then that the sun shines in its majesty through the clouds, and mountain, lake and valley are filled with the glory of its beams.

The Church of Wales has of late years been recovering from Henry VIII.'s scheme of disendowment. The policy of the Ecclesiastical Commissioners, and the benefactions of its sons and daughters, have done much to furnish it with the means necessary to send forth clergy to do its work; for in this northern clime and inhospitable age it is useless to weave fanciful dreams of carrying on work without funds. Clergymen are not exempted by their sacred office from the ordinary necessities of humanity, and even a celibate ministry would need food and clothing, and some amount of shelter for their heads.

It has been proposed to repeat the act of the infamous Henry VIII.; and those who profess to dread the interference of the State in religion, with strange inconsistency call upon the State to despoil the Church of the scanty remainder of those pious gifts which were offered by men of old time to God and His saints. If the policy of Norman plunderers and of Tudor tyrant be repeated in the nineteenth century, the Church of Wales, according to all human probability, will again be crippled for centuries. But even though man may injure, he cannot destroy the Church of God. Still, as ever, the Welsh Churchman will remember the promise of his Lord: 'In the world ye shall have tribulation; but be of good cheer: I have overcome the world.'

APPENDICES TO CHAPTER XIV.

A.

ANNUAL VALUE OF THE WELSH MONASTERIES AT THE DISSOLUTION.

(*From Tanner's 'Notitia Monastica,' 1744; Wales, pp. 699-721; Monmouthshire, pp. 327-332.*)

	£	s.	d.	
1. Holyhead, College of Prebendaries	24	0	0	
2. Glannach, Priestholme, St. Cyriol, Praestol, or Penmon ...	47	15	3	gross.
	40	17	9	net.
3. Brecknock... ...	112	14	2	(D.)[1]
	134	11	4	(S.)[2]
4. Black Friars, Brecknock. Converted into College of Christ Church, and College of Abergwili joined with it.				

[1] (D.) Dugdale. [2] (S.) Speed.

		£	s.	d.	
5.	Kidwelly	38	0	0	gross.
		29	10	0	net.
6.	Whitland, or Alba Landa	135	3	6	(D.)
		153	17	2	(S.)
7.	Talley	136	9	7	(D.)
		153	1	4	(S.)

Had 8 canons at dissolution.

		£	s.	d.	
8.	Carmarthen	174	8	8	gross.
		164	0	4	net.

Had 6 Black canons.

		£	s.	d.	
9.	Abergwili College	42	0	0	

(Annexed to Brecon College.)

		£	s.	d.	
10.	Bardsey	46	1	4	(D.)
		56	6	2	(S.)
11.	Beddgelert	70	3	8	(D.)
		69	3	8	(S.)
12.	Bangor Friary. Made a free school.				
13.	Strata Florida	118	7	3	(D.)
		122	6	8	(S.)
14.	Cardigan	32	0	0	gross.
		13	4	9	net.
15.	Llanllyr	57	5	4	
16.	Llanddewi Brevi	40	0	0	gross.
		38	11	0	net.
17.	Valle Crucis	188	8	0	(D.)
		214	3	5	(S.)
18.	Maenan	162	15	0	(D.)
		179	10	10	(S.)
19.	Ruthin College. (No valuation given.)				
20.	Basingwerk	150	7	3	(D.)
		157	15	2	(S.)
21.	Ewenny	78	0	8	gross.
		59	4	0	net.

		£	s.	d.
22.	Margam	181	7	4 (D.)
		188	14	0 (S.)
23.	Neath	132	7	7 (D.)
		150	4	9 (S.)
	(8 monks at dissolution.)			
24.	Swansea hospital	20	0	0
25.	Cymmer	51	13	4 (D.)
		58	15	4 (S.)
26.	Strata Marcella	64	14	2 (D.)
		73	7	3 (S.)
27.	Llanllugan	22	14	8 (D.)
		22	13	8 (S.)
28.	St. Dogmael	96	0	2 gross.
		87	8	6 net.
29.	Monkton	113	2	6 (S.)
		57	9	3 (D.)
30.	Haverford	133	11	1 (D.)
		135	6	1 (S.)
31.	Pill	67	15	3 gross.
		52	2	5 net.
32.	Caldey	5	10	11
33.	Slebach	211	9	11 gross.
		184	10	11 net.
34.	St. Mary's College, St. David's	111	16	4 gross
		106	3	6 net.
35.	Pembroke Hospital	1	6	8
36.	Tenby Hospital, or Lazar-house	2	0	0
37.	„ Free Chapel of St. John the Baptist	6	0	0
38.	Cwmhir	28	17	4 gross.
		24	19	4 net.
	(3 monks at dissolution.)			
39.	Abergavenny	129	5	8 (D.)
		59	4	0 (S.)
	(Prior and 4 monks at dissolution.)			

	£	s.	d.
40. Llanthony	87	9	5 (MS. of Corpus Christi College, Cambridge.)
	99	19	0 (D.)
	71	3	2 (S.)
41. Goldcliff (previously granted to Eton College) ...	144	18	1
42. Monmouth	56	1	11
43. Tintern ...	192	1	4 (D.)
	256	11	6 (S.)
(13 religious at dissolution.)			
44. Malpas ...	14	9	11 net.
	15	6	8 gross.
45. Striguil	32	0	0 (D.)
	32	4	0 (S.)
(3 monks at dissolution.)			
46. Grace Dieu, or Stow	19	4	4 net.
	26	1	4 gross.
(2 monks at dissolution.)			
47. Usk Nunnery	55	4	5 (D.)
	69	9	8 (S.)
48. Llantarnam	71	3	2
49. St. Kinemark Priory	8	4	8

The alien priories had been previously suppressed. The friars had no endowments, but their churches were appropriated frequently as parochial churches. There were various hospitals besides, the value of which is not mentioned.

B.

The tone and temper of the party of plunder and of private gain towards Wales, the Welsh people, and ancient Welsh traditions may be accurately gauged by a perusal of the following letter written by Bishop Barlow to Cromwell, just as the visitors of the monasteries were entering Wales. The writer himself, though undoubtedly sincere in his 'Puritanism,' was not of the stuff of which martyrs are made, and not long before, in 1533, had humbled himself to the dust in a letter to the King, wherein he professed that he had been in 'darcknes' and 'deadly ignoraunce,' through the 'fendes instygacyon and fals perswasyones' in his treatises, erring 'agaynst the blyssed sacrament of the altare, dysalowyne the masse and denyenge purgatorye, with slawnderous infamye of the pope and my lorde cardynall, and owtragious raylyng agaynst the clergye, which I have forsaken and utterly renownced.' To such pitiful poltroons did Henry VIII. commit the policy of oppression and disendowment of the national Church of Wales, a policy which the following letter shows was then, as now, utterly anti-national.

From 'Three Chapters of Letters relating to the Suppression of Monasteries,' edited from the originals in the British Museum by Thomas Wright, Esq., M.A., F.S.A., etc. London: Printed for the Camden Society, by John Bowyer Nichols and Son, Parliament Street, 1843. Pp. 206-210.

CI.

BISHOP BARLOW TO CROMWELL.

(*From MS. Cotton. Cleop., E. IV., fol.* 260.)

After my right humble commendacions, I considere my dutie tadvertise your lordship, that according to the purporte of your lettres latly receaved, signifienge the

kynges highnes pleasour for the removynge of ydolotrous
abused ymages, wherewith this contrey horribly dyd
abounde, in satisfyenge of the same I have diligently done
myne endevour, and that quyetly every where withyn my
diocesse unresisted, without tumulte, commotion, or disturbance, with no frustrate expectacion (as I trust) of
forther effectuall redresse, yn all causes of Christen re-
ligyon and godly purposes of the kynges most honorable
and no lesse profitable proceadinges. The people now
sensibly seinge the longe obscured veryte manyfestly to
displaye her brightnesse, wherby their inveterate accustomed supersticion apparantly detected, all popish delusions shall sone be defaced, so that erudityon, the parente
of vertue and unfallible foundacion of all ordinate pollecye,
which by the kynges most renowmed fortherance beawty-
fully florisheth yn all other his royall domynions, might
also be planted here in his graces principalyte of Wales,
where knowlege utterly unknowen, scyence ys litle regarded, barberouse ignorance pyteously pleatinge in
possession, notwithstandinge wolde easely be redressed,
without hyndraunce of the kynges advauntage, yee with
notable augmentacion of his most worthy honour, small
expences therto requysite of any partie, with moch
commodytie of many, to the incommodotie of none that
preferre an unyversall weale before a private sensuall
pleasure. In case my peticion thorow your good lordships medyacion maye be attayned of the kynges highnes,
for the translacion of the see to Kermerddyn, and trans-
posinge of Abergwilly college to Brecknok, the princypall
townes of Sowthwales, where provision had for lernynge
as well yn gramer as yn other scyences and knowlege of
Scripture, the Welsch rudenesse wolde sone be framed
to English cyvilitie, and their corrupte capacyties easely
reformed with godly intelligens, which moveth me to be
so instante a suter and a contynuall peticyoner, especy-
ally for the translacion of the see, beinge sytuated in soch

a desolate angle and in so rare a frequented place (excepte of vacabounde pilgremes), that evill disposed persons, unwillinge to do good, maye lurke there at lybertye in secrete withowt restraynte, and they that wolde fayne do well can have no convenyente oportunyte profitablie to utter their well doinge to the commodytie of the comon weale. Which, yf there were no nother causes, as ther be ynfinyte more reasonable then maye be justly disalowed, and so evydente that they can not be shadowed, yet yt mighte seme sufficient necessarylie to persuade a translacion of the see. But forthermoare, yt hath be allwayes estemed a delycate doughter of Rome, naturally resemblinge her mother in shamelesse confucion, and lyke qualified with other perverse properties of execrable malignitie, as ungodly ymage service, abhomynable ydolatrye, and lycentiouse lybertie of dishonest lyvinge, popish pilgremages, disceatefull pardons, and fayned indulgences, in whose lawde yt ys written,

> Roma semel quantum dat bis Menevia tantum.

And as the bisshop of Rome crepte up by policye, and rayninge by tyranny was more then man, little lesse then God, whose authorytie never knowen was contynually obeyed, no reason admitted to aske why, but as he wold so did yt avayle, even thus hath our Welsh David byn avaunced to be patrone of Wales, as he that had signiory not only in erth, by lawles pryveleged exempcions, but power also in heven to geve it whom he wold, to discharge hell, to emptie purgatory, to pardon synne, to release payne, yee to save his beneficiall frendes, to curse and kyll his unfavourable adversaries, whose legende ys so uncerten of trueth, and certenly full of lyes, that not only his sayntly holynesse ys to be suspected, but rather to be dowted whether any soch person was ever bisshop there, as ys surmysed, experyence in semblable cases latly tryed owte by Dervelgadern, Conoch, and soch other Welsch godes, antique gargels of ydolatry. And verely, yf credence ought to be geven to the most auntyente writinges that can be exhibited, whereof I have certain pamflettes testifyeng antiquitie, both in barbarouse letters and incongrue Latyne, agreable to the maners of that season, also mencyonynge soch enormyous faschion, that scarsly Rome myght be comparable with saynte Davids terrytorye concernynge presumptuous usurpacyon apon their princes, crafty yncrochinge of possessions, subtyle defeatinge of enherytances, extorcion, brybery, symonye, heresie, ydolatrye, supersticion, etc. Wherfore, consideringe that where Rome with all her popish pageantes (praysed be God!) thorow the kynges most prudente provysyon ys exiled forth of England, the unfayned fydelitie of myne allegeaunce enforseth me to wysh all memoryall monymentes of her popetry yn lyke maner to be banyshed owt of Wales, which hytherto remaynynge yn the terrytory of S. David, unneth maye be extincte without translacion of the see. For excepte the manyfolde occasions of ydolatrous infidelytie and papisticall practyses (notwithstandynge compulsory inhibycions and tongue professions) be clerely abolyshed, shall allwayes renovate new fangled ymaginacions to contrefayte the olde exercysed wickednes. Wherein reducynge to remembraunce the prysed memoryes and perpetuall renowned factes of the famouse princes of Israel, which did not only abarre ydolatrye and other ungodlynesse, but utterly abolished all occasyons of the same, lykewise notifyenge their terreble reproches and aggravated punyshmentes that were neglygent, I dowte not but that my supplyante sute shall seme reasonable. And though peraventure some will objecte the contrarye, the causes not prepensed, which partly I have uttered yn these and other my former letters, omittinge the resydew, lest I shud molest your lordship; yet havinge the kynges most benynge and gracyous favour with your assistente supportacion, I trust so to justifie the equytie of my peticion that no adversarye shalbe able to emblemish yt. And yf urgente ymportunytie of hasty sute shall neade excuse in this behalfe, I have sufficiently to allege the importable charge and costly expences of a sumptuous buyldynge (a comorthe latlye graunted for the same), which bestowed yn Kermerddyn or some other frequented place, myght be pleasante, profitable, and commodyous for the kynges subjectes, whereas other wyse yt shalbe wasted yn vayne and unprofitably perysh in a barbarous desolate corner, as knoweth our Lorde, who have you in his tuicion. From Lantfey, the xvj[th] daye of August.[1]

Your lordeshyppes to commaund,

W. MENEVEN.

[1] A.D. 1538.

INDEX.

Aaron, 17, 18, 21
Aberconway, 219, 276, 303, 305, 311, 313, 314, 323, 325, 344, 345, 376, 408, 420
Abergavenny Priory, 290, 291, 315, 408, 415, 421
Abergwili College, 331, 416, 419, 420, 424
Act of Union, 403
Adam, Bishop, 191, 197, 204-207
Adelfius, 18, 39
Afan, 58
Alan, 236
Aldhelm, 55, 126-131, 134, 135
Alexander de Monmouth, 351
Alfred the Great, 155-159
Alleluia Victory, 34-36, 38
Anatolius, 15
Anian, Friar, 333
Anian I. (of St. Asaph), 322
Anian II., 323-327, 340
Anian I. (of Bangor), 322, 353-355
Anian Seys, 356
Anselm, 165, 166, 168
Anselm le Gras, 314, 346
Ap Rice, 405
Archbishops of Welsh sees, 225, 226
Ariminum, Council of, 19
Aristobulus, 4, 5
Arles, Council of, 18, 98, 111, 139
Arminius, 18, 20, 21
Arthur, King, 15
Asaph, 21, 57, 79

Asaph, St., bishopric founded, 57; cathedral burned, 358, 362, 368; rebuilt, 373; its bishops, etc., 79-81, 153, 154, 190, 191, 194, 196, 197, 204-208, 219, 313, 314, 318, 319, 322-327, 331, 333, 340, 344, 353, 355, 356, 359-361, 367-373, 376-380
Asser, 155-159, 161, 162, 226
Assheby, Nicholas, 398
Aubrey, Richard de, 248
Augustine, 17, 61, 107, 111-113, 117, 125, 136, 137
Augustinian canons in Wales, 295, 296

Bache, Alexander, 356
Baldwin, Archbishop, 189, 193-195, 216-220, 278, 326
Bangor bishopric founded, 56; cathedral burned, 358, 362; rebuilt, 374-376; its bishops, 79, 132, 166, 169, 189, 190, 192-197, 218, 236, 308, 309, 312-314, 318, 322, 353-357, 361, 367, 373-376
Bangor Deilo, 77
Bangor Friary, 334, 406, 416, 420
Bangor Iscoed, 61, 78, 79, 110, 115, 118, 119, 124
Baptism, British, 136, 137
Baptism, rules respecting, 244
Bardsey, 75, 79, 83, 275, 293, 296, 354, 383, 388, 420
Barlow, William, 377-379, 387, 397, 423
Barret, Andrew, 351
Barrow, William, 373

Index

Basingwerk Abbey, 304, 305, 383, 408, 420
Bassaleg Priory, 291
Beck, Thomas, 321, 331, 340, 346, 397
Becket, Archbishop, 192
Beddgelert, 276, 296, 354, 420
Bedwd, 190
Bells, Celtic, 144, 145, 270, 271
Benedictines, 290-295, 307
Bernard, Bishop, 167-169, 181-185, 190, 191, 301
Beuno, 64, 83, 84, 138, 402
Birkhead, Edward, 376
Bishops, consecration of, 139
Blakedon, James, 374
Bledri, 165
Bleduc, 165
Boia, 64
Boniface, 123
Bottisham, William de, 351, 352
Bran, 5-7, 13
Branwen, Mabinogi of, 6, 7
Brecon Friary, 334, 416, 419
Brecon Priory, 292-294, 408, 413, 416, 419
Bretoña. See of, 107, 108
Brian, Bishop, 346, 348, 349
Brittany, 52, 70, 73, 77, 82, 101-107, 116, 130, 133, 146-149, 196
Bromfield, 351, 352
Brute, Walter, 390
Brychan, 41, 64, 103, 143
Brynach, 44
Burghill, John, 351

Cadfan, 82, 83, 142, 143
Cadfrawd, 39
Cadoc, 15, 38, 43-46, 52, 56, 61, 62, 67, 71, 73, 79, 80, 86, 103-105, 108, 110, 116, 140, 147
Cadwgan, Bishop, 309, 318
Caergybi, 58, 83
Caerleon, 17-20, 74, 125, 225, 304, 316
Caerwent, 85
Caldey Priory, 300, 301, 421
Calixtus II., Pope, 180, 181, 184
Cameleac. See Cyfeiliawg
Caradog, 169, 273
Caratacus, 5-7, 13
Cardiff, 176, 187, 415

Cardiff Friaries, 359, 380
Cardiff Priory, 293, 359, 380
Cardigan Priory, 293, 420
Carmarthen Friary, 334
Carmarthen Priory, 296, 321, 408, 413, 420
Catterick, John, 393
Ceneu, 39, 145
Chad, 119, 121
Chepstow Priory, 290, 416, 422
Cherbury, David, 394
Cheryton, Thomas, 374
Chester, Battle of, 78, 118
Chicheley, 346, 350, 381, 393, 397
Child, Lawrence, 356
Churches, Early Celtic, 23, 36, 39, 40, 138, 140, 145-148
Cistercians in Wales, 279-289, 297, 299, 307
Claudia, 4, 5
Cliderow, 366, 373
Cluniacs, 280, 299
Clynog Fawr, 64, 304
Columba, 30, 56, 61, 97, 109, 116, 119, 120
Columbanus, 15, 109, 113, 115, 117
Conoch, 425
Cornwall, Church in, 146-148
Coventry, John, 351
Cradock, 351
Craswall Priory, 300, 381
Cuhelm, 169
Culdees, 275, 277
Cunedda, 101
Curig, 389
Cuthbert, 120, 125
Cwmhir Abbey, 302, 304, 306, 323, 358, 421
Cybi, 15, 58, 83, 84, 138, 147
Cydifor, 172
Cyfeiliawg, 160-162, 169
Cymmer Abbey, 303, 313, 323, 344, 421

Dafydd ap Bleddyn, 355
Dafydd ap Iorwerth, 376
Dafydd ap Owen, 376
Dafydd Dhu Hiraddug, 391
Danes, the, 159, 160, 169, 173, 174
Daniel ab Sulien, 167-169

Index 431

David, St., 15, 21, 46, 51, 52, 57, 58, 61, 62, 64, 67, 73-77, 79, 80, 85, 87, 101, 108-110, 116, 119, 139, 140, 143, 146, 147, 184, 225, 391, 425
David's, St., bishopric founded, 57; cathedral, 209, 347-349, 393, 395, 396; its bishops, etc., 73, 74, 153, 155, 156, 161-163, 165-170, 181-189, 197, 202-204, 208-217, 222-237, 252-254, 280, 301, 309, 314, 319-321, 331, 345-350, 378, 379, 392-397, 413, 414, 423-427. *See also* Menevia.
David (of Bangor), 189
David Fitzgerald, 185-187, 195, 198, 203
Dean, Henry, 374, 375
De Attica, George, 391
Deiniol, 56, 78, 79, 100
De la Bere, 392-395
De la Zouche, 398
Denbigh Friary, 334
Deorham, Battle of, 118
Derfel Gadarn, 388, 389, 425
Diacon, Michael, 376
Docwinnus, 85
Dore Abbey, 304
Dubricius. *See* Dyfrig
Dunawd, 78, 100, 126, 226, 400
Dyfan, 13, 14, 225
Dyfrig, 38, 40, 44, 56, 57, 67, 68, 70, 74, 75, 77, 126, 225

Easter controversy, 99, 112, 113, 116, 117, 120-122, 134, 135, 151
Ednam, Richard, 355, 374
Edward I., 325-327, 331, 337, 338, 344, 347, 390
Elbod, 132, 152, 169, 226
Eleutherius, 11, 12, 225
Elfod (of St. David's), 165
Elias de Radnor, 315-317, 338
Eliseg's Pillar, 173, 304
Elvanus, 12
Euaggultheu, 326
Eugenius III., Pope, 185, 190
Evaristus, 11
Ewenny Priory, 292-294, 408, 415, 420
Ewias Harold, 292

Fastolfe, Bishop, 349
Ffagan, 12-14, 225
Fitzhamon, 176, 179, 414, 415
Foliot, Reginald, 222, 229
Friars, 333, 334

Gall, St., 131
'Gemma Ecclesiastica,' 235, 238-268
Genealogies, Welsh, 40-42
Geoffrey de Henelawe, 223, 224, 229, 237, 253, 254
Geoffrey of Monmouth, 191, 196
Gerald de Barri, 17, 18, 47, 57, 70, 188, 195, 197-289, 295, 297-300, 303, 305, 306, 314
German, 27, 33-39, 66, 67, 99, 269, 270
Geruntius, 126, 129
Gervase de Castro, 356, 357
Gilbert, Bishop of St. Asaph, 191
Gilbert, Bishop of St. David's, 346, 349, 357
Gildas, 1, 2, 9, 17, 27, 39, 40, 46-56, 61-64, 67, 73, 100, 103, 105, 108, 110, 116, 131, 137-140, 389
Giraldus Cambrensis. *See* Gerald de Barri
Gloucester, St. Peter's, 176, 412
Gloucester bishopric, 412, 413, 415, 416
Glyndwr, Owain, 312, 353, 357-361, 363, 367, 376, 380, 397
Godfrey, Bishop, 191
Goldcliff Priory, 291, 310, 315, 381, 416, 422
'Golias the Bishop,' 234, 281, 284, 286
Golven, 104
Gower, Bishop, 346-348
Grace Dieu, 304, 422
Grandmontines, 299
Gruffydd ab Yr Ynad Coch, 326, 336
Gruffydd ap Iorwerth, 356
Guy de Mone, 349, 350
Guy Rufus, 218, 236
Gweslan, 58
Gwynlliw, 71
Gytto'r Glynn, 382

Haverfordwest Friary, 334
Haverfordwest Priory, 296, 377, 414, 421
Henllan, 74
Henry, Bishop, 315
Hervé, 166
Herwald, 165, 166, 179, 196
Holgate, Robert, 398, 399
Holyhead, 419
Honorius II., Pope, 180, 181
Honorius III., Pope, 310
Houghton, Bishop, 346, 349
Howel I., Bishop, 319
Howel ap Ednyfed, 318, 319, 322
Hubert Walter, 222, 223, 226-229, 236, 297
Hunden, John, 398
Hywel Dda, 154, 162, 163

Illtyd, 38, 45, 61, 67-71, 73, 85, 86, 92, 116, 143, 146, 147, 391
Incest in Wales, 272
Ingleby, John, 398
Innocent II., Pope, 182, 185, 190
Innocent III., Pope, 225-236
Iorwerth, Bishop, 298, 309, 346
Ireland, Church of, 23, 28, 29, 31, 60-64, 66, 67, 82, 86, 87, 90, 108-110, 113, 115-117, 119, 121-123, 130, 132, 133, 136-138, 140, 141, 144, 145, 151, 170-173, 192, 193
Irenæus, 16
Ismael, 21

John IV., Pope, 123
John, Bishop of St. Asaph, 322
John de Eclescliff, 351
John de Monmouth, 340, 341, 351
John de la Ware, 320, 321
John de la Zouche, 351
Jones, Roderick, 299
Jordan, Archdeacon, 203
Joseph, 165, 166
Julius, 17, 18, 21
Juvencus Manuscript, 172

Kenfig, 173, 177
Kentigern, 22, 44, 53, 57, 64, 79, 80, 85, 119, 126, 139
Keri, 170, 204, 207

Kidwelly Priory, 292, 408, 420
Kinsi, 166
Knight, Thomas, 373

Laleston, 177, 315
Lampeter, 218
Landevennec, 102, 116, 130
Langton, John, 394
Langton, Thomas, 395
Laurence, Archbishop, 113, 114
Lay Abbots, 277, 278
Legends of Saints, 42-47
Leonorius, 105
Lewis, Abbot, 382, 384, 386
Lewis Glyn Cothi, 389
Lewis Morganwg, 306, 386, 390, 399
Libiau, 161
Lifris, 179, 197
Llan, 145-147
Llanafan Fawr, 58
Llanbadarn Fawr, 57, 59, 218, 277, 278, 413
Llanblethian, 36, 177, 316, 317
Llancarfan, 38, 43, 52, 62, 71, 79, 80, 85, 86, 105, 172, 174-176, 179
Llandaff, bishopric founded, 56; its limits settled, 162, 163, 179-182; its bishops, etc., 74-77, 153, 160, 161, 164-166, 168, 169, 179-183, 196, 197, 217, 220, 310, 314-318, 338-341, 351, 352, 397-399, 415, 416
Llandaff, Book of, 10-13, 40
Llandaff Cathedral, 75, 182, 183
Llandaff, church founded at, 13
Llanddewi Brefi, 58, 67, 74, 143, 218, 331, 420
Llandough, 85, 96, 177
Llanelwy. *See* Asaph, St.
Llanfaes, 312, 330, 334, 358
Llangenith, 282, 293, 350, 381
Llangwyn, 293, 382
Llanllugan Nunnery, 304, 421
Llanllyr Nunnery, 304, 420
Llansantffraed, 283
Llantarnam Abbey, 304, 422
Llanthony Abbey, 295, 374, 416, 422
Llantwit Major, 5, 23, 38, 53, 61, 68-71, 85, 86, 90 96, 105, 140, 173-176, 179, 316

Lleision, 386, 397, 400-402
Lleurwg. *See* Lucius
Llunwerth, 161, 162
Llywarch ab Llywelyn, 335, 342
Llywelyn Bifort, 361
Llywelyn, Bishop of St. Asaph, 355
Llywelyn of Bromfield, 340
Llywelyn ap Gruffydd, 296, 319, 321-327, 337, 353
Llywelyn ap Iorwerth, 195, 231, 246, 296, 303, 308-312, 315, 317-319, 333
Llywelyn ap Madoc, 355
Lollardism, 371, 390
London, Dr., 406
London, Council of, 187
Lowe, John, 368-370
Lucius, 10-14, 40
Lupus, 27, 33-36, 38, 66, 67, 269, 270
Lyndwood, William, 394

Maclovius, 105
Madawc ab Gwallter, 336
Maelgwn Gwynedd, 42-45, 49, 53, 56, 77, 79, 80
Maenan. *See* Aberconway
Maen Llythyrog, 142
Maglorius, 105
Malpas Priory, 300, 422
Mapes, Walter, 234, 286
Margam Abbey, 173, 182, 304, 305, 315, 316, 408, 415, 421
Marriage of clergy, 169, 170, 197, 203, 209, 243, 265-269, 274, 375
Marshall, John, 398
Martin, St., 66
Martyn, David, 346, 347
Martyn, Richard, 395
Mass, rules respecting the, 239-243; scepticism, 249; abuses, 257-262
Matthew de Englefeild, 356
Medwy, 12-14
Meilyr, 275
Melanus, 154, 190
Menevia, 52, 57, 59, 62, 64, 74. *See also* David's, St.
Merthyr Mawr, 173
Meurig, Bishop, 184, 190, 192
Meurig, King, 56, 105

Mevanius, 103, 104
Mitford, Bishop, 349
Mochros, 74
Monkton Priory, 292, 381, 421
Monmouth Priory, 291, 415, 422
Mor, 39
Morgan Hên, 162, 164
Morgan, John, 396, 397
Morgeneu, 85, 169

Neath Abbey, 301, 305, 306, 315, 382, 383, 385, 386, 399-402, 407, 408, 415, 421
Newcastle (Bridgend), 177, 315
Newport Friary, 334
Nice, Council of, 19
Nicholas, Bishop, 175, 176, 178, 197
Nicholls, Benedict, 361, 373, 393
Non, 74, 147, 386, 399
Novis, 155, 226

Origen, 8
Osbert, 229
Oswiu, 120, 123
Oudoceus, 40, 45, 77, 105, 126, 153
Owen Gwynedd, 190-194

Pace, Thomas, 375
Padarn, 57, 58, 67, 76-78, 139, 146, 147
Padarn, Bishop of Llandaff, 164
Paganism, 24-32, 65, 271, 389
Parfew, Robert, 380
Paris, Council of, 70
Pascal, Bishop, 351
Patrick, St., 22-25, 27-29, 42, 46, 60, 63, 64, 66, 68, 72, 86, 109, 110, 136, 138, 139, 145
Patrington, Stephen, 393
Paul, St., 3-5
Paul Aurelian, 104
Paulinus, 58, 67
Pavy, Hugh, 396
Peblig, 39
Peckham, Archbishop, 324-334, 342, 353
Pecock, Reginald, 369-373
Pedilavium, The, 137
Pelagian heresy, 28, 33, 34, 99, 122
Pelagius, 33
Pembroke Hospital, 421

Penitentials, 51, 52, 110, 121, 122
Penmon, 83, 293, 408, 419
Penny, John, 375
Penrhys, 390
Peter de Leia, 188, 189, 208-217, 229, 252-254, 280
Peter Manducator, 266
Petroc, 147
Peverell, Bishop, 351, 352
Phaganus. *See* Ffagan.
Philip de Staunton, 339, 340
Pigott, Thomas, 375
Pill Priory, 300, 421
Piro, 53, 70, 96
Portionary churches, 170, 204, 269, 332
Premonstratensians, 296
Price, Ellis, 388
Priestholm, 275, 419
Provisions, Papal, 310, 340, 343, 347, 349, 351, 352, 355-357, 369-371, 373-376, 393-396, 399
Pudens, 4, 5

Rawlins, Richard, 397
Redman, Richard, 373, 376
Reiner, Bishop, 191, 318
'Repressor,' Pecock's, 371
Rhayader Friary, 334
Rhuddlan, 219, 330, 331, 333
Rhygyfarch, 169, 172
Richard, Archbishop, 193, 208, 209
Richard, Bishop of St. Asaph, 191
Richard, Bishop of Bangor, 312, 318, 322
Richard de Carew, 320, 321, 346
Ringstede, Thomas, 356
Roath, 176, 415
Robert, Bishop, 308
Robert, Bishop of Dover, 406
Robert de Chandos, 291
Robert de Haya, 291
Robert de Lancaster, 361, 367-369
Robert of Gloucester, 181, 292
Robert of Shrewsbury, 236
Rodburne, Thomas, 393, 394
Rum map Urbgen, 132
Rushooke, Bishop, 351
Ruthin College, 420
Ruthin Friary, 334

Sacerdos, 18
Sadyrnin, 169
St. Clears, 300, 350, 381
St. Dogmael's Priory, 218, 228, 229, 233, 300, 421
St. Kinemark's Priory, 416, 422
St. Mary's College, St. David's, 421
St. Winifred's Well, 65, 388, 389
St. Woolos, Newport, 413
Salcot, John, 376
Salley, Miles, 398
Samson, 21, 46, 52, 53, 58, 70, 86, 104, 105, 116, 147, 225
Samson, Abbot, 69
Sardica, Council of, 19
Sawyl Benuchel, 79
Seiriol, 83, 84, 100, 389
Sherborne, Robert, 396
Sion Cent, 390, 391
Slebach, 408, 421
Smith, John, 398
'Speculum Ecclesiæ,' 278-289
Spytty Jevan, 364
Stanbery, John, 374
Standish, Henry, 376, 377
Stones, monumental, etc., 20, 67-69, 140-144, 172, 173, 270, 271
Stowe Missal, 137
Strata Florida, 218, 280, 287, 302-304, 306, 323, 331, 358, 380, 383, 407, 420
Strata Marcella, 282, 283, 303, 306, 323, 376, 405, 421
Striguil Priory. *See* Chepstow
Succession system, 170, 269
Sulien, 169, 172, 174
Sulien, son of Rhygyfarch, 169
Swaffham, John, 357
Swansea Hospital, 421

Talley Abbey, 296-298, 303, 305, 383, 385, 405, 408, 420
Teilo, 15, 40, 44, 54, 57-59, 67, 75-77, 101, 105, 126, 139, 146, 147, 391
Teilo Churches, 179
Tenby Friary, 334
Tenby Free Chapel, 421
Tenby Hospital, 421
Tertullian, 7, 9, 10
Tewkesbury Abbey, 176-178, 414, 415

Index

Thenew, 22
Theodore, Archbishop, 121, 122, 124, 125
Thomas ap Ieuan, 390
Thomas Wallensis, 319, 320, 346, 397
Thoresby, Bishop, 346, 348, 397
Tintern Abbey, 301, 305, 408, 416, 422
Tironians, 299
Toledo, Council of, 108
Tonsure, Celtic, 127, 135. 151
Tours, Council of, 107
Tremerin, 165
Trentals, 258, 259
Trevor I., John, 355
Trevor II., John, 358, 369
Triads, 4, 6, 10, 13. 64, 68, 77. 79
Tully, Robert, 395
Tydeman de Winchcombe, 351
Tyfei, 54
Tŷ Gwyn, 58

Uchtryd, 197
Urban, Bishop, 40, 168, 179-184, 197
Usk Nunnery, 291, 292, 408, 416, 422

Valle Crucis, 304, 305, 323, 369, 376, 382, 408, 420

Vaughan, Edward, 396, 397
Verulam, Council of, 34
Viriconium, 20
Vortigern, 37, 38

Wecheleu, 220, 221
Wells. Holy, 65. 388, 389
Wells. John, 398
Whitby, Synod of, 15, 120
Whitland, 67, 297, 301-303. 305, 309, 323, 385, 407, 408, 420
Wilfrid, 15
Wilfrid, Bishop of St. David's 166, 167
William, Prior of Goldcliff, 310, 315
William de Bottisham, 351
William de Breuse, 321, 338
William de Burgh, 314, 320, 321, 338
William de Spridlington, 356
William of Radnor, 320, 321
William of Saltmarsh, 197, 217, 315
Winwaloe, 101, 102, 116
Wrexham Church, 376
Wright, Thomas; his theories, 2, 8, 9
Wynn, Meredith, 365

Young, Richard, 357. 361

THE END.

www.ingramcontent.com/pod-product-compliance
Lightning Source LLC
Chambersburg PA
CBHW021233300426
44111CB00007B/533